Leadership Transformation

The Klein Group Instrument® Facilitator's Guide

Leadership Transformation

The Klein Group Instrument® Facilitator's Guide

Robert R. Klein

CENTER FOR APPLICATIONS OF PSYCHOLOGICAL TYPE, INC.

2815 NW 13th St, Suite 401 ׀ Gainesville, FL 32609

Published by
Center for Applications of Psychological Type, Inc.
2815 NW 13th Street, Suite 401
Gainesville, FL 32609
352.375.0160
www.capt.org

Printed in the United States.

DEDICATION

To my wife,
Deborah Scanlon Klein
whose support has meant so much to me.

With special appreciation
for an excellent research advisor:
Dr. Terrence Tivnan
Harvard University

TABLE of CONTENTS

ACKNOWLEDGEMENTS

This book evolved over a six-year period, as I interacted with scores of people related to Klein Group Instrument® training, coaching, and research. To start, I would like to thank the CEO of my publisher, Betsy Styron, who is a marvel of patience, insight, and support. I also want to express my appreciation to my friends at the Center for Applications of Psychological Type, who have sailed with me for so many years on the KGI journey. Thanks to John Amerson and Christy Freeman in graphic design, Rob Rothschild in marketing, Kesstan Blandin, Judy Breiner, and Logan Abbitt in research, Naima Cortes, my project manager, Mark Enting and Glenn Grenade in the technology department, Lisa Orr in training, Sandy Peterson and Michelle Cohan in customer service, and Greg Adams in accounting, who is also one of my key informants for Gator Nation!

Several people provided me with invaluable editorial assistance: Mark Richardson, who has helped me with my writing since we were flatmates in London so many years ago; Lee C. Barrett, one of the great, all-time Yale guys; and Kesstan Blandin, who has a keen eye for the flow of psychological ideas.

It is important to express my gratitude to the many people at Western New England University who have provided encouragement and support for my work: President Anthony Caprio, Dean of Arts and Sciences Saeed Ghahramani, who, as a mathematician and a short-story writer, is the perfect man for his job, Assistant Dean of Engineering Richie Grabiec, Professor Emeritus Russell Fanelli, my friends from D'Amour Library—Priscilla Perkins, Mary Jane Sobinski-Smith, Vicky Ludwig, Lindsay Roberts, and Linda Chojnicki, and administrative personnel Donna Utter and Jackie LeHouiller.

A special thanks to my Co-Director of the Sport Leadership and Coaching Program at Western New England, Sharianne Walker, whose vision and energy are terrific. And to Head Football Coach Keith Emery, who saw the potential for KGI applications in sport.

I want to express my gratitude to my colleagues at the C.G. Jung Institute in Zurich, Switzerland who embraced the KGI–MBTI model. I also want to thank Joseph Cambray, whose encouragement and professional guidance have meant so much to me. I also want to thank my trusted professional colleague, Tuula Haukioja, to whom I always turn for advice. Also, my friend and colleague Daniel Clement, who helps me prepare my PowerPoint® presentations and offers such astute feedback. And a warm thanks to my colleague Rhonda Tranks who has provided so much support along the way.

I want to extend a word of gratitude to Professor Mary Vollaro of Florida Polytechnic University, who has been a key collaborator in the study of leadership training for engineers.

Over the years, there has been a variety of family members, friends and associates whose engagement with the KGI ideas helped to inspire me in this pursuit. I want to express my appreciation to: Jim Andersen, Christian Boesen, Gary Brown, Tess Castleman, Nick Connell, Eve Davis, Mike Doyle, Tom Doyle, Peter Dufresne, Michael Erba, Jonathan Hayes, Andrea Henschen, Robert Hinshaw, Katherine Hirsh, George Hudson, Ted Jasnos, Bruce Klein, Peter Klein, Michelle Klein, Rudy Klein, Margaret Lynch, Gary Mayer, Steven Melino, Victor Messina, Jack Murphy, Veronica Murphy, Alesha Pisano, Gottfried Polage, Robert Scanlon, R.B. Scanlon, James Scherer, Alexandra Sielecki, Dean Soucie, Jan-Petter Skullerud, Ursula Weiss, and Christopher Zorn.

INTRODUCTION

My colleague, Jack Greeley, is a former bank vice president with a background in personnel training in the financial field. Now a Professor of Business Management at Western New England University, Jack teaches leadership courses and directs the Leadership Institute, a program the university puts on each year for the Affiliated Chambers of Commerce of Greater Springfield (MA). The institute trains

a select group of business and professional people in an assortment of leadership skills that equip them to advance their careers.

In his role as director, Jack sat in on my presentation for the program, becoming acquainted with my training design which utilizes the Klein Group Instrument® for Effective Leadership and Participation in Teams (KGI®)˙ and the Myers-Briggs Type Indicator® (MBTI®) assessments. The model informs people about their personality preferences, the essential elements of effective teamwork, and how the two intersect. It helps participants gain a better understanding of their personality styles, the styles of others, and trains them in very specific behavioral strategies that allow them to refine their leadership and membership roles in small groups. With this formula, all of the participants have been able to increase their group expertise, making it a popular presentation.

A focused, practical man, Jack liked the concrete approach I took in teaching these skills. So he invited me to collaborate with him in his Masters of Business Administration course, Foundations of Leadership. My role would be to

instruct the students in the model, while Jack would guide their skill development during the rest of the semester. Since the majority of students are employed, they have been able to apply the new strategies in their job settings. Our collaboration has proven highly effective: during the term, the students have honed their leadership abilities in many productive ways.

In the most recent round of this partnership, a dramatic incident occurred in class that demonstrates the power of the model. I would like to share it here.

On the sixth meeting of the course, I delivered a presentation on the basic elements of the MBTI and KGI systems, identifying how they intersect in the skill-building design. Prior to the class, all of the students had taken the assessments so they had personal results in hand. By introducing anonymous case studies, I explained how users can employ the Myers-Brigg's® clarity indexes (which illustrate the strength of a person's scores in the four MBTI dichotomies) and the KGI Composite Subscale Graph (depicting a person's outcomes in nine critical areas of group behavior) to determine their strengths and challenges in small-group activities. With this information, they can construct a sound plan for improvement. Drawing on multiple examples, I showed how people with different personality preferences and different patterns of group behavior could make the necessary adjustments to become well-rounded team leaders and group members. By utilizing this system of analysis with their own results, the students could then choose growth statements from their KGI® Individual Profiles and build a series of new skills.

At that point, after answering a few questions, my expectation was that the students would now work independently for an upcoming assignment—the task of designing their own plans for personal improvement. But Professor Greeley spoke up and said that one of the students in the class had volunteered to have his personal results put up on the screen so we could do a live analysis and instruct him on how to proceed. Always enjoying the challenge of a case analysis, I happily agreed.

The student turned out to be a young engineer, in his mid-twenties, employed with a local firm. His Myers-Briggs' results indicated he was an ISTJ, an Introvert with Sensing, Thinking, and Judging preferences. His KGI results demonstrated high scores in Perspective Taking, Task Analysis, and Task Implementation; however, the Leadership subscales portrayed low scores in Assertiveness, Group Facilitation, and Initiative.

As we discussed the results, the student announced that he prided himself on being a good listener in a group, always staying in touch with other members' ideas and concerns. He also relished analyzing a task, and then finding smart adjustments to successfully execute it.

We all conceded that these were key strengths for him, but there was the matter of his social reserve—his Introversion—restricting him in the leadership areas.

Jack Greeley strode up to the screen, a laser pointer clutched in his hand. He waved a red dot of light across the high KGI columns for Perspective Taking, Task Analysis, and Task Implementation. "If you have these strengths," he said in his usual straightforward manner, "the obvious question is why don't you do more to speak up, share your ideas, and lead here?" He flashed the dot across the trio of low leadership scores. "That's the issue."

"From my experience," I said to the student, "with your listening skills, which keep you in touch with other people's ideas, and with your interest in designing a strong plan and executing it well, I think there's an eighty percent probability your suggestions in a group would be on target. The odds are in your favor that you'll make meaningful contributions. But you have to develop some Extraversion to speak up and take action."

With a thoughtful expression on his face, the student stared at the graph scores on the screen, but he didn't say anything more.

Shortly thereafter, I concluded the presentation and departed. The class is four hours long, with my segment taking up the middle portion. In the final hour, the class dissected an organizational case study, an entirely separate assignment.

Later that evening, Jack called me on the phone to debrief the session.

"You're going to love what happened," he said. "After you left, we did that case study. As I led the discussion, the engineer jumped right in at the beginning and shared some useful points. In previous weeks, he'd never, ever done that. In fact, when he spoke up so quickly, all of the other students paused and looked at him for a moment, as if in disbelief. He looked back at them and said: 'Well, I was listening to them!'"

"So the feedback had an immediate impact," I said with a smile.

"Absolutely! He changed his approach right then and there. After class, I spoke to him about it. Part of it was I wanted to ask him if I had been too aggressive with my analysis of his results, but he said, no, that was fine. He's there to learn, and he didn't mind my being direct. But he said the materials helped him to see clearly the issues, and it motivated him. He told me this is his first MBA class, and he decided to take leadership because he thought it would help him with all of the other courses that follow. He said that after tonight's session, he is sure this will help him in important ways, with the future courses, but just as significantly, it will help him with his group projects at the engineering firm. He's excited about the possibilities for his personal skill development."

"That's terrific, Jack. That is just what we want to achieve."

I decided to share this story for several reasons. First, it illustrates how readily people can get their minds around this model. The Klein Group Instrument provides a clear structure for understanding foundational group dynamics and productive group behaviors. The Myers-Briggs Type Indicator assessment provides a basic compass for comprehending the patterns of one's psychological energies, and how these energies flow in social settings. Together, the two measurements create a lucid, accessible design for enhancing and refining social performance.

Second, this case demonstrates how quickly people can transfer insight into practice. It reveals how individuals can make prompt adjustments that impact the here and now.

And third, the example offers a small demonstration of how the approach positively affects people's attitudes, helping to stir a growth orientation that can have transformational effects.

All of these points will be elaborated in greater detail in the coming chapters, as people encounter a design that has helped thousands of people obtain new leadership and group skills, and, hopefully, will help many thousands more do the same. ✕

CHAPTER 1

Why the Klein Group Instrument®Assessment?

As we travel through our life journeys, we become involved in small-group work in a wide variety of contexts: family life, educational classrooms, sport teams, business enterprises, professional and community organizations, and religious communities. In each of these settings, we are expected to work effectively with others for team success and for our own social development. We need to be able to participate, to contribute, and to lead, as appropriate. However, it requires thoughtfulness and flexibility to be a

capable group member. So over time, as we get immersed in these assorted group activities, it becomes increasingly relevant to cultivate a battery of skills that make us more competent team players. These skills are critical for the achievement of group goals and, just as meaningfully, for our personal advancement in life, enabling us to climb to higher levels of satisfaction, influence, and success.

But acquiring these skills is not always an easy task. Part of the problem is that assessing and managing small-group dynamics is a complicated process. In any group setting, there's a diverse mixture of elements with which to contend: leadership and membership issues; task and interpersonal concerns; negotiation processes; and various personality styles. All of these factors can impact a small group in a shifting, unpredictable way. It is no wonder that people often find it difficult to get a handle on group dynamics, and then guide a team in the best direction.

To address this challenge, a new tool was

designed: the Klein Group Instrument for Effective Leadership and Participation in Teams (KGI) assessment. The KGI tool provides a compass for interpreting small-group dynamics, offering a way to understand essential aspects of group life and the interplay of these elements, making them clearer and more accessible. Grounded on the points of this compass, the KGI measurement furnishes a system for strengthening individual performance for leadership and membership roles, promoting skill acquisition and long-term growth. It helps any individual become a stronger player on any team. In addition, the KGI measurement can also speak to teams themselves. It supplies a method for bolstering overall group performance, enabling teams to evaluate and selectively adjust a variety of their interactive processes to generate synergy. Team synergy occurs when members blend their talents in ways that produce smarter task analysis, greater creativity, and higher productivity.

Constructed over a twelve-year period, utilizing quantitative and qualitative analyses, the KGI tool has demonstrated its effectiveness for people from around the world. The instrument is based on the primary components of group life that are comprehensible for all people and for every team.

On the individual level, the KGI assessment will put in motion a transformative developmental process that allows a person to attain a much higher level of social skillfulness. The method positively influences how a person thinks, feels, and behaves in group settings, empowering an individual to acquire a greater sense of self-confidence founded on real achievement. Used with coaching and counseling, the KGI tool allows clients to tap new parts of their potential to become more fully functioning group participants.

After exposure to the KGI model, individuals exhibited the following characteristics:

1. Greater understanding of small-group dynamics,

2. Increased insight into effective team leadership and team membership,

3. Increased skill in employing appropriate leadership techniques in small groups,

4. More openness to other group members, with greater ability to build relationships,

5. Increased creativity in response to the fluctuating demands of small-group life, and

6. Greater ability to promote efficient collaboration and strong task outcomes.

On the group level, the KGI assessment promotes a team development process that can spark the synergy that lifts a group to a higher plane of performance. With this approach, the members' KGI® Individual Profiles are anonymously combined to construct the KGI® Group Profile. This report illustrates the patterns of group interaction, and it offers suggestions on how the team can refine its practices. It encourages a group to become a learning team, one that can plot new strategies, balance the skill sets of its members, and make ongoing adjustments that will perfect its operations.

After exposure to the KGI team-building approach, groups have exhibited the following characteristics:

1. Greater clarity about how the team is functioning,

2. Improved communication among members during group activities,

3. Increased awareness of how to blend individual skills to improve teamwork,

4. More openness to mentoring opportunities to support members' skill development, and

5. Greater knowledge about how to adjust team practices to improve performance.

The aim of this volume is to provide counselors, coaches, consultants, and teachers with the means to employ the KGI assessment for training their diverse clientele in leadership and group skills. The text explains all of the fundamental elements of the instrument, the available materials, and step-by-step procedures for individual and team development. It also supplies professionals with very precise details about how to guide particular clients and teams based on their specific KGI results. Offering a wide range of case studies, it presents talking points for professionals that will allow them to direct robust social growth for their trainees.

Additionally, the volume outlines a method for using the Klein Group Instrument measurement with the Myers-Briggs Type Indicator (MBTI) assessment for individual coaching and for team building. The MBTI tool is the most widely used psychological instrument in the world for the general population. It measures individual psychological preferences, and it has valuable applications for leadership and group training. Over the years, thousands of people have been instructed with the two instruments. People have learned how to expand their leadership and group skills, and how their personal psychological energies could be enlisted in this process. When the two instruments have been utilized in combination, they have created a very substantial learning dynamic. This text diagrams how the two instruments intersect and articulates approaches for individual and group application, supplying the particular talking points that professionals may use with their clients, students, and teams.

In the final analysis, this book is about empowerment: the empowerment of individuals and teams by helping them increase their interpersonal skills, thereby boosting their competence. It is also about the empowerment of counselors, consultants, coaches, and teachers, providing them with information that will allow them to employ the KGI materials and expand their professional repertoire. In a world that needs more quality leaders and greater teamwork, the intent of the KGI model is to make a worthwhile contribution to their development. ✘

CHAPTER 2

The KGI® Diamond Model

The Klein Group Instrument for Effective Leadership and Participation in Teams assessment focuses on small-group activities (in general, groups of 2 to 10 members) where there is a specific task to accomplish, such as in business, sport, professional, organizational, and educational settings. The KGI model embraces the "team" concept, addressing a small group in which members collaborate on a project with a common, shared outcome, as well as any other small-group activity in which people

work on a task without an intentional joint goal. An example of the latter would be a discussion group in a college seminar. While the students share information designed to expand their personal knowledge, they are not trying to produce a collective product. In a business or professional environment, a similar example would be a training session where members exchange ideas about a topic meant to support personal development.

In these situations, group dynamics has to do with the interactive processes that occur when a cluster of people come together to discuss, to work, to collaborate. It examines how members interact, how they influence each other, and how member relations evolve during their time together. With respect to these interactive processes, there are a number of fundamental elements that come into play. Of these, four of the most central are:

- Leadership
- Task execution
- Interpersonal relations
- Negotiation

The intent of the KGI measurement is to bring these components into a coherent design that illustrates their significant interrelationships and underlying energy patterns. When people are able to clearly comprehend this design, they obtain a compass that allows them to navigate group waters with greater confidence and expertise.

The four major scales of the instrument are Leadership, Negotiation Orientation, Task Focus, and Interpersonal Focus. The design of the measurement can be expressed visually using a diamond model:

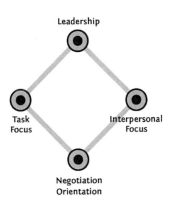

Leadership is essential for any task-oriented group venture. Whether there is a designated leader or not, someone must take the initiative to coordinate the efforts of the group—this is a primary dynamic. It may be one person (but can also be more than one) who steps up to influence the direction of the activity and engages other members in the effort. Leadership guides the group in two main areas: Task Focus (working towards competent task completion) and Interpersonal Focus (promoting positive member relations). An underlying goal of Interpersonal Focus is to foster team cohesion that inspires the group to achieve its best results. Negotiation Orientation enables the group to manage both task and interpersonal issues. With respect to the task, it seeks to resolve strategy differences so the team can arrive at a unified plan, with all members committed to the project. With regard to interpersonal relations, it strives to resolve personal conflicts that may emerge, as well as to connect members' interests and enthusiasms to the work to increase their motivation for the enterprise. Negotiation always plays a crucial role when discord occurs in the group, relating to either the task effort or interpersonal relations. It pursues agreements that encourage meaningful collaboration and favorable task outcomes.

Concise definitions for the four major scales:

Leadership, as measured by the KGI tool, is the ability of members to guide the group towards effective collaboration and successful task completion.

Negotiation Orientation measures the ability of members to listen closely to one another and to construct mutually acceptable agreements.

Task Focus measures the ability of mem-bers to devise a sound strategy for the task and to carry out the plan fruitfully.

Interpersonal Focus measures the ability of members to develop a team spirit and to address the feeling issues in the group.

When people from around the world have been trained in the KGI model, they have acknowledged a similar point: no matter what continent you come from, when you work in some small-group context, you need to pay attention to these four functions to make the group highly success-ful. The design has thus demonstrated a very prac-tical and universal appeal.

To continue with the issue of group dynamics, it is always important, when assessing a group, to ask these questions: How are the members engaged? Where's their attention, their interest? How are they channeling their efforts? In essence, which way is the energy flowing? The flow of energy informs us about the focus and activity of the group, and what might be needed to maintain a positive balance that will be most productive. Using the KGI diamond diagram, it is possible to detect some natural energy streams that are very significant in group life.

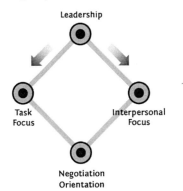

Effective leadership pays attention to both the task and interpersonal sides of the group enter-prise. At the most basic level, the group must con-centrate on the task because that's why it has assembled. But doing the job requires a collective effort, and how the members get along affects the levels of their participation and the quality of the final outcome. So attention must be paid to the people, because team harmony impacts productiv-ity. Accordingly, leaders need to be flexible and stay alert to both of these domains.

One of the bedrock theories about small-group dynamics was articulated in the 1950s by Robert Bales (Bales 1950, 1955), a researcher who examined the relationship between task execution and the socioemotional aspect of group life. He found that when a group zeroed in on a task, trying to get it done directly, there were times when disagreements occurred among members due to competing strategies, values, and visions. Consequently, tensions could surface, and members could become angry, aggressive or withdrawn. At those times, it was important for the group to switch focus from the task to its social relations in order to reestablish harmony among the members. The goal was to resolve interpersonal problems and remove the emotional disturbances. Only then could the group go back to the task in a unified way, drawing on its full complement of human resources to achieve a quality outcome.

Bales saw that an elemental rhythm existed in groups, as the members' attention shifted back and forth between the poles of group task and group maintenance. Interestingly, the research on these twin aspects of group life indicated they were negatively correlated, so that focusing on one by necessity draws attention away from the other. Since a group can concentrate on only one at a time, there is a back-and-forth motion in group life, as the focus fluctuates between task and interpersonal concerns. This fundamental movement is the source of a core interactive dynamic, common to all small groups and teams. Being aware of this tension and managing it capably is an essential skill for leaders and team members. Attention to this dynamic is at the heart of the KGI diamond model.

Whether a group attends to the task, or examines interpersonal issues, negotiation plays an influential role. Members must strike agreements that provide the basis for their collective efforts. When a team constructs a task strategy, negotiation comes to bear as the group sorts out the options and decides on a joint plan. When the group implements the strategy, negotiation plays a role in the evaluation of appropriate adjustments to sharpen the plan's effectiveness. When conflicts emerge among members, negotiation helps to resolve the issues. When a team decides to take steps to build a more positive group spirit, negotiation assists in the strategizing. So in a variety of ways the negotiation process applies to the task and interpersonal functions of group life. Negotiation operates to ensure that voices are heard, that people remain involved, and that the team, to the best of its ability, stays unified. In the KGI model, energy from Negotiation Orientation rises up to address these different concerns.

As can be seen, the KGI diamond identifies the movement of primary energies in small groups that enable members to gain a better understanding of fundamental processes. By monitoring the movement of these energies, and by guiding them in constructive directions, members can influence the group's efforts in beneficial ways and increase the potential for superb results. In the next chapter, the specific KGI skills that members can employ in this effort are outlined and explained. ✄

CHAPTER 3

Description of Major Scales and Subscales

The Klein Group Instrument diamond model distinguishes four essential functions in small-group life and shows how they are interrelated, orienting people to a series of pivotal group dynamics. This is the first step in the method. The next is to help group members become more proficient in operating in each of these domains, and more flexible in moving among them to nurture high-quality individual and team performance.

Toward these ends, the KGI tool defines a number of subscales for each major scale. The subscales designate *specific skill sets* for the four sectors of group activity, identifying the practical skills people can employ to refine their behavior. As a result, the information that guides individual improvement and team improvement in the KGI system flows through the subscale sections of the KGI® Individual Profile and KGI® Group Profile, respectively.

To familiarize readers with the subscales, a two-step procedure will be utilized. First, one-sentence definitions of the subscales will be presented, permitting readers to grasp the initial concepts. This will be followed by paragraph-long descriptions of the major scales and subscales, providing a more elaborate explanation of their operations.

Leadership Subscales

1. **Assertiveness:** the expression of ideas in the group.

2. **Group Facilitation:** the coordination of the group's efforts with regard to negotiation, task, and interpersonal relations.

3. **Initiative:** the willingness of members to assume primary leadership roles in different aspects of the group's work.

Negotiation Orientation Subscales

1. **Perspective Taking:** the skill of investigating and understanding other people's values, interests, and needs.

2. **Constructive Negotiation Approach:** the promotion of a win-win negotiation method so that all members benefit from an agreement.

Task Focus Subscales

1. **Task Analysis:** the examination of problems, opportunities, and task solutions.

2. **Task Implementation:** the competent execution of a plan with appropriate strategic adjustments along the way.

Interpersonal Focus Subscales

1. **Positive Group Affiliation:** the promotion of mutual respect, acceptance, and rapport among members, with the aim of forging a team spirit.

2. **Feeling Orientation:** attention to the emotional issues in the group.

The following paragraph-long descriptions of the major scales and subscales explain more fully these concepts.

Leadership

In a small-group setting, leadership means that people take the initiative to help guide the group with the task and, at the same time, promote positive, cooperative relations among members to ensure successful collaboration. A leader is able to influence group members about what path should be taken to get the job done, and then enables their effective participation. Leaders provide ideas, structure, support, and encouragement to other members.

1. Assertiveness

To take a leadership role, a person must have his or her ideas heard by other members. Expressing ideas and inviting reaction to them is a leadership function that moves the task along. As much as possible, an individual should present relevant, supporting facts to persuade others about the accuracy of his or her position.

2. Group Facilitation

In taking a leadership role, a person becomes engaged in the facilitation of various group processes. With respect to the task, facilitation can be accomplished by promoting a thorough analysis of the assignment, or inciting creativity in the problem-solving enterprise, or organizing the effort in the most efficient manner. With respect to the interpersonal component, facilitation can occur by establishing a positive environment where people can do their best work, or helping build stronger relations among members, or promoting ethical behavior by the group.

3. Initiative

To be an important group leader, a person must be willing to be in the spotlight and take the glare. Therefore, a leader is in the middle of the action, eliciting the best efforts from all members. The leader moves the team forward and provides key energy to get the task done.

Negotiation Orientation

To be effective in negotiation, a person needs to listen closely to others, and appreciate their aims and interests with respect to the topic under discussion. Understanding multiple points of view allows one to broker an agreement that can meet various members' needs. Finding a solution that provides some benefit for everyone helps to ensure successful implementation of an accord. A competent negotiator wants to have, as much as possible, all members on board with an agreement in order to promote personal commitment to the work and a unified effort in the follow-up.

1. Perspective Taking

To be a competent negotiator, a person listens thoughtfully to what others say and considers empathically their underlying values and interests. When one is able to empathize with others' perspectives, to "get inside their shoes," one is better able to construct proposals that others can buy into and support. Through the process of active listening, a person obtains essential information with which to advance effective agreements.

2. Constructive Negotiation Approach

This approach inspires a person to set a positive tone for a discussion, to investigate group members' concerns as fully as possible, and to propose solutions that bring together various interests in a way that satisfies the members. Obviously, it is not possible to please everyone all of the time, but this method attempts to address the varying interests as much as is feasible. Whenever a group devises a "win-win" agreement, in which all members receive some benefit, the agreement boosts morale, energizes members, and encourages their best efforts. When members hold out in the final phase of a negotiation, someone with these skills helps the group find acceptable accommodations to achieve a reasonable solution.

Task Focus

A group begins a task by analyzing the assignment: members propose ways to accomplish the objectives, assess the strengths and liabilities of different strategies, and then determine a structure for the action plan. The project advances to the next level with plan implementation, which requires clear communication, coordinated effort, strategic adjustments, increasing efficiency, and consistent investment of energy until the work is completed.

1. Task Analysis
Task analysis is the initial step in accomplishing a project. A group needs to look at a range of possible solutions, evaluating which ones have the most promise of success. Thinking about potential problems is important, as is identifying potential opportunities and resources. Being flexible in the analysis is critical. People need to be able to shift perspectives, brainstorm, and consider the outcomes of different alternatives. The group then designs a workable structure for the effort. Key goals include coming up with a step-by-step, practical plan, and designating appropriate responsibilities for the members.

2. Task Implementation
Once a group constructs a sound plan, follow through becomes the all-important next phase. As the work proceeds, members need to maintain clear communication to stay attuned to necessary responsibilities, to collaborate efficiently, and to introduce appropriate tactical adjustments that deliver strong outcomes. All members need to sustain a significant energy level and commitment to the project for the group to produce its best effort. It is imperative that members take personal responsibility for accomplishing their part of the task.

Interpersonal Focus

If group members nurture positive interpersonal relations and develop a team spirit, their collective performance usually ascends to a higher level. When members demonstrate mutual acceptance and are able to share feelings, values, and personal experiences with each other, they usually develop greater rapport which enhances their ability to collaborate and to be productive. It is important that all members feel included in the group's efforts and that they believe their ideas and concerns have been heard and respected, whether their ideas are integrated into the group's final solutions or not.

1. Positive Group Affiliation
In building up the personal relations in a group, the ultimate goal is to create a team spirit so members have a sense of positive interconnection. The foundation for this is a respect for the personal dignity of each member, which includes respect for ideas, values, experiences, and personhood. When members feel respected and accepted within a group, a sense of positive affiliation is fostered. Rapport-building activities can then further strengthen these bonds.

As members grow in mutual understanding, the group is able to operate more smoothly and more efficiently. As people establish stronger relationships, including friendship, they usually become more aware, supportive, and considerate. They can harness this positive social energy to expand creativity and productivity.

2. Feeling Orientation
When conflicts occur among members, they need to be able to speak about their concerns and feelings to address the issues. This process helps a group work through interpersonal conflict in a timely fashion, instead of letting it fester, which is destructive for any team. On a positive note, members should also pay attention to each other's enthusiasms, in order to channel constructive emotional energy into the enterprise. An important objective, therefore, is for all members to be comfortable in expressing their feelings, values, and ideas to promote broader communication. When members get clearer about their personal feelings and motivations, as well as those of others, they can manage positive and negative emotions more capably, which is essential for superior group performance. Members can stay

attuned to the emotional undercurrents in the group by watching the facial expressions and physical gestures of teammates, as wells as by listening to the tone and intensity of verbal communication.

These descriptions of the major scales and subscales reveal core information about the focus and purpose of the KGI assessment. They identify activities that produce flourishing team life, and they serve as guidelines for the skill development system. It should be noted that the model is grounded in the best research in the fields of team leadership and group behavior. In the next chapter, the connection to this research is explained to further illustrate the power of the measurement to inform dynamic personal and team improvement. ✕

CHAPTER 4

Research and Scholarship Underpinning the Klein Group Instrument® Model

The aim of the Klein Group Instrument (KGI) assessment is to bring together the best research on team leadership and group dynamics into a practical design for skill development, a system that is clear, accessible, and actionable. Accordingly, the model rests on a set of expert theories that address leadership, growth, group behavior, and team building. This chapter examines these connections to disclose the potency of the instrument for promoting exceptional individual and team achievement.

Group Synergy

The KGI design is structured to promote synergy in teams. Since the creation of synergy results in the highest performance, it is always the goal of group life, the gold standard for it. KGI leadership and membership skills zero in on the areas that foster this peak performance, integrating task, interpersonal, and negotiation operations in a substantial way. As a result, the model helps leaders and members cultivate sharper thinking and versatile problem solving to attain excellent task outcomes.

Researchers from the Massachusetts Institute of Technology, Carnegie Melon University, and Union College, published a study in the journal Science about their investigation of group intelligence and group dynamics (Wooley et al. 2010). They analyzed situations where the problem-solving ability of small groups jumped to a peak level, higher than what the smartest person in the group could have done alone, or what the simple combination of member skills would produce. In common language, they were targeting "synergy," that much sought after dynamic where a group vaults to an exceptional level of performance, beyond the simple sum of its parts. In an impressive piece of research, they quantified this dimension and identified the forces that make it happen. What they found is that social awareness and inclusion are critical elements for igniting synergy in a team, the key ingredients that propel a group to superior problem solving, creativity, and productivity. Based on this study, it becomes clear that when group members pay attention to each other, demonstrating social alertness, and when they include each other, making everyone feel a part of the team, a spirited interactive process can be achieved that brings out the best in people.

These results fit perfectly with the KGI model, aligning with its diamond design.

Leadership

Task Focus

Interpersonal Focus
Social Awareness

Negotiation Orientation
Inclusion

Interpersonal Focus strengthens social awareness by promoting positive member relations and by encouraging emotional sensitivity, which keeps members attuned to one another. Negotiation Orientation champions inclusion by deepening mutual understanding through perspective taking and by increasing member involvement through a win-win approach. Both of these KGI domains operate in support of Task Focus; they inject the extra social energy that sparks outstanding performance.

Leadership

Every team needs someone to take a leadership role. With or without a designated leader, a member must step up to guide the group, sharing ideas on how to properly complete the task and involving other members in the enterprise. For high-performing teams, experts assert that a shared leadership model often works best (Hackman 2002; Katzenbach and Smith 1993). The KGI model advances shared leadership in several ways. First, it introduces a basic compass to identify the specific skills that are necessary to induce high performance, putting everyone on the same page. Second, it assists individuals in understanding their own personal leadership abilities and defines ways they can expand their skills. Third, it prompts all members to rise up and become involved when their talents are most relevant to the undertaking, so the team makes maximum use of members' abilities and leadership potential.

Well-known psychologist Mihaly Csikzentmihalyi adds his voice to those extolling the benefits of a shared leadership approach. He formulated the theory of "Flow," describing a state where people have deep concentration and optimal engagement with their work (2002). In his research with Charles Hooker, he notes that sharing leadership roles has the effect of increasing opportunities for Flow, as members become more engrossed in the group effort. Shared leadership increases personal motivation for the work, creating more optimal experiences for the members and for the group as a whole. The researchers state that this approach can also enhance a group's creativity and potential for innovative work (2003). Allied with this perspective, the KGI model nurtures shared leadership opportunities, setting the stage for positive interpersonal relations, strong motivation, and larger creativity.

One way the KGI accomplishes this is by allowing people to refine two essential leadership traits: Assertiveness and Initiative (Brown 2000). Attention to these skill areas enables people to become more involved in the conversation, while also helping them avoid being so domineering that they block others' participation. When a team balances its members' Assertiveness and Initiative in a conscious manner, it can really advance a shared leadership agenda, stimulating member inclusion and, again, contributing to synergy.

With the Group Facilitation subscale, the instrument addresses two other important leadership concerns: task and social/relational issues (Bales 1950, 1955; Jay 1999). When leaders remain aware of both task and interpersonal interests, focusing attention in either direction as appropriate, they enable the team to maintain the equilibrium that produces steady and stout performance.

A Win-Win Model

In win-win bargaining, a team pursues solutions that will benefit every member. Fisher, Ury, and Patton (2011) state that this method supports good working relationships among participants, making it easier for members to cope with personal differences and to achieve significant task outcomes. Kouzes and Posner (2006) point out the win-win approach strengthens group morale, increases team cohesiveness, and boosts members' motivation to contribute considerable effort for the collective cause. In short, the win-win model seeks to include everyone and benefit everyone, as much as is reasonably possible, thereby creating an atmosphere that promotes synergy and, as a result, noteworthy achievement. When members feel respected, heard, and included, when they feel part of the fabric of the team, they usually develop the strongest identification with group goals and, consequently, have the deepest desire to accomplish them.

The Negotiation Orientation scale focuses on actions that enable a small group (or team) to resolve both task and interpersonal issues by applying a win-win approach. By definition, a team is a group of people working interdependently towards a common outcome (Hackman 2002). Because a team participates in a shared enterprise, the win-win model will often play an integral role in achieving the goals, a philosophy supported by a number of other theorists (Conger 2011; Covey 2004; Gordon 2004).

Toward these ends, the KGI subscale Perspective Taking inspires group members to investigate seriously one another's ideas, interests, and values to gather necessary information to strike mutually beneficial agreements. The Constructive Negotiation Approach subscale incorporates the elements of the win-win model, providing participants with direct feedback for employing this highly advantageous approach.

Focus on Tasks

With regard to the Task Focus scale, task expert J. Richard Hackman (2002) states that a team begins a project by making an assessment—it evaluates potential problems and favorable opportunities related to the assignment. The team then determines strategies to sidestep the difficulties, exploit the opportunities, and mobilize the best tactics. The analysis concludes with a structured plan to advance efficient operations and achieve outstanding outcomes. The KGI Task Analysis subscale promotes this approach, assisting individuals and teams in dealing with tasks in a logical, systematic manner.

Regarding the execution of the plan, Hackman (2002) declares that a team needs to do the following: communicate well, coordinate the effort smoothly, monitor the progress of the job consistently, use collective resources properly, and make necessary adjustments to the strategy in order to

guide the project to success. The Task Implementation subscale puts these specific elements into place so a team can obtain rewarding outcomes.

Emotional Intelligence

The Interpersonal Focus scale addresses the socio-emotional aspect of team life and connects with major theories in the Emotional Intelligence field. The concept of "Emotional Intelligence," which was first introduced by Peter Salovey and John Mayer (1990), and later became popularized by the work of Daniel Goleman (1995) and his associates, is an approach that has many valuable applications for group life. As Goleman, Boyatzis, and McKee (2009) indicate, when people feel good emotionally, they work at their best. In group settings, when positive feelings exist, people comprehend information more clearly, think more flexibly, and show a greater willingness to be helpful. Positive feelings truly enhance collaboration, contributing to the achievement of high-quality results. As these authors point out, an enthusiastic, cooperative mood on a team puts it on the path towards success.

The Positive Group Affiliation subscale inspires members to examine the social atmosphere of the team, motivating them to enrich relationships and strengthen team unity. Affiliation begins with a respect for each member's personal dignity and talents (Hicks 2011), which can engender mutual acceptance and mutual support. As these elements get established, people communicate more openly, look out for each other, and develop a camaraderie that enlivens the team. Hard work can then turn into fun because of a positive esprit de corps. As world-class entrepreneur Sir Richard Branson states, "So put people together in a way that will have them bouncing ideas off each other, befriending each other, and taking care of each other, and suddenly they are coming to you, not with gripes and problems, but with solutions and great ideas." (2008, p. 20)

On the other side of the spectrum, Goleman, Boyatzis, and McKee (2009) note that when emotional conflicts drain members' attention and energy, group performance suffers.

So it becomes imperative for members to

stay in touch with their feelings and those of their teammates. Basic goals with Emotional Intelligence are being mindful of your own feelings, as well as being aware of and empathizing with the feelings of others (Caruso and Salovey 2004; Goleman 1995; Goleman, Boyatzis, and McKee 2009; Salovey and Mayer 1990). When members stay alert in these ways, people can be attentive to emerging emotional issues and address them in a timely, constructive manner. This is critical for keeping a team on a productive track.

The Feeling Orientation subscale highlights these concerns. It offers information to promote emotional self-reflection, as well as attentiveness to others' feelings, with the aim of fostering effective management of emotional energy. It helps people notice when emotions turn negative, spurring them to reverse that trend. It also encourages people to watch for other members' enthusiasms and excitements, with the goal of funneling that energy into productive work for the group. As Caruso and Salovey (2004) state, the overall goal is to help members identify, understand, use, and manage emotions in the most beneficial manner. When this occurs, it moves a group towards first-rate collaboration.

Summary

As can be seen from this analysis, the KGI scales and subscales concentrate on group functions that major theorists identify as integral for achieving excellent performance. The model organizes these elements into a clear, practical system that allows leaders and members to come together in the pursuit of great results.

How the KGI design makes this possible is twofold: through the development of each individual member's social skills, and through the refinement of the team's overall interactive processes. As each member grows in skillfulness, and as the team as a whole plays smarter, there's an upsurge in performance that takes a team to new heights.

Social psychologist J. Richard Hackman asserted that individual skill development alone is not enough to propel a team to superlative performance (Coutu 2009). It's also necessary to refine the group's processes: the collective methods by which the team solves problems, implements strategies, and manages interpersonal relations. This is exactly where the KGI assessment's versatility comes to bear. The individual members' results can be combined to form the KGI® Group Profile, identifying team strengths and team challenges across the nine subscale dimensions. The profile furnishes suggestions about how the group can refine its practices in each area. With the KGI compass in their hands, members can attack a variety of issues straight on, related to leadership, task, interpersonal, and negotiation concerns. They can analyze their range of talents, determine key priorities, and experiment with new strategies to improve how they interact. Putting their heads together, they can implement fresh approaches that strengthen their collaboration. The method can empower any small group in its pursuit of potent performance.

In this final application, the true flexibility of the KGI model can be detected. Not only does it stimulate individual growth through the acquisition of new leadership and group skills, it invigorates the team as a whole through the refinement of its interactive processes. Individuals and teams can now interpret group life in a more systematic manner, identifying adjustments that lead to superior achievement.

In the next chapter, a remarkable aspect of the KGI model is explained: how the implementation of this method can transform an individual's social personality in ways that will have broad, lifelong benefit. ✄

CHAPTER 5

A Process of Psychological Transformation

At the beginning of the research project that created the Klein Group Instrument assessment, the simple goal was to design a measurement that would allow people to expand their leadership and membership skills in small groups. With the new assessment, people would become more capable facilitators, negotiators, task executors, and collaborative players. Grounded in established cognitive and behavioral methods, the model would offer a clear compass to interpret group events

and identify specific actions that would produce higher performance. Through years of rigorous investigation, the KGI measurement demonstrated again and again that it could meet these early objectives. When people received training with the model, they learned to read group dynamics more astutely, and they acquired some of the targeted skills to enhance their effectiveness.

Over time, however, additional benefits emerged during the ongoing research with the instrument. While every participant gained at least one or two new skills, there were those who persevered with the method, gaining five, eight, even twelve new skills, propelling them to a very accomplished level of performance. There were also people who developed new skills across a range of subscales, in ways that really stretched their personalities. As they integrated new techniques across numerous subscales, they acquired a remarkably different attitude about group life, one that was much more positive, confident, and rewarding.

In these instances, a significant psychological transformation took place. People didn't merely gain skills—their thinking processes, their feelings, and their attitudes about leadership and group life changed considerably. Their former fears about, or indifferences to, leadership or group participation diminished. A greater sense of self-efficacy emerged, a stronger belief in their own competence, based on their ability to employ their talents in constructive ways in group settings. A richer appreciation for other people also surfaced, generating a greater comfort level in groups, along with an increased ability to build relationships and develop friendships.

When these people now entered group events, they were much more potent players. They were alert to the subtleties of group dynamics, more intentional about how to make worthwhile contributions, and more ready to collaborate. With a broader array of skills, tapping into a broader range of psychological energies, their personalities became more balanced and more harmonious.

They acquired a new social maturity. Because of their knowledge and their valued contributions, they also became role models for their teammates, leaders in every sense of the word.

The connection with the MBTI instrument aided this process. As individuals drew on their understanding of personality preferences—their own and those of others—this knowledge assisted them in making useful changes in an array of social contexts, and expanded their psychological understanding of these experiences. Later in this volume, the relationship between the MBTI and KGI tools in this approach will be explained.

From studying these changes, it became evident that **when individuals gained skills in five KGI subscale areas, they appeared to cross a threshold, passing into a new territory with regard to their social development.** Their evolution into more fully functioning performers altered their sense of social self, so that they opened up and thrived in new ways in group settings.

Consequently, people came to view interpersonal relations with greater awareness, sensitivity, and acceptance. They learned to listen, reflect, and communicate more effectively, enabling them to build bridges with others to establish more cohesive, energetic teams. They also obtained a stronger conviction about their ability to nurture their own development, learning how to challenge themselves, how to make adjustments, and how to expand their perspectives and skills. In short, they learned to embrace a growth mindset, with lasting consequences.

This process of psychological change occurred in a four-step sequence:

1. Cognitive Insight
2. Behavioral Adjustment
3. Emotional Change
4. Psychological Transformation

The details of this experience will aid counselors, coaches, trainers, and teachers in appreciating a remarkable transition that can take place with this method, one that can be truly life changing for their clients and students. By understanding this process, professionals will be able to support people in their movement through the phases, maximizing their clients' potential growth using the instrument.

1. Cognitive Insight

The voyage begins when a person comprehends the KGI diamond model, the design that illuminates the fundamental operations in small-group life. As an individual grasps this design, fathoming the core concepts, the person begins to perceive group dynamics in a brand new way. What may have been confusing before now becomes clearer, more intelligible. The individual acquires a fresh way of looking at, and thinking about, group events, bringing a new order to experiences that may have previously seemed random or even chaotic. The individual is now able to interpret what's happening with greater precision and certainty.

The next element is personal reflection. Aware of the KGI compass and utilizing a KGI® Individual Profile, a person can evaluate his or her performance in the essential aspects of group life. What are one's strengths? What are key challenges? A person can now engage in a process of self-analysis, assessing the data, considering the personal patterns of social involvement. Through the reflective process, a person now becomes more self-aware, distinguishing important opportunities for skill development and determining what skills to acquire to become a well-rounded leader and group member.

One learns a way to think more deeply about personal development and to make thoughtful adjustments that cultivate a greater portion of one's potential. Of course, when a coach, consultant, or teacher who is knowledgeable about the KGI system becomes part of this process, the client's position is greatly enhanced. A professional explains theoretical fine points, asks probing questions to expand self-reflection, and assists in formulating an energetic plan for skill development.

Together, a professional and a client ponder subscale interrelationships and seek to balance the various skills in the individual's repertoire. They determine a set of priorities and evaluate which growth suggestions in the individual profile are most relevant to pursue, shaping an integrated plan for skill development. The dialogue between client and professional broadens thinking about all of these issues, setting up the next step in the procedure.

2. Behavioral Adjustment

The individual can now experiment with one or two behaviors in small-group contexts, which begins the first stage of behavioral adjustment: a person takes action to practice new skills.

During this experimentation, a person should be aware that things may not go smoothly in the initial attempt; there may be awkwardness and imprecision. Like all worthwhile skill development, behavioral adjustment takes time, effort, and perseverance. The operative word is boldness—a person needs the courage to go forward and practice the skills. Without the courage to push forward, the project can come to a standstill. Given that a client has an intelligent strategy in mind, it's best to plunge ahead and try out the skills.

When things don't go smoothly, the second aspect of behavioral adjustment is brought to bear: making appropriate modifications to the strategy to get better results. In the pursuit of new skills, particularly challenging ones, there is always trial and error. After the first attempt, an individual needs to take stock of the effort and consider ways to refine the practice.

In evaluating the application of the skill, what might have gone awry? Was it the timing of the action, emerging at the wrong moment? Was it the way the person expressed certain ideas, not communicating them clearly? Was it a lack of confidence that surged and somehow undermined the effort? What didn't go well, and why? Perhaps the effort did go pretty smoothly, only needing a minor adjustment for next time. In any case, sorting through the details of the action will help determine the adjustments that will bring greater success.

For example, an individual decides to acquire skills with Feeling Orientation, paying closer attention to the emotional issues in the group, in order to help the team manage them. As the individual attempts to tune in to the emotional currents, he experiences moments of confusion in reading specific feelings, and there may be some awkwardness in raising points with the team. The path to skill acquisition turns out to be a bumpy road, not a smooth one. Despite the bumpiness, he persists in monitoring emotional patterns, checking them out with teammates, and getting a better feel for the emotional nuances of group life. Seeking to find the correct language and the correct instant to communicate these issues, he tinkers with ways to diagnose feelings and ways to open up discussion with the team. With some experimentation, he eventually becomes more expert with the process, becoming better at picking up on clues and addressing them. He has now acquired useful skills that can aid his teams in maintaining better emotional balance, which will contribute to higher productivity.

By persevering and making refinements along the way, an individual gains deeper insight into the application of specific skills. With practice, the new behaviors are reinforced, strengthened, and integrated in the person's regular pattern of participation.

Importantly, in the initial phase of practice, people state that, in general, it takes three attempts to get firm traction with the new skill, a place in which one is much more confident with the application. **So making three attempts, with appropriate adjustments, is imperative.** This is a critical idea to instill in a client. It encourages persistence and also indicates that a person can achieve competent use of a skill in a relatively short time. One or two poor attempts may cause some people to get discouraged and want to quit, but better performance may be just around the corner if the individual tries again.

After the third attempt, which increases confidence in using the skill, smaller adjustments, based on different group contexts, will enable a client to further sharpen it. Over time, a person will be able to apply the skill nimbly whenever it is needed, exercising the correct technique in situations without even thinking; the skill has become second nature.

3. Emotional Change

Behavioral adjustments occur in a social context. A person is not working alone but with others, helping a team attain greater cohesion and enabling it to accomplish a task. As a result, there's an audience for these efforts. Other members notice a person's positive contributions to the group—whether the efforts are in facilitation, negotiation, task execution, or interpersonal relations.

Because the contributions are visible, because they enable the team to be more successful, other members appreciate these efforts. They express praise, gratitude, and other forms of affirmation. The individual's efforts get repaid with increased social standing.

What is refreshing to see is the way that social appreciation significantly impacts how an individual feels in a group, and also in general. When other members are affirming, it lifts a person's self-esteem. When others praise one's skillfulness, it raises self-confidence. When others call someone a valuable team player, it increases a sense of belonging.

Where before someone may have lacked self-assurance in certain roles, a new sense of confidence arises. Employing new skills, the individual is valued by the team in fresh ways and, consequently, the person feels better about himself. Since the group's affirmation is a response to real performance, practical actions taken during the team's work, the new feeling of achievement has a firm basis. With it, the individual starts to gain a stronger belief in his capacity to be a capable leader and group member.

Not only does the group reaction constructively impact an individual's sense of social self, it also alters the way a person responds to other people. Acceptance and appreciation from others enable an individual to feel more comfortable in a group. Trust grows and a greater openness to others begins to blossom. An individual can reciprocate by expressing appreciation to teammates—an acknowledgment of their skills, talents, and perspectives—resulting in an increased ability to build rapport and collaborate with them. Appreciation begets appreciation, fostering a greater mutual acceptance, which strengthens a team. From a person's successes with KGI skill development, a whole cluster of positive social emotions can begin to flourish, including feelings of sympathy, empathy, and a sense of unity with others.

In the past a person may have been restricted by fear, distrust, or suspicion, but constructive experiences, connected with skill development, help reduce negative feelings and replace them with more positive ones. The individual may feel surprise at this reversal in emotional circumstances. But given a taste of a more satisfying emotional state, many individuals become inspired to expand on it, pursuing their skill development even further. As they experience uplifting group encounters and achieve a sense of personal effectiveness, they are motivated to greater effort and greater accomplishment. This favorable momentum and deepening motivation has been evident in many KGI participants.

4. Psychological Transformation

As an individual passes through these phases, a significant transformation can take place with respect to attitude and consciousness. In the past, a person may have endured many frustrations in groups, which produced a negative outlook. People didn't work well together; there were tensions, difficulties, and mediocre outcomes; it wasn't clear how to move in better directions. With a shrug, the individual staggered into the next group event with low expectations—nothing felt rewarding in the situation.

But exposure to the KGI model begins to change that experience. Having clearer ideas about essential group dynamics and possessing new skills for competent participation, a person grasps how to operate more adeptly in groups and is better equipped to assume a leadership role that helps to make a group successful.

An individual recognizes that taking responsibility for improving her performance brings multiple benefits. It makes her a more vibrant team player. When she contributes thoughtful insights, it stimulates everyone's thinking, elevating the team's problem solving. When she helps the group achieve its goals, it lifts everyone's morale, adding fresh energy to the atmosphere. She discovers a deeper satisfaction in her group roles, along with an increased enjoyment in working with others. These factors help a person to fashion a more positive social identity.

An exciting element in the KGI system is that it puts people in touch with a process of self-improvement that spawns a growth mindset, supporting ongoing skill cultivation. They gain a new consciousness about the importance of self-development, one that will further the psychological processes of individuation and self-actualization, with broad applications for all types of social relations.

Since the KGI® Individual Profile contains fifteen to twenty growth suggestions, there's a tremendous opportunity for continued expansion. Success with initial efforts whets someone's appetite for more. As one climbs up the ladder, gaining more skills across more subscale domains, a remarkable transformation takes place—he becomes a strikingly different leader, with greater versatility and adaptability. The skills achieved in one or two group contexts can be transferred to many others, including intimate personal relationships and also family life.

By taking charge of one's developmental destiny, an individual gains a sense of direction, a sense of purpose, and a sense of control. Group situations are now colored by a different attitude: seen as opportunities for on-going learning and skill refinement.

Experiencing these changes, an individual acquires greater pluck for sailing group waters, aware that he or she can be an impact player on any team, one who not only performs well personally, but one who can also assist others in elevating their performances. In an alert, conscious way, the person can be the one who kindles synergy in a team. In this process, the individual becomes a different social being.

Theoretical Underpinnings for Personal Transformation

This system of personal development is grounded in the ideas of several major psychologists: Carl Jung, Abraham Maslow, Alfred Adler, and Carol Dweck. Jung articulated the process of individuation, a series of actions in which a person commits to the fullest possible development of his or her capacities (1921/1971; Jacobi 1967; Stein 2006). Consequently, an individual strives to realize a broad array of personal abilities to become well-rounded and whole. A valuable component in this process is the acquisition of skills that increase a person's ability to relate well to others, to interact effectively with them (Jung 1921/1971; Hannah 1997). This social development is exactly what the KGI model advances. It assists people in maximizing their present abilities and in cultivating new, previously undeveloped capacities in leadership, interpersonal relations, and negotiation skills. By

guiding the expansion of the personality in these directions, the KGI model permits people to realize a greater portion of their potential and become more fully individuated in the social realm.

Of course, Jung's individuation process includes the development of the various personality preferences, which are identified in his work Psychological Types (1921/1971). Jung's typology serves as the basis for the Myers-Briggs Type Indicator (MBTI) instrument. As noted earlier, the MBTI tool operates as a complementary measure with the KGI assessment, a relationship that will be explained in Chapter 19. Importantly, there is a remarkable correlation between Jung's psychological preferences and the fundamental operations in small groups, as defined by the KGI model. As a result, the MBTI and KGI assessments combine to deepen the understanding of both personality energies and social relations, allowing people to manage both more intelligently. The instruments support the acquisition of insights and skills that sustain the social growth intrinsic to Jung's individuation process.

Abraham Maslow, the humanistic psychologist, presents a theory of self-actualization displaying many similarities to Jung's individuation process. Maslow (2014) emphasizes a learning process that spurs people to cultivate their unused, neglected, and overlooked capacities in order to reach their greatest potential. Through astute choices and concerted effort, people become more self-determined. The KGI design supports people in making informed choices in the development of leadership and group skills, guiding them in a learning process that furthers Maslow's self-actualization. Maslow points out that by practice and overcoming difficulties, people extend their capacities and turn them into serious strengths. In this manner, real achievement occurs, and realistic self-confidence ensues. This is perfectly in line with the system espoused by the KGI method. As people practice new group skills, they expand their competencies, experience meaningful growth, and become more self-confident leaders and team members.

Alfred Adler, founder of the individual psychology movement, was a colleague of Sigmund Freud and Jung, and later mentored Maslow. Of the early depth psychologists, he placed the greatest emphasis on the value of social relations, seeing it as a cornerstone of a person's mental health (1927/2010). Adler recognized that as social beings, we are bound up in community, and critical for our development is the nurturing of a social interest that enables us to cooperate with others and cultivate meaningful relationships. By striving for social competence, we can contribute productively to the group, which, in turn, provides us with a feeling of self-worth. We need to find the courage and energy to face social challenges and manage them constructively. As we do, we are able to enrich the lives of others, as well as our own, something that can be a lifelong enterprise which will continue to broaden and strengthen our personalities (1927/2010; 1964; Adler and Ansbacher 1979). These ideas are entirely in accord with the KGI system; in fact, the KGI model helps to operationalize these goals in an important way, by providing guidance with the best contemporary research on team leadership and group skills to support the pursuit of greater social dexterity.

Carol Dweck, a psychologist from Stanford University, emphasizes the critical "mindset" that sustains this growth process, an attitude that makes all the difference with regard to what one achieves in life (2008). The growth mindset cultivates a belief that our personal qualities are things to be nurtured through effort—through passion, toil, and training. The important first step is to gain accurate insights about our abilities and limitations. We then pursue an appropriate learning process, which requires love of challenge, belief in the value of effort, resiliency in the face of setbacks, and the creative pursuit of greater success. Dweck declares that we never know our true potential because it's an unknown, but if we implement these principles, we are on the correct path to the fullest realization of our talents.

The KGI model concurs with Dweck's reasoning. A person's full leadership potential is an unknown because it doesn't simply apply to a business, profession, religious group, sport team, or social club. It also applies to family life, and to the most personal of one-on-one relationships. Leadership cuts a wide swath through all realms of social existence. So as a person gains a clearer understanding of the central elements of small-group leadership, acquires insights into his or her strengths and limitations, and then commits to the persistent practice of new skills, the applications can be sweeping. Over time, as more skills are added to one's repertoire, a really remarkable improvement can occur, bringing outstanding levels of success. During years of training with the KGI assessment, thousands of people have developed their talents as Dweck describes. Through insight, practice, adjustment, and persistence, they have not only amassed an array of new skills but have cultivated an attitude and grasped a process that would support their ongoing growth far into the future. In short, they have realized and actualized the right mindset.

These theorists offer influential ideas about the process of personal growth that reside at the heart of the KGI method. While this system can be pursued independently by an individual, it becomes even more compelling when it is nurtured within a team context where all members work together on KGI results. In this setting, people can inspire, reinforce, and mentor one another in their skill building, extending further the potency of the learning. With the KGI method, members have a common language, a common focus, and opportunities for personal and group gain. It's another variation on the win-win theme: all members can benefit by a shared learning process and, as they sharpen their skills, the team itself becomes healthier and more proficient.

Over the years, many people experienced these developmental changes from their training with the KGI model. In the next chapter, several case studies reveal how this pattern emerged in a variety of contexts. ✕

CHAPTER 6

Case Studies

The studies in this chapter demonstrate how the Klein Group Instrument assessment can influence social behavior, causing striking transformations. The first example depicts a corporate CEO who had everything going for him except a leadership style that alienated his top people. The second presents a young businessman who caught a vision with the KGI tool that put him on a fast track to accomplishment and success. The third portrays a talented student whose rigid attitudes about group life stifled her

leadership development. In each instance, the KGI model opened the person's mind, provided guidance on behavioral modification, and put in motion a process of consequential change. The examples draw from diverse contexts: an executive coaching situation, a leadership training program, and a college course on leadership skills. They illustrate the flexibility of the model to empower people with new insights and more enlightened decision making.

Executive Coaching

As Chief Executive Officer of a major corporation, William sat atop an empire that controlled sixty percent of its market in the Western United States. With plenty of name recognition and plenty of profits, everything seemed to be going swimmingly for the business. An accountant by training, William had made a steady climb to the executive seat through diligent attention to detail and a fixation on task performance. Displaying a tremendous

patience with fine points, he methodically analyzed the practical issues in business operations.

Wishing to maintain a keen competitive edge for the company, William hired a consultant to do coaching and team building with himself and his executive council of vice presidents. The consultant utilized the Klein Group Instrument tool for these purposes.

The initial phase of training proceeded in a fairly standard manner. The consultant introduced the team to the model, and then met individually with the members to set personal agendas for skill building. The executives had the opportunity to practice new skills for a month before follow-up sessions, when they would bridge into the team-building aspects of the project. The participants all seemed receptive in the opening round.

When the consultant returned to meet one-on-one with the participants, most had made solid progress in obtaining new skills. The conspicuous exception was William. Dragging his feet, he became reluctant to do things differently. His attitude appeared to be that the training should focus on his subordinates because they needed to refine their leadership performance much more than he did. He stated that the board of directors was pleased with the job he was doing; in fact, they had rewarded him with a major bonus at the end of the previous year. So he directed the consultant to concentrate on the vice presidents. Though the consultant tried to explain the benefits William would receive from participation, the CEO turned a deaf ear.

What really startled the consultant was a conversation that transpired a short time later in the lunchroom of corporate headquarters. Walking in to pick up a snack, the consultant was tugged to a table by two vice presidents. They sat at a distance from others in the room. After glancing around, the vice presidents leaned in and talked in a confidential tone. They stated that the consultant's efforts had been worthwhile; they had acquired new skills that would be valuable for them—valuable in their next positions with other companies! Both planned to leave as soon as possible. They explained that this had been the pattern for some time at the executive level in the organization.

Despite a prestigious company name and sizable profits, they said that the elite people found working with William suffocating. He remained remote, controlling, and nitpicking. For example, when they submitted expense reports for travel, he fought over nickels, dimes, and pennies. All of the best people decided to grab some useful experience, bide their time, and jump to another company as soon as an opportunity presented itself.

One of the VPs, staring coldly into the consultant's eyes, said: "William is a rock. You can't budge him. You can't change him. Because he won't change, the quality people will be leaving, like always."

Hearing those words, the consultant felt a chill.

Later, reflecting on the conversation, the consultant began to experience a sense of panic. This intervention was sliding into a tailspin, and he felt it could crash. How could he convince William to try to change? What leverage did he have? Apparently, the board of directors really liked him, bestowing a large bonus. The money kept rolling in. Because the company dominated the regional market, it could always attract replacements for those who departed. Still, it was a terrible waste of talent and money. The company kept grooming new executives who planned to skip out when the time was right. Hiring fresh people required more investments of time, training, and capital. Losing its most expert people, the company had to wait for the next executives to get acclimated and really gear up but, eventually, they too would want to abandon ship.

The consultant felt his back was against the wall. He needed to speak with William and put the cards on the table. He decided to be direct and honest with him, in a respectful way, and see where it might lead. He had to try to lift the rock out of the ground, despite knowing how seriously embedded it was. One thought consoled him: William was a straightforward type of person, so the approach wouldn't be totally off target.

In his meeting with the CEO, the consultant took a deep breath and told William that by not participating in the training, he had become detached from the executive group. He was disconnecting from his team. The consultant said that he'd become aware that these actions distressed some of the team members. Maintaining confidentiality, the consultant brought up the fact that this type of action alienated people; it was the kind of thing that drove people away from the company.

William became defensive and pointed to his record as CEO. He'd achieved exceptional profits for the company, which everyone recognized. There were always disgruntled people, he said, and it was inevitable that some left.

But the consultant responded that the executive group was becoming like a revolving door—a number of talented people, with really important knowledge and skills, had departed. The company had to train new leaders, at great expense, and there was the time lag before they fully mastered the business. That was tremendously inefficient. Plus, the situation caused low morale, further reducing the quality of performance. While the company held a splendid position, these factors could erode that position, and it would eventually affect him.

William didn't rebut these points, but paused for a moment, thinking.

The consultant then asked about the toll that this leadership style had on William. He pointed to the long hours William invested each week, fighting to maintain a tight grip on the organization, and the stress that put on him. What if they could establish a greater esprit de corps with the executive group? What if they could create a positive atmosphere, one that bred more commitment to the organization? What if, instead of low morale, there was increased trust and camaraderie? Wouldn't that reduce stress—his and theirs? And if they could operate like a real team, it would make the company much more productive. That could make him comfortable enough to take a little more time for his family and other interests. He wouldn't have to be a slave to this job. The truth was that real, authentic teamwork could help him accomplish that.

"This has been rather inefficient," William conceded. "What would the new approach entail, specifically? Tell me the points."

The consultant took out a copy of William's KGI® Individual Profile, opening it to the composite subscale graph, and laid it on the desktop. They examined it. The subscales that fell in the low range of the Medium section included: Group Facilitation, Initiative, Constructive Negotiation Approach, and Positive Group Affiliation. At the very bottom of the Low section, barely visible on the graph, was Feeling Orientation.

"As we've discussed before," said the consultant, running a finger across the page, "all of these subscales offer meaningful opportunities for growth. Constructive Negotiation Approach and Positive Group Affiliation would be the most important to start with, in my opinion, to build better team morale. But Initiative is also crucial, because if the others see you step up and lead in new ways, it will be influential."

Much to everyone's surprise, William organized a weekend retreat for the executive group the following month. Out at a secluded center, he made himself accessible in a way he had never done before. He told those gathered that he wanted to open up communication, understand others' views, and create greater dialogue so they could work together more effectively. He wanted to establish a new atmosphere that would promote shared decision making and better collabo-

ration. He asked people for ideas on how to go forward in these directions, and they had initial discussions.

Back at the office, William showed his sincerity by literally opening his door and having people come to meet with him more frequently, one-on-one. Slowly, he began to build better rapport with his people. He discovered that their shared analysis and mutual problem solving did produce beneficial results. People became more willing to bring up creative ideas, and their work moved forward more quickly in the process.

At meetings, he tried to facilitate open-ended discussions about topics. In the past he believed that once he thought through a problem, that was it, the matter was settled. Now, it became a process of thinking through the problem together, seeking a group consensus.

During one meeting, he asked his team what they thought he should do to provide greater motivation for all of the employees in the company. There was a stilted silence.

"Come on," he prodded, "there must be some ideas."

A female VP spoke up, "I am not sure you want to hear this, but I think you could publically express your appreciation to the employees for their hard work at the next full-company meeting."

The comment gave William a pause. It challenged him with his most repressed area—the expression of feelings, connected to the Feeling Orientation subscale. That had always been a major roadblock for him because he wasn't one to express any feelings at all. In addition, his value system said that people were paid to do a good job. That was expected; it didn't require extra praise or appreciation. Having been brought up that way, the idea was central to his personal belief system.

"I will think about that," he replied. Fortunately, the next major meeting was months away, so there was time to ponder the matter.

However, a crisis emerged just a few weeks later. One of the VPs, the head of a critical division in the company, left for another job.

William directed the consultant to organize a one-day workshop for people in that division, in order to gather their input about the issues in that sector. In their opinion, what type of job description would be appropriate to find the right person to fill the position? The consultant said he could facilitate these activities but told William he should attend all of the sessions of the workshop.

The CEO resisted, declaring that the loss of such a prominent division leader created a crisis that demanded his full attention. He didn't have time to be involved in the workshop. He just needed the data it would generate. The consultant replied that William had been working diligently to build more connections with people. This dilemma presented an opportunity to advance that effort in a serious way. By participating, he would show the employees his concern and that he was with them in solving the problem. After considering these points, William said he would compromise and come to the first hour of the workshop.

What transpired became a pivotal moment in changing the culture of the organization. Attending the opening hour of the workshop, William became engaged in the conversation. He decided to cancel his other appointments and stay for the day's events. Not only that, he stayed after the closing session and chatted with a number of key managers, getting to know them more personally. No one had ever seen him take initiative in this way.

Together, the participants constructed a detailed report, one that targeted central issues for the division and identified the type of leader who could address the concerns and enable the organization to flourish. In a follow-up meeting with the division, William publicly thanked everyone for their hard work with the report. People thanked him for his involvement with the process. It was a new moment of mutual respect and authentic collaboration. William became increasingly comfortable working with his people, and it changed his thinking, attitude, and style of leadership. He became aware of the power of building interpersonal rapport, how it supported sturdy performance and high task achievement. The insight influenced him as he moved into the future, allowing him to respond to people in a more personal, direct way. This approach made everyone more comfortable and reduced the underlying tensions that were undermining the company.

For ten years, I have been an instructor with the Springfield Leadership Institute, sponsored by the Western New England University College of Business and the Affiliated Chambers of Commerce of Greater Springfield (MA). The program offers a series of training events that focus on prominent aspects of leadership development. The last session showcases the Klein Group Instrument and Myers-Briggs Type Indicator method for acquiring team leadership skills. The program attracts an impressive cross-section of business and professional leaders, from both the for-profit and nonprofit sectors.

A number of years ago, a young man lingered after my presentation. As it turned out, James, in his early thirties, was a middle manager in a manufacturing company. Dressed in a jacket and tie, with a smart, stylish cut, he appeared every bit the aspiring young businessman. Right away, I picked up on his intensity and serious-mindedness.

With his KGI® Individual Profile in his hand, he stated: "This material really spoke to me. I think there are a number of points here that could help me strengthen my team leadership."

I asked him what points resonated with him.

He identified the ideas related to balancing the task and interpersonal skills. From his experience, he recognized the need to manage both elements in a team. You had to keep the task moving, and you had to keep the people involved. But it wasn't always easy, especially finding the best ways to deploy people and keep them motivated.

Together, we looked over a number of growth statements in the profile, featured in Group Facilitation, Task Focus, and Interpersonal Focus. With his concerns in mind, we roughed out an agenda that involved several skills. We conferred about how to align the points in a skill-building sequence. I mentioned the importance of persistence in practicing the behaviors and refining them as he went along.

As the conversation concluded, he said: "Would you be willing to do a presentation at the national conference for our industry?"

His question surprised me, but I replied: "Sure, I'd be glad to. Give me a call and we'll work something out."

He thanked me for my time and assured me

he would be in touch.

Almost exactly a year later, I received the call with the invitation. The organization booked me for an afternoon event, asking me to attend the luncheon that preceded it. When I arrived at the hotel, James was there to greet me, and we had time to chat before going into the dining room.

"During the past year," he announced, "I kept my KGI profile in the top drawer of my desk. Every month I took it out and selected a new skill to work on. I did that for twelve months, and I have gained twelve new skills!"

He beamed with satisfaction.

"That's outstanding," I replied. "That's what I hoped for when I designed the instrument, that people would pursue a series of skills that would really make them versatile, highly effective leaders."

"Well, my team runs much smoother now. We discuss things thoroughly; we ask each other a lot of questions and analyze problems from a lot of angles. We tinker with ideas and refine them. Everyone's involved, sharing opinions. As you suggested, I use probe questions and really pay attention to people's interests. I tap into those when we split up the assignments. It really helps to keep people in the game. Plus, we always take time to celebrate our successes. We try to appreciate everyone's contributions."

"It sounds like there's a lot of positive energy on your team."

"There is. It's great. But the thing is I really feel comfortable leading the group. I know what to do—how to facilitate, how to keep people involved, how to motivate them based on their interests. My leadership is much better now. I feel like I'm a much different person as a leader."

"When you develop that range of skills, it's natural that your leadership identity evolves. You're becoming an excellent team leader."

"Thank you. It's all about the practice. Once I learned how to make improvements, I just kept pursuing the model. I added more skills. Since I was getting results, it was the logical thing to do. It's been a real difference maker. I really look forward to working with my team now, and I'm not afraid of being on any team."

"That's the beauty of it. The same skills can be applied to any group situation."

He nodded.

Shortly thereafter, we went to the banquet room for our luncheon. Our upbeat exchange really lifted my spirits, and it carried over into an animated afternoon presentation. But I didn't have any more opportunities to speak with James again.

About a year later, I experienced a bit of luck. At a business banquet, with random seating, it turned out that I sat at a table with the Vice President of James' company. As the dinner concluded, I intentionally walked out with the VP, seeking the opportunity to inquire about James. I mentioned to him my previous association with his employee.

"It's funny you mention that," he replied, "James was recently promoted to Director of Marketing for our company. We've been impressed with his growth as an employee, and with his leadership abilities. We've got our eye on him. We see great things for him in our future. In fact, if things continue to go well, he could be a candidate for executive leadership."

"That doesn't surprise me at all," I answered. "During my conversations with him, I was impressed by his commitment to self-improvement. He took skill development seriously, and he worked hard at it. With his attitude and energy, I agree with you: I think great things are going to happen for him and for your company, because he's going to make them happen."

Leadership and Team Skills Course

Jessica, an undergraduate senior, was a student in my Leadership and Team Skills course. A science major, she had a studied reserve about her, as she sat silently in the corner and watched the various class interactions to start the term. Always neatly attired, yet with certain aloofness, she seemed content to remain on the sidelines simply observing.

After exposure to the KGI assessment, she received an assignment to develop new leadership skills in an out-of-class team. The project required writing several application papers, spaced several weeks apart, in which she would evaluate her progress with these efforts. In addition, she participated in a ninety-minute interview with me at the end of the semester to analyze her experiences.

Jessica belonged to an academic honor society,

in which she was assigned to an ad hoc committee tasked with coordinating a fundraising dinner at the end of the semester. She said that when she joined the committee she noticed the other students began the meeting by engaging in personal conversation, taking up time with small talk. This irritated her. A busy lady, she attended the meeting to get the job done; she wanted to get down to work. This chitchat seemed like a waste of time. As a result, she never conversed with the other students in this manner, remaining standoffish. She sensed that some of the other students were starting to dislike her and she didn't fit in with the team, but that didn't matter to her. Her personal value was to get the work done as promptly as possible and then move on to the next task. She would stick to her value, regardless of what others thought.

While she had a high KGI score in Task Implementation, the Positive Group Affiliation score was much weaker, languishing in the Low section. It was obvious that attending to group spirit was irrelevant to her. In addition, her Leadership scores for Assertiveness, Group Facilitation, and Initiative all landed in the Low section. Challenged by these results, she decided to become more participatory in her honor society committee. It seemed like an appropriate setting to stretch herself, especially given the way things were going.

Jessica started taking part in the informal conversations, seeking to become more acquainted with others, practicing new skills from Assertiveness and Positive Group Affiliation. Bit by bit, she began to feel accepted by her groupmates. Then some surprising things started to happen. Not only did she stop to talk with other committee members on campus when she encountered them, she actually developed meaningful friendships with two of them as they began to socialize together. Jessica stated that she never thought friendships could result from this kind of association!

As greater rapport developed, she became more committed to the group. Increasingly, she felt integrated into the fabric of the team. Given these conditions, it seemed that she could now begin to work on the Leadership subscales of Group Facilitation and Initiative to broaden her skill development.

On the evening of the fundraising dinner, an interesting transition took place. Normally, she declared, she would have tried to meet her obligations at the beginning of the event and then split at the earliest opportunity, leaving the messy, closing details to others. At a fundraising dinner, the dirtiest work, of course, is always at the end with the cleanup process. This she had always steadfastly avoided. But this time her conscience bothered her because she didn't want to leave her friends in the lurch—the situation had become personal. So she decided to stay to the bitter end.

As the cleaning up process began, with people scurrying in different directions, Jessica stepped up and took charge of the operation. Her practical, organizational skills had found a perfect showcase. She smoothly guided people in a more efficient effort, while maintaining a friendly banter with her teammates. Communication flowed as the group handled its job adroitly. Her initiative, and her ability to facilitate the effort, impressed all of the group members, making the job quicker and easier for everyone. At that moment she really became established with the team, one of the leaders.

The experience triggered a compelling insight for her. She recognized that when teammates develop rapport, it increases their commitment to the work and helps to achieve strong task outcomes. Members are willing to do more for the group because of the personal connections. She had always been about strong task outcomes, but now she saw how building relationships supported that in a consequential way. She also realized that as she became more comfortable with her teammates, she became more confident in stepping up to lead them. Feeling like one of the group made it easier to pick up the leadership reins. Since she had always been one to linger on the sidelines, she never fully appreciated this dynamic before. She noticed that becoming really immersed in the group created leadership opportunities, allowing her to display practical talents that others respected and valued.

At the end of the interview, Jessica emphatically stated that she would never again approach any group situation with such a narrow attitude. She recognized that making interpersonal connections and building rapport with people counted for a lot. It mattered for teamwork and, just as significantly, for her own leadership development. By relating to people, there was a chance for a whole range of her social skills to grow. As she approached her new career in science, she intended to stay connected with the people in future teams so she could further refine her leadership and group talents.

These cases display the substantial changes that can take place when people are trained with the KGI model. Participants expand their thinking, acquire new skills, and develop a very different point of view about collaborating with others. They fashion new social identities that make them more engaged leaders and team members.

In the next chapter, the reader will be introduced to the administration of the KGI assessment and the scoring system. ✄

CHAPTER 7

Administration and Scoring

The Center for Applications of Psychological Type (CAPT), the publisher of the Klein Group Instrument assessment, has created an online website for the administration of this leadership tool. The site is informative, efficient, and user friendly. Administration is only offered electronically; no paper-and-pencil version is available. While any individual or group may go online and take the assessment independently, the website is designed with professionals in mind. It contains special features for counselors, coaches, consultants, trainers, and teachers, making it easy to direct the flow of information for professional applications. The site includes a series of pages that explains all aspects of the instrument, including administration, as well as answers to frequently asked questions about the measurement.

It requires fifteen-to-twenty minutes to complete the KGI measurement, which presents straightforward statements about basic group behaviors. A sample KGI item: "I will analyze a problem for the group and suggest a strategy for solving it." Using a five-point rating scale, an individual responds by identifying the frequency with which the person employs that particular behavior in a small-group setting. The five choices include: (1) Never, (2) Rarely, (3) Half-the-time, (4) Usually, or (5) Always.

A respondent can approach the questions in one of two ways: how the individual generally performs in small-group settings, or how the person performs in a particular small group of choice. The latter offers a respondent specific advice on how to adjust behavior in that express context. When a person finds him-or-herself in a regular, important group situation, such a tailored strategy can be a tremendous asset to improve performance. This approach also allows an individual to take the instrument multiple times, from the perspectives of various small-group affiliations, to examine variations in behavior in these settings. This can provide insights into how an individual adapts to different groups according to the person's role, colleagues, and task expectations. For example, a person can evaluate how she operates in a group of peers, compared to a group of administrative superiors. This will facilitate an even deeper analysis of one's patterns of social behavior.

Individual scores are based on the percentage of the time the person endorses the behaviors connected to particular scales. A high score on any of the major scales or subscales indicates that a person performs the specific behaviors in that area 75% to 100% of the time; a medium score signifies the person performs the behaviors 50% to 74% of the time; while a low score points to performance from 0% to 49% of the time.

The respondent receives a KGI® Individual Profile, which displays results for all major scales and subscales on colorized graphs, presenting a visually attractive, straightforward way to evaluate patterns of behavior. The report also includes detailed, bulleted feedback in each subscale area to guide specific skill development. Feedback points are clear, focused, and easy to put into action. All of this information will be illustrated in Chapter 9.

When members of a particular team wish to improve their collective performance, their individual scores can be anonymously combined to create the KGI® Group Profile. This report includes an overview of the team's performance on all scales and subscales, recommendations for improvement, and directions for implementing an action plan. While the KGI® Individual Profile introduces precise, personal information for coaching a client, the KGI® Group Profile presents a broad range of group data to orchestrate an energetic team-building process.

Professionals who coach or train with the instrument can establish a special account to manage the KGI experience for their customers. The benefits of the system include:

1. **Easy Access.** Clients or students are able to take the assessment without having to create separate accounts on the CAPT website.

2. **Controlled Pace.** Consultants decide when, and how, to deliver the KGI® Individual and KGI® Group Profiles to the group members. This can be done via email or printed copy.

3. **Confidentiality.** Because individual results are confidential, group members must grant access to the consultant. This can be done as a person takes the instrument, and the consultant can also send an email reminder to grant access.

4. **Oversight.** Consultants are able to monitor all activity through their CAPT account. They receive automated email notifications as their clients move through the KGI process.

Here are the steps a consultant would follow to set up a professional account and work with clients:

1. **Get Started**
Point your browser to CAPT.org and look for the KGI section under assessments. You'll find many resources here, including sample profiles and information on preparing to take the KGI assessment. Look for the Purchase section and choose either Group or Individual administrations. When buying for a group you must know the number of members, so be sure you have that locked down before making your purchase.

2. **Understand everyone's role**
Let's define the roles for you as the facilitator, and for your clients as the people who take the assessment. You will act in the **Consultant/Coach** role, a term you will encounter as you set up the administrations. The table below outlines the roles:

Consultant/Coach	Client
Must have a CAPT account	No need for a CAPT account
Does not take KGI	Takes the KGI
May have access to Individual Profile	Can grant access to Individual Profile
Has access to Group Profile	Receives profiles via email or printed copy
Controls timing and delivery of profiles	

3. **Set up KGI administrations for your clients**
All of your work with the KGI assessment begins by logging into your account at CAPT.org. Proceed as follows:

› On the Your Account page, choose **Klein Group Instrument®** under Digital Product Purchases. Note that Individual and Group administrations are managed separately, but everyone takes the same KGI assessment.

› Choose **Individual Administrations** to access these purchases, and then choose *Have a client or colleague take the KGI*.
  a. Read and follow the instructions in the Overview.
  b. Fill in the blanks on the *Set Up Administration and Send Orientation Email*

(name, email address, optional deadline) page. Note that your relationship to the individual will be Consultant/Coach. If you choose Colleague you will not have access to his or her profile.

Here you will also choose how the person should respond to the KGI items—as the person is in a specific group or in small groups in general.

  c. When you complete these steps your client will receive an email with instructions for taking the assessment.

• Choose **Group Administrations** to access these purchases, and then look in *Unassigned* to see these raw groups. Once you get started you will see sections here called *In Process and Complete.*

  a. Choose *Set Up Group*; read and follow the instructions in the Overview.

  b. On the following *Set Up Group* page, choose a group name and your relationship to the group (Consultant/Coach). Here you will also choose how group members should respond to the KGI items—as if they are in a specific group or in groups in general.

  c. In *Send Orientation Email*, add the names and email addresses for each member of the group (be careful to get these right— you won't get another chance!)

  d. When you complete these steps your clients will receive an email with instructions for taking the assessment.

4. After your client(s) complete the KGI assessment

You can monitor the status of both Individual and Group administrations in your account.

Individuals who have not yet taken the KGI appear *In Process*. Those who finished are moved to *Complete*. You will see links in each section that allow you to remind clients to take the assessment, grant you access to see their profile, and download or email their profile.

Groups who have not completed the assessment appear *In Process*, and it is here that you will choose to *Score the Group Profile*, available once everyone completes the assessment. Once this is done the group gets moved to the Complete section.

As a consultant/coach, you control when and how clients receive their profiles, either via email, or as a handout from you. When your clients have completed the assessment, you can schedule your feedback sessions and begin the work of enhancing leadership and team performance.

In the next chapter, reliability and validity data on the Klein Group Instrument offer additional evidence about the power of the measurement, illustrating why it is such a dynamic training tool. ✕

CHAPTER 8

Reliability and Validity

The Klein Group Instrument for Effective Leadership and Participation in Teams assessment was developed over a twelve-year period, which involved intensive quantitative and qualitative research to determine its reliability and validity. During the development phase, thousands of participants took the assessment and hundreds of the people were interviewed about their skill-building experiences in business, professional, organizational, and educational settings. Results from all of these studies are

contained in the Klein Group Instrument Manual (2007). By the end of the research period, the KGI assessment demonstrated that it was an accurate and potent measurement tool.

For the present purpose, it would be worthwhile to highlight the key points from the statistical and qualitative analyses, which display the power of the instrument.

Reliability

Reliability has to do with the consistency with which an instrument measures the specific behaviors it is targeting. Does the KGI assessment consistently evaluate the intended group behaviors? To examine this issue, two kinds of reliability are considered. First, within the instrument itself, how well do the items for the scales consistently measure their constructs? This is known as internal consistency reliability. Second, how consistently does the instrument measure the

same behaviors for a given population over time? This is known as test-retest reliability.

For internal consistency reliability, using Cronbach's coefficient alpha analysis, the coefficient alphas for the four major scales of the KGI assessment ran from .82 to .86. (A coefficient alpha of .70 is considered good, and as the figure goes higher, it reflects greater reliability.) Given that the instrument has just 63 items, these scores reflect very substantial reliability. In addition, the coefficient alphas for the KGI subscales ran from .70 to .80, from the good to very good range.

For test-retest reliability, the KGI assessment was administered to the same group of people on two occasions, with an interval of thirty days, which is a standard test-retest interval. Using the Pearson correlation coefficient analysis, results for the major scales and subscales ran from .78 to .92, falling in a very good range.

Validity

Validity is concerned with the question: Does the instrument actually measure what it intends to measure? Does it really assess the behaviors on which it claims to focus? One way to investigate this issue is for research participants to take the Klein Group Instrument along with another established assessment. The results from the two measurements can be statistically compared to see if they correlate in the ways that would be expected based on the underlying theories. This is called concurrent validity. Another way to examine validity is to determine if participants can actually employ instrument results to develop and refine the intended group behaviors. Do the results give people accurate information so they can go forward and acquire the intended group skills? This can be evaluated with qualitative research, using both written documents and interviews.

A concurrent validity study, conducted with a thousand participants who took both the Klein Group Instrument and Myers-Briggs Type Indicator measurements, yielded very strong validity results for the KGI assessment. Correlations between the two instruments indicated the KGI tool measured patterns of group behavior that would be expected given the theoretical constructs underlying the two instruments. The study consistently demonstrated significant and meaningful correlations between these assessments, providing evidence of their potential power when used in combination. (This relationship will be discussed in detail in Chapter 19.)

In a smaller concurrent validity study, participants took both the Klein Group Instrument and the Fundamental Interpersonal Relations Orientation-B (FIRO-B) measurements and, again, there were strong results. The correlations showed that the KGI tool measured behaviors that would be expected given the theoretical constructs underpinning the two assessments.

In a qualitative study with two hundred business and professional people, who were enrolled part-time in a Master's of Business Administration program at Western New England University (Springfield, MA), all of the participants acquired at least one or two new leadership/group skills when they applied their KGI results to job-related group activities. Based on surveys and application papers, all participants acknowledged that the KGI model deepened their understanding of group dynamics in their work settings. Participants with a cross-section of scores on different KGI scales and subscales, working in a broad range of organizational contexts, made meaningful adjustments grounded on KGI results. Importantly, those who persevered with their skill building achieved even greater success, acquiring four or five new skills. These participants experienced a very significant increase in their effectiveness as leaders and group members. Since these accomplishments were guided by KGI information, the results yield solid validity data about the instrument's effectiveness.

In semester-long studies with three hundred and fifty undergraduate engineering students at Western New England University, after being trained with the KGI and MBTI measurements, all of the students gained two new group skills while working in project teams. Students were assessed through questionnaires about their experiences, application papers they wrote describing specific actions in team settings, and faculty observations of their group behaviors.

In semester-long studies with one hundred and fifty undergraduate students who participated in the course Leadership and Team Skills at Western New England University, all of the students obtained two new group skills which they applied to in-class and out-of-class teams after being trained with the KGI and MBTI assessments. Students were assessed through surveys, papers they wrote about their skill development, and interviews conducted with key informants.

The above studies impart pertinent data about the reliability and validity of the KGI assessment. They demonstrate the power of the measurement, and its strength for training people in social skills.

In the next chapter, the information contained in the KGI® Individual Profile is described in detail, along with the *KGI® Individual User's Guide* accompanying the report. ✕

CHAPTER 9

Design of the KGI® Individual Profile and User's Guide

After completing the Klein Group Instrument assessment online, a participant receives two documents via email: the KGI® Individual Profile and the KGI® Individual User's Guide. The profile presents customized data about the person's current level of group participation and information to direct future skill acquisition. The user's guide explains the elements of the profile, details about fundamental group dynamics, two short case studies, and an outline of steps on how to use the information to become a more proficient leader and team member.

The KGI® Individual Profile

Information in the KGI® Individual Profile proceeds in the following manner:

1. *An introduction that describes the profile's structure.* The first page outlines the document's design, which is divided into four sections according to the major scales of the instrument:

Leadership, Negotiation Orientation, Task Focus, and Interpersonal Focus

For each section, the most vital data are delivered in the subscale categories. They identify the following information: group behaviors that are personally enjoyable to perform; behaviors that are difficult or challenging; and new behaviors that will foster social development. It is useful to note that for the second item—behaviors that are difficult or challenging—if an individual already functions at a very competent level in that skill area, there may be no data reported for the category.

An **important qualification** is emphasized in the introduction: the individual must evaluate all of the profile feedback and select the most accurate, relevant ideas with which to work. While data derive from extensive quantitative and qualitative research, each individual must validate the information personally and apply it in an appropriate manner. A counselor or coach, working with a client, will assist in this analysis.

2. *Results for the Leadership section.* The profile then moves into the Leadership section, with information structured in this manner:

A. *A color graph.* The segment opens with a graph containing columns for the composite Leadership scale (the aggregate of all subscales), the Assertiveness subscale, the Group Facilitation subscale, and the Initiative subscale. The columns indicate high, medium, or low frequency of performance in each area.

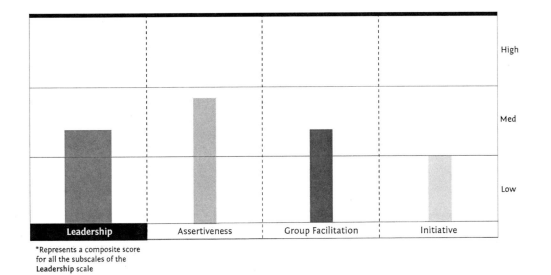

High

Med

Low

| Leadership | Assertiveness | Group Facilitation | Initiative |

*Represents a composite score
for all the subscales of the
Leadership scale

The graph promotes a rapid appraisal of the individual's performance, with the opportunity to compare performance across the various domains. A high score indicates that a person performs the specific behaviors in the scale or subscale 75% to 100% of the time; a medium score indicates that a person performs the behaviors 50% to 74% of the time; while a low score points to performance from 0% to 49% of the time.

B. *Information about the Leadership scale and the respondent's personal results.* The section then introduces a brief explanation about the essentials of group leadership, followed by a statement describing the respondent's orientation in this area. This statement corresponds to the score in the first column in the graph, the composite Leadership score. The statement is calibrated to a low, medium, or high result.

C. *Information about the Assertiveness subscale and the respondent's personal results.* The report progresses to the first of the critical subscale areas, which supply the real meat of the profile. It starts with the KGI definition for Assertiveness, followed by a statement about the respondent's fundamental orientation in this area, which, again, is reflected in the graph in the column score for Assertiveness.

The report then provides detailed, personal information to analyze, breaking out behavioral data in three categories:

› What You Enjoy

› What You Find Difficult or Challenging

› Behaviors That May Help You Grow

For each of the categories, points are rendered in a *bulleted fashion*—clear, focused statements. This facilitates a *fast absorption* of the information, enabling the user to quickly transform ideas into action.

The information about What You Enjoy confirms what a respondent likes and is doing well in this area of group activity. The data can help a person become aware, or more aware, of specific skill sets, allowing that person to acquire a greater confidence in these abilities. The information can also encourage an individual to pursue these preferred behaviors more vigorously in group settings, thereby applying the strengths to greater advantage.

Example of What You Enjoy from the Assertiveness subscale:

› When you are knowledgeable about a topic and believe other members will be receptive, you express your opinions in the group.

The statements about What You Find Difficult or Challenging identify behaviors that tend to be problematic for the respondent. The individual, in turn, may be fully aware, partially aware, or unaware of these issues. In any event, the feedback allows a person to become more conscious of these challenges, with an opportunity to conduct problem solving. When a coach is working with a client, this is essential information to analyze and address. There is a real growth opportunity here, as a client turns a difficult situation into a more productive one by adopting different, more constructive behaviors and attitudes.

As noted earlier, however, it is possible for a respondent to receive no information in this category, which means that the individual is performing solidly in this area, based on the personal responses to the instrument items.

Example of What You Find Difficult or Challenging from the Assertiveness subscale:

> Dealing with a fear of saying the wrong thing in a group.

The statements from Behaviors That May Help You Grow assist a client in two ways. First, if an issue is identified in What You Find Difficult or Challenging, there will be a growth statement that corresponds to it, providing a client with a strategy to improve performance. The statement imparts guidance for practically managing the problem.

Second, in situations where no difficulties have been highlighted, the statements offer ways to elevate an already solid or strong performance to an even more advanced level. The growth suggestions have been formulated from interviews with professionals who have been high-achieving role models in this domain and from a review of research literature targeting superior performance in this sector of activity.

This is *one of the real strengths of the KGI model*: whether a person has a high, medium, or low score on any given subscale, there are always growth suggestions to help a person refine performance. The paths to further development are spelled out.

Example of Behaviors That May Help You Grow from the Assertiveness subscale:

> Think through your ideas carefully. When you are confident of their accuracy, state them in a clear, focused way. Remember, even if people disagree, they are rejecting the ideas, not you as a person.

(This suggestion came in response to the previously identified challenge: Dealing with a fear of saying the wrong thing in a group.)

D. *Information about the Group Facilitation subscale and the respondent's personal results*. Information in this subsection flows in the exact same manner as the information in the Assertiveness section. There's a description of the subscale's focus, with a statement summarizing the respondent's basic orientation in the area. Information then appears about What You Enjoy, What You Find Difficult or Challenging, and Behaviors That May Help You Grow.

E. *Information about the Initiative subscale and the respondent's personal results*. Data appear in the same way as in the previous subscale categories.

3. *Results for the Negotiation Orientation, Task Focus, and Interpersonal Focus sections*. The information in these subdivisions is structured in the same manner as the Leadership section.

4. *Composite Graphs*. On the final page of the profile are two composite graphs: the first displays the scores for the four major scales; the second depicts all of the subscale scores in a continuous sequence. These are the indispensable tools for evaluating client performance and establishing a plan for skill development. As will be seen, based on the interpretation of these graphs, a consultant can organize a very powerful plan for a client's social development.

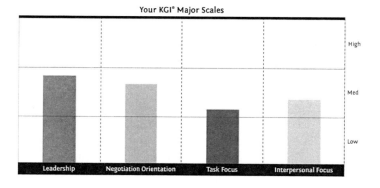

This graph brings together the scores for the major scales, allowing the recipient to evaluate frequency of performance in the large domains.

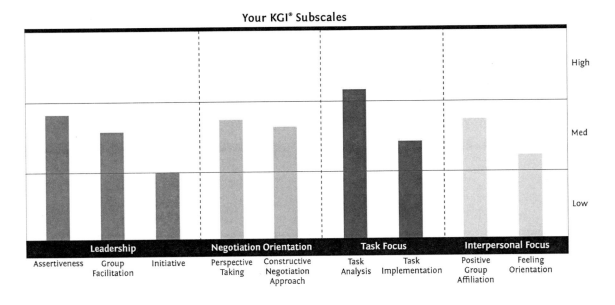

What is useful to examine here are the *highest* score and the *lowest* score.

The highest score pinpoints the individual's primary focus in small-group events. This aspect of group life stimulates the greatest interest (even fascination), and it is the easiest area for active participation. The lowest score, on the other hand, holds the least interest and may be avoided to a small or a large degree. It takes greater exertion for the individual to engage in this activity. These scores establish benchmarks for individual performance: what I tend to like most; what I tend to like least. They depict fundamental currents of energy in the person's social personality.

The subscale graph is the most crucial element in the profile. With it, a consultant and client evaluate performance across all of the skill domains, promoting a broad examination of group behavior. The graph displays areas of strength and areas of softer performance. It helps identify relationships among the skill areas, which will aid in balancing overall performance. In short, the graph serves as the *foundation for constructing a plan for personal development*. The next chapter explains the ways to interpret this graph, from a simple, direct approach to a more complex, sophisticated one. As a professional delves into this information, a potent plan for skill development can be constructed for any client.

In the next chapter, professionals will see how interesting it is to fashion such a strategy. It can be like solving a puzzle, putting the pieces together in a meaningful design for the client.

The KGI® Individual User's Guide

Accompanying the KGI® Individual Profile, a customer receives the *KGI® Individual User's Guide*, which is structured in the following manner:

1. *Introduction*. The document begins with a brief overview of the guide's contents, which are described below in 2–9.

2. *Basic elements and dynamics in groups*. The section defines core ideas about small-group life that inform the KGI diamond design.

3. *Design of the Klein Group Instrument assessment*. This segment describes the fundamental aspects of the instrument.

4. *Description of the four scales and nine subscales*. The one-sentence definitions of the major scales and subscales are presented.

5. *KGI® Individual Profile*. The blueprint for the KGI® Individual Profile is explained.

6. *Interpretation and skill development for the individual user*. This section summarizes the process for interpreting data from the assessment, which will be explained in detail in Chapter 10.

7. *Ethics for using the Klein Group Instrument*. This subsection emphasizes respect for persons, confidentiality, and the creation of a trusting environment for building new skills.

8. *Developing a plan for improving your group performance*. This segment outlines a step-by-step procedure for expanding leadership and membership skills in small-group settings. (The process is described in Chapter 11.)

9. *Case studies*. Two personal stories illustrate how individuals obtained new group skills by employing the KGI materials. They describe a self-improvement process that a customer can now embrace.

These two documents introduce the basic building blocks in the KGI system. The individual profile lays out personalized data to direct social growth, while the user's guide articulates the strategy to accomplish the mission. An individual now has the necessary materials for a journey of self-improvement.

The next chapter explains the system for interpreting the Individual Composite Subscale Graph, which paves the way for this journey. ✄

CHAPTER 10

Interpreting the Individual Composite Subscale Graph

The earlier chapters highlight central features of the Klein Group Instrument measurement: its precision (major scale and subscale definitions); its theoretical strength (supporting research and scholarship); and its power (reliability and validity results). In this chapter another aspect is revealed: the instrument's ease of use. When a professional and client concentrate on the Individual Composite Subscale Graph, found on the last page of the KGI® Individual Profile, they can translate fresh insights into direct action

to achieve impressive results. Just how easily this can be done is part of the attraction of the KGI assessment.

As noted previously, this graph displays the subscale scores in a continuous sequence, looking something like an urban skyline, with high, medium, and low scores in the various domains side-by-side. The layout allows for a rapid assessment of group behavior, with the opportunity to compare different skill sets and balance them to fashion a well-rounded practice, related to both leadership and membership roles.

To explain the interpretive process, the basic principles for evaluating a graph will be introduced first—how to assess low, medium, and high levels of performance. These principles ground any analysis and, in many instances, may yield a satisfactory strategy for skill development. They offer a direct means for interpreting how an individual participates in group activities and illuminate ways to improve that participation.

But there's a secondary technique that adds further richness to the discussion. After years of research, another interpretive perspective emerged: a series of Inter-Subscale Combinations (ISC), which focuses on ways that certain skills play off each other to expand the skill-building process. With this approach, a counselor, coach, consultant, or educator can take the analysis of the composite graph to a more sophisticated level, harnessing the full power of the instrument. In the second part of the chapter, this design will be introduced, showing its strength and suppleness.

Let's begin with a sample graph (see page 44).

As can be seen, there's a range of scores, falling in the Low, Medium, and High sections, as is often the case. It's possible to open up a conversation with a client by discussing any of these areas, according to what seems most relevant. For the purpose of this analysis, we will start with the low scores and move systematically to the high results.

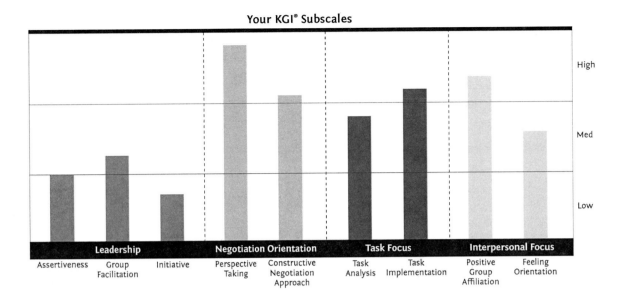

1. **Low Scores:** These domains are significantly underdeveloped, posing a serious test. They present meaningful opportunities for growth, but a person really needs to dig in and take on the challenge.

Because the domains are undervalued, it requires more effort and greater persistence to improve these skills. The fact is they may arouse anxiety and fear about performance. In the past, a person may have seriously avoided these areas of participation. Now, clearly seeing the pattern in the KGI graph, a client can be prompted to take action and address the challenges. The graph creates the opportunity to make changes that will really alter performance. Many people have done this. They observe the low areas and choose to tackle them head on. With steady persistence, they turn soft spots into hard skills.

It is useful to talk to a client about the underlying reasons for low performance. By identifying the thoughts and feelings that are inhibiting the person's actions, the coach and client can develop new strategies that will promote growth. Part of the strategy is to investigate any negative self-talk that the person may employ ("I'm no good in that area of group activity. I'll only embarrass myself.") and change it to more positive affirmations ("With practice, I can be much more effective and really help the team."). The intent is to create a positive vision for skill acquisition, to encourage a belief that new skills can be obtained, leading to more competent participation. Then the coach and client can identify a reasonable group setting to

practice the new skills. With a willingness to reflect on performance, make adjustments to improve it, and diligent practice, a person can develop durable skills that overcome the previous limitations.

In the sample graph, the Initiative subscale column falls into the Low section of activity. The Assertiveness column, just touching the line between the Low and Medium sections, is also considered an area of low performance.

Important: The Initiative subscale, for a significant majority of people, is often the lowest, or one of the lowest scores on the graph. The reason for this phenomenon has been researched for years. What has become apparent is that a large percentage of people feel anxiety about occupying the seat of the primary leader. While they may have skills in Assertiveness, Group Facilitation, Negotiation Orientation, Task Focus, and Interpersonal Focus, they fear the glare of the spotlight that shines on that principal player.

When people were interviewed about factors that held them back, many said they found it difficult to represent all group members' ideas and interests in a competent, balanced way, in a manner that would satisfy everyone, so they shied away from the responsibility. In addition, many stated they felt uncomfortable when everyone looked at them to make things happen, which produced a lot of pressure to consistently say and do the right thing. For others, they were waiting for the "ideal circumstances" before stepping into that major role. Given that they wanted perfect conditions, it was easy to dodge anything that was less than perfect, which often meant they could squander years in a waiting game.

What has become evident is that the variety of skills defined by the KGI model provide the right antidote to address these concerns. People can learn a range of techniques to handle being the primary leader. They can practice skills in the immediate circumstances in which they find themselves, "imperfect" or not. Through intelligent practice, they can acquire the methods and the confidence to manage a leader's critical responsibilities.

With respect to leadership development, let it be said: *the Initiative subscale is the engine that drives the KGI ship.* When evaluating the composite subscale graph, a professional will always want to assess where a client stands in this category and determine what battery of skills from the other KGI domains will help the individual acquire the necessary techniques in task management, interpersonal relations, and negotiation to become a flourishing leader.

On an optimistic note, many individuals with a very low score for Initiative have found the courage to address the situation and embrace their leadership development with real gusto. What is interesting is that as an individual adopts a bold attitude and pushes forward, really splendid outcomes can be achieved in a matter of a few months! Once a person breaks down the walls of inhibiting ideas and achieves favorable results with skill-building, a positive momentum occurs that really changes the individual's approach, producing wonderful consequences.

Across the board, people have made various adjustments to perfect their leadership performance, creating a new confidence in their capacity to be the point person for the team. This is an outstanding feature of the KGI method.

2. **Medium Scores:** These represent areas of solid, more capable performance. Generally speaking, an individual feels more at ease participating in these areas of group activity. Within the Medium section, however, there are subtle and significant differences. They appear as follows:

A. For low-Medium scores, an individual is still significantly challenged with skill development. He or she has emerged from the Low section but is only beginning to gain confidence in the movement towards mastery. In the sample graph, the Group Facilitation subscale depicts this condition.

In this scenario, it is useful to have an individual move in small steps to practice the new techniques and slowly build up belief in his or her ability. Some of the inhibitions lurking in the Low sector, mentioned earlier, can still be affecting the client, and it would be valuable to discuss these issues and address them, as appropriate. A key goal is to move in a step-by-step manner to achieve steady improvement with skill development.

B. For middle-Medium scores, a person has reached a substantial level of skill development and is poised to advance in a significant way. Usually, the person feels secure in the use of the action but needs to expand the practice in various contexts to further strengthen it.

On the sample graph, Feeling Orientation reflects this situation. Some thoughts to share with a client are the value of the skill and the benefit of its usage. With deeper appreciation for what the skill will accomplish, the person increases attention to it and becomes more motivated to employ it.

C. For high-Medium scores, an individual has attained a very consequential level of usage. The person is usually quite comfortable participating in this aspect of group life. In fact, the high-Medium level is a strong position to be in, since the person can usually exercise the skill with good flexibility.

The Task Analysis column on the chart represents this status. In this situation, an individual can develop a more nuanced, polished application of the skill, and exercise it more regularly in group activities. With further refinement, the individual can elevate it to the high sector of performance.

Important: When beginning a skill-building process with the KGI system, it can often be worthwhile to start with a skill in the Medium section. The individual already has some traction with the activity, and starting with a skill that is accessible and easier to employ can rapidly move the effort in a positive direction. This builds confidence in the overall process and makes the pursuit of a second skill, such as one from the Low section of the graph, more agreeable.

Everything depends on the client's personality. Some individuals like the challenge of selecting a skill from the Low section right from the start, and then climbing the mountain. Others prefer to start out with something less strenuous and, after accomplishing it, move on to a second, harder challenge. It is always important to pay attention to the client's inclination. In general, for many people, starting with something less demanding will create an initial success, build up self-confidence, and make a difficult challenge in the next round less painful. The ultimate goal is to set an agenda that will help a client persist with skill-building, so the candidate will acquire an array of skills and not quit in the early going.

3. High Scores: These scores reflect a very proficient level of performance. An individual exercises such skills with interest and confidence; they have become primary assets in the social arsenal. When refining an individual's leadership and membership talents, these abilities are important tools in the operation. They are skills that can be wielded right now with good effect. However, this comes with a caveat: there is a point where a high-level score can be overused, thereby turning it into a liability. The Individual Composite Subscale Graph indicates where this tipping point resides.

A. For low-High scores, the result falls in a range just above the Medium-High dividing line,

on up to the mid-point of the High section. On the sample graph, columns for Constructive Negotiation Approach and Positive Group Affiliation portray such results. They signify strong performance, places where an individual acts with assurance and, most often, with discrimination. A person can pick the right moments in group situations and take the correct actions.

Important: As it turns out, *the low-High area is the best section on the graph, the target zone for skill development.* Within this range, a person normally has flexible control of the technique. By and large, the individual is not so enamored with the skill that it becomes overused. (See diagram below regarding the range for low-High.)

It is worthwhile to discuss with a client the ways in which the individual employs the skill. For example: What successes have you had in using the skill? What situations allow you to use it to its best advantage? What refinements might make the skill more effective? At this level, it's mostly a matter of small strategic adjustments to maximize the benefit. Seeing the high score on the graph can give a client additional confidence about possessing the skill and using it. Generally speaking, it doesn't pose much of a problem to tinker with a few adjustments and fine-tune the application of such a skill.

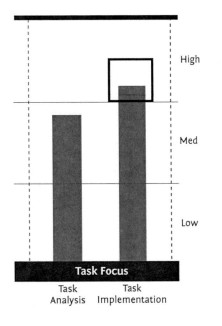

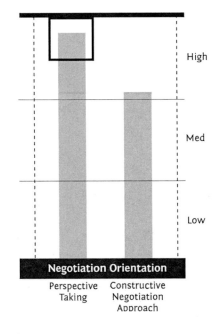

B. For high-High scores, the results land in an area from the mid-point of the High section up to the top of the graph. On the graph on the previous page, the Perspective Taking subscale fits this description. While this score can appear like a super strength, it has a serious liability. From our research, it's become apparent that people investing this much energy in the skill can develop a distorted view about it. The skill is a major asset for them; they fall in love with it, and the love turns blind. Regardless of the appropriateness of the skill for the group situation, they feel they need to employ it—to the point of overkill—with detrimental effects for themselves and their teammates.

What is important to evaluate with such a score is the level of control with which the skill is deployed. Does the individual use discrimination with the skill, selecting the right time and context to employ it? Or does the person employ it compulsively? This often reflects the attitude that because a skill was successful in earlier group experiences, it must be valuable now, in increasingly larger dosages. So, it is vital to investigate the level of employment of the skill, and a client's awareness of the problem of overutilization.

From qualitative interviews with participants, many people recognize they have tripped into the overkill zone; nevertheless, they have had trouble making appropriate adjustments to back out. One informant, with a very high Assertiveness score, recognized that he talked so much in a group that other people found him overbearing. Yet he felt so zealous about participating that he had a hard time containing himself. Less easy to work with are the people who think that more is always better and remain oblivious to the effect on other people. They haven't even glimpsed their groupmates' reactions to the problem of overdoing it.

In these situations, it becomes a matter of teaching an individual to throttle down the excessive energy, so the skill can be utilized more selectively, to better effect. In so doing, the individual can then redirect some of the energy into other aspects of skill development while returning the talent, like Assertiveness, to the asset column and eliminating the fallout from overuse. When people exercise better decision-making in this regard, it proves extremely profitable for them and for the groups in which they operate.

This example clearly demonstrates how the KGI model can help people to strike the right balance with their social skills. Everyone understands the importance of building up low areas of performance, or further advancing the medium areas, but it can also be a matter of adjusting the very high areas, deemphasizing them to the degree they are employed with greater effectiveness. By adjusting group participation in this way, a client is better able to harmonize various KGI capacities and exercise all of them with more beneficial results.

For the nine KGI subscales, it would be productive to mention briefly what the high-High level of overuse tends to look like:

Assertiveness: an individual comes across as too talkative, self-absorbed, and unable to listen to anyone else.

Group Facilitation: a member can seem too pushy, too controlling.

Initiative: a person appears too independent or autocratic, unable to involve others.

Perspective Taking: a participant becomes too deferential to others, not recognizing the value of his or her own point of view.

Constructive Negotiation Approach: an individual becomes too ardent for win-win, not noticing when that option really won't be viable and something else is needed.

Task Analysis: a member seems ready to analyze unto death, in pursuit of a "perfect" strategy.

Task Implementation: a participant pushes forward too quickly with the task, trying to drive it to conclusion, regardless of low quality or mediocre results.

Positive Group Affiliation: an individual seems to make the group a social club and doesn't stay in touch with the task.

Feeling Orientation: a person comes across as hypersensitive and overreactive to emotional issues.

When a coach works with a trainee who has high-High scores in certain areas, these points can be examined to see potential disadvantages from overuse of the skills. The client can reflect on group situations where his or her behavior may have come across in these ways. This may introduce a fresh perspective on the behavior, opening up an opportunity to consider adjustments that will generate more productive results.

After a professional and a client evaluate these issues with the Individual Composite Subscale Graph, they can target particular subscales for improvement. They can look into those subscale sections of the KGI® Individual Profile and investigate suggestions in Behaviors That May Help You Grow. The suggestions identify particular behaviors the client can practice. The movement from a general analysis of behavior to specific practice is as simple as that. The graph enables a broad evaluation of performance and a prioritizing of skill areas for refinement. After checking those sections of the profile, one can pinpoint exact behaviors that will further the effort. There are often two or three growth behaviors per subscale, so the most attractive one can be chosen from the list. Much of the work that puts the client into action has now been completed. The whole

process of coaching will be explained in the next chapter, supplying the fine details to inform this effort, but the graph analysis is the central aspect of the approach.

As mentioned earlier, there is a second level of analysis that will take the examination even further. It's based on the Inter-Subscale Combinations (ISC). The ISC system identifies connections among subscales that have a powerful relationship to leadership functions and group dynamics. As a professional becomes acquainted with this design, she or he can integrate the ideas into coaching sessions in a variety of ways. A professional may even use them immediately in the initial graph evaluation, as appropriate topics surface. In situations where clients have a series of strong results, *with no results below the middle-Medium level*, the ISC assessment will be especially useful to open up a more complex level of interpretation and strategy construction.

To introduce the ISC system, graph examples with one-sentence descriptors will be presented first, followed by detailed explanations.

Graph One: Assertiveness with **Perspective Taking**
This pairing enables a person to strike the right balance between speaking and listening, in order to cultivate a more competent leadership and membership style.

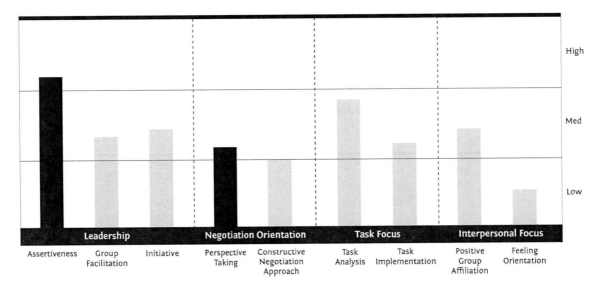

Graph Two: Group Facilitation with **Task Focus** and **Interpersonal Focus Subscales**
This combination allows a client to refine group facilitation across the two primary dimensions
of group life: task and interpersonal.

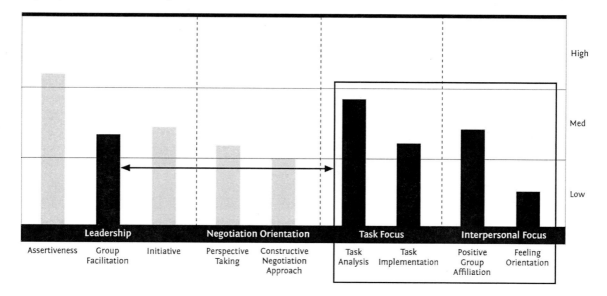

Graph Three: Initiative with **Negotiation Orientation, Task Focus,** and **Interpersonal Focus Subscales**
This sequence permits a participant to evolve into a flexible team leader, by integrating a battery
of practical skills.

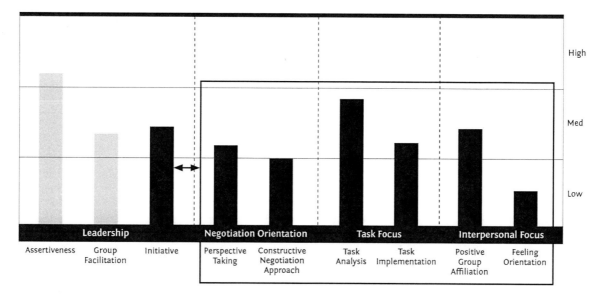

Graph Four: Constructive Negotiation Approach with **Positive Group Affiliation**

This pair targets factors that spark synergy on a team, propelling a group to its highest level of performance.

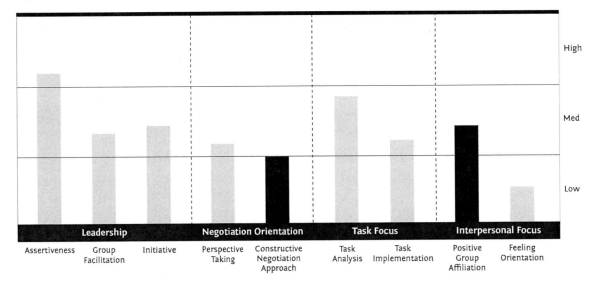

Graph Five: Task Analysis with **Task Implementation**

This set allows one to strike a better balance between the complementary skills in the task enterprise, leading to higher quality outcomes.

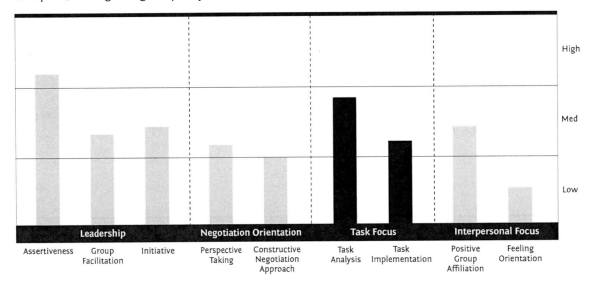

Graph Six: Positive Group Affiliation with **Feeling Orientation**
This combination enables a client to nurture team spirit through the effective management of emotional issues within the group.

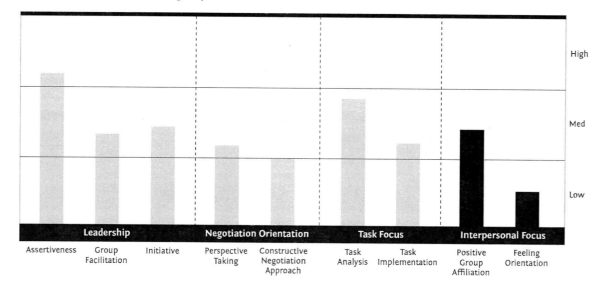

1. Assertiveness with **Perspective Taking**
This pair evaluates the relationship between two foundational group skills: speaking and listening. When Assertiveness is much higher, it usually means a person needs to slow down, listen more, and be more selective about when to participate. If Perspective Taking is much higher, the individual should try to talk more, perhaps by asking questions, or by sharing ideas on a subject, or being assertive in *reacting* to the points made by others. A person can also present a summary of what's been said during a discussion, helping a group keep its ideas alive and accessible.

For any individual, there is a **rhythm** to how much one listens and how much one speaks in a group. By inspecting these scores together, a consultant and client can analyze this pattern. Striking a solid balance is the correct path to pursue. Usually, when both of these elements are located in the low-High section, it produces excellent performance.

For leadership that energizes group members, the general axiom is to listen, understand, and then speak. By following this principle, one can react constructively to the ideas of other members, increasing the possibility of engaging their interest and energy. When this happens, group members develop increased motivation to commit their best efforts. Of course, a leader may also

have creative ideas to share, but the trick is to put these forward and then solicit others' reactions. The goal is to initiate a dialogue that engages everyone's creative thinking.

2. Group Facilitation with **Task Focus** and **Interpersonal Focus Subscales**
When a leader organizes a group, two items immediately appear in the mix: task needs and interpersonal relations. The art of leadership is to manage these elements so that people get along, collaborate effectively, and achieve strong outcomes.

Reviewing graph results, a consultant can actually interpret a Group Facilitation score in terms of the Task Focus and Interpersonal Focus subscales. Whatever the Group Facilitation score may be, results in Task Focus and Interpersonal Focus indicate **where** the primary strengths reside, and **where** the deficiencies may be. By inspecting the Task Analysis, Task Implementation, Positive Group Affiliation, and Feeling Orientation scores, a consultant can identify the assets and the areas of challenge. The high scores indicate where a client tends to focus when facilitating a group, while lower scores reveal what is overlooked and neglected. To become a superior facilitator, a client works to have all task and interpersonal subscales fall in a low-High section.

A client with high Task Analysis and Task Implementation scores usually feels comfortable attending to the practical aspects of the job, while a client with high Positive Group Affiliation and Feeling Orientation enjoys organizing the interpersonal side.

Remember the point about the tension between the task and interpersonal poles of group life? As you focus on one, by definition, you take your eyes off the other. It requires alertness and practice to be able to distribute awareness between the two spheres, to find the right rhythm that will be most productive for a group. Usually people prefer one over the other, so these four subscale scores provide information about how to bring these elements into better balance, resulting in more versatile, competent facilitation.

3. Initiative with Negotiation Orientation, Task Focus, and Interpersonal Focus Subscales

The Initiative subscale drives leadership growth in the KGI model. But many people are reluctant to step up and take action. Not only is this true for younger, less experienced people, but for many seasoned business and professional veterans as well.

The antidote to this predicament is **courage**. To break the bonds of fear and lethargy, people need the boldness to assume a critical leadership position and work to master the challenges. Naturally, things don't always go smoothly, but by taking the leap, there is an opportunity to gain insights, make adjustments, and refine practice. When someone takes on a significant leadership role, there is fertile ground for learning and a terrific opportunity for growth.

With the graph results, a professional can determine where a client's strengths reside among the Negotiation Orientation, Task Focus, and Interpersonal Focus domains. As a client seeks to assume a leadership role, it's important to know where one's best resources lie and to deploy them consciously to greatest advantage. This contributes to success. For example, with a talent for Constructive Negotiation Approach, an individual can intentionally take a greater role in promoting win-win agreements. Or, with a high score in Task Implementation, a person can step up to promote fluid communication as the group executes a task.

Along the way, he can help the team make strategic adjustments that yield better results. Drawing on their best skills in a conscious way, people are well-positioned to be competent leaders. The graph results lend themselves to this type of analysis and practical action, a sound approach for leadership skill building.

It is also beneficial to consider how the softer subscale areas can be built up and integrated over time, to develop a complete set of leadership tools. With the graph results, a counselor and client can design a comprehensive strategy for leadership development that will reap excellent dividends. This can incorporate skill building in three, four, or five subscale areas, culminating in a well-rounded style.

One final point: there are times when a person possesses a very high score on the Initiative subscale. In this situation, research has shown that an individual may take on too many responsibilities and, as a result, become exceedingly stressed out by all of the demands and deadlines. In this case the question is how can an individual pare down obligations in order to focus on the most meaningful actions, the ones which bring the best rewards? Here, less is more. The other high scores on the graph can reveal activities that give the most satisfaction, and it's preferable to select leadership roles that employ these skills. It is also important to consider which leadership opportunities may bring the most long-term career benefits, which will serve as a way to prioritize options and find the right ones to pursue.

4. Constructive Negotiation Approach with Positive Group Affiliation

There is a meaningful connection between these subscales, related to the creation of synergy in a team. What ignites synergy in a group, according to the research, is an inclusive, positive social atmosphere. The Constructive Negotiation Approach subscale, with a win-win orientation, introduces the necessary inclusion, while Positive Group Affiliation promotes a team spirit, which heightens social awareness and strengthens mutual support. When a leader, or a group member, brings these two elements together, it triggers potent collaboration.

A counselor should alert a client to this important connection and help the person integrate these complementary skills. Often a client has a higher score in one compared to the other, sometimes with a significant disparity. A coach can advise the individual to distribute her attention more evenly between the domains. If a client already invests substantial energy in one, it is usually not a difficult step to invest more in the other. This increases the client's influence in a group in a major way. Whether from a leadership position or from a membership role, this action will unquestionably enhance team performance.

In situations where a client is sluggish in both areas, the individual can approach skill building with the two in tandem. As a leader promotes win-win agreements in a team, it boosts group morale. Conversely, as he helps to build up interpersonal relations and team spirit, the members become more inclined to construct win-win accords. So the two subscales resonate with each other. Given this association, a coach and client may design strategies to address the two subscales in combination, maximizing gain from the effort and accelerating a client's development into a consequential team player.

5. Task Analysis with Task Implementation

Both subscales reside in the Task Focus sector, and there are critical issues to consider when interpreting this pair of results.

Each subscale displays a serious liability with overuse (when the score appears in the upper half of the High section on the graph). For Task Analysis, a very high score points to the problem of perfectionism with task planning. Too enamored with the analytic process, an individual persists in the pursuit of the *ultimate solution* (which remains tantalizingly elusive) and loses a lot of time in the bargain. It can become paralysis by analysis, overthinking of the situation, without pursuing action within a reasonable time frame. As time slips away, it creates mounting pressure and stress for a team.

The overuse of Task Implementation has the opposite effect, but with a similar result. A person pushes for rapid closure of a project, trying to wrap it up too quickly, which leads to missteps and errors, byproducts of hasty action. When a group goes back to clean up the mistakes, it is time, again, that is lost.

Keeping these concerns in mind, it becomes useful to evaluate these issues even when a client's scores don't actually fall in the high-High section of the graph, because these problems may be percolating just below the surface with any set of TA and TI scores. Here's what to do:

Whenever Task Analysis is significantly higher than Task Implementation, the consultant should ask the client about the attraction of analysis, and how it plays out in group activities.

- What motivations/interests push the client towards the stronger use of task analysis?
- Does the client feel some perfectionist tendency in trying to construct a plan?
- How does the client see the relationship between creating a plan and implementing it?
- What makes it hard to stop task analysis and move on to implementation?
- Does the client ever experience the loss of time from over planning?

Whenever Task Implementation is notably higher, the client should again be asked about motivation and the consequences of this approach.

- What pressures does the client feel to push a task forward?
- How does the client see the relationship between planning and successful task execution?
- What problems have been encountered when the work moves ahead too quickly?
- What things tend to get overlooked?

In the first situation, with higher Task Analysis, the client needs to take action sooner: to adopt a reasonable, solid strategy, test it, and refine it through application, instead of chasing the illusory perfect plan. In the second case, with Task Implementation, the client should think longer about the plan before jumping into action.

If the two scores fall in the Low section, or low-Medium section, then, clearly, an individual does not pay adequate attention to the task venture. The consultant can guide the client to first consider a task from multiple angles in order to construct a healthy strategy. If the client has a solid score in Perspective Taking, the consultant can suggest the client pose questions to other members to hear their thoughts about attacking the task. The client can help facilitate the discussion while learning how other members prefer to construct the plan. This technique exposes the client to a variety of ideas about plan preparation. If a particular person on the team has a knack for task analysis, that individual, in particular, would be someone to listen to in order to learn practical ways to analyze a project.

The consultant can also advise a client about how to monitor the group when implementing a task strategy. A client wants to focus on facilitating communication among members, paying attention to unanticipated things that disrupt the work, and then making modifications to correct the strategy and move the work towards successful completion. A client should promote a dialogue on a team about planning and implementation, one that allows for continuing strategic adjustments that will move a project through difficult phases to successful realization.

6. Positive Group Affiliation with Feeling Orientation

These subscales comprise the Interpersonal Focus domain, in which we encounter a key concern: the repressed nature of feeling in group life. Out of all the KGI subscales, the two most repressed are Initiative and Feeling Orientation. Concerns with the former have already been discussed. For Feeling Orientation, a large number of people believe that attending to emotions in a group can open Pandora's Box, derailing the task effort by releasing raw, destructive feelings. With this attitude, people see conversation about emotions as turning into a never-ending, circular argument, wasting a lot of time. Even people who are emotionally sensitive become fearful about raising such issues in a group, because others may become hostile and negative when they do. So they conclude it's better to remain silent, knowing that critical points about emotions will remain unstated.

But when members stay alert to various emotional events in group life, it helps to maintain a healthy environment that contributes to a positive team spirit. This is a highly relevant connection that people need to understand. As they do, it can help to reduce the phobia about emotional expression.

Quite a few people receive high scores for Positive Group Affiliation. They realize the benefit of building the team's esprit de corps, and they prize it. At the same time, they often have a significantly lower score for Feeling Orientation. While valuing team spirit, they pay less attention to emotions in the here and now as the group is operating. This type of gap is often visible. People want one result, without cultivating the other side. But the truth is that ignoring difficult emotions can erode team spirit and, as a consequence, undermine productivity. Proper management of emotions is essential for robust personal relations and strong collaboration.

When a consultant notices this discrepancy—high Positive Group Affiliation with lower Feeling Orientation—it's necessary to explore the client's thinking about the gap. It's imperative to determine what attitudes are at play, and if the fear factor might be causing this split. It can be useful to talk about recent group experiences where this pattern might be evident. Ultimately, a counselor will want to change the client's thinking about the matter, pointing out that a thoughtful treatment of emotions contributes to a positive atmosphere, one in which a lively team spirit can thrive. When people are able to work through testy emotions, it builds confidence about their ability to resolve problems and to collaborate. When they regulate emotions well, it increases their esprit de corps.

When a client's eyes are opened to this issue, it initiates a process of change, permitting a person to alter previous prejudices and acknowledge what an asset emotional awareness can be. Over the years, a remarkable number of people have been transformed in this way. They see this connection and are encouraged to cultivate their emotional awareness and emotional expression. As mentioned in the research and scholarship chapter, this is what the Emotional Intelligence field is about. These skills make people more capable leaders and group members.

Less frequently, a client scores higher for Feeling Orientation than Positive Group Affiliation. While an individual displays sensitivity to feeling issues, there can be anxiety in working with other people. This person doesn't feel "part of" the team. It is important to investigate the reasons for these feelings. It can be useful to encourage such an individual to spend time talking to other members before or after meetings. Informal conversation can instill a sense of connection with one or two other members, which can be the first steps in becoming more connected to the group. There have been instances where a friendship with a single teammate can assist someone in developing greater rapport with the group as a whole. Also, if an individual contributes to a group in some constructive way, others often respond favorably, which can advance positive affiliation. In building up relations with others, the individual can use the feeling awareness to fashion emotionally intelligent responses, helping to build bridges. As a person begins to feel more connected, more relaxed, it's very natural to feel more immersed in the team spirit.

For some people, neither Positive Group Affiliation nor Feeling Orientation has a substantial score. With this pattern, a person is usually preoccupied with Task Focus, as Interpersonal Focus falls into neglect. There can be a serious bias about staying totally absorbed in the task. Again, the individual needs to be aware of how essential the interpersonal domain is for sparking synergy on the team, prompting the highest performance. This idea must be part of the conversation. When a person who is preoccupied with strong task outcomes is able to grasp how much interpersonal skills aid the cause, it can be very persuasive. Many such individuals then put Interpersonal Focus on their radar screens and attend to these skills. When they see the exciting results—enhanced task performance because of improved social relations—they become converts to the cause.

These subscale interrelationships address themes that are the most significant for client development within the KGI system. While some other subscale combinations may be relevant at times, these six are the most important.

The Individual Composite Subscale Graph presents the core data for assessing a client's patterns of group behavior. An easy-to-use device, the graph promotes straightforward evaluation of performance and the construction of a sound action plan. As a professional becomes more expert with this method, he or she will be able to guide major skill acquisition in an efficient manner. The next chapter explains the coaching process, the larger enterprise that surrounds the graph analysis.

CHAPTER 11

Coaching and Counseling with the KGI® Individual Profile

With colorful, informative graphs, bullet points about strengths and challenges, and growth statements to improve performance, the KGI® Individual Profile is an excellent coaching tool. It introduces a sturdy system for interpreting the patterns of a person's group behavior, and provides a precise method for constructing new skills, skills that can transform an individual into a highly competent leader and group member. What follows is a step-by-step procedure for counseling a client with a KGI® Individual Profile,

a standard approach that will ground any counseling or coaching activity. As a professional becomes better acquainted with the method, one may modify the sequence in ways that seem relevant for a particular situation. With any design, there's always room for creativity and adjustment.

1. At the beginning of the coaching process, review the KGI diamond model, along with the design of the KGI® Individual Profile.

This orients a client to the underlying ideas in the KGI approach and the structure of the materials, setting a foundation for the interpretation of data. The *KGI® Individual User's Guide*, which accompanies the individual profile, presents a focused overview of this information, making it a handy resource. If a client has pre-read this guide, which is highly recommended, it prepares him or her for the session. (To assist a consultant in preparing for this meeting, see Appendix: The Basic Script for Introducing the Klein Group Instrument Assessment.)

In particular, raise these points:

▸ The KGI model is grounded on four basic functions in small groups, featured in its diamond design. Using the diamond diagram, explain the four major scales and their interconnections, described in Chapter 2.

▸ Each of the major scales has subscales that define specific skill sets to improve performance in that area of group life. Introduce and briefly explain the subscales.

Leadership subscales: Assertiveness, Group Facilitation, and Initiative.

Negotiation Orientation subscales: Perspective Taking and Constructive Negotiation Approach.

Task Focus subscales: Task Analysis and Task Implementation.

Interpersonal Focus: Positive Group Affiliation and Feeling Orientation.

- Utilize the one-sentence descriptions of the subscales to introduce them, and the paragraph-long descriptions to explain further details. This information is found in Chapter 3.

- The structure of the KGI® Individual Profile proceeds along the four major scales—Leadership, Negotiation Orientation, Task Focus, and Interpersonal Focus. Each section begins with a graph, depicting the client's results for that particular major scale and its subscales.

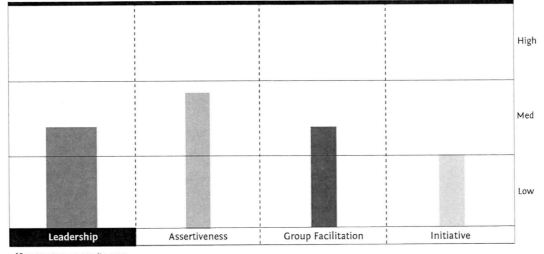

*Represents a composite score
for all the subscales of the
Leadership scale

- The graph is designed with Low, Medium, and High sections. Low signifies that a person uses the particular skill 0–49% of the time, Medium from 50–74% of the time, and High from 75–100% of the time. The graph enables a quick assessment of performance in these areas.

- This graph is followed by information for each of the subscales. They offer information about what one enjoys in that area of group life, what one might find difficult or challenging, and suggestions for new skills that will improve one's performance. The suggestions will be important for setting behavioral goals to expand leadership and group membership.

- For each subscale in the profile, there is a statement identifying its rank among the nine scales, e.g., Assertiveness: your score on this subscale ranks third out of nine. The first of nine will be the highest score on the graph, while the ninth is the lowest one which presents the greatest challenge. There is also a statement about the person's basic approach in this area of group life.

- Two composite graphs appear at the end of each profile: one presents the four major scale scores together; the other all of the subscales scores in a sequence. These will play a primary role in devising a plan for skill development.

2. *If the client has not already done so, have her read through the entire KGI® Individual Profile, with the goal of evaluating the accuracy of the results.*

It is necessary to have a client validate the personal results in the profile, in order to establish a realistic baseline from which to work. When the client has reviewed the material, introduce these questions:

- In the client's view, which information seems to be most accurate?

- Which information seems questionable?

From research on the KGI® Individual Profile, most people say their scores fit them well to very well. They believe the information is accurate, affirming the strength of the model for assessing behavior. In this discussion, as a person explains his or her reactions, the client's self-concept begins to emerge. For example, a person declares that her high leadership scores are accurate because she often takes an active role in leading small groups or, alternately, a person declares the low leadership scores fit because she rarely, or never, takes a leadership role.

When a client states that certain information is *questionable*, it provides the opportunity to explore why the client came to that conclusion. This sheds additional light on patterns of behavior and self-perception. When the conversation moves in this direction, a consultant should employ *probing questions* to extract details about performance.

Some worthwhile questions:

• What examples from recent group events can you give that illustrate a different pattern of behavior (compared to the KGI score)?

• What factors most influence you in this area of activity (positively or negatively)?

• When you took the assessment, did some recent group experiences significantly affect your responses?

With these questions, a counselor can examine the issues that are influencing the client's interpretation.

Sometimes, upon further analysis, a client sees that the KGI result is reasonable. But other times, the client may still disagree. In either scenario, the discussion will offer useful information for the construction of a plan for skill development. The counselor will consider adjustments to a plan, addressing the issues raised in this conversation. For example, a person with a low Initiative subscale score may feel that he generally takes more leadership initiative. In response, a coach and client may want to identify a meaningful leadership challenge in the early phase of skill development to practice this skill and then evaluate the results.

3. ***Analyze the Individual Composite Major Scale Graph at the end of the KGI® Individual Profile.***

On the last page appear two composite graphs. The first, the Individual Composite Major Scale Graph, displays the scores for the four major domains. Each column indicates a high, medium, or low score.

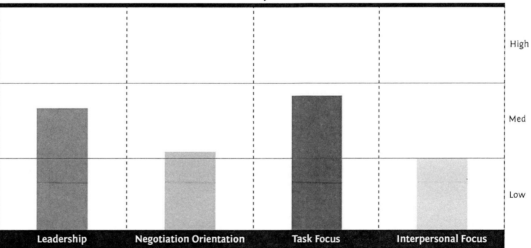

Your KGI® Major Scales

When evaluating this graph, identify the column that exhibits the highest level of performance, and the one that exhibits the lowest. The highest indicates the main area of attention, the place a client invests the most energy; accordingly, it is the place where the client will tend to be most comfortable. Conversely, the lowest score usually indicates the area of least comfort. The client may be avoiding or repressing activity in this domain.

With respect to the highest score, ask the client about what is satisfying and interesting for her when she participates in this area of group activity. What engages her? Later on, tapping into this positive energy, wherever possible, can provide valuable motivation for the skill-building process.

With respect to the lowest score, ask the client what might be uncomfortable or difficult in this sphere of activity? Find out what things may be inhibiting the client's performance. This will be helpful information for designing strategies to address these problems and for building new skills that can empower the client in this area.

Essentially, these two scales provide the fundamental benchmarks about how a client operates in small groups, representing the basic flow of energy. They set an initial framework for the skill-building process. After discussing these patterns with the client, a counselor can then proceed to a more complex level of analysis.

4. *Evaluate the Individual Composite Subscale Graph from multiple angles.*

The second graph features the nine subscale scores in a sequence; it displays the levels of energy investment in the specific skill areas. As mentioned in the previous chapter, significant variations can be evident: high, medium, and low scores, side by side, illustrating the different levels of participation in different aspects of group life. This graph provides a clear portrait of how a client tends to operate in groups and will be crucial for customizing a plan for skill development.

Your KGI® Subscales

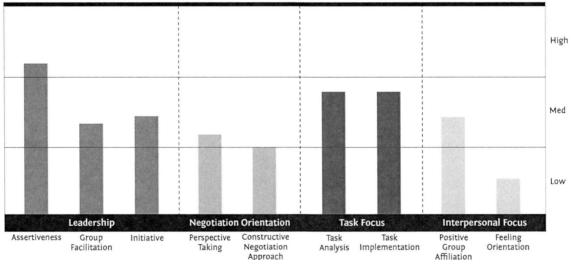

As mentioned in the last chapter, a general review of the graph is the first step in the analysis.

> Invite the client to offer an initial response to the graph data, articulating the most significant elements from his perspective. The respondent may direct attention to low, medium, or high scores.

> What are the client's main concerns and interests? What skill areas does the client wish to develop? *Investigate the client's*

interests. Above all, get a *clear idea* about the key goals and core values for the client and work to develop strategies that will address them.

If the client zeroes in on a score in the Low section, investigate the obstacles that have been holding the client back in this area. Why has it been an area of low performance? What attitudes and fears may be involved? (This may follow up on points that were raised in the discussion of the

Composite Major Scale Graph, mentioned above. If so, pursue additional details.)

If the client concentrates on a score in the Medium section, what is the current level of performance with the skill? What situations encourage use of the skill? What situations block usage? How does the client wish to modify performance in this area? Refer to the previous chapter to investigate significant differences in low-Medium, middle-Medium, and high-Medium levels of performance. Discuss these with the client, as appropriate.

If the client fixes on a score in the High section, evaluate how to further refine the skill.

> • If the client has a score in the high-High section of the graph, raise the issue of over-use and the liability that presents. Ask the client about situations where overuse of the skill has produced negative consequences—explore any of these circumstances. Refer to the points about overuse presented in the previous chapter. With this situation, it will be meaningful to assess ways the client can *reduce* action with this skill, so it can be employed more selectively and with greater benefit.

> • As part of the conversation, examine the client's **Initiative subscale score** and determine what skill development would enhance this aspect of performance. That is *central* to the enterprise.

Following this phase of the discussion, the client and coach can designate certain subscales for improvement. It is possible to prioritize the top two and begin a process of new skill acquisition. For those subscales, go directly to their sub-sections in the KGI® Individual Profile and inspect the suggestions in Behaviors That May Help You Grow. They identify behaviors to practice for skill development. (This process will be explained in detail in point #6 which follows.) This is the simplest, easiest way to use the KGI materials, and it will guide a client directly into skill acquisition.

However, research with the KGI model has shown that people who go on to acquire skills in **five KGI subscale areas** really have a transformative social experience; they vault to a much higher level of social development, self-confidence, and leadership effectiveness. The full developmental

dynamic with this experience has been described in Chapter 5. Accordingly, the coach should encourage the client to think in terms of five subscales as providing the richest experience. It should be noted that some clients choose to simply work on a couple of subscale areas, ones they deem most important, and conclude the skill-building exercise right there. That is fine. But working on five subscales offers the greatest benefit and will extend the time for practicing new skills, usually for a number of months.

At this point, a coach can explain to the client the opportunity to take the analysis to another level, introducing the Inter-Subscale Combinations (ISC), which allow for the construction of a more elaborate plan. Even if a client doesn't wish to advance to a five-subscale skill level, the ISC model will enhance this part of the consultation. In situations where a client has a composite graph with strong scores across all domains, the ISC system introduces a way to broaden the analysis and identify suitable paths to refine such a strong performance.

According to the client's graph results and goals, select appropriate subscale pairings to discuss. The combinations include:

1. **Assertiveness** with **Perspective Taking**: creating an appropriate balance between speaking and listening skills.

2. **Group Facilitation** with **Task Focus** and **Interpersonal Focus Subscales**: refining facilitation skills across the two primary sectors of group life—task and interpersonal.

3. **Initiative** with **Negotiation Orientation**, **Task Focus**, and **Interpersonal Focus Subscales**: building a versatile leadership style by integrating skills from these pivotal areas.

4. **Constructive Negotiation Approach** with **Positive Group Affiliation**: perfecting skills that will promote synergy on a team, resulting in high-quality group outcomes.

5. **Task Analysis** with **Task Implementation**: achieving a better balance between these complementary skills in the task area.

6. **Positive Group Affiliation** with **Feeling Orientation**: nurturing team spirit through the effective management of emotional issues within the team.

The counselor may draw on ideas from any of these combinations to initiate a more nuanced analysis of the graph data. At the minimum, this will elevate the previous phase of analysis and expand the client's understanding of group dynamics. It will add an important perspective to the skill-building enterprise. By integrating the ISC ideas, it will also be easy to establish a skill-building plan with five subscales, or even six. The client can then climb to a really excellent level of team leadership and group performance.

5. *Construct a priority list for skill development.*

After the ISC analysis of the graph, there's plenty of data to design a plan for skill development. Selecting a series of subscales to work on, the coach and client can now make a ranked list, with the top item the number one priority. In this process, consider the following:

> ‣ What subscales hold the greatest interest for the client?
>
> ‣ What combination of subscales could bring the greatest and most immediate benefit from the effort?
>
> ‣ What series of items enable the client to evolve into a multifaceted group performer, integrating task, interpersonal, and negotiation skills?

As counselor and client consider these issues, subscale priorities can be sorted out. The actual skill development process will then proceed with one or two subscales at a time.

6. *Review the "Behaviors That May Help You Grow" for the top two subscale choices.*

Once the list is set, counselor and client can delve into the appropriate subscale sections of the profile and evaluate the behavioral growth statements.

There will be at least one growth statement in a section, but most of the time two or three. With multiple options, the coach can help the client select the most attractive and, possibly, opt to work on more than one.

If, for a particular subscale section, the client has statements for What You Find Difficult or Challenging, then look at the growth statements that directly address these issues. Tackling the

challenges will promote substantial growth for the client. Keep this in mind with planning.

If a client has no challenge statements, then simply pick the growth statements that are most appealing.

Once the growth statements have been selected, the conversation should focus on the group settings where the client will practice. The consultant and client should reflect in a detailed way about these contexts.

For example, the client may wish to assume more leadership based on the Initiative subscale in a certain group or groups. How, when, and under what circumstances will the individual take action? What issues will be most challenging for the client? Where might there be anxiety about the effort? Based on the KGI results, what current strengths can the client draw on to support this effort? Consider these details and plan strategies accordingly, to maximize the potential for success.

A particular KGI growth statement may be the exact fit for a situation, but under certain circumstances it may not. This is where a consultant's background in leadership development and group behavior comes into play. While a growth statement offers a concrete suggestion for improving performance, the consultant and client may want to tinker with it, devising an adjusted strategy that will more precisely addresses a specific setting.

Ultimately, the client would do well to practice one new skill at a time, and not more than two. Self-regulation theory (Mithaug 1993) proclaims that focusing on one new skill is optimal. Two would be the maximum. The key is not to overload, but to keep the practice clear and simple, and to move forward in focused steps. By maintaining focused attention, a client can more easily make small adjustments as the effort proceeds, increasing the potential for success.

A couple of other things to consider with the client:

> ‣ *The importance of positive self-talk.* Too many people defeat themselves with negative self-talk, saying things like "I can't really do this," "I am not good at this," or "What if I mess up and people think I am incompetent?" This undermines conviction and effort.

In this enterprise, it is critical to create a positive self-talk mantra:

"I am going to jump in and try this new skill. I will take action and learn from it. Even if it is not exactly right the first time, I will make adjustments and get it right. It will be excellent to acquire this new skill."

It is valuable to point out that KGI research has shown that people get *real traction with a new skill on the third attempt*. The first attempt may work decently, the second may go better, *but the third attempt can be the charm*. A person usually achieves much greater competence and self-confidence at that moment. This is an important concept for a client: it enables a client to be patient and to persist. These are critical ingredients for self-improvement.

> • *The importance of envisioning success.* For any individual, trying out new skills in neglected or undeveloped areas poses risks. A person can become hampered by envisioning feeble outcomes and bad reactions from others. Like negative self-talk, a creeping, negative vision will have a detrimental effect.

It is necessary to create a constructive mental image, that is, a person should envision taking a positive action that will benefit the group. Other people will appreciate this contribution, and they will have positive reactions. The individual will become more effective socially, which will feel satisfying. Ask a client to envision this scenario, in order to strengthen the motivation to apply the new skills. It should be noted that many KGI participants over the years have been very pleasantly surprised by the positive reactions from others in response to their efforts. They began to wonder why they had such negative expectations in the first place! The experience taught them about the value of having positive expectations.

After reviewing these points, the client will be well prepared to go out and take action. Action is the key. Encourage the client to have the boldness to begin and see what happens.

7. *Follow-up session with the client.*

After the client has had two, three, or four weeks to practice the new skills, another conversation is in order to assess the results. During this discussion, review the following points:

> • What things went well? What successes should be celebrated?

> • What could use further refinement? What might the client do differently?

> • What surprises occurred in the process, positive or negative?

> • What insights did the client gain about the process of skill development?

The common experience is that people feel uplifted by this endeavor. They learn to look at group dynamics with fresh eyes and acquire new skills to increase their social competence. The practice puts KGI ideas in the forefront of their minds, alerting them to things to watch out for in groups and the appropriate actions to take. They become more aware, more thoughtful, and more proactive. They also cultivate a self-reflective practice, learning to analyze their actions and make adjustments to improve the quality of their performance.

When people do not reach this level, it's usually because they have not put in enough effort. If an attempt went poorly, they may have retreated and avoided making adjustments and trying again. Or perhaps they did not seek out opportunities to begin with, or failed to take advantage of those they did encounter. They may have dealt with situations passively, not energetically, which produces meager results. With such clients, it's necessary to evaluate what is blocking their actions and find ways to reduce the problems. It is useful to assess their motivations and see what might light their fire. The coach will want to refine the strategies and encourage greater expenditure of effort.

What the counselor can do is set up a very precise assignment—a focused, small behavior in a very specific situation. Encourage the client to take *baby steps* in the right direction. Whenever a client experiences trouble in advancing a skill, it is always useful to break things down into smaller, easier steps. Once a person starts to achieve results, the experience of some success generates positive momentum, and the practice can accelerate with larger strides. While some people feel disdain for the idea of reducing things to "baby steps," this prejudice should not obscure the fact that tiny progress is progress, and it is essential for building a larger success.

In general, the goals for this session are the following:

- *Reinforce strengths.* Identify the client's assets in the situation and encourage their further use and refinement. What thoughts and feelings contributed to the client's successful behaviors? Build on these in the next phase of skill development.

- *Look for concrete ways to further improve the performance.* Distinguish practical actions that can refine a skill(s) for the next application. As was noted about clients who are experiencing problems, keep the actions small, clear, and focused.

- *Reward success.* Praise the client's successful efforts. It is also valuable to encourage a client to reward him-or-herself in some way when successes occur. This builds self-esteem and reinforces a desire to improve.

- *Encourage a deeper analysis of group dynamics.* As the client looks at group situations with a more knowledgeable eye, discuss the client's insights. What new things did the client notice that weren't so evident in the past? What ideas from the theory became clearer from practice? What dynamics will the client pay more attention to in the next group event? By reflecting on these issues, the consultant will be able to evaluate the client's ability to read group dynamics and reinforce key concepts.

The counselor and client can then discuss the next round of skill development. Imitating the earlier procedure, take these steps:

- Identify the next subscale area(s) to work on.

- Investigate the Behaviors That May Help You Grow in the appropriate subscale domains of the profile.

- Select some of these behaviors to practice.

- Analyze the group setting and consider any modifications that might be needed to make the behaviors a correct match for the situation.

The client is now ready to embark on the next round of skill acquisition. *The procedure outlined in this section will then be repeated throughout the rest of this skill-building process.*

8. *The consultant should be sensitive to, and support, a process of psychological transformation in the client.*

After the next phase of practice, the counselor and client will have a further conversation, following the pattern just outlined. They should assess progress, refine strategies, and extend the skill-building process. As noted previously, acquiring new skills in five subscale areas should be the aim, a journey that will span a number of months.

As a client adds more skills, attaining a greater mastery of group techniques, an interesting metamorphosis can take place. The fact is a client doesn't gain the skills in isolation but in social contexts. Other people observe the actions and appreciate the contributions. Flowing back at the client from other members can be a ripple of appreciation. When your actions benefit the team, when you help your teammates, they respond more positively to you—praising you, thanking you, treating you with more regard. This provides a very powerful reinforcement. A client not only amasses skills, but also starts to feel very differently about being in groups. Based on the successes, the client becomes more comfortable, more self-confident. As a sense of self-efficacy increases, it nourishes the belief that one can build more positive relations with people and constructively impact group events. The client's whole attitude about group life can transform into a much more favorable point of view. And this can then apply to all kinds of small groups, including families, and the most intimate of one-on-one relationships.

A coach will want to pay attention to these changes, helping the client to reflect on them and nurture them. Indeed, a powerful social transformation can take place through KGI training.

In the next chapter, a series of composite subscale graphs, with talking points, will aid professionals in mastering the KGI method, so they can foster this type of social transformation in their clientele. ✂

CHAPTER 12

Individual Composite Subscale Graphs with Talking Points

To help professionals use the KGI method in their coaching practice, this chapter presents twenty-four individual subscale graphs, along with interpretive points that can be employed in consultations. Offering a wide cross-section of cases, these graphs enable practitioners to become better acquainted with KGI graph analysis, while supplying reference points for actual counseling sessions. By comparing a real client's results to this set of examples, a counselor can find a close match and utilize the ideas

in an analysis. If there is no exact match, two sample graphs may be combined to address the relevant issues. In this way, professionals can accelerate their mastery of graph interpretation and increase their confidence in applying the model. Over time, they will be able to refine the process, adding their own creative insights to the approach.

As described in Chapter 10, in the initial evaluation of an Individual Composite Subscale Graph, it is enough to identify the columns that fall in the Low or Medium sections. If a client acknowledges issues in these areas and wishes to address them, it is possible to move directly to Behaviors That May Help You Grow in those subsections of the profile and set up a strategy for the practice of new skills. However, it is also possible to extend the analysis, by using the Inter-Subscale Combinations system, which advances the evaluation to a more sophisticated level. The talking points for the subscale graphs demonstrate both of these approaches in an inte-

grated fashion. With this two-step method, a professional can provide a detailed interpretation of a client's group behavior and guide skill development that will convert an individual into a more dynamic leader and group participant.

The twenty-four cases are divided into two parts. First, the opening example provides not only the diagnostic points, but also direct references to the Behaviors That May Help You Grow sections in the individual profile. As noted previously, in a coaching session, the first step is to study the composite subscale graph and make a determination about which subscales to pursue for skill building. The second step is to select growth statements from those subscales to guide the practice of new behaviors. With the initial example, the bridge between graph analysis and the selection of growth statements is clearly displayed to show the connection.

The other twenty-three cases simply lay out the interpretive points for the graphs, supplying further examples for the first phase of the process.

These graphs exhibit a wide range of scores, demonstrating ways to approach diverse results and construct coherent plans for development. For all twenty-four examples, there are five interpretive points, which refer to at least five different subscales. With the KGI model, when a participant makes adjustments in five subscale areas, he may experience a significant transformation, not only with regard to leadership development but with respect to social identity and self-confidence. Picking up five new skills causes people to obtain greater interpersonal flexibility and to adopt more positive attitudes about group experiences and social interactions in general. The five talking points for each graph set the foundation for this type of transformation and would enable a counselor to work with a client for a number of months to achieve these goals.

Graph One

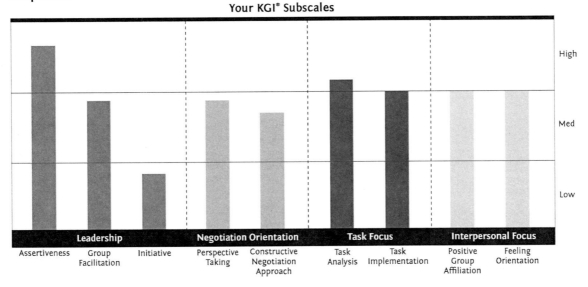

1. **Assertiveness with Perspective Taking:** The client represented in Graph One should reduce the number of times he or she speaks in the group, in favor of more listening and observing. A useful tactic would be to ask more questions of other members to assess their positions on various issues. The client can then respond to their points in a more thoughtful way, creating a richer dialogue in the group.

Assertiveness Growth Statement
(which speak directly to the client):

A. It's best to use controlled assertiveness: be patient, pick your issues, and select what is most important to you.

B. Watch people's reactions when you speak, so you can adjust to the situation and control your input. If people are distracted or are pulling back, you should slow down. If they are perking up, you are on track and should keep going.

Perspective Taking Growth Statement

Be willing to ask a number of questions to get a deeper understanding of people's concerns and how they want to approach the task. Use this information to help the group find mutually agreeable ways to get the work done.

2. **Group Facilitation with Task Focus:** The client can refine skills in Group Facilitation by taking a more active role in the Task Focus enterprise, which is a strength area where the individual should feel comfortable in an expanded role. The client can help the team look at a project from multiple angles to construct the best strategy. As a plan is implemented, the client can promote discussion of strategic adjustments that will increase efficiency.

Group Facilitation Growth Statement

Be aware of people who haven't contributed to the discussion and, at the appropriate time, invite them to share their ideas.

Task Analysis Growth Statement

Be willing to be the devil's advocate (but do it respectfully) in order to assess all ideas thoroughly.

Task Implementation Growth Statement

Be alert for opportunities where you can give support—such as ideas, encouragement, praise, or resources—to other members.

3. Constructive Negotiation Approach with Positive Group Affiliation: The client's interest in building team spirit in Positive Group Affiliation can be more directly connected with efforts in Constructive Negotiation Approach. As members build greater rapport, they are more inclined to seek win-win agreements. The client can become more actively involved in helping the team find common ground in its negotiations.

Constructive Negotiation Approach Growth Statement

Pay particular attention to quiet members. An agreement is truly strong only when the last reserved person has spoken. Invite input and assess the buy-in for strategies being proposed.

Positive Group Affiliation Growth Statement

At the start of a group session, make an effort to get input from everyone as soon as possible, so all of the members feel valued, respected, and involved.

4. Task Analysis with Task Implementation: The client shows a slight propensity towards Task Analysis over Task Implementation. It is always useful to investigate if the person may fall into overanalysis at times, delaying action on a task due to excessive analysis. Striking a solid balance between analysis and implementation would strengthen performance.

Task Analysis Growth Statement

Be aware that there can be flaws in your own analysis. Pay attention to your own biases about how to do the task.

Task Implementation Growth Statement

Always fine-tune the work strategy as the task moves along. Solicit input from others about adjustments that need to be made to help improve performance.

5. Initiative: The client should select a meaningful team project to lead, drawing on established skills in Task Focus and Interpersonal Focus to guide the team towards a successful performance. The client has considerable skills on which to draw, and it would be beneficial to employ these tools in a leadership role to gain experience and confidence.

Initiative Growth Statement

A. When you speak in the group, focus on the key points in your position. Try to express them clearly, present your conclusion, and invite feedback on your ideas. Remember, it is difficult to persuade everyone. There is always disagreement and criticism, which is a judgment about the ideas, not you as a person.

Graph Two

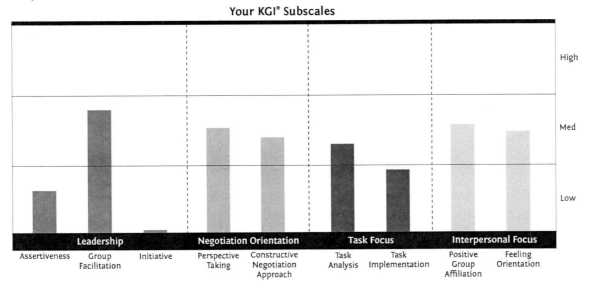

Your KGI® Subscales

1. **Assertiveness:** This client should try to speak up more in groups, sharing ideas and insights. Responding thoughtfully to other members' points would be one worthwhile way to contribute. At the beginning of group events, the client should try to get into the discussion early, creating a positive momentum for participation.

2. **Group Facilitation with Interpersonal Focus:** The client can take a more active role in promoting Positive Group Affiliation, which will inspire group cohesion and higher productivity. The client has a solid interest in facilitation, which can be comfortably applied with other strength areas. If that goes well, the client can also assist the group in paying more attention to Feeling Orientation issues, making people aware of the group's emotional undercurrents.

3. **Task Analysis with Task Implementation:** The client has more affinity for analysis than implementation. For the former, the client should speak up more and share task ideas with the group, increasing his participation. The client can also observe other leaders in the group who are effective in prosecuting a task. What approaches and techniques do they use? By paying closer attention, the client could imitate these actions, practicing them later in appropriate situations.

4. **Constructive Negotiation with Positive Group Affiliation:** These subscales are interconnected. As one promotes Positive Group Affiliation, building team spirit, it inclines people to seek win-win agreements with Constructive Negotiation Approach. The client can make more proposals in favor of win-win, which, in turn, supports the efforts with Positive Group Affiliation. The client has an inclination to listen to others, as seen in the Perspective Taking score. Use insights gained from Perspective Taking to configure the win-win proposals.

5. **Initiative:** The client is challenged in this area. It would be beneficial to build up performance in a series of small steps. First, have the person speak up more often to become more active in the group. On the right occasion, sharing leadership with an appropriate teammate would be a way to try out a leadership role. Eventually, with a certain project of interest, the client could move up to a solo leadership position.

Graph Three

Your KGI® Subscales

Leadership			**Negotiation Orientation**		**Task Focus**		**Interpersonal Focus**		
Assertiveness	Group Facilitation	Initiative	Perspective Taking	Constructive Negotiation Approach	Task Analysis	Task Implementation	Positive Group Affiliation	Feeling Orientation	

1. **Assertiveness with Perspective Taking:** This client shows a strong interest in other members' concerns and positions. By asking probing questions to explore more fully other people's positions, the client can become more vocal in the group, and can also share some personal reactions to points that are raised. The client may express agreement, or share a different perspective. As the client establishes a greater verbal presence, it will become easier to participate in other aspects of group life as well.

2. **Group Facilitation and Constructive Negotiation Approach:** Her skills create an opportunity to help organize the group's negotiations. Being very aware of other members' positions through Perspective Taking, the client can suggest win-win proposals and promote a dialogue to find mutually agreeable decisions. The client should become more active in this major strength area.

3. **Feeling Orientation:** The client can draw on existing skills with Perspective Taking to pay more attention to the feeling issues in the group. She can watch for teammates' emotional reactions, both positive and negative, which will enrich her understanding of their concerns. The client can use this information to promote greater emotional understanding among members, which will enhance Positive Group Affiliation.

4. **Task Analysis with Task Implementation:** Does the client push ahead to complete a task without enough analysis and strategy development? The graph results seem to indicate this impulse, which needs to be investigated. With regard to Task Analysis, the client may want to develop more patience in looking at the task from multiple angles, making sure to construct a sound plan before pressing forward with implementation. The client can benefit from observing how group members with TA skills evaluate a task and then practice some of their techniques.

5. **Initiative:** The client should select a significant project with which to take leadership, utilizing established skills in Negotiation Orientation and Positive Group Affiliation to guide the team towards a successful performance. She can invite others to share task strategies in Task Analysis, and then try to negotiate a plan everyone can buy into.

Graph Four

Your KGI® Subscales

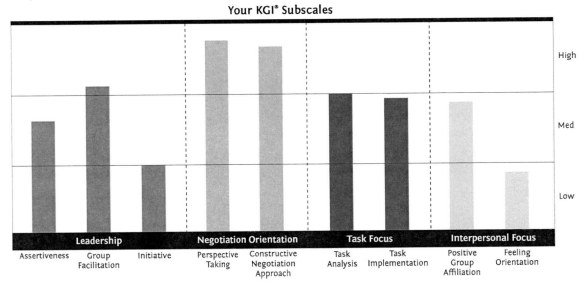

Leadership			**Negotiation Orientation**		**Task Focus**		**Interpersonal Focus**	
Assertiveness	Group Facilitation	Initiative	Perspective Taking	Constructive Negotiation Approach	Task Analysis	Task Implementation	Positive Group Affiliation	Feeling Orientation

1. **Assertiveness with Perspective Taking:** This client's concern for knowing others' ideas and values may come at the expense of not sharing his own thoughts. It would be useful to strike a better balance, reducing some of the energy in Perspective Taking, and channeling it into self-expression. The client should offer more personal opinions on the issues and invite the group members to respond.

2. **Group Facilitation with Task Focus:** The client can take advantage of a leadership opportunity by facilitating the group's task effort. This may include prompting the group to investigate a broader range of options when constructing a strategic plan and also helping the group to assess what adjustments need to be made during task implementation to make the effort more efficient and successful.

3. **Constructive Negotiation Approach with Positive Group Affiliation:** The two subscales are interrelated. When members develop greater interpersonal rapport in PGA, they are more inclined to seek the win-win consensus in CNA. With the client channeling so much energy into Constructive Negotiation Approach, redirecting some of it towards PGA would be an effective strategy to balance his performance and to create a more positive overall atmosphere on the team.

4. **Feeling Orientation:** The client would benefit from acquiring skills with Feeling Orientation, paying greater attention to feeling issues in the group by watching out for members' positive emotions (enthusiasm, excitement) and negative emotions (anger, hostility). The client could then assist the group in responding to these issues, helping the team manage its emotional life more successfully.

5. **Initiative:** The client should pick a team project and become the key leader, drawing on established skills in Negotiation Orientation, Task Focus, and Positive Group Affiliation. Get everyone involved in the discussions, find win-win accords that keep people committed to the task, and work to sustain high morale. By taking a significant leadership role, the client can showcase the array of skills in his possession.

Graph Five

Your KGI® Subscales

Leadership			**Negotiation Orientation**	
Assertiveness	Group Facilitation	Initiative	Perspective Taking	Constructive Negotiation Approach

High
Med
Low

Task Focus		**Interpersonal Focus**	
Task Analysis	Task Implementation	Positive Group Affiliation	Feeling Orientation

1. **Assertiveness with Perspective Taking:** The individual can use Assertiveness to ask more questions and investigate others' views. This will fortify Perspective Taking, bringing it more into balance with Assertiveness.

2. **Constructive Negotiation Approach:** As the client refines skills with Assertiveness and Perspective Taking, it opens the door to build up the CNA skill sector. By developing listening skills and gaining more knowledge about teammates' interests, the individual can take an active stance in promoting win-win agreements in discussions.

3. **Task Analysis with Task Implementation:** The client seems to be much more engaged in analyzing the task than in implementing the strategy. It would be worthwhile to investigate the individual's motivations in this regard, to explore the reasons for the imbalance. The goal is to balance these two elements, particularly by having the client become more engaged in the execution of the plan.

4. **Positive Group Affiliation with Feeling Orientation:** Interpersonal Focus is the most underdeveloped component of the client's profile. Taking time to become more acquainted with other members could enhance the client's effectiveness and influence in two other areas of the group's work, Negotiation Orientation and Task Implementation. Paying more attention to feeling issues would help the client connect with other members.

5. **Initiative:** As the client develops the skills outlined above, he should take the next step by assuming an important leadership role in the group. At the appropriate time, the client should select the right project and take the helm. This will offer a valuable challenge and the opportunity to gain experience with leadership practice.

Graph Six

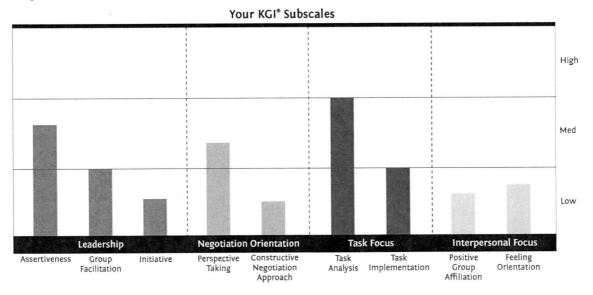

Your KGI® Subscales

1. **Assertiveness with Perspective Taking:** The client should ask more questions of other members to gain insights about their thoughts, values, and concerns regarding both task and interpersonal issues. The client can also share opinions about the various topics that emerge.

2. **Perspective Taking and Constructive Negotiation Approach:** Using the information gained from Perspective Taking, the client can make proposals for possible win-win agreements during negotiations, helping the group pursue decisions that would benefit all members.

3. **Task Analysis with Task Implementation:** This graph suggests the client overuses Task Analysis at the expense of Task Implementation. Discuss the client's attraction to analysis versus implementation. Does the client tend to over-analyze and then move rather slowly to implementation? Why the big difference between these two aspects of Task Focus? The client should try to strike a better balance here.

4. **Positive Group Affiliation with Feeling Orientation:** The client should pay attention to other members' body language and facial expressions, observing their emotional reactions, noticing what things positively excite people and what things turn them off. The client can use the information to help the team assign work when people have enthusiasm for it, and also address negative emotions that may cause people to pull back and withdraw. This will promote mutual respect and help establish a better social atmosphere on the team.

5. **Initiative:** The client should identify a meaningful group project and take on a specific leadership role. To start off, the client could exert leadership in helping the group analyze a task, which would utilize an established strength. With some initial success, the client could then branch out by taking leadership in other aspects of the group's work.

Graph Seven

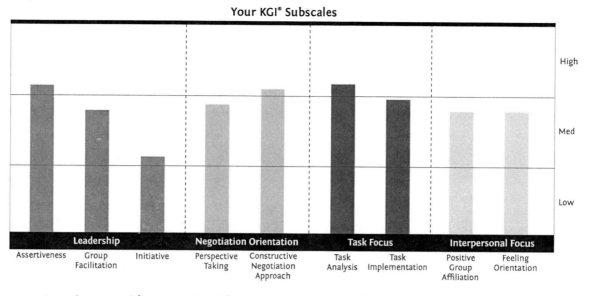

Your KGI® Subscales

| | | | | | | | | | | High / Med / Low |

Leadership — Assertiveness, Group Facilitation, Initiative

Negotiation Orientation — Perspective Taking, Constructive Negotiation Approach

Task Focus — Task Analysis, Task Implementation

Interpersonal Focus — Positive Group Affiliation, Feeling Orientation

1. Assertiveness with Perspective Taking: The client can ask more questions to better understand other members' positions, interests, and values, and share responses to their ideas. In addition, she could raise her own points about the topic, promoting more dialogue on the issues.

2. Constructive Negotiation Approach with Positive Group Affiliation: The client can take time to assist the group members in getting better acquainted, stepping up to promote rapport-building conversation. This will boost team morale and encourage members to seek win-win agreements, which the client naturally supports.

3. Task Analysis with Task Implementation: There's the possibility the client may have an impulse to overanalyze the task. It is worth talking about. She can look for ways to become more active during implementation. Taking more of a role with Group Facilitation in the task area would also be a growth opportunity.

4. Feeling Orientation: The client can pay more attention to emotional reactions in group discussions, especially when negative emotions are being stirred up. She can help investigate the underlying issues for the conflict and seek to restore harmony.

5. Initiative: The client can seek an opportunity to be a key leader. She is able to draw on a variety of group skills in the negotiation, task, and interpersonal areas, and can refine these skills in an active leadership position.

Graph Eight

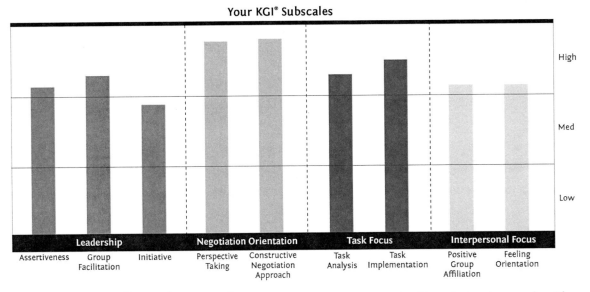

Your KGI® Subscales

| | Leadership | | | Negotiation Orientation | | Task Focus | | Interpersonal Focus | |
| Assertiveness | Group Facilitation | Initiative | Perspective Taking | Constructive Negotiation Approach | Task Analysis | Task Implementation | Positive Group Affiliation | Feeling Orientation |

1. Perspective Taking and Constructive Negotiation Approach: Are these skill areas being overused? Does the client focus too much on other members' opinions and not express enough of his own? Are there times when win-win isn't reachable and the client has trouble recognizing it? Investigate how much time the client invests in these areas, and how efficiently the skills are being used. The client may not recognize when there's enough information, or when win-win isn't feasible, so an alternative agreement may be the better answer. In general, redirect some of this energy, as indicated below.

2. Assertiveness with Perspective Taking: The client can utilize some of the Perspective Taking energy for speaking up and stating his own views. The goal is to strike a balance between Assertiveness and Perspective Taking. The optimal zone for both is in the lower part of the High section on the graph.

3. Constructive Negotiation Approach with Positive Group Affiliation: With such a high CNA score, it would be beneficial for the client to direct some of that energy toward PGA, to further refine that skill area. He can put additional time into building rapport with group members, finding ways to lift team morale. This will, in turn, increase the members' desire for win-win agreements. By facilitating some rapport-building activities, he would move people in the right direction.

4. Task Analysis with Task Implementation: Examine with the client the relationship between TA and TI. At times, does the client push the work forward a bit too quickly? It might be prudent for the client to ease up on the rush to implement a plan. He should make sure that all members are involved to create a unified team effort.

5. Initiative: The client should take on a leadership position, practicing a more sophisticated, nuanced approach to the role, based on the feedback in the previous points.

Graph Nine

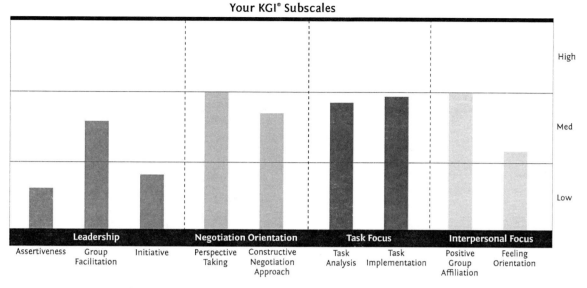

Your KGI® Subscales

1. **Assertiveness:** The client should look for opportunities to speak up more in the group. The client can respond to other members' interests, based on insights gleaned from Perspective Taking. The client can also share thoughts about Task Analysis and Task Implementation to assist the team in moving work along.

2. **Group Facilitation with Task Focus:** The client can become more active in facilitating the task enterprise. She can invite others to contribute ideas about task strategies, while also sharing personal thoughts on the matter. She should try to keep the conversation going, looking at task issues from multiple angles.

3. **Constructive Negotiation Approach with Positive Group Affiliation:** The client can shift some of her interest in building rapport with teammates (PGA) towards the pursuit of finding common ground in negotiations (CNA). Team morale goes up after people hash out win-win agreements. As the client intentionally connects efforts in these domains, it can help the team develop greater cohesion.

4. **Positive Group Affiliation with Feeling Orientation:** The client can boost team spirit by paying closer attention to the emotional currents in the group and making efforts to guide emotional energy in positive directions. Responding quickly and constructively to negative emotions can keep these feelings from seriously eroding team morale.

5. **Initiative:** The client should look for a significant group project and assume a leadership position, employing skills with Negotiation Orientation, Task Focus, and Positive Group Affiliation to guide the team in constructive directions.

Graph Ten

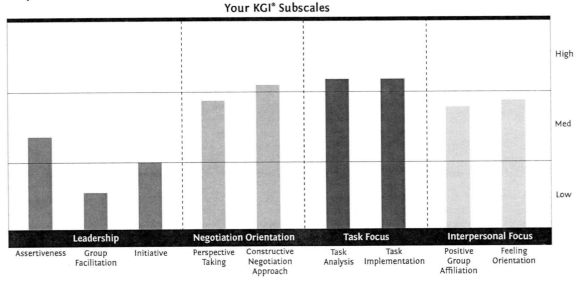

1. Assertiveness with Perspective Taking: The client should speak up more, particularly expressing opinions in the task and negotiation areas. Also, the client can ask questions to explore other members' interests, strengthening the Perspective Taking domain.

2. Group Facilitation with Task Focus: The client pays close attention to task functions and could assist the group in organizing and executing its work. There is a real leadership opportunity here. The client could begin by sharing ideas, inviting feedback, and asking others to participate in a creative dialogue about the task enterprise.

3. Constructive Negotiation Approach with Positive Group Affiliation: The client can take time to become more acquainted with other members, talking with them before and after meetings, getting to know their interests and concerns more fully. This information would then be useful for constructing win-win options when the team debates various strategies.

4. Feeling Orientation: Given the client's attention to feeling issues, this could be valuable information to share at times, helping other members in the group to be more aware of the influence of feelings on the team. Combining this "feeling content" with Assertiveness, in an appropriate and selective way, would be astute skill integration.

5. Initiative: The client should be less hesitant about stepping into a prime leadership position. The client has a cluster of skills that could be effectively employed in a leader's role. The individual should pick an advantageous project, an interesting one, and take the helm.

Graph Eleven

Your KGI® Subscales

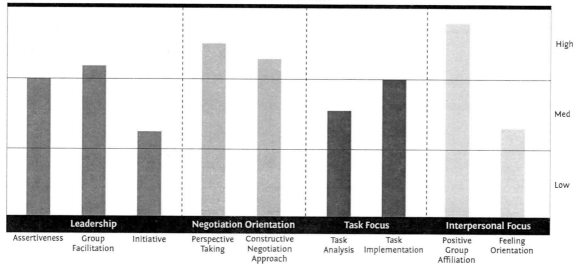

1. **Feeling Orientation:** This client can employ skills with Perspective Taking to focus more on other members' emotional reactions. He can pay attention to people's enthusiasms and look for ways to guide this energy into appropriate work (delegating job assignments based on member interests). Also, he can watch for negative emotions and address them as they emerge, in order to maintain team harmony.

2. **Task Analysis:** The client should listen closely to members who present solid task strategies, and see how they make their cases. He should attempt to structure and present his own ideas in a similar manner.

3. **Task Analysis with Task Implementation:** The graph suggests the client may jump ahead and try to conclude a task without thinking through the strategy. Explore this issue. Guide the client to be more patient with strategy development, before turning to action. Help him to establish more equilibrium between analysis and implementation.

4. **Positive Group Affiliation:** The client shows a strong interest in developing member rapport and team cohesion. However, this may be going over the top. Too much PGA can make the group a social club, without a strong enough task focus. Dialing down PGA and directing some of that energy towards developing Task Analysis would create more balance in the client's participation style.

5. **Initiative:** The client should take a leadership role in a relevant group project. He can utilize skills with negotiation and Positive Group Affiliation to establish a positive team spirit. He can invite all members to participate in Task Analysis, so people work together to structure the steps for completing the task.

Graph Twelve

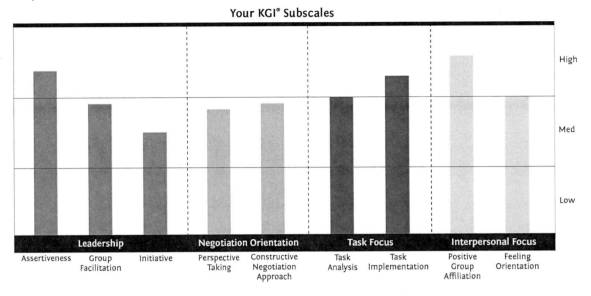

Your KGI® Subscales

1. **Assertiveness with Perspective Taking:** The client can use Assertiveness to ask more questions, probing others' positions to gain insights about their concerns. He can make more of an effort to get inside their shoes in order to understand their values, which will aid in negotiating agreements that address members' interests and thereby build greater commitment to the work.

2. **Constructive Negotiation Approach with Positive Group Affiliation:** The client should redirect some of the energy from PGA to support efforts in CNA, the work of forging win-win agreements. Win-win boosts team morale and resonates with Positive Group Affiliation.

3. **Task Analysis with Task Implementation:** It appears that the client may have an impulse to push for closure with the task, while analysis lags a bit behind. Explore this issue. He should balance patience with the planning process with his concern for timely execution of the task.

4. **Group Facilitation with Interpersonal Focus:** Given the client's interests and skills, he should consciously lead the group in the interpersonal area, promoting a positive atmosphere through rapport-building conversation and by paying attention to feeling issues. He should help the group address positive and negative feelings in constructive ways.

5. **Initiative:** The client should take on a challenging leadership position. He should avoid being too assertive about his own ideas; rather, he can facilitate a broad discussion of issues, fostering an inclusive dialogue and team decision making. That will engage people and draw out their best efforts.

Graph Thirteen

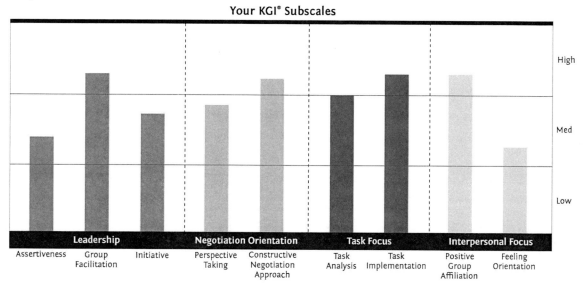

Your KGI® Subscales

1. **Assertiveness:** The client should take the opportunity to voice ideas in group discussions, particularly related to Constructive Negotiation Approach, Task Focus, and Positive Group Affiliation. She could invite members to respond to these ideas to expand the conversation.

2. **Feeling Orientation:** The client can use Perspective Taking skills to pay more attention to the emotional currents in the group, watching out for positive and negative reactions from others. When emotional expression occurs, she can ask questions to obtain a deeper understanding about teammates' motivations, feelings, and values, and then assist the group in managing the situation.

3. **Constructive Negotiation Approach with Positive Group Affiliation:** The client has valuable skills in these areas, which are vital for creating team cohesion and synergy. Tapping skills with Group Facilitation, she can assume a larger leadership role in advancing rapport-building conversation in the group, strengthening member relations, and guiding the group towards win-win decision making that will enhance unity and increase productivity.

4. **Task Analysis with Task Implementation:** Investigate with the client the relationship between TA and TI. There is some impulse here to spring ahead and conclude a task before the plan is completely considered. Check the client's patience with the TA process, and how TA and TI are being balanced. Consider possible refinements that would strengthen Task Focus.

5. **Initiative:** The client should pick a very substantial team project and assume a leadership role. With a broad array of skills in negotiation, task, and interpersonal, she is well positioned to embrace a meaningful challenge and push her leadership development to the next level.

Graph Fourteen

Your KGI® Subscales

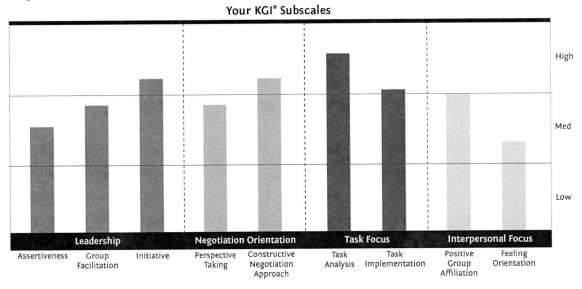

Leadership			**Negotiation Orientation**		**Task Focus**		**Interpersonal Focus**	
Assertiveness	Group Facilitation	Initiative	Perspective Taking	Constructive Negotiation Approach	Task Analysis	Task Implementation	Positive Group Affiliation	Feeling Orientation

1. **Assertiveness:** The client can speak up and express more ideas in group discussions. After sharing various views, the client can invite feedback to promote dialogue about the issues under discussion.

2. **Perspective Taking:** The client should ask probing questions to learn more about other members' positions—their interests, values, and concerns. The client can then use this information to build thoughtful proposals for Constructive Negotiation Approach, a domain where the client has significant interest. Better CNA proposals can boost morale and deepen commitment to the work.

3. **Task Analysis with Task Implementation:** Such a strong TA score suggests a potential perfectionism with task analysis. Excessive analysis can be time consuming and non-productive. Explore how the client approaches the relationship between TA and TI. The goal would be to redirect some of the energy from TA towards Task Implementation, to strike a better balance between the two, with both scores ultimately landing in the low-High region of the graph.

4. **Positive Group Affiliation with Feeling Orientation:** The client can cultivate skills in Feeling Orientation that will support efforts in Positive Group Affiliation. By paying attention to body language and facial expressions to assess other members' emotional reactions, the client can help the team consider current levels of morale and motivation.

5. **Initiative:** The client has a strong score and may already be effective in assuming prime leadership responsibilities. However, an important question is: Does the client take too much initiative, picking up leadership responsibilities for too many projects, thus leading to feeling overloaded? Explore with the client the consequences of too much initiative. Less may be more. Becoming more selective with Initiative may be valuable for delivering higher quality work on chosen tasks.

Graph Fifteen

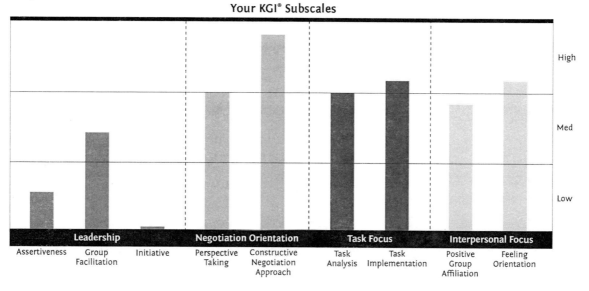

Your KGI® Subscales

1. **Constructive Negotiation Approach with Positive Group Affiliation:** This client channels tremendous energy into CNA, which seems to be too much. It would be beneficial to explore the reasons for the client's strong focus. The client may see this effort as so important that it can blind her to other group issues. In general, it could be useful to direct some of the CNA energy towards PGA. Taking time to get to know other members will provide useful information about their concerns, which will support efforts to find win-win agreements.

2. **Assertiveness with Perspective Taking:** The client can speak up to ask probing questions, investigating more fully other group member's perspectives on various issues. Two particular areas could be targeted: Task Analysis and Feeling Orientation. The client can assist the group in discovering more information in these areas. She can then become more active with the development of task strategies and in identifying emotional currents that affect productivity.

3. **Task Analysis with Task Implementation:** The client leans a bit towards implementation. As always, it is worthwhile to investigate how she looks at the relationship between TA and TI. Does the client jump the gun occasionally to get the work done, without being patient with TA? Some fine tuning in this regard could improve performance.

4. **Group Facilitation with Task Focus:** There is an opportunity for the client to assume a more active leadership role with the task effort. The individual can help the team examine the task in a thoughtful way, and assist the group in making adjustments as a plan is implemented. With her interest in these areas, it would be a natural direction to develop leadership skills.

5. **Initiative:** The client exhibits a great deal of inhibition in this domain. If she can co-lead different aspects of the group' work, it would be a meaningful way to build skills and, later on, prepare her to take on a solo leadership position. The client has significant skills in negotiation, task, and interpersonal, so there are several options for shared-leadership positions.

Graph Sixteen

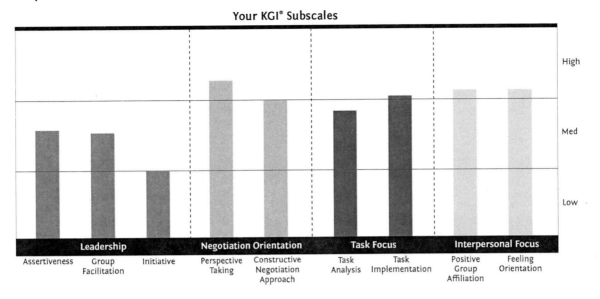

Your KGI® Subscales

Leadership			Negotiation Orientation		Task Focus		Interpersonal Focus	
Assertiveness	Group Facilitation	Initiative	Perspective Taking	Constructive Negotiation Approach	Task Analysis	Task Implementation	Positive Group Affiliation	Feeling Orientation

1. **Assertiveness with Perspective Taking:** The client appears to be a good listener, with a healthy score in Perspective Taking. He could respond more to others' statements by expressing support, or offering alternative ideas. Since the client demonstrates interest in the negotiation, task, and interpersonal areas, there are a variety of ways to join the conversation.

2. **Group Facilitation with Interpersonal Focus:** The client can take a more proactive role in helping the team pay attention to and manage emotions, and also in promoting rapport-building activities that foster team cohesion.

3. **Constructive Negotiation Approach with Positive Group Affiliation:** The client can be more intentional about investigating others' interests during social conversations with teammates. This information can be used during group discussions to forge win-win agreements.

4. **Task Analysis with Task Implementation:** The graph indicates that the client may, at times, feel the impulse to jump ahead and complete the task without fully thinking through the plan. Investigate this possibility. The client can develop skills for examining a task from multiple angles to construct a more thoughtful strategy. This would bring TA and TI into greater balance.

5. **Initiative:** The client should select a worthy team project and step up to be a key leader. Using negotiation and interpersonal skills, he can create a positive team atmosphere. With respect to Task Analysis, he could invite all members to share ideas and construct a group plan.

Graph Seventeen

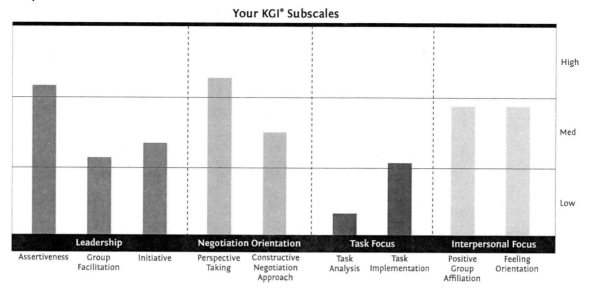

Your KGI® Subscales

1. **Group Facilitation with Interpersonal Focus**: The client can step up to play a more prominent role in promoting rapport-building activities that foster team cohesion. The client can also help the members attend to the emotional issues that arise during group sessions.

2. **Perspective Taking:** The client can ask probing questions to get a clearer grasp of other members' perspectives with Task Analysis, observing how members with skills in this area logically construct a strategy. The client can imitate these approaches and begin to build new skills with analysis.

3. **Constructive Negotiation Approach with Positive Group Affiliation:** The client can utilize skills in PGA to strengthen Constructive Negotiation Approach by talking with teammates before and after meetings and becoming more familiar with their concerns and issues. This information will provide insights that can later be used for constructing win-win solutions during negotiations. Also, as members get to know each other better, they are more inclined to be mutually supportive in negotiations.

4. **Task Implementation:** The client can take an active role in improving communication when the team works on a task. She can be in touch with others, instigating a regular flow of information, and help the team make adjustments that will produce a more efficient effort.

5. **Initiative:** When an interesting project appears, the client should rise up to be the leader. She can draw on teammates' talents in the Task Focus area, assigning roles so that people can employ their skills with analysis and implementation to help the team. Rather than trying to do everything herself, she can facilitate a mutually supportive atmosphere and a team effort.

Graph Eighteen

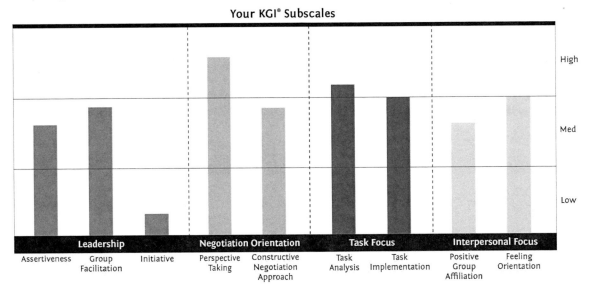

Your KGI® Subscales

1. **Assertiveness:** The client can speak up more to share ideas, particularly related to Task Analysis and Task Implementation. There is also an opportunity to share insights about emotional currents in the group related to Feeling Orientation.

2. **Group Facilitation with Task Focus:** The client can be proactive in facilitating discussions about Task Analysis, inviting others' participation, sharing his own ideas, and helping the group look at a task from multiple angles to construct the best plan. He can also assist the group in monitoring its actions as it implements the plan, helping guide it to a strong outcome.

3. **Perspective Taking:** The client expends significant energy to understand others' perspectives. But this "other focus" could be reduced slightly in favor of sharing his ideas in discussions. The client could also consciously use the insights gained from PT to propose more win-win agreements that would build team cohesion.

4. **Positive Group Affiliation with Feeling Orientation:** This client pays attention to feeling issues in the group. The next step is to use these perceptions to help the group manage its emotional resources in constructive ways. He could help connect members' enthusiasms with the right work and address negative emotions in a timely way so they don't erode team morale.

5. **Initiative:** The client could start with shared leadership opportunities, partnering with others to help guide efforts in the negotiation, task, and interpersonal domains. As the individual gains confidence, it would be profitable for him to take on full leadership responsibility for a team project.

Graph Nineteen

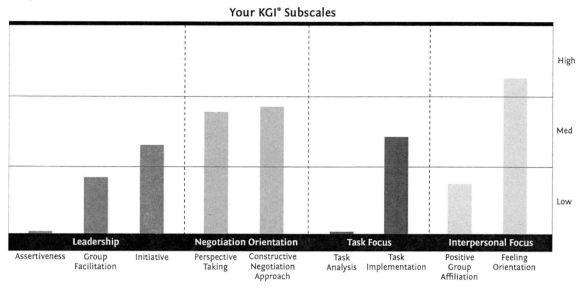

Your KGI® Subscales

1. **Assertiveness with Perspective Taking**: This client needs to participate in group discussions. To start, he can ask more questions about other people's interests and concerns, tapping into the PT skills. The client can then respond to these ideas, identifying points of agreement, or sharing other information that will expand the conversation. The client should, in a patient, step-by-step way, practice expressing his ideas to develop a greater social presence.

2. **Group Facilitation with Constructive Negotiation Approach**: The client can start becoming more proactive in the negotiation area. As people share their interests and concerns, he can help the group construct win-win agreements, proposing options that will be mutually beneficial and inviting feedback so the group can fashion acceptable agreements.

3. **Constructive Negotiation Approach with Positive Group Affiliation**: The graph shows client interest in the win-win approach to negotiation. Having him develop more rapport with teammates (PGA) will support this approach. The client could build better relations with other members by taking the time to talk with them before and after meetings. As people get more acquainted, they are better able to identify common ground in agreements.

4. **Task Analysis**: With such a low score, the client would do well to observe how other members, who have strength in this area, participate in group discussions. How do they structure arguments that are clear, logical, and persuasive? He needs to use observational learning to absorb these techniques and then practice them to build skills in this domain.

5. **Initiative**: The client should select a meaningful project and take a leadership role using negotiation skills to strike mutually beneficial agreements. He should be ready to draw on other members' strengths in the Task Analysis area, inviting their input and working as a team to construct effective strategies. He should help the team maintain effective communication when implementing the plan in order to make adjustments and bring about strong outcomes.

Graph Twenty

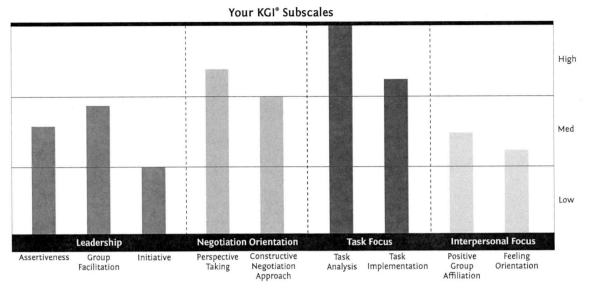

Your KGI® Subscales

	High
	Med
	Low

Leadership — Assertiveness, Group Facilitation, Initiative
Negotiation Orientation — Perspective Taking, Constructive Negotiation Approach
Task Focus — Task Analysis, Task Implementation
Interpersonal Focus — Positive Group Affiliation, Feeling Orientation

1. **Task Analysis:** This client needs to evaluate the amount of time and energy going into the Task Analysis. Is she in pursuit of the "perfect" strategy? There can be overemphasis on finding an ideal, air-tight plan, which wastes time and will only need adjustment later. It would be better to direct some of this energy to underdeveloped areas, such as Positive Group Affiliation and Feeling Orientation.

2. **Assertiveness with Perspective Taking:** The client could speak up more in group settings. She possesses solid listening skills, as indicated by the Perspective Taking score. The client could provide thoughtful responses to others' views and describe her own ideas. This can be especially useful when articulating win-win proposals that would build team harmony.

3. **Constructive Negotiation Approach with Positive Group Affiliation:** The client demonstrates interest in win-win agreements. An important way to support this interest is to build greater team rapport. The client can make time to get better acquainted with other members, building personal bridges. Also, she can promote rapport-building activities with the whole team to help members bond. As they do, they become more inclined to strike mutually agreeable accords.

4. **Feeling Orientation:** It would be useful for the client to expend time observing the emotional reactions of other members, their body language, facial gestures, and tones of voice. She can then use these data to discern what others care about and what they value, which can inform negotiations. Also, she can note people's excitements relating to the work at hand and try to delegate assignments accordingly, matching interests with task assignments.

5. **Initiative:** The client should look for an opportunity to be the primary team leader, making sure everyone's voice is heard in the task effort and in negotiations. She should be careful to establish a positive atmosphere by paying attention to the Interpersonal Focus domain, which will boost team productivity.

Graph Twenty-one

Your KGI® Subscales

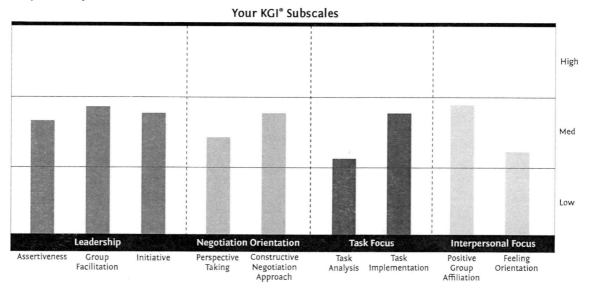

Leadership			Negotiation Orientation		Task Focus		Interpersonal Focus		
Assertiveness	Group Facilitation	Initiative	Perspective Taking	Constructive Negotiation Approach	Task Analysis	Task Implementation	Positive Group Affiliation	Feeling Orientation

1. **Assertiveness with Perspective Taking:** The client should ask more questions of other members, including probing questions to understand more accurately their ideas, values, and interests, which will strengthen PT skills.

2. **Constructive Negotiation Approach:** Using information gained from an increase in Perspective Taking, the client can construct more win-win proposals for the group, boosting participation in this area of activity. As the client becomes more comfortable with this process, it would be advantageous to take a leadership role, employing Group Facilitation. The client can help guide the group's efforts during negotiations.

3. **Task Analysis with Task Implementation:** The client appears more comfortable on the implementation side of this equation. Task Analysis is underdeveloped. Explore this situation, examining the client's approach to the task effort. More patience and attention to the planning process (TA) would be in order. When the group analyzes a task, the client should ask members to share their reasoning to gain insights into how they attack a problem. The client can pick up techniques that will be useful to employ later.

4. **Feeling Orientation:** The client can pay more attention to the emotional patterns in the group: the things that excite people and motivate them; the things that cause conflict and undermine them. The client should try to direct the excitement into appropriate work for the team, while promptly addressing emotional conflict to help reduce it. These efforts support Positive Group Affiliation in a potent way.

5. **Initiative:** The client is positioned to take on a significant leadership role. But it will be important to include all members in discussions, paying close attention to their thoughts, feelings, and values. Urge the client to empathically consider others' positions and construct mutual agreements that motivate people. Also, the client needs to make sure there is broad discussion with Task Analysis so the team develops a strong plan.

Graph Twenty-two

Your KGI® Subscales

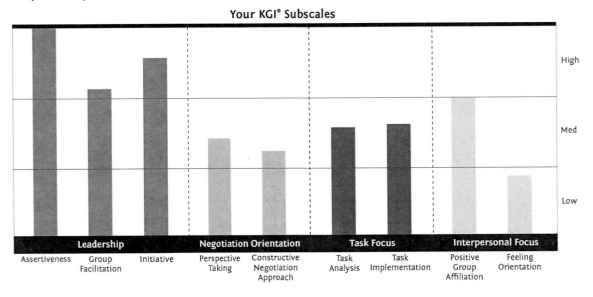

	Leadership			Negotiation Orientation		Task Focus		Interpersonal Focus	
Assertiveness	Group Facilitation	Initiative	Perspective Taking	Constructive Negotiation Approach	Task Analysis	Task Implementation	Positive Group Affiliation	Feeling Orientation

High / Med / Low

1. Assertiveness with Perspective Taking: The client should reduce the amount of personal speaking in group discussions. This level of Assertiveness can come across as domineering, and can be counterproductive to good leadership practice. As an alternative, he can build up Perspective Taking, asking questions to draw others into the conversation, listening patiently to what they have to say and gaining insight into their perspectives and interests. He can share ideas that respond to their positions, as well as articulating his own ideas on the subject.

2. Group Facilitation with Positive Group Affiliation: The client should pursue his interest in Positive Group Affiliation. He could suggest that the group spend time at the beginning of a session for some personal sharing so that people get to know each other better. This will strengthen team cohesion.

3. Constructive Negotiation Approach with Positive Group Affiliation: As a group gains team spirit, members are more inclined to pursue win-win agreements that benefit everyone. Such agreements increase people's commitment to the work. The client should look for opportunities to not only build greater member rapport, but to promote the win-win approach. He can attend to CNA by utilizing insights obtained through Perspective Taking and then constructing mutually beneficial accords.

4. Feeling Orientation: The client should pay attention to emotional reactions in the group. If there's a conflict and someone withdraws, at the right moment the client should invite that person back into the discussion. Also, he should pay attention to what positively motivates members and direct that energy into relevant assignments.

5. Initiative: The client should be selective in taking leadership positions in teams. There is a strong interest in being the prime leader, but he can take on too many leadership posts, becoming over-burdened and losing effectiveness. He should pick the most significant and rewarding tasks and pay attention to the feedback in the previous points to become a well-rounded, productive leader.

Graph Twenty-three

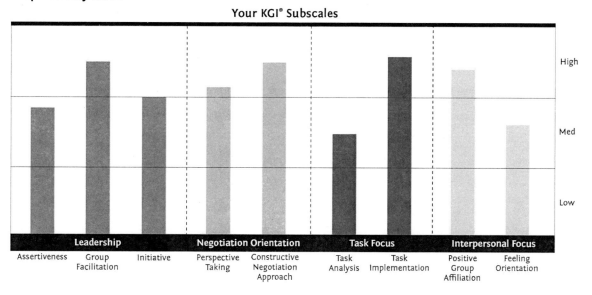

Your KGI® Subscales

1. **Assertiveness:** The client should look for more opportunities to speak up in a group, particularly in areas of interest, such as win-win negotiations (Constructive Negotiation Approach), advancing the work (Task Implementation), and building member rapport (Positive Group Affiliation).

2. **Task Analysis with Task Implementation:** The client has an intense focus on Task Implementation while tending to neglect Task Analysis. This indicates a drive to get the work done without first developing a sound strategy. Investigate why the client operates in this manner. What are her motives? Point out the value of having more balance here. The client should direct some of the TI energy into TA and develop more patience with that aspect of the process.

3. **Group Facilitation with Task Analysis:** The client can lead a discussion by asking other members to help analyze the task. She can listen for the logic and persuasiveness of their points, and then share her own ideas about constructing a strategy. She should invite people to respond to each other's ideas and promote a strong collective analysis.

4. **Positive Group Affiliation with Feeling Orientation:** The client can pay more attention to the emotional currents in the group. She can watch for displays of enthusiasm from members and look for ways to connect that energy to task assignments and to build win-win agreements. If negative emotions appear, she can help lead a discussion to manage the issues in a timely way. All of these actions support a constructive team environment, the aim of Positive Group Affiliation.

5. **Initiative:** The client has a valuable impulse to take a primary leadership role. The key is to select the best opportunities, the ones that offer the most rewards and benefits for her career. She should avoid picking up too many responsibilities, which can dilute the quality of her work and overwhelm her.

Graph Twenty-four

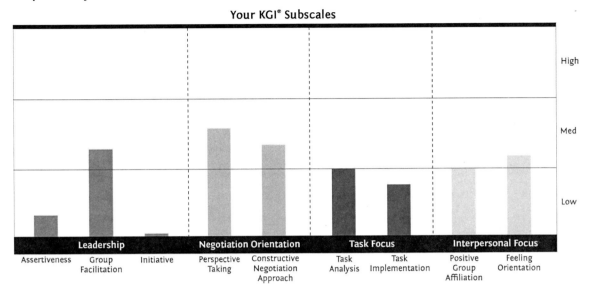

Your KGI® Subscales

| | Leadership | | | Negotiation Orientation | | Task Focus | | Interpersonal Focus | |
| Assertiveness | Group Facilitation | Initiative | Perspective Taking | Constructive Negotiation Approach | Task Analysis | Task Implementation | Positive Group Affiliation | Feeling Orientation |

1. **Assertiveness with Perspective Taking:** The client should take a more active role in group discussions. Part of the effort can focus on the client's sharing reactions to other members' points, following up on Perspective Taking. When listening to other members' positions, the individual can identify points of agreement and offer supporting ideas for those positions, initiating a relationship of mutual support. The client can consciously build bridges with like-minded teammates, which, over time, can make it easier to speak up in a group.

2. **Group Facilitation:** The client can seek to facilitate discussions in the Negotiation Orientation area. He can ask questions of other group members to gain further insights about their positions and then help the group craft win-win agreements that will address various members' interests.

3. **Task Analysis with Task Implementation:** The client can begin by observing other members who are strong in the task domain. How do they analyze a task? How do they coordinate the group's efforts to execute a plan? What are their best techniques? He can then select certain approaches and practice them until they become part of his own repertoire.

4. **Positive Group Affiliation:** The client should take some time to get to know other members. He should engage in small talk, finding areas of mutual interest and developing some rapport with people. Not only will the client feel more a part of the group, these efforts will also support his interest in Constructive Negotiation Approach, helping to identify the points to build win-win agreements.

5. **Initiative:** The client should look for opportunities to share leadership with other members on appropriate projects. He can pursue these opportunities to build his leadership skills. Also, he can study those who are effective leaders in the group. What techniques do they employ? He can consciously imitate their best practices. After building skills in these ways, he should be willing, at the appropriate time, to step into a full leadership role and direct the team on a meaningful project.

The above cases introduce a broad range of results and demonstrate a flexible method for interpretation, showing how a consultant can customize a plan for any client, according to the pattern of the individual's graph scores. Professionals have stated that it is like solving a puzzle. You see how the pieces fit together to create an effective design for skill development, one that enables the client to become a fully functioning leader and group member. With this agenda in hand, the client practices new techniques in a step-by-step manner and advances to a fuller realization of his or her social potential.

Importantly, with the KGI system, improvement is not restricted to the individual alone. A whole team can join together to refine its interactive processes, ascending to a higher plane of performance. In the next chapter the device for making this happen is unveiled: the KGI® Group Profile. ✕

CHAPTER 13

Design of the KGI® Group Profile

When the members of a team take the Klein Group Instrument assessment, the scores can be anonymously combined to construct the KGI® Group Profile. Participants then receive a pair of reports: individual and team. With the former, a consultant directs personal growth, with the latter, a team-building process that maps out strategies to refine collaboration. With this method, members pursue progress on two fronts to spur greater productivity.

In a number of ways, the format of the KGI® Group Profile imitates that of the KGI® Individual Profile. The heart of the report flows in the same manner, moving systematically through the major scale domains, presenting a graph for each segment and offering suggestions for improvement in each subscale area. The graph displays the range of member scores for the major scale and each of the subscales, supporting an intricate analysis of group dynamics and group learning needs. The materials permit an examination of diverse issues related to leadership, communication, task execution, feedback processes, and team cohesion, presenting a series of options to address these concerns so that the team can choose the most appropriate strategies for its particular situation.

Other features of the profile, likewise tailored to promote a potent team-building process, will be explained as the components of the document are now spelled out in a systematic manner.

1. **Introduction.** The report starts with the KGI diamond model, presenting the conceptual design of the instrument, and introduces the major scales and their subscales. It announces the goal of making the group a learning team, one in which members learn from and with each other to create a high-performing unit.

2. **Communication and Confidentiality.** This section explains that as the group analyzes its issues, the members will also refer to their individual results. This needs to be done with mutual consent, a respect for persons, and appropriate confidentiality. Through this enterprise, individuals gain personal skills and the team rises to a new level of competence.

3. **Team Results: Composite Group Graphs.** The report moves into the team's collective results, which are displayed on two graphs.

A. *Group Composite Major Scale Graph*
The first graph reveals the results for the major scales: Leadership, Negotiation Orientation, Task Focus, and Interpersonal Focus. The graph has High, Medium, and Low sections, depicting

the various levels of performance. Critically, the column for each scale contains a rectangular box indicating the range of members' scores in that domain. The top line of the rectangle identifies

the highest score, while the bottom identifies the lowest. Inside the rectangle is a diamond line, indicating the average score for the team.

Team Major Scale Scores

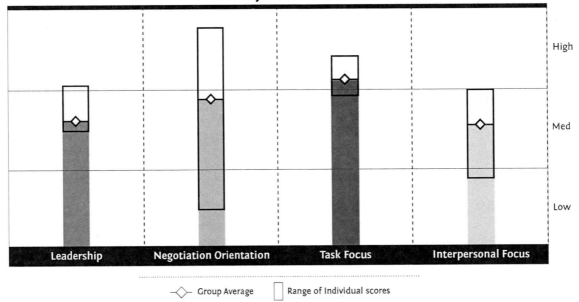

Leadership   Negotiation Orientation   Task Focus   Interpersonal Focus

◇ Group Average   ☐ Range of Individual scores

Important: When one analyzes this graph, it is necessary to be aware of a statistical fact that is *counterintuitive*. In evaluating team performance on a specific column, pay attention to the diamond line marking the average score. **The greater cluster of member scores will be in the smaller area above or below this line in the rectangular box.** An initial assumption might be that there are more scores in the larger area on either side of the line when, in fact, the opposite is true—more members are clustered in the smaller area. **That's necessary to remember when interpreting the graph results.**

This section also includes points for interpreting the Group Composite Major Scale Graph, with an emphasis on the evaluation of the highest and lowest scale results, which serve as benchmarks for team performance.

B. *Group Composite Subscale Graph*

The second graph unveils all of the subscale scores in a continuous sequence, similar in design to the graph at the end of the KGI® Individual Profile. Each column contains a rectangular box with the range of member scores. This graph is an invaluable resource for the analysis, permitting a team to assess strengths, needs, and ways to balance group performance. *This graph is the centerpiece for determining team strategies.*

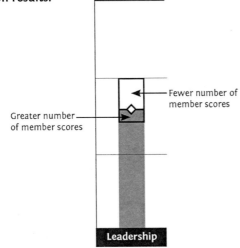

Greater number of member scores

Fewer number of member scores

Leadership

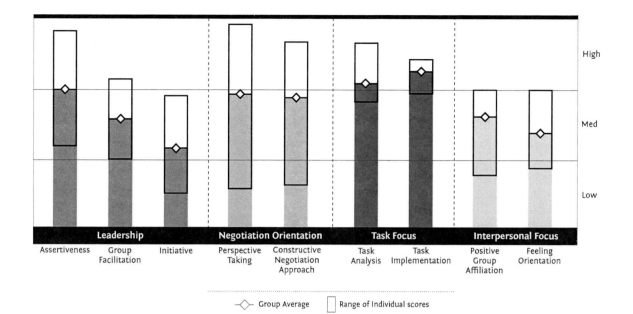

Assertiveness | Group Facilitation | Initiative | Perspective Taking | Constructive Negotiation Approach | Task Analysis | Task Implementation | Positive Group Affiliation | Feeling Orientation

Leadership   **Negotiation Orientation**   **Task Focus**   **Interpersonal Focus**

◇ Group Average   □ Range of Individual scores

This section likewise includes points for interpreting the graph, including how to analyze it using the Inter-Subscale Combinations system. It also contains information about how to interpret the range of member scores located in the rectangular boxes.

4. **Action Steps.** The next section outlines the steps for choosing subscale categories to address, finding suggestions to improve the team's interactive processes in the appropriate subscale areas of the report, implementing those strategies, and pursuing an ongoing developmental process that will make the group a high-performing team.

5. **The Four Major Scale Sections.** The report now introduces specific information for each of the major scales and their subscales. Like the KGI® Individual Profile, the details in each section appear in the exact same format, so the first section to be described, Leadership, serves as a template for the later ones.

The information in the Leadership section proceeds as follows:

A. *A color graph*

The section begins with a graph displaying columns for the overall Leadership scale, the Assertiveness subscale, the Group Facilitation subscale, and the Initiative subscale. The graph has lines that differentiate high, medium, and low frequency of performance. A high score indicates that a group performs the specific behaviors in the scale, or subscale, 75% to 100% of the time;

a medium score signifies the group performs the behaviors 50% to 74% of the time; while a low score points to performance from 0% to 49% of the time. As noted previously, each column contains a rectangular black box indicating the range of member scores.

Graph Example

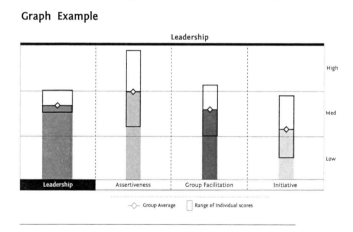

Leadership

Leadership   Assertiveness   Group Facilitation   Initiative

◇ Group Average   □ Range of Individual scores

B. *Information on the Assertiveness subscale*

The report then presents data about performance in the Assertiveness sector. It includes information in the following three categories:

i. *In Brief:* Explains the significance of Assertiveness for effective team operations.

ii. *Team Assessment:* Provides a short summary of the team's results in this domain.

iii. *Suggestions to Improve Your Team's Performance:* Lists 5 to 8 recommendations on how to upgrade performance in this area, according to the team's specific score. The number of options allows the team to choose the most appropriate strategies, which may be modified to create a more exact fit.

C. *Information about the Group Facilitation subscale and Initiative subscale*

Data for these subscales follow and are presented in the same manner as the Assertiveness section, with the *In Brief, Team Assessment*, and *Suggestions to Improve Your Team Performance* categories.

The profile then introduces information for the Negotiation Orientation, Task Focus, and Interpersonal Focus segments, delivering data in the same format outlined above in the Leadership section.

6. **One-Sentence Descriptions of the KGI Major Scales and Their Subscales**. On the last page of the profile are brief descriptors of the scales and subscales, providing an easy reference for the essential ideas in the KGI system.

With the material contained in the KGI® Group Profile, a consultant can lead a team into exciting new territory, enabling the members to refine their communication, strengthen their collaboration, and sharpen their task execution. The next chapter explains the methodology a professional employs in this team-building endeavor. ✕

CHAPTER 14

Team Building with the Klein Group Instrument® Model

Team development with the Klein Group Instrument model combines the use of the individual profile and the group profile. The approach operates on the guiding principle: as individuals thrive, so, too, the team can flourish. Personal growth takes place within the context of collective improvement. By extending an opportunity for group members to cultivate their own skills while they perfect their teamwork, the model motivates people to summon their best efforts. By taking care of individuals as well as the team, the method creates a win-win system for the project.

With this formula, individual coaching is combined with group meetings to establish a lively learning atmosphere. For group sessions, the analysis targets a key item: the Group Composite Subscale Graph, the chart that allows a team to quickly assess patterns of performance and determine areas for improvement. Once members identify subscales to work on, they can go into the body of the profile and examine suggestions in those domains. They can select the most appropriate options, make any necessary adjustments, and then practice the new techniques. The method is focused, direct, and easy to carry out.

The outline below explains the steps for a consulting intervention. Included in the outline are time suggestions to help a professional gauge the length of each segment. Clients will take the assessment online and receive individual profiles prior to the training. Usually, the consultant will wait until the second phase of the training to supply the group profile. The aim is to avoid overloading participants with too much information too soon, and instead establishing the concepts in a well-paced, sequential manner.

1. *Begin with an overview of the KGI model, and explain the KGI® Individual Profile and the personal development process.* (Time: 45–60 minutes)

(To assist a consultant in preparing for this session, see Appendix: The Basic Script for Introducing the Klein Group Instrument® Assessment.)

The overview would cover these points:

A. Explain the KGI diamond design with the four major scales, and their interconnections.

B. Provide a systematic description of the subscales for each of the major scales. The one-sentence descriptions for the subscales, found in Chapter 3, furnish an appropriate introduction.

The consultant can elaborate on this information using data from the full-paragraph descriptions also located in Chapter 3.

C. Mention the two separate KGI reports: individual and group. State that both have a similar design, which makes it easy to work with them in combination.

D. Move to the KGI® Individual Profile, explaining the components contained in each of the main sections: Leadership, Negotiation Orientation, Task Focus, and Interpersonal Focus.

i. Graph material.

ii. A statement about an individual's basic approach in that area of group life.

iii. Subscale data on What You Enjoy, What You Find Difficult or Challenging, and

Behaviors That May Help You Grow. With this information, an individual obtains insights into how one operates in small groups, along with suggestions for skill building.

E. Show illustrations of the composite graphs at the end of the individual profile—the graph with the major scales, and the graph with all of the subscales. Explain their importance. The major scales allow one to establish basic benchmarks for performance (see Chapter 9).

The composite subscale graph permits a detailed analysis of group behavior with the goal of balancing performance across the different domains to increase individual effectiveness. *The subscale graph is the most critical component in the individual profile* (see Chapter 9).

Your KGI® Major Scales

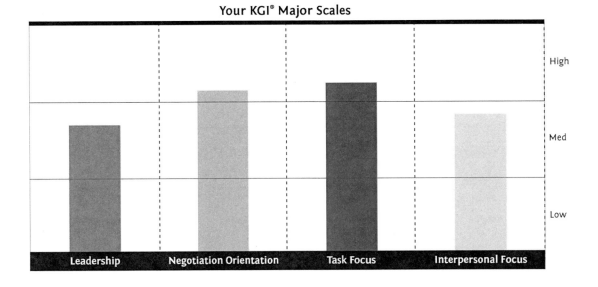

Your KGI® Subscales

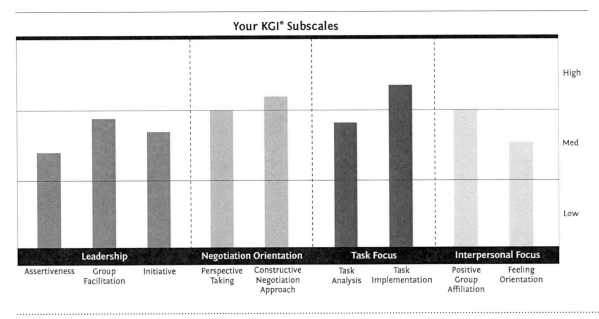

F. Describe the use of the Inter-Subscale Combinations to evaluate performance in the composite subscale graph. (Draw on information described in Chapter 10 of this guide.)

The combinations:

- Assertiveness with Perspective Taking
- Group Facilitation with Task Focus and Interpersonal Focus
- Initiative with Negotiation Orientation, Task Focus, and Interpersonal Focus
- Constructive Negotiation Approach with Positive Group Affiliation
- Task Analysis with Task Implementation
- Positive Group Affiliation with Feeling Orientation

Working on these subscales in combination can help individuals balance their skills in core areas of small-group behavior.

G. Review the steps an individual will follow to develop leadership and group skills, using the KGI® Individual Profile:

- Identify subscale strength areas in the various domains.
- Assess subscale areas that are problematic.
- Decide which subscale areas would be the *most valuable* and *most meaningful* to develop in order to expand one's leadership and group skills. How can one balance the various skills to become a multidimensional group leader and group member?
- Decide which skill areas would be most important to develop within the context of the current team.
- For the selected subscales, investigate those domains in the KGI® Individual Profile to find suggestions in Behaviors That May Help You Grow. Identify the suggestions that appear most advantageous for new skill development.
- Prioritize the new skills and establish a learning agenda.
- Experiment with one or two new skills in current group setting(s).
- Continue to practice and refine the skills until they become more comfortable, more integrated into one's style. Mention that the research shows **three attempts** in practicing a new skill usually create a reasonable comfort level with its use.
- Develop a relationship with a team colleague who can give feedback about these efforts. It is beneficial to get objective feedback about one's performance.
- Continue to build skills. After a person masters the initial skills, he or she can continue to pursue additional ones, further expanding leadership and membership effectiveness. Building skills in **five subscale areas** can have a transformative effect, making an individual a multitalented group performer. This will boost self-confidence and a sense of personal effectiveness **in any group setting**.

H. Discuss **the issue of confidentiality** in working with individual materials as part of a team-building enterprise. Individual profiles are the property of the individual respondents. Members have a right to select what information they want to share. In group settings where members choose to share personal information, guidelines for confidentiality need to be established.

Guidelines are necessary for the ethical use of these materials. They create an atmosphere of respect and trust that puts people at ease, enabling them to share information in an honest and open manner. When members can share personal information in a frank, trusting way, it helps to build team cohesion, enabling a team to rise to higher levels of performance, a key goal with this training.

Guidelines to establish: Allow individuals to select the specific information from their profiles that they are comfortable sharing with other members. These decisions need to be respected. It should be noted that such respect can, over time, encourage members to be freer and more open in sharing information. Also, information shared in the group must stay within the group, unless some other agreement is made with the participants' free consent.

2. *Have the team members raise any questions, issues, or points for clarification.* After responding to the issues, announce the next phase of the training will be individual coaching sessions. A schedule of meetings may have been arranged in

advance, or it can be done at this moment. Allow extra time, as needed, when booking the schedule right then.

3. **Proceed with individual coaching sessions with each of the members.** (Time: 90 minutes per person) The content of these sessions will follow the guidelines set forth in Chapter 11: Coaching and Counseling with the KGI® Individual Profile. However, since these sessions take place within the context of a team-building enterprise, a number of additional points are important to consider.

A. As the consultant works with an individual member, it will be worthwhile to explore the member's perspective on the team. How does the individual view the team's current dynamics: its strengths, its weaknesses, and the nature of leadership roles in the group? Also, how does the individual view his or her role in the group?

B. Ask the individual to identify the members of the team that *he or she collaborates with most effectively*, and why. This can be helpful later on when the consultant considers establishing mentoring roles with different participants.

C. Ask the individual to identify which members of the team *he or she has the most difficulty collaborating with*, and why.

› As part of the training, **it is possible for a consultant to work with pairs of individuals in separate sessions** to resolve conflicts and establish better working relationships. With the KGI data, a consultant can assess how different patterns of results may be contributing to the conflict. Example: a certain member might be a "task person," while another might be an "interpersonal person." When different orientations put people at odds with each other, identifying that pattern and then building appropriate subscale skills can help remedy the situation. Therefore, asking members about group-mates with whom they have problems can flush out issues that can later be addressed as part of the training.

D. Based on the KGI graph data and growth statements, set personal goals for the individual to obtain new skills. Utilize the Inter-Subscale Combinations as a part of the analysis.

4. **After the individual coaching sessions are complete, hold a group session with the members and introduce the KGI® Group Profile material.** (Time: 90 minutes)

At the appropriate time prior to this session, the consultant will electronically send a copy of the KGI® Group Profile to each member for review. This is the most efficient way to proceed. However, it is also possible for the consultant to print paper copies and distribute them either beforehand, or during the group session. Since the profile contains a significant amount of information, it is important to remember it will take a while for people to go through it. So, if members have the group profile for a reasonable time before the session, they will be best prepared to participate in the team meeting.

Briefly review the structural components of the group profile, as follows:

› The **Introduction**, which presents the diamond model and spells out the goal of forging a learning team.

› **Communication and Confidentiality.** This segment establishes ethical guidelines for the sharing of personal results as part of a team-building process.

› **Team Results: The Composite Graphs.** The section displays the Group Composite Major Scale Graph and the Group Composite Subscale Graph, with points about how to interpret them so members can assess their collective performance.

› **Action Steps.** This segment outlines the steps for choosing subscale categories to address, finding suggestions to improve the team's interactive processes in the appropriate subscale sections of the report, implementing those strategies, and pursuing an ongoing developmental process that will make the group a high-performing team.

› **The Four Major Scale Sections.** The team receives feedback across the four major domains (Leadership, Negotiation, Task, and Interpersonal). Each section includes a graph that identifies the range of member scores for the major scale and its subscales, a team assessment statement for that area, and suggestions on how to improve group performance in each of the subscale categories.

• **One-Sentence Descriptions of the KGI Major Scales and Their Subscales.** On the last page of the profile are brief descriptors of the scales and subscales, providing an easy reference for the essential ideas in the KGI skill-building system.

5. *Present for team analysis, the Group Composite Subscale Graph.*

This is a **critical phase of the training** in which the team will assess how it operates. The Group Composite Subscale Graph presents indispensable information. It includes all of the subscales and helps to target particular skill areas the team needs to address. The consultant can be selective about what to emphasize from the graph (which will vary from group to group), but should certainly allot significant time for the discussion of this graph. **As will be seen, analysis with this graph is focused, practical, and a powerful mechanism for creating effective team strategies.**

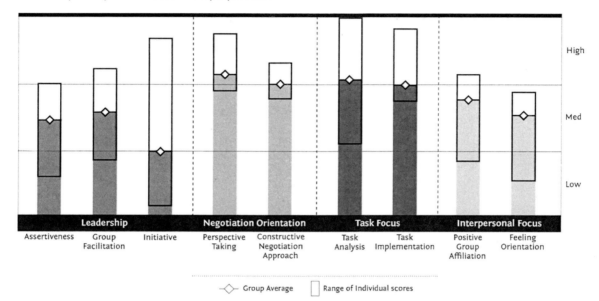

Here are discussion points the consultant can introduce:

• In surveying the sweep of the graph, what insights do the members gain about how they invest their energies across the various domains?

• In the opinion of the members, do the top scores seem like the team's greatest strengths? Do people see these skill areas actively in use when they work on a task?

• Are any of the top subscales being overused to the team's detriment?

• For example, Perspective Taking has the highest result on the above graph. It appears that all of the members participate in this area of activity. But do people get so deferential, always soliciting others' perspectives, that members are reluctant to take an assertive stance and express their own opinions, especially if their ideas are controversial?

Overuse of a skill area can be as much of a problem as underuse. The team will want to examine this issue and see if it wants to use certain skills more selectively.

• How does the team evaluate the lowest scorers in the graph? Do they seem accurate as areas of low performance? Which domains, in the team's opinion, need the most attention? Why?

• Draw on the Inter-Subscale Combinations (ISC) to assess the graph. What combinations of different subscales would it be beneficial to address?

The ISC groupings, with relevant questions for the team to discuss, are:

1. **Assertiveness** with **Perspective Taking**. How is the team balancing the management of speaking and listening in its discussions? What might be adjusted?

2. **Group Facilitation** with **Task Focus** and **Interpersonal Focus Subscales**. How is the team managing the pivotal task and interpersonal operations? How can the members better attend to these areas to orchestrate smoother execution of projects?

3. **Initiative** with **Negotiation Orientation, Task Focus,** and **Interpersonal Focus Subscales**. Where do people have substantial skills in these domains? How might members share leadership roles, based on their strong skill sets, to make the team more productive?

4. **Constructive Negotiation Approach** with **Positive Group Affiliation**. How does the team balance its energy investment in these sectors? Since they are related, how might the team adjust its actions to maximize this connection? The interplay of these two subscales helps to create synergy on the team, leading to exceptional performance.

5. **Task Analysis** with **Task Implementation**. Which item has a higher score? Does the team lean too much in one direction? How can members strike a better balance between these two task operations?

6. **Positive Group Affiliation** with **Feeling Orientation**. Is the group neglecting either one, or both? How can the group build greater team spirit and manage feeling issues more competently?

Example: Based on the graph, if the team struck a better balance between Assertiveness and Perspective Taking, it could generate a more effective interactive process during a discussion. Members can consciously work to elevate Assertiveness and bring it more in line with Perspective Taking, thereby enhancing the quality of the team dialogue.

The Group Composite Subscale Graph also enables the team to determine the exact pattern of performance for a subscale by examining the range of member scores in the rectangular box on the specific column. If there is a wide distribution of scores, then some members have stronger skills while others are less developed. People with stronger skills can become leaders in helping the group refine its efforts in that domain. They can also offer mentoring tips to groupmates who are trying to build skills in that area. If it's a narrow

cluster of scores, particularly in a Medium or Low section of the graph, the team as a whole might benefit from some form of group training to acquire new skills. (See Chapter 15 for further details on the analysis of the range of member scores.)

▸ Following this phase of the conversation, facilitate a discussion about the particular subscales to address for skill building. Which **two or three subscales** does the team wish to start with to improve its performance?

6. *Based on the subscales the team selects, the members should examine the particular suggestions for those subscales in the body of the report.*

A. Since each subscale section offers a menu of 5 to 8 suggestions about how to refine interactions in that area, the team can choose the suggestions it would like to adopt.

B. As new strategies are selected, the consultant can help the group assess how these strategies might be tailored to best suit its needs.

Example: With Positive Group Affiliation, there may be a recommendation to conduct rapport-building activities with the team. How could these be organized in a way that would be most convenient? A team might devote the first ten minutes of a meeting to a short, rapport-building activity, such as sharing positive news items with each other. Or the team could hold an informal, after-work event where people can mingle and get to know each other in a relaxed setting.

C. Important: as the team identifies new procedures to employ, *be sure to set up clear, measurable goals for its actions*, so the team can determine its success in implementing the new tactics.

Example: The team needs to spend more time with Task Analysis to develop better project strategies.

Based on the time frame of meetings, decide on a specific amount of time that would seem reasonable for the discussion, and have a member keep time. Don't let the team quit too early. Also, make sure that people share all perspectives that would be worth considering. Make sure everyone speaks and raises points. These would become benchmarks for evaluating how well the strategy was executed.

7. *Assist the group in identifying opportunities for shared leadership, more effective delegation of responsibilities, and mentoring relationships.* As a group analyzes the various KGI data and comes up with strategies for improving performance, a consultant should be alert to ways that members can share leadership responsibilities and delegate work assignments more effectively, based on people's skill sets. This is where people can share information from their personal KGI profiles to create a more powerful plan.

One of the assessment's strengths is the way that it supports this form of analysis. Members can share information about their personal skill sets and take on duties related to their most significant talents. They can also organize mentoring relationships, in which a person with a high score guides less developed colleagues in the application of certain techniques.

For example:

- A person with a high score in Perspective Taking can lead the team in asking more probe questions, so members get a clearer picture of everyone's interests and concerns.

- A member with a high score in Task Analysis can aid the group in evaluating tasks from multiple angles, in order to thoroughly examine the problems, opportunities, resources, and possible solutions.

- An individual with a high score in Positive Group Affiliation could take the lead in conducting some focused rapport-building conversation to enhance team cohesion.

- Members with fewer skills in these areas, but who are interested in acquiring them, can, at first, observe how capable members lead these activities. The leader can also provide pointers about the use of specific tactics. Over time, the developing members can assist in these actions in order to acquire more competence with the skills. Eventually, they can take a lead role, building mastery with the new techniques.

8. *Support the team in implementing its strategies.* As the team makes adjustments in conducting its meetings, the consultant can, at the team's discretion, serve as a process observer. The consultant can assess the group's interactive dynamics, offering practical insights about the team's manner of operating. From this vantage point, the consultant can help the team fine-tune its KGI strategies.

Under any scenario, the consultant should schedule a follow-up meeting (or meetings) to help the group assess the implementation of its new strategies. The consultant should organize group reflection on what went well, what unexpected issues emerged, and what adjustments would produce further improvement. **The team can also identify additional group processes that it wishes to address, moving down its list of priorities.** As described above, the group will identify subscale domains to target and select process suggestions to implement.

The consultant always wants to assist the team in strengthening its capacity to self-reflect, so, in the future, members can analyze their practice in a systematic way, identifying adjustments that will increase their effectiveness. Over time, the team will become acclimated to this process and become a self-directed learning team.

The consultant can also conduct follow-up individual sessions with the members to promote further refinement of their skills. **A second session with each individual to perfect the practice is highly recommended.** They will also identify additional skills to perform.

As noted earlier, it is possible for **the consultant to work with pairs of people** who are experiencing conflict or other difficulties in order to remedy these situations. The consultant can draw on information in the KGI materials to assist in these interventions.

Example: Significantly different scores for a particular domain, such as Constructive Negotiation Approach, can be a source of conflict because people approach the issues from different perspectives. Also, when two or more people are weak in a certain area, it can be a struggle to establish quality collaboration. The KGI materials provide insights about how to approach such issues.

This chapter establishes a basic procedure for team building. The method addresses individual and team needs, initiating a growth process that will benefit all members. Since the training focuses on central operations in group life, members always feel they are striving towards meaningful goals in a manner that is clear, practical, and empowering.

Integral to the team-building process is the interpretation of the Group Composite Subscale Graph. This graph plays a decisive role in the formulation of a team improvement strategy. In the next chapter, there are additional points about how to interpret this graph, including ways to orchestrate a deeper analysis using the Inter-Subscale Combinations framework. ✄

CHAPTER 15

Interpreting the Group Composite Subscale Graph

With team building, like individual coaching, the centerpiece of the enterprise is the composite subscale graph, which permits an analysis of the team's levels of engagement with various subscales and a consideration of strategies to balance the pattern of performance. In this evaluation, a consultant and team can employ the Inter-Subscale Combinations (ISC) system. The ISC elements distinguish important relationships among the subscales, injecting an innovative approach for harmonizing the team's efforts.

In the previous chapter, reference was made to the ISC design for interpreting the Group Composite Subscale Graph during a consultation, presenting initial points for the application of this framework. Now it is necessary to introduce a more complete explanation of the method, so the richness of the application can be seen. In addition, further explanation is provided about how to interpret the range of member scores displayed in the rectangular box on each column, details that also influence how a group should proceed. As a consultant learns how to weave these ideas into a group analysis, the process will yield powerful strategies for team development.

Assertiveness with Perspective Taking
How do team results fall in these skill areas, targeting the vital speaking and listening functions? Is there a reasonable balance, at a solid level of performance (scores in the high-Medium to low-High sections of the graph)? Is there broad

participation among the members? The answers to these questions influence how to advise a group. If Assertiveness is too high, members may turn aggressive, fighting for air time. It becomes hard to have a calm, thoughtful discussion. The group may wish to set guidelines to harness this energy, perhaps establishing a time limit for how long someone may hold the floor, or by designing a rotation that gives all members a chance to speak. *The group should guarantee that quieter members get their voices heard in every meeting.* This is essential for establishing an authentic group dialogue.

If there is too little Assertiveness, KGI data can embolden people to sit up and express themselves, participating in a more active way. In this case, members should not only speak up themselves but also encourage others to do so. Providing mutual encouragement will aid the cause.

With regard to Perspective Taking, the group

should ensure that enough questions are asked so that members have a clear understanding about everyone's interests and concerns. A useful principle to adopt is that people need to know more. By asking additional questions, members gain a deeper understanding of their teammates' perspectives. This is particularly useful for problem-solving with the task. The group wants to make sure that all relevant data are on the table, that no information is held back, so the best decisions can be made.

In evaluating the Assertiveness and Perspective Taking scores, the consultant wants to help the group establish a more comprehensive dialogue among members. Everyone needs to be included and have adequate time to share ideas. This is necessary for creating a real sense of inclusion on the team, which, in turn, helps to stimulate synergy.

Group Facilitation with Task Focus and Interpersonal Focus

How does the team fare in balancing the task and interpersonal concerns? The leadership function of Group Facilitation is central to this enterprise. A capable leader wants to pay attention to both areas and maintain a stable connection. As noted previously, there is a rhythm in the group as attention moves back and forth between task and interpersonal issues. Both elements need to receive adequate attention if the team is going to perform at its best.

The group can consider how it might share leadership in managing this dynamic. Based on various members' strengths with the task and interpersonal subscales, how can different people, at different times, share their expertise and help facilitate? This will keep more people engaged in the process and can strengthen overall team performance. And how might the expert players mentor others about the nuances of facilitation techniques, so the group, as a whole, becomes more competent in this leadership function?

Initiative with Negotiation Orientation, Task Focus, and Interpersonal Focus

How can the team support members in taking relevant leadership initiatives? Where do members have specific skills that would benefit the team? How can they take more leadership for appropriate projects? The team can analyze its assets and set up a smart plan for delegating responsibilities. For individuals who don't yet have established skills but want to learn, the team can designate shared-leadership opportunities, wherein a novice plays a smaller role at first while partnering with a more experienced teammate. Over time, the novice can assume more responsibilities and, by acquiring additional skills, eventually take on a solo leadership role with a selected project. Again, mentors will provide pointers about techniques that will accelerate skill acquisition. A team that becomes conscious of developing its leadership potential in these ways will, over time, rise to new heights.

Constructive Negotiation Approach with Positive Group Affiliation

Where does the team stand with respect to the complementary activities that ignite group synergy? Is the team strong in one area but not in the other? How can it pay better attention to both? An active pursuit of win-win agreements raises group morale. A spirited effort to build social rapport inclines people to seek win-win accords. How can the team address these issues with this relationship in mind, in order to vault to a superior level of performance? As a team blends its efforts in these domains, it can unleash an intense energy for the task enterprise.

Task Analysis with Task Implementation

What are team results in the twin aspects of task performance? Does the team lean toward over-analysis with its planning, or toward under-analysis? With implementation, is it too quick to implement a plan, or, perhaps, too slow? For any project, thought without action leads to paralysis. Action without thought can lead to calamity. Where does the team fall in this regard? What would be the right balance for optimal production? Which players have the requisite skills to guide the team toward task efficiency and quality outcomes? The team can have the most proficient players in analysis and implementation share leadership responsibilities to engineer high-caliber task execution.

Positive Group Affiliation with Feeling Orientation

How attuned is the team to its social and emotional issues? Is there a positive rapport among members, sparking a team spirit? How can that spirit be built up or refined? Does the team pay attention to feeling issues in the here and now? Do members respond to these concerns in constructive ways? The timely management of feelings certainly impacts team morale. Who will provide leadership in the social and emotional areas? As a team makes emotional issues more discussable, it creates a healthier environment. As team spirit rises, team productivity will also rise. This is an important relationship to pay attention to, one that can be worth its weight in gold.

Through a thoughtful examination of the Inter-Subscale Combinations, a group can perform a systematic analysis of its operations, finding ways to balance performance and spur productivity. It can create a customized plan to meet its precise needs.

Assessing the Range of Member Scores

When evaluating the Group Composite Subscale Graph, examine each column and determine the range of member scores in the black rectangular box. The box identifies the levels of member involvement in that domain, running anywhere from high to low. The distribution of scores will affect the strategies for skill building. With regard to the arrangement of scores, the following points are valuable to consider with a team.

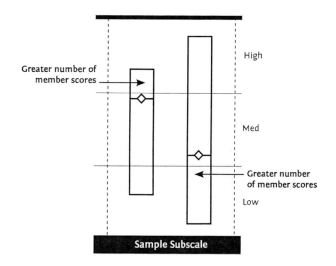

Sample Subscale

A Wide Range of Member Scores

With a wide distribution of scores, *the rectangular box runs through all three sections of the graph, from high to low.* In this scenario, there is a tendency for the high-scoring members to dominate and for others, particularly those with the lowest scores, to passively tag along. Members with high scores may feel they are exerting appropriate leadership, but it is necessary, over time, to get the other people more involved. The group should consider adjustments that will bring all members into action. For example, a team can invite a quieter member with a solid Task Analysis score to share ideas when the group is drafting a plan for a project. As the person becomes more

comfortable participating in the discussion, it would be possible to have the individual co-lead such a conversation in the future. Another option is to have higher-performing members share tips and mentor the lower-performing teammates. At the minimum, it would be necessary to include all members in the discussion and to create an atmosphere of mutual support.

When a wide range exists, it is important to notice how the members' scores cluster above and below the diamond line (which identifies the group average). *The smaller area above or below the line indicates the greater number of member scores.* The proportion of strong or solid players compared to more challenged players in a particular skill area influences the strategy. If just a couple of people fall into the lower zone, it would be easier to provide personal support for their development, such as mentoring or coaching, than if there are many. If there are many in the lower area, perhaps some type of focused training intervention related to KGI suggestions would be appropriate. This way, all of the challenged members can gain skills at once. The consultant and the team should consider what would be the best options, given the proportion of people who require skills.

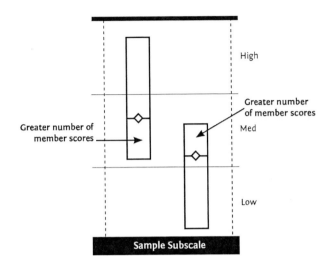

Sample Subscale

Moderate Range of Scores

With this configuration of scores, *the rectangular box stretches between two sections of the graph*: High-Medium or Medium-Low. In this case, the member scores fall closer together, compared to the more radical split occurring in the wide range. For High-Medium, the team lands in a positive area, well-positioned to elevate its performance. All members possess some skills, and it is easier to assist the lower-scoring members in raising their performance. There is valuable expertise with high-scoring members who can lead the way, modeling effective behaviors, sharing thoughts about correct techniques, and providing general guidance as the team executes subscale suggestions.

For Medium-Low, the situation is more challenging. In this instance everyone has a distance to go for the team to achieve a strong performance. Again, some type of focused training intervention with KGI suggestions would be appropriate, so that all members can gain skills at once. This would elevate performance in an efficient way.

It's also helpful to examine where most of the scores cluster, above or below the diamond line. Is the group leaning up, or is it leaning down? How the box is configured can affect the team's tactics. If the cluster is dense at the bottom of the rectangle, more people lack skills. Some kind of group training may be the answer. But if it is dense towards the top, more members possess solid skills, creating leadership opportunities for them to guide the group in skill development. The team can be innovative in its approach.

For example, an ambitious member could research a special topic related to that skill area and deliver a presentation to the group, injecting some extra ideas on how to improve performance. Similarly, several members could cooperate in a broader research investigation, and then share their findings to promote team learning. Certainly, the suggestions in a subscale section will offer worthwhile options to pursue, furnishing direction for the group. But these other tactics can engage members in active problem-solving that further strengthens the group's identity as a learning team.

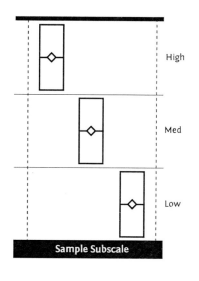

High

Med

Low

Sample Subscale

Narrow Range of Scores

With a narrow cluster of scores, *the rectangular box resides in one section of the graph,* meaning that all of the members perform in a similar fashion. When the box is in the High section of the graph, the team as a whole possesses significant skills in this category. Usually the team is very effective operating in this domain, but it may also produce a blind spot. When everyone is really engaged in a certain skill area, it can cause group think. For example, with Feeling Orientation, everyone enjoys discussing emotional issues related to the group's life. But this can go on and on, with the group losing sight of task concerns. Because everyone engages in the process, no one wants to mention that the group is failing to take task action. Or if someone does suggest less talk and more action, the group may still be slow to conclude the analysis, wasting more time. When everyone thinks the same way, it's harder to redirect the current of energy.

This phenomenon is important to notice, evaluate, and correct. The group needs to design a structure that keeps it from going overboard. With regard to the above example, a team can set a time limit for the conversation, or it can designate a certain member with the authority to hit the brakes when the conversation runs on too long. The goal is to keep a strength area from turning into a liability from blind overuse.

A tight cluster occurring in the Medium or Low sections of the graph can indicate a collective need for skill building. It would be appropriate to arrange a training session. For example, if the subscale of Perspective Taking is low, a brief session on listening skills and the use of probe questions may well do the trick, enriching the quality of discussion and enabling the team to better negotiate win-win agreements.

Also, as mentioned for the moderate range, members can take actions to research topics for a particular skill domain and share the information to expand the team's knowledge base.

As can be seen, by paying attention to the distribution of member scores, a consultant can employ discrete strategies to help raise performance. Since every group is unique, this method helps to address that specialness and find the right tactics for the particular team.

Significantly, when a group implements this team-building approach, a very substantial transformation can take place, reshaping its style of operating. In the next chapter, this transformation will be examined, along with an illustrative case study. ✕

CHAPTER 16

A Process of Team Development with a Case Study

Just as an individual may experience a compelling social transformation through the Klein Group Instrument coaching process, a group can also have a significant transformation through the KGI team-building procedure, one that alters its method of operating in decisive ways. The KGI process can broaden a group's thinking, enliven its social atmosphere, and incite spirited collaboration. It can fashion a situation where people learn from and with each other, establishing a growth mindset that over time enables a team to become a much more cohesive, vigorous force.

Specifically, the KGI method spurs transformation in these ways:

1. Introduces a Sound Structure for Analysis

The method initiates a logical, systematic evaluation of team performance, setting the stage for thoughtful adjustments along the major domains of group life: leadership, negotiation, task, and interpersonal. Every team is like an individual, having its own unique personality, with certain strengths and certain deficiencies. Members can decide how to employ their strengths more intelligently, while being aware of, and working to improve, softer areas. Colorized graphs facilitate this analysis, providing convenient materials for evaluating strengths, shortfalls, and the range of member skills. Since the KGI model zeroes in on the primary skills in group life, members focus on essential issues that will enhance performance.

2. Strengthens Communication

By presenting objective, anonymous feedback, the KGI® Group Profile makes it easier for team members to communicate. Because personal scores are not identified, people can feel free to more openly address issues. As levels of trust and comfort increase on a team, members may choose to share some or all of their individual results. But the starting point is a respect for confidentiality, so that members can address team data with openness and candor. In this process, they also develop a common language to share ideas and build new strategies. As they learn the KGI system, they talk more directly about core topics of group functioning; the terminology creates a shorthand to get to the point when analyzing team operations.

3. Promotes Shared Leadership

As team members analyze their data, making decisions about how to improve, there is an opportunity to expand shared leadership. People become more conscious of their skill sets and how their particular skills fit into the team configuration. As a result, they can pinpoint ways to contribute more to the team effort. Members acquire a deeper appreciation for each other's skills and how to blend them to make the best use of each person's talents. Part of the program can involve designating more skillful members to mentor the less skillful, which is also a leadership function. A team that assigns leadership responsibilities more broadly and nurtures the development of these skills in all members is more likely to ascend the ladder to terrific team performance.

4. Creates a Learning Team

As KGI materials promote logical analysis, open communication, and the creation of shared leadership opportunities, they enable a group to form an active learning team. With a clearer grasp of team operations and a better understanding of their own roles, members can discuss strategies for enhancing team performance. This includes the personal acquisition of new skills, along with the refinement of the team's interactive processes. Members will learn to reflect together on personal and collective issues and to collaborate in a concerted effort for improvement, opening up a dialogue that aids everyone in making smarter assessments about group life and more precise adjustments that lead to greater personal and team success. The ongoing dialogue creates a positive interdependence among members that lifts team morale and sparks synergy. The team that learns together is the one most able to vault to an exceptional level of performance.

Team-Building Case Study

This case chronicles how the KGI model was applied in a business setting, showing how the method stimulates communication, inspires healthy collaboration, and triggers sturdy performance. It also reveals how a group of talented people can fall into a dysfunctional rut, spinning their wheels, unable to pull out of the ditch. After exposure to the model, the group gained a deeper appreciation of its situation, got reoriented, and steered itself back onto a productive track. With the KGI materials, any team can discover a way to get on a better course; for a floundering team, the approach is especially rewarding.

A partner in a large insurance company contacted a consultant regarding a troubled team within his division. When the two met, the partner described the details of the situation. As it turned out, the team had been in turmoil for years. Members had never connected, didn't communicate well, and the group rattled along at a mediocre level of performance. For a long time, people in the organization thought the team would "eventually get its act together," since it was comprised of capable junior and senior executives who formed the eight-member unit. But that never happened and, adding to the predicament, the group occupied an increasingly significant place in company affairs. So a decision was made to conduct an intervention to put the impaired team on a better path. The consultant suggested that the Klein Group Instrument assessment would be an excellent tool in this context. When he provided an overview of the design, the partner agreed to employ it.

The consultant arranged for a group administration of the instrument so the individual scores would be combined for a team report. After the participants completed the assessment, he conducted the initial meeting in which he familiarized the group with the KGI information and outlined the steps in the program—first, individual coaching sessions to set personal agendas for skill building, then a group session to improve the interactive processes of the team. In four weeks there would be follow-up sessions to evaluate progress. He stated that the goal was to make the group a learning team, a circle in which every member would gain new skills while the team as a whole would upgrade its practices. In this approach members would contribute ideas to strengthen each individual, as well as the team itself.

As the consultant met with each executive, they reviewed personal scores and fixed priorities for skill building. Critically, the consultant interviewed the person about his or her perspective on what had transpired with the team. This prompted a litany of complaints. Some senior executives thought that junior members were dependent individuals who needed a lot of guidance, who didn't take initiative, and who let little issues become major obstacles to the work. Some junior members thought the senior people were aloof, authoritarian, and in certain cases, personally biased against others on the team.

What the consultant noticed was a rash of negative projections, people interpreting others' behaviors in hostile ways, which, in turn, inhibited communication. The members had come to believe that it was "a waste of time" to raise issues in the group, foreseeing the "usual" lack of constructive response. The more these assumptions undercut communication, the more dysfunctional the team became. Collecting everyone's opinions on the matter, the consultant felt prepared for the full-group session. The Group Composite Subscale Graph, he believed, would open up the conversation about a number of relevant topics, a pivotal step for moving the team in a better direction.

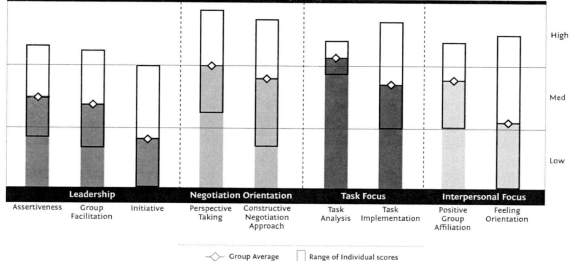

With the participants assembled in the conference room, the consultant flashed the image of the team's graph up on a screen. To start, he noted that the group's top three scores were Task Analysis, Perspective Taking, and Constructive Negotiation Approach. Wishing to establish a positive tone, he pointed out that these results were excellent assets for the job at hand. Task Analysis would be instrumental for diagnosing issues and for designing new strategies. Perspective Taking would be essential for grasping each other's interests and concerns. And Constructive Negotiation Approach would be influential for constructing win-win agreements that could bring the team together. In short, the team had considerable resources at its disposal. When the consultant glanced around the table, it appeared that people appreciated this affirmation.

He then led a discussion about the lowest scores. At the bottom stood Initiative, followed by Feeling Orientation, Group Facilitation, and Assertiveness.

"Do you agree with these results?" the consultant asked. "Do they seem accurate?"

Members stared at the screen. A number nodded their heads in agreement and no one objected.

"Well," the consultant continued, "a good question would be: why is the Initiative score so low?"

There was a chilly silence.

Finally, one of the junior executives spoke up. "For some time, I have felt that if I took initiative and went out on a limb, if that limb broke and I crashed to the ground, there was nobody there to offer me a hand, nobody there to pick me up. So why risk it?"

After a pause, one senior member replied, "I didn't know you felt that way. I would be there to offer a hand."

The two members locked eyes.

Another junior colleague spoke up: "On one project, I sent two emails, left a phone message, and never heard anything back. I thought: this is no big priority and just dropped it."

There was no answer to that comment.

"Silence is always the enemy of teamwork," interjected the consultant. "Let's look more closely at the graph to see how we might address some of these issues."

Pointing to the Assertiveness and Perspective Taking columns, the consultant stated that it would be beneficial to strike a better balance between these two. While there were substantial skills with Perspective Taking, the group needed to hear more voices with Assertiveness, to make sure that everyone was in the mix. They needed to balance speaking and listening. The group examined the suggestions in the Assertiveness section of the group profile. They targeted a point that made sense: encourage quieter members to share their ideas, which should be valued and discussed respectfully. This would be a step in the right direction.

Focusing on the low Initiative score, the consultant asked where people with high personal scores in Negotiation Orientation, Task Focus, or Interpersonal Focus might step up to help lead the team? Several people mentioned places where they could possibly take action, particularly with Constructive Negotiation Approach and Task Implementation. The consultant reminded the participants that, with their personal goals to guide them, there would be opportunities for everyone to take on some new leadership roles as the work evolved. But it was imperative that people rise up and get engaged. They should look for situations where members were excited about some aspect of a project and give them opportunities to lead in those contexts. Finding places where they could share leadership roles would also be a smart strategy, infusing extra energy into the team.

Returning to the graph, he directed attention to the Feeling Orientation subscale, where, according to the rectangular box, over half the scores fell in the low area of activity. The consultant mentioned that a real concern for the team was that people weren't in touch with how others were reacting to different issues. Feeling Orientation could address that by helping them respond to the emotional currents in the group. He stated that the participants should flip to that section of the profile to study suggestions about what measures the team might adopt. After some deliberation,

they chose the following:

- Support one another in expressing feelings in honest, thoughtful ways. Encourage anyone who is feeling frustrated or confused to speak up.
- Promote the expression of positive emotions, such as may follow a success for the team or an individual. This can be a starting point to help create a positive climate for expressing all feelings.

Finally, the consultant targeted the Group Facilitation score. What could the team do to get better traction here? After investigating the suggestions for that subscale, the group selected:

- Share previous learning experiences in which constructive feedback helped members improve their skills. Create a climate for constructive feedback.

All of the members agreed they would make the effort to implement these new processes with the team. For some, the goals coincided with personal goals they had set from their KGI® Individual Profiles.

At the conclusion, the consultant stated that he looked forward to returning in four weeks to see what progress had been made. In the interim, people could send him an email if there were any concerns or issues.

The next weeks passed quietly, without an email exchange. Then the consultant received a note from the partner, as the four-week date approached. The partner mentioned that constructive things had happened as a result of the initial round of training. When the consultant returned, the partner brought him into his office.

"I'm so pleased," said the partner, smiling, "we've observed more initiative, more effort from this team in recent weeks than we've seen in years—believe me! The team's become much more focused, and people are working together more collaboratively. Everyone in the top executive group is excited about this turn around."

"Excellent," replied the consultant. "We knew there was talent on the team. But they needed to communicate better and support each other."

"They have been, and it's really ramped up their productivity. When I've talked to different members, they seem more relaxed and more comfortable with each other."

"That's great. We'll try to expand on that in the next round."

In this phase, the full-group event came first. The consultant asked members to comment on their experiences during the recent interval and about how they were progressing toward their goals.

A number of people stated that after the last session, members became, in general, more candid in their conversations and listened to each other with greater attention. They also sought to support each other more by including everyone in the discussions. A number of times, they shared updates about their personal skill-building efforts, and people offered helpful feedback to one another. When various members achieved certain successes, other teammates praised them. All of this brought fresh energy to the team. They felt more like a team, not just a collection of individuals, as a spirit of mutual respect and mutual concern began to emerge.

The consultant replied that by making these adjustments, the team had altered the atmosphere, unleashing new energy. He congratulated them on their progress. He suggested that they look at information in the Constructive Negotiation Orientation and Positive Group Affiliation subsections, to see how they might build further on this headway. He stated that these two subscales highlight factors that produce synergy on a team, propelling it towards highest performance. They proceeded to examine those sections of the group profile.

After some evaluation, they focused on the following suggestions:

For Constructive Negotiation Orientation, they liked the proposal to rotate the facilitator's role for various discussions, so different members could assume positions of leadership. This could aid the group in scrutinizing issues from multiple angles in the pursuit of common ground. It would also help in the quest to expand everyone's leadership skills.

For Positive Group Affiliation, they selected:

‣ Invite members to reflect on the best ways to fit their different talents together when they work on a project.

The team did some brainstorming, right then and there, about how they might operationalize this goal in an upcoming project, and how they could configure assignments in the most fruitful way.

The consultant pointed out that the application of this new strategy could also be integrated into an effort to improve Task Implementation. As they defined ways to put their talents together in a more dynamic manner, they could monitor how the strategies worked out during actual execution. As the task moved along, they could provide each other with feedback so people could further refine their actions, enabling the team as a whole to perfect its task performance. This would foster stronger outcomes.

The members liked the way these various subscales strategies could be woven together to maximize the benefits.

The consultant announced that after he conducted the next round of one-on-one sessions, assisting members in identifying additional skills for personal development, they would have more ideas they could blend into this analysis. They would gain other insights about how to merge their skills in innovative ways, creating a more flexible, integrated team effort. This would be another step in making the group a thriving learning team.

When the consultant conferred personally with the participants, they expressed appreciation for the new climate on the team. They felt stimulated by the sharing of ideas and the element of mutual support. Some members wished they'd progressed further with their own skill development, and the consultant helped them to modify their strategies to realize these ambitions. The consultant mentioned that as the team embraced their shared learning, the situation would be ripe for everyone's next phase of skill building. People could do more to help each other hone their skill acquisition. With every member, the consultant identified additional skills to practice.

A month later, at the concluding session, it became evident the team had really advanced to a new level. People readily exchanged ideas, responded flexibly to each other, and reveled in the team's high productivity. The members had made significant progress in learning how to integrate their talents in rewarding ways. A real pride in the team had surfaced. On the individual level, members felt satisfied with their personal progress, everyone having acquired some new skills. The consultant mentioned that through this enterprise, they now understood a critical method for nurturing personal development in the future. Every member could select additional skills to practice, reflect on the applications, and make appropriate refinements. With commitment to the practice, they could become really polished players. The team, in turn, could continue to refine its methods and rise to even greater heights.

Among the happiest of all was the partner who initiated the intervention. In a show of thanks, he contacted the company's national headquarters, speaking to the Vice President of Human Resources. He offered a glowing testimonial to the effectiveness of the consultant and the KGI method and created a bridge for the consultant to expand his work with the company on a national level.

This story reveals the type of positive environment the KGI method generates, a lively forum for ideas that guide individual skill expansion and the enhancement of group processes. The method channels people's energies in productive directions, transforming a sputtering collection of individuals into a real team.

The next chapter introduces a series of Group Composite Subscale Graphs, with the interpretive points, so consultants, trainers, and teachers can gain a deeper appreciation for the method and bring its power to their professional practices. ✄

CHAPTER 17

Group Composite Subscale Graphs with Talking Points

To assist professionals with the team-building application of the KGI system, this chapter presents fourteen group subscale graphs along with interpretive points that will be a resource for training events. They exhibit ways to evaluate different patterns of scores and how to guide teams in suitable directions. Like the earlier individual graph examples, the group graphs establish reference points for actual consulting situations. When results from a current team correspond to one or more of the case examples, a professional can

draw on these ideas in a team analysis, grounding a consultant's interpretation and accelerating mastery of the method.

Similar to the individual graph examples, the group graphs include interpretations with the Inter-Subscale Combinations framework. There is also analysis, as appropriate, of the range of member scores displayed in the rectangular boxes on graph columns. For the first of the fourteen graphs, there are references to Suggestions to Improve Your Team's Performance found in the subscale sections of that specific group profile. With the KGI method, the intent is to distinguish which subscale domains need to be addressed,

and then evaluate the suggestions in those areas to determine practical strategies. The first graph makes this connection explicit. The other thirteen examples simply provide the basic interpretive points for an analysis.

As professionals read through these examples, they will acquire a feel for the process of deciphering the graphs. With practice, they will become proficient with the method and be able to introduce innovative strategies that will propel their client teams to impressive levels of performance.

continued on next page ›

Team One

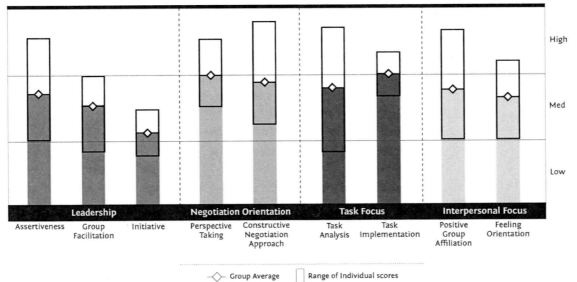

High
Med
Low

| Leadership | | | Negotiation Orientation | | Task Focus | | Interpersonal Focus | |
| Assertiveness | Group Facilitation | Initiative | Perspective Taking | Constructive Negotiation Approach | Task Analysis | Task Implementation | Positive Group Affiliation | Feeling Orientation |

◇— Group Average   ▢ Range of Individual scores

1. Initiative:

> The team should investigate opportunities for various members to take on leadership roles. Members should pursue opportunities according to their interests and strongest skill sets. Given the range of member scores, everyone should become more involved in this activity.

Suggestions to Improve Team Performance from Initiative subsection:

A. Members who are not accustomed to initiating ideas or tasks should try to be proactive and not wait to be asked. When members think of something, they should verbalize it, even an unformed idea. The comment may trigger a contribution from another team member and move the process forward.

B. The team should rotate the role of group leader to help members practice Initiative skills, as well as to foster variety.

2. Task Analysis with Task Implementation:

> With a tight, high cluster of scores in Task Implementation, the team may be in a rush to complete tasks without fully thinking through its strategies. The team can have blinders on, pushing work forward while quality declines along the way. More thoughtful Task Analysis could produce better outcomes. Members with the highet scores in

this domain can be role models for analyzing tasks and constructing quality strategies.

Suggestions to Improve Your Team's Performance from Task Analysis subsection:

A. Invite members to collaborate in a thorough analysis of the task, including different perspectives on both the big picture *and* the details. Assign a facilitator to insure opportunities for quiet members to share their thoughts.

B. Work on the problem, or analyze the task, by first identifying the facts in the case. Then generate solutions and evaluate (both logically and in human terms) these ideas. Seek plans that everyone can live with.

Suggestion to Improve Your Team's Performance from Task Implementation subsection:

Conduct an in-depth analysis of both the processes used by the team to accomplish its tasks, and the performance indicators you use to measure success. Suggest and discuss more efficient processes and more powerful measures. Look for measures that will tell the team precisely how well it is doing a particular job.

3. Perspective Taking and Feeling Orientation:

▸ Use the team's overall strength with Perspective Taking to increase awareness of feeling currents. Seek to channel member enthusiasms into work assignments.

Suggestions to Improve Team Performance from Perspective Taking subsection:

A. Group members can ask about the critical factors and the history that have led teammates to their views.

B. Team members can seek to get to know one another better. This can be done during meetings, as time permits, or during time set aside for social interaction. Members can explore each other's concerns, interests, and priorities.

Suggestions to Improve Your Team's Performance from Feeling Orientation subsection:

When emotions are not being expressed, consider an anonymous poll of each group member's emotional reactions to different proposals/issues. The team can have a discussion about the collective results.

4. Assertiveness:

▸ Members with high scores should invite quieter members to participate, so everyone is included in the discussion.

Suggestions to Improve Your Team's Performance from Assertiveness subsection:-

A. Assertive team members should not rush to fill every silence. Pausing for ten seconds to allow time for others to weigh in and then letting them finish without interruption is a useful strategy to practice.

B. Quieter members should be encouraged to contribute ideas and opinions, which should be valued and discussed respectfully. According to different members' areas of expertise, invite them to share comments on that aspect of the work.

5. Positive Group Affiliation:

▸ Members with high scores can facilitate short, team-building sessions, creating opportunities for members to get to know each other and increase team cohesiveness.

Suggestions to Improve Your Team's Performance from Positive Group Affiliation subsection:

A. Invite team members to reflect on the best ways to fit their different talents together when they work on a project.

B. Encourage team members to get to know one another on a personal basis. This can be done as a group exercise or by pairing less-acquainted members to interview one another. Seek to learn the following:

▸ Conditions under which each member does his or her best work.

▸ Work history, with past successes and career high points.

▸ Goals, hobbies, interests, or how a person likes to spend leisure time.

Team Two

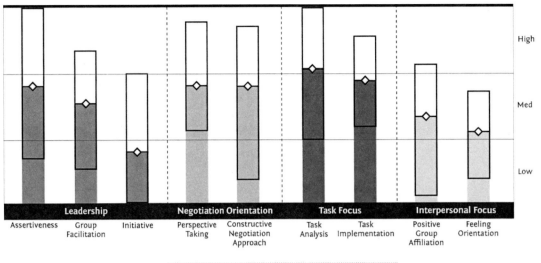

- Group Average   □ Range of Individual scores

1. Assertiveness:

‣ Some members may be taking up considerable air time in discussions, while others are not participating at all. For best outcomes, the team needs to create a better balance, with all members speaking up at appropriate times.

‣ The most assertive team members should monitor their behavior and try to balance talking and listening time.

‣ Make sure that all voices are heard before the group makes a significant decision.

2. Perspective Taking and Task Analysis:

‣ Most members fall in the middle range of Perspective Taking. The team should strive to have more members share their views. This would be particularly helpful in the Task Analysis area, where some members may contribute many ideas while others share few or none.

‣ By having everyone participate in Task Analysis, the group can increase its ability to design thoughtful plans. Members should ask more questions of one another, and then play off one another's ideas to increase creativity and better refine their strategies.

3. Constructive Negotiation Approach:

‣ The group has a wide diversity of scores for this subscale. The group would do well to strengthen the win-win focus of the team, which can increase member motivation and improve team cohesiveness.

‣ The group has solid skills with Perspective Taking. Using information gained from this activity, the team should make a more conscious effort to find the middle ground in decision-making, devising solutions that benefit all members.

‣ All members should seek ways to modify their positions to support the pursuit of win-win accords.

4. Positive Group Affiliation:

‣ The group has very diverse scores for this subscale. Promoting team spirit could increase group unity and could help create a win-win atmosphere for group negotiations. It could also assist the team in delegating responsibilities more precisely, based on members' talents and interests.

‣ Ask those who are less involved: What does the team need to do differently to help you feel more comfortable?

5. Initiative:

‣ Many team members may be sitting back, allowing one or two people to assume all of the leadership roles. To utilize the team's talents more fully, all of the members need to step up at appropriate times to take on meaningful leadership positions.

‣ Investigate members' interests. Identify the tasks that excite people and then create opportunities so they channel that energy into leadership responsibilities.

Team Three

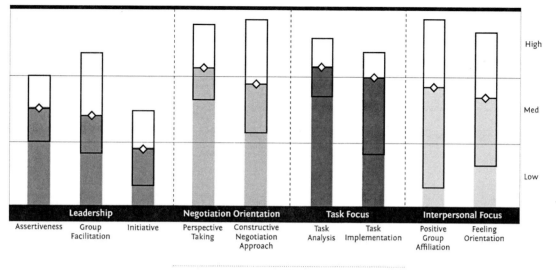

High
Med
Low

| Leadership | | | Negotiation Orientation | | Task Focus | | Interpersonal Focus | |
| Assertiveness | Group Facilitation | Initiative | Perspective Taking | Constructive Negotiation Approach | Task Analysis | Task Implementation | Positive Group Affiliation | Feeling Orientation |

◇ Group Average ☐ Range of Individual scores

1. Assertiveness:

‣ The people in the top half of the rectangle may well be running the group. Ask the group about its pattern of participation. Are some people chronically silent, not sharing ideas?

‣ Team members should be asking more questions of one another to get people involved in the discussion.

2. Group Facilitation:

‣ Most member scores cluster below the diamond line. This indicates that quite a few are not active in helping facilitate the work of the group.

‣ According to their skill strengths in the areas of negotiation, task, or interpersonal relations, more members can become involved in facilitating these aspects of a project.

‣ The goal would be to develop greater shared leadership that would more fully utilize the strengths within the team.

3. Initiative:

‣ What are the members' thoughts about how the group is functioning with respect to leadership initiative?

‣ From the column score, it appears that most, if not all members, could contribute greater leadership energy within the group.

‣ Where are members interested in stepping up to help lead the group? Identify those interests and give members opportunities to take the captain's seat. Have members support and encourage one another in these efforts.

4. Perspective Taking:

‣ Perspective Taking is one of the team's main strengths. There is significant member interest and energy here.

‣ The team can draw on its PT energy and use it to improve performance in the Feeling Orientation area. Members can pay closer attention to, and ask questions about, feeling currents in the group, responding more quickly to negative, disruptive emotions while also seeking to align people's passions to appropriate work opportunities.

5. Constructive Negotiation Approach with Positive Group Affiliation:

‣ The team can spend time doing rapport-building activities, so members get to know each other better. This will increase team cohesion.

‣ As members develop greater rapport, they are more capable of pursuing win-win agreements since they have more knowledge about others' interests and concerns. This knowledge can buttress efforts with Constructive Negotiation Approach.

6. Task Implementation:

- According to the range of scores, there is at least one member, maybe more, who are not fully integrated into the team's task efforts. The group should improve member communication and keep everyone actively involved with the task, thereby enhancing performance.

Team Four

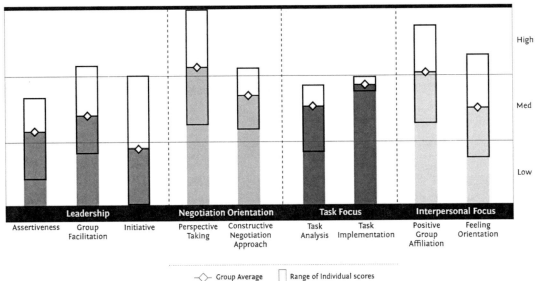

◇ Group Average   ☐ Range of Individual scores

1. Task Analysis with Task Implementation:

- The team has a tight cluster in the Task Implementation domain, indicating that members share a healthy ambition to get the job done.

- But with the lower Task Analysis score, does the team just plow ahead to complete the task without adequate effort to develop a solid strategy?

- The team will benefit from spending more time considering its task strategies, making sure it has not overlooked any issues that are important for achieving quality outcomes. Make sure that all members share ideas in the discussion.

2. Assertiveness with Perspective Taking:

- All of the members should take an active role in discussions. Those who speak up more often should invite those who haven't contributed to join the discussion, fostering a broader dialogue about the issues.

- People can channel their interest in Perspective Taking into Assertiveness. Members with the strongest PT scores can model for other members the questioning and listening skills that deepen interpersonal understanding. Members can share insights about questioning techniques that will enrich a conversation and then apply them in the next meeting.

3. Group Facilitation:

- The team should give a variety of members the chance to facilitate aspects of the work related to their strongest skills in negotiation, task, or interpersonal focus.

- More shared leadership would encourage greater commitment to the team and its pursuits.

4. Initiative:

- Based on the team score, it seems that a number of members are content to let one or two others carry the ball in the Initiative domain. How does this play out for the team?

- Where can other members take important leadership actions that will benefit the team and advance their own development?

5. Feeling Orientation:

‣ The team could acknowledge feeling issues in the group and make the issues discussable.

‣ Members with high scores in this area can help the team be more alert to feelings—both positive and negative—so the group can manage these energies constructively.

Team Five

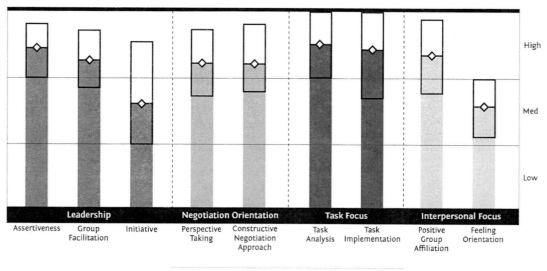

| Leadership | | | Negotiation Orientation | | Task Focus | | Interpersonal Focus | |
| Assertiveness | Group Facilitation | Initiative | Perspective Taking | Constructive Negotiation Approach | Task Analysis | Task Implementation | Positive Group Affiliation | Feeling Orientation |

◇ Group Average   ▫ Range of Individual scores

1. Assertiveness:

‣ The team has a lot of conversational energy. This can create competition for air time. How does the team manage its discussions, given this high score?

‣ The team can design a structure for how long someone may speak in order to promote a point-counterpoint discussion, opening up the dialogue. (Teams with this challenge have deployed this strategy successfully.)

2. Initiative:

‣ A significant number of members fall into the low-Medium area of this category.

‣ How can the team create more opportunities for all members to take leadership roles, as appropriate?

3. Task Analysis with Task Implementation:

‣ Given the team's very high score in Task Analysis, does it devote too much time to analysis before moving into action with the plan?

‣ When implementing a strategy, members should be alert to any adjustments that would make the effort more efficient. Find quick ways to put such insights into action.

4. Feeling Orientation:

‣ The team could pay greater attention to emotional currents in the group, seeking ways to productively harness this energy.

‣ What attitudes or concerns may be holding the team back from attending to feeling issues?

‣ The group may want to do some skill-building activities from the Emotional Intelligence field to enhance its effectiveness.

5. Group Facilitation:

‣ The score indicates that all team members have significant energy in this domain.

‣ Is the team creating enough opportunities for various members to facilitate the work when a person's expertise warrants it?

‣ How can the team delegate group facilitation responsibilities more broadly to promote shared leadership opportunities?

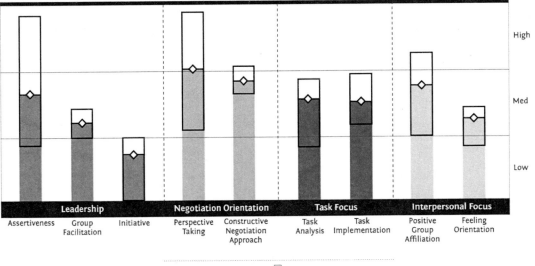

◇— Group Average   ☐ Range of Individual scores

1. Group Facilitation with Task Focus:

▸ The team needs to discuss ways to improve its facilitation process to lift task performance.

▸ The team should draw on KGI® Group Profile suggestions to refine group facilitation, as well as reading other materials that would identify techniques for organizing the group.

▸ Members with higher scores in Task Analysis and Task Implementation can lead a discussion about how the team might refine its techniques in each of these domains. Members need to be patient and think practically about ways to increase their effectiveness, and then experiment with fresh ideas, modifying them along the way to increase positive outcomes.

▸ The team should put the task issues at the top of their agenda and devote ample time to this enterprise. Given the team scores, members appear reluctant to directly attack task concerns, and they need to overcome this resistance.

2. Assertiveness:

▸ In light of the score, how can members balance their participation so everyone participates on a regular basis?

▸ Members with high scores can use their Assertiveness energy to ask more questions, drawing others into the conversation.

3. Initiative:

▸ Where can members step up to take more leadership roles for the team?

▸ How can the team structure opportunities so members can build leadership skills? They should make this an ongoing priority and support those who step up to assume new responsibilities.

4. Perspective Taking:

▸ The team displays a significant range of skills in this domain. Higher scoring members can share insights to assist others in refining their practice, mentoring them to increase their competence.

▸ By strengthening all members' skills in Perspective Taking, the group will obtain valuable data to orchestrate agreements for Constructive Negotiation Approach, an area of high interest. Making people aware of this connection will help motivate them to put in the extra effort for PT skill building.

5. Positive Group Affiliation with Feeling Orientation:

▸ In response to the range of issues already identified for this team, members would do well to openly share their feelings and concerns about these points. The group should use frank talk to establish an authentic dialogue, setting a solid foundation for problem solving.

- Opening up the dialogue could help the team appreciate the Feeling Orientation subscale and spur development of other skills in this area. In general, the team should consider ways to pay closer attention to feeling issues.

- The team should conduct rapport-building activities, finding time to schedule these efforts. This builds up Positive Group Affiliation, which inclines people to construct win-win accords, something in which the group has an interest. By pointing out the connection between Positive Group Affiliation and Constructive Negotiation Approach, members will find additional motivation to pursue PGA activities.

Team Seven

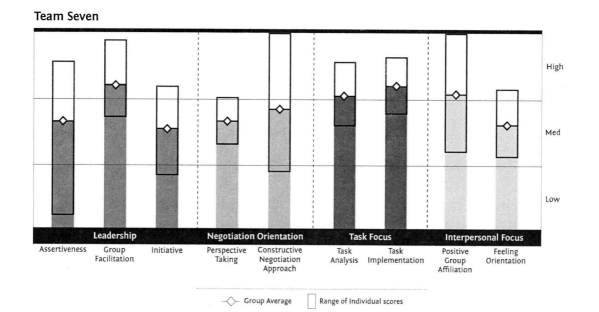

1. **Perspective Taking:**

- The team has a narrow range of responses in the Medium area. Expanding the team's skills could significantly improve performance across the negotiation, task, and interpersonal domains.

- How do the members view their ability to listen closely to one another and collaborate? Are there situations when individual members, in leadership roles, just go forward without consulting with teammates? What are the characteristics of the team's decision-making process?

- All team members should ask more probe questions to investigate each other's positions. Mirroring back what has been said would help to ensure correct understanding.

2. **Feeling Orientation:**

- The majority of the members fall in the lower half of Medium. This is a skill area that could be fortified. Such action would deepen interpersonal understanding related to Perspective Taking.

- Members can select activities to increase their emotional awareness, perhaps drawing on Emotional Intelligence materials. Members with higher scores can take leadership roles, helping the team pay attention to the flow of feelings.

- In a respectful way, members should practice openness in talking about feeling issues related to their collaboration.

3. **Assertiveness:**

- The team needs to make sure that quiet members are invited into the conversation. With such a wide range of scores, pay attention to those at the lower end.

4. Task Analysis with Task Implementation:

▸ In comparing the scores on these scales, there is a slightly stronger preference for Task Implementation. Does the team find itself jumping ahead at times to complete a task without a fully developed strategy?

▸ How can the team fine-tune its overall task approach?

5. Constructive Negotiation Approach with Positive Group Affiliation:

▸ The team could try some focused rapport-building activities to help members become better acquainted and create more team unity.

▸ Such rapport building can provide information that will help members construct win-win agreements with Constructive Negotiation Approach. Building member rapport, boosting team morale, and developing win-win strategies all tend to play off one another, making a team more cohesive and higher performing.

▸ Members with higher scores on PGA and CNA should provide leadership, bringing members with lower scores into active involvement in these areas.

Team Eight

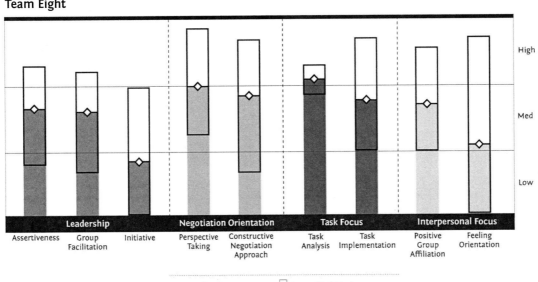

High

Med

Low

Leadership			Negotiation Orientation		Task Focus		Interpersonal Focus	
Assertiveness	Group Facilitation	Initiative	Perspective Taking	Constructive Negotiation Approach	Task Analysis	Task Implementation	Positive Group Affiliation	Feeling Orientation

◇— Group Average   ☐ Range of Individual scores

1. Task Analysis with Task Implementation:

▸ The team has a tight cluster of scores in the High zone for Task Analysis. With so many members having this preference, does the group spend too much time with analysis—to the point of overanalysis? Is the team wasting time in this area?

▸ The team would do well to settle on a reasonable strategy, not a "perfect" strategy, and then move forward to implementation, refining the task strategy during practical application.

▸ The team has quite a few members operating in low-Medium with Task Implementation. It needs to improve communication during task activities and to get all members focused and integrated into the group effort.

2. Initiative:

▸ A significant number of members are performing in the Low section of this subscale.

▸ The group could have a discussion to investigate what factors prevent members from taking initiative.

▸ The team should determine how all members can take appropriate leadership initiatives and then create a supportive environment for these actions. Members can help each other identify goals and strategies, and encourage personal growth. They can also look for ways to create shared leadership opportunities.

3. Feeling Orientation:

▸ A majority of the group fall into the bottom zone of this subscale.

▸ The team could discuss any negative emotional currents in the group that may be thwarting member efforts. They can also investigate people's enthusiasms and interests, so these can be harnessed to create satisfying work assignments for members.

▸ What the group may discover by frank conversation on the emotional level could be connected to the points for the Initiative subscale listed above. Identify feelings that are holding members back and discover interests that need to be tapped.

4. Assertiveness:

▸ The team should make sure all members are able to share ideas in discussions, and everyone feels comfortable expressing their views.

▸ The group may want to institute a procedure for going around the table and having each person share thoughts on the subject under discussion.

5. Positive Group Affiliation with Constructive Negotiation Approach:

▸ The group could explore some team-building activities to increase member rapport. By getting to know one another better, members can collaborate more effectively on tasks.

▸ By increasing team spirit, members will, in turn, be more motivated to work towards win-win agreements to everyone's benefit. Encourage more attention to the win-win approach.

▸ Working on PGA and CNA inter-relatedly will assist the team in creating the synergy that will lift it to a higher level of performance.

Team Nine

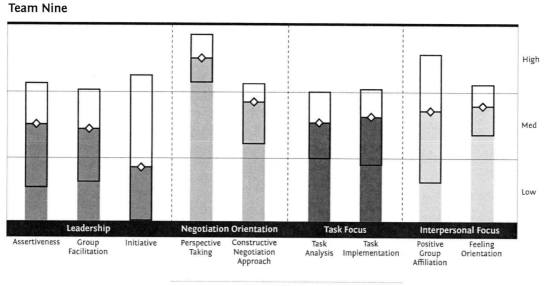

-◇- Group Average   ☐ Range of Individual scores

1. Perspective Taking and Constructive Negotiation Approach:

▸ The team has a narrow range of scores in the High section of Perspective Taking.

▸ Does the team tend to overdo this skill area? Does it get too caught up in exploring everyone's views, to the point that it becomes difficult to move forward into concrete action?

▸ With such a high, tight score for PT, the team can become too deferential, losing

the ability to give honest, direct feedback to members for fear of hurting someone's feelings. In what ways does the team struggle with these issues?

▸ The team should channel some of its high PT energy into a more active pursuit of win-win agreements with Constructive Negotiation Approach. As members investigate others' points of view, they should look for ways to bring these positions together in agreements that are mutually beneficial.

2. Perspective Taking and Task Analysis:

▸ The team could direct some of its Perspective Taking energy towards Task Analysis to strengthen performance in that sector.

▸ Members could explore one another's viewpoints on different task strategies. They should examine a variety of options and also the consequences of those options, assessing problems and potential opportunities. They can play off each other's ideas to create a more refined task strategy.

3. Positive Group Affiliation:

▸ The greatest number of member scores is concentrated in the upper section of the column, indicating that there is significant attention to team morale in the group.

▸ The group should build on this strength, conducting some team-building activities, to help the group become a more cohesive unit. By this means, it can bring members in the lower area of this subscale into the fold. As cohesion increases, it will enhance collaboration in the task and negotiation domains.

4. Initiative:

▸ According to the team's score, most members are languishing at the bottom end of this column, with just a member or two showing significantly greater skill development.

▸ How has the team been operating with regard to leadership initiative? Are one or two people carrying the load for the team? What are the team dynamics here?

▸ How can the team diversify the leadership opportunities, tapping into various members' strengths and interests? By getting more people involved in this undertaking, it will develop people's personal talents and give the team flexibility in how it might manage its tasks.

5. Assertiveness and Group Facilitation:

▸ Both subscales have numerous members in a solid level of performance.

▸ But the team should ensure that more reserved members regularly participate in group discussions and, as appropriate, are given opportunities to facilitate aspects of the group's work where they have skills. This will promote leadership development and will utilize member talents more fully, strengthening the team.

Team Ten

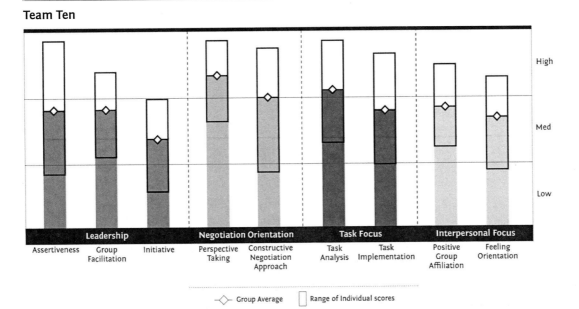

1. Assertiveness:

▸ The wide range of member scores for this subscale suggests that people at the top may be dominating air time while others are without consistent voices. How do the members assess the pattern of verbal participation on the team?

• The team needs to make sure that all voices are heard. People with stronger Assertiveness scores can ask more questions, invite others to share perspectives, and bring everyone into the conversational mix.

2. Constructive Negotiation Approach:

• The team has significant energy invested into Perspective Taking. This energy could be channeled more intentionally into the Constructive Negotiation Approach domain, which is a natural direction that would increase team cohesion and member commitment to the work.

• The team should get these members with lower CNA scores more involved in the negotiation process. One way this can be accomplished is by soliciting their input and making sure that everyone understands their interests and concerns. Then the team can look to address these interests more fully as it develops its plans.

3. Task Analysis with Task Implementation:

• The graph results indicate the team leans in the direction of Task Analysis. It would be useful to investigate how the team operates. Is there a tendency, at times, to overanalyze? How can the team strike the right balance between reasonable analysis and timely action?

• With respect to Task Implementation, there are some members who are less engaged in this area. Developing ways to get these members more involved in the effort will boost productivity and team cohesion.

4. Initiative:

• While some members have a solid level of leadership initiative, others do not. The team should consider ways to provide appropriate leadership opportunities for its members related to their skill levels and interests.

• The team should create a forum for analyzing leadership Initiative, providing support and encouragement for those who wish to step up. Various members could share insights gained from their challenges and successes with leadership to help others refine strategies and grow skills.

5. Feeling Orientation:

• The group has a Medium score with Feeling Orientation, which can be enhanced. Members with High scores can help facilitate discussions that assess the undercurrent emotions in the group.

• The team should address negative emotions that are inhibiting people's performance and resolve these issues. It should also listen for positive emotions, members' enthusiasms and excitements, and direct this energy into work that enhances team performance.

Team Eleven

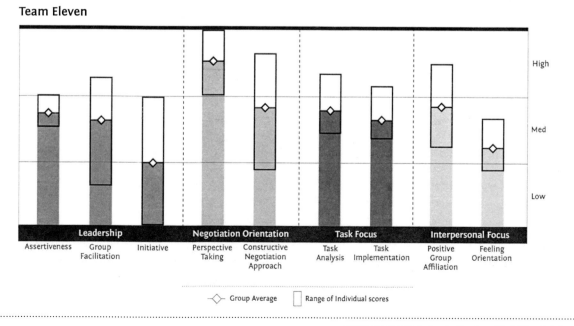

1. Assertiveness with Perspective Taking:

▸ With such a high score in Perspective Taking, this team might be overly concerned with gathering information about everyone's opinions. People can be too solicitous, and then defer too much to others' opinions, becoming reluctant, on occasion, to share their own ideas. In light of these concerns, how do members view the team's pattern of participation?

▸ The team could channel some PT energy towards Assertiveness. Although the Assertiveness score is in a solid, upper-Medium range, infusing more energy could expand the team's conversation, making it more dynamic. This, in turn, could increase the number of ideas the group generates when working with Constructive Negotiation Approach and Task Analysis.

▸ The team could also use Assertiveness energy to initiate opportunities for group facilitation. Members can identify their personal interests in the negotiation, task, and interpersonal domains. The group can allow these people to step up at appropriate times and assume a leadership role, so they can practice facilitation skills.

2. Constructive Negotiation Approach with Positive Group Affiliation:

▸ Members can structure opportunities to do more interpersonal sharing (within appropriate time boundaries), to help build greater rapport in the group. Doing so could increase team spirit and team cohesiveness.

▸ As members increase their team spirit, it disposes them to work more collaboratively to construct win-win agreements, thereby enhancing their efforts with Constructive Negotiation Approach, which could use some attention and strengthening.

3. Initiative:

▸ Like the Group Facilitation area, Initiative could be better balanced so that more members are willing to take important leadership actions.

▸ All members should earnestly pursue the opportunity to take on a key leadership role for an appropriate group project or team activity.

4. Feeling Orientation:

▸ If members gained a better understanding about how people felt about different issues, it would assist them in their negotiations and task enterprises.

▸ When members notice facial expressions and gestures that indicate emotional reactions by others, they can inquire about what is going on to gain further perspective on their teammates' concerns. This will deepen worthwhile understanding.

▸ With this investigation of emotional reactions, the aim is to move the group in positive directions, straightening out potential misunderstandings or conflicts, and translating member excitements into worthwhile group contributions.

5. Task Analysis with Task Implementation:

▸ With both of these subscales, most of the members fall in the middle of the Medium sector of performance. In each instance, there are some members with higher results. The team should identify these people and have them offer suggestions about how to sharpen the team's task efforts.

▸ The team needs to improve communication in the Task Focus domain. Make sure that all voices are heard during the construction of initial strategies and during the refinement of these strategies when the team moves the project along.

Team Twelve

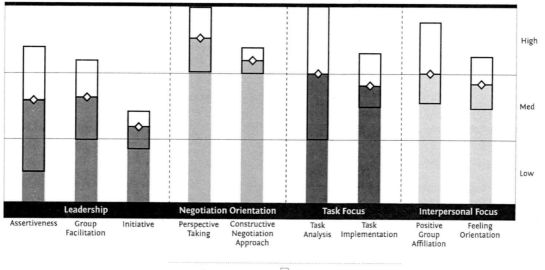

- ◇ Group Average
- ▯ Range of Individual scores

1. Initiative and Feeling Orientation:

▸ The team has a meaningful asset with its Feeling Orientation score, showing a tight cluster in the high-Medium range. All members appear comfortable with discussing emotional issues in the group.

▸ The team could use this asset to evaluate the Initiative skill area. Members can share feelings about the obstacles that prevent them from assuming a leadership position. What attitudes and feelings hold them back? How, with mutual support, could members overcome their anxieties and begin to experiment with being active leaders?

▸ Members could also explore what passions, interests, or visions might be harnessed to create enthusiasm for leadership development. How can positive emotions prompt people to take risks and develop their latent leadership potential?

2. Assertiveness:

▸ The team should investigate ways to balance the participation level so all members are involved. It seems a few may dominate while others sit back.

▸ Members with higher scores should invite quieter members to speak and make sure that no decision is made without hearing everyone's ideas and concerns.

3. Perspective Taking and Task Analysis:

▸ The team has a sturdy score for Perspective Taking, which could be utilized to strengthen efforts with Task Analysis.

▸ Members need to do more investigation of other people's thinking when developing task strategies. What insights can people share about problems, opportunities, and smart solutions for doing specific tasks?

▸ The team needs to open up the discussion to hear from everyone, and play off each other's ideas to fashion more effective task strategies. Asking more questions and sharing reactions to people's ideas would move the team in a favorable direction.

4. Group Facilitation with Task Implementation:

▸ A number of members have significant skills with Group Facilitation, which could be more directly applied to Task Implementation.

▸ The group should pay more attention to how it facilitates Task Implementation. It can grant appropriate members more leadership responsibilities based on their facilitation and task skills. It can thoughtfully delegate work to people who will play supportive roles, tapping into their interests and talents. All members should help analyze how to better orchestrate their efforts to boost productivity.

5. Constructive Negotiation Approach with Positive Group Affiliation:

▸ To improve Positive Group Affiliation, the team can organize some rapport-building activities so members become more familiar with each other ("familiar" means belonging to the family). This can increase team cohesion.

▸ This effort can also provide information to assist members in designing win-win options when they collaborate. Since the team has such a strong impulse towards Constructive Negotiation Approach, there is a natural motivation to take this strength to a higher level. By refining and elevating PGA, it will benefit CNA. Together, they will fuel greater synergy on the team.

Team Thirteen

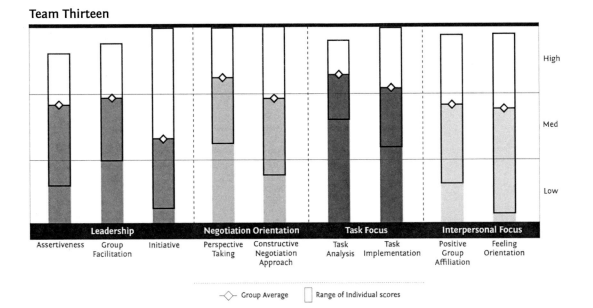

- ◇- Group Average   ☐ Range of Individual scores

1. Task Analysis with Task Implementation:

▸ The Task Analysis subscale has the highest team score; it is also the domain where individual members' interests and energies cluster the most. This can be a critical asset as the team analyzes and tries to balance performance among other subscales which display a wide diversity of scores. Sound analysis will be the foundation for this group development venture.

▸ However, the team must be careful not to fall in love with analysis and fail to take concrete action, thus experiencing "paralysis by analysis." It needs to use this skill in a focused way, one that supports thoughtful problem solving and timely, effective action.

▸ The team will want to look at ways it can design mentoring opportunities across the other subscales, to have members with high scores share insights and tips to educate members with softer scores. Such efforts

will build team unity and raise overall performance.

▸ The group can utilize its analytical skills to determine ways to improve communication and coordination with Task Implementation, making the team more efficient. The team needs to turn solid, practical ideas into action and then refine them with adjustments along the way. They need to get all members in the mix with Task Implementation, and not leave it to members with high scores.

2. Constructive Negotiation Approach with Positive Group Affiliation:

▸ A significant number of members are in the upper half of the rectangular box for Positive Group Affiliation. They should assist the team in conducting rapport-building activities, helping groupmates to become better acquainted, thus increasing team cohesion and establishing a positive atmosphere for the group.

• As members develop more harmony, they can strive for more win-win agreements, pulling people even closer together and creating greater commitment to the task effort.

3. Assertiveness with Perspective Taking:

• The group should pay attention to people who are reserved and make sure their voices are heard. Inviting people into discussions helps them to develop their social identities and increases their comfort level in the group.

• Having people speak up is one thing, but it is also critical to make them feel they are being heard. The members could refine their Perspective Taking skills by asking more probing questions to better understand each other's positions. Members should then repeat back what they have heard, checking to ensure there is clear communication.

4. Initiative:

• One or two members appear to be carrying most of the leadership load, with others content to follow along.

• The team needs to distribute opportunities for leadership more broadly. Members should discuss their interests in this regard.

In what projects, or parts of projects, would members like to step up to help lead the group? Members with greater Initiative skills can offer guidance on how to successfully organize and conduct projects based on their experiences. They can then encourage others to experiment with new leadership roles in selected projects.

5. Feeling Orientation:

• Members should pay closer attention to feeling undercurrents and make feeling issues more discussable in the team.

• With such a diverse array of scores in this domain, team members can assist each other by discussing their feelings about the challenges of developing various skills in the different KGI subscale areas. Members who have strong skills in certain areas can talk about the problems they faced in obtaining these skills and how they overcame them, offering insights to those who are currently struggling in these ways. People can talk about their inspirations and challenges, which can help the group to become a learning team, with members supporting each other in their efforts to acquire new skills.

Team Fourteen

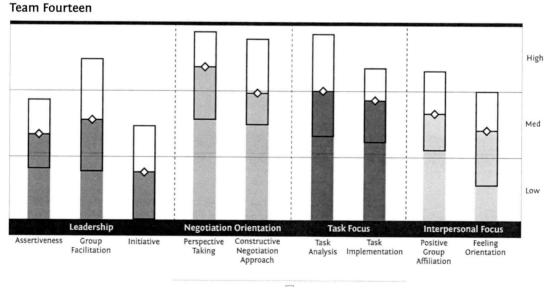

-◇- Group Average   ☐ Range of Individual scores

1. Assertiveness with Perspective Taking:

• A majority of members score above the diamond line in Perspective Taking, indicating a significant interest in understanding others'

positions and concerns.

• Members can use their PT energy to invite people into the discussion and ask probing questions to investigate their positions, drawing out the quieter members and encouraging them to express themselves in the group.

- The group could simply go around the table and ask people to share reactions to a topic, which would get the conversational ball rolling. The team could then build on these ideas to shape a strategy.

2. Initiative:

- With regard to this subscale, all of the members have work to do.

- What future projects or assignments do members have an interest in? Where can people's best skills be put forward to help lead the team? Where do people want to gain new skills related to new leadership responsibilities? All members should be involved in the discussion, and all members should take on assignments at some point in the future.

- When members take new leadership actions, the group should discuss what went well and what could be improved. By including a group reflection on the practice of leadership, members will learn from each other and build on their collective experience, thereby furthering personal growth and team effectiveness.

3. Task Analysis with Task Implementation:

- The team, based on its graph, tends to favor Task Analysis over Task Implementation. When this is evident, it's always worthwhile to ask members--do they tend to overanalyze when deciding on a task strategy? Does the discussion run on, even when there is a very reasonable plan on the table? Is there a delay in putting a plan into action?

- The team needs to refine Task Implementation, bringing it into better alignment with TA. How can members improve communication and collaboration when implementing a plan? The team can brainstorm ways to monitor and perfect its collaboration during actual plan implementation.

4. Constructive Negotiation Approach with Positive Group Affiliation:

- Most member scores fall below the diamond line towards the low-Medium area of Positive Group Affiliation. The team would benefit from members developing more familiarity with one another and more camaraderie. The team should introduce some rapport-building activities to get better acquainted.

- As members become better acquainted, they acquire useful data to construct win-win agreements, since they better understand each other's interests and concerns. The team already has significant energy investment in Constructive Negotiation Approach, and increasing member rapport would enhance its ability to pursue that interest.

5. Feeling Orientation:

- A significant number of members pay attention to the feeling issues, evidenced by the fact that the smaller part of the rectangle is above the diamond line. These members could open up a discussion about feeling undercurrents in the group. People could analyze what emotions are at play during conflicts and how to manage them constructively. They could also identify where people have enthusiasms and how that energy can be channeled into specific work tasks or leadership opportunities.

- Having a discussion about what obstacles are holding members back in the areas of Assertiveness and Initiative could move the team into productive problem solving that could generate increased participation in these areas. People can share what they are experiencing in these domains and support one another in embracing positive attitudes about their future leadership development.

The team examples, with a diverse array of graphs, showcase a versatile system of analysis. By following these examples, a professional can construct a sound plan for improvement based on a specific team's scores. As a team refines its practices, it will move in directions that inspire synergy, resulting in first-rate performance.

As mentioned earlier in this volume, when information from psychological typology is added to the KGI skill-building system, the approach can be enhanced. Typology offers insights into energies that are present in all individuals and that affect group participation. The next chapter explains how psychological typology impacts group life. This will be followed by data on how the type system and the KGI system merge, with powerful applications for individuals and teams. ✕

CHAPTER 18

Psychological Typology and Group Behavior

In 1921 Swiss psychiatrist Carl Jung published a seminal book, Psychological Types. In this text he identifies a series of personality attitudes and functions which, in various combinations, create a system of psychological typology. Jung describes the attitudes and functions as pairs of opposites, or dichotomies, where an individual comes to prefer one side over the other and therefore invests more energy and effort in that direction. This significantly influences the shape of a person's thoughts, actions, and development.

The model enables people to appreciate how psychic energy flows in different ways in the personality and it provides a deeper understanding of human motivation and behavior. With respect to group activity, the model contributes many practical insights.

Extraversion and introversion, the first dichotomy, defines a primary life attitude in which an individual's main interest centers on either the outside world of people and things (extraversion) or the inner world of thought and personal experience (introversion). The second pairing, sensing and intuition, identifies the perceiving functions, indicating the manner in which an individual prefers to take in information. With sensing, a person likes to use the five senses and attend to here-and-now details; with intuition, a person chooses to utilize the unconscious in order to see potential associations and future possibilities. Finally, there are the two judging functions, thinking and feeling, classifying the way someone prefers to make decisions. With thinking, a person

wishes to employ objective, logical analysis; with feeling, a person favors a system of feeling-toned values.

Jung's concepts supply a meaningful design for a broad audience—for psychological clinicians, their clients, business and professional people, educators, and researchers—in fact, for anyone who seeks a clearer understanding of the primary patterns of the human personality. But the system doesn't simply paint a clear picture of personality traits; it introduces a method for growth and development. Using this model, people can more selectively employ their natural strengths while also nurturing undeveloped aspects of their personalities, thereby expanding their ability to handle a wide range of life events. This personality expansion connects to Jung's idea of individuation, central to his analytical psychology, the procedure by which a person intentionally cultivates previously untapped parts of the personality to become a more fully functioning, well-rounded individual.

Psychological Types caught the attention of an

American mother-daughter team, Katherine Briggs and Isabel Myers, who had a long-standing fascination with personality typology. As they studied Jung's theory, they recognized the soundness of the model. They decided to create an assessment based on the design, an instrument that would bring the benefits of this practical psychology to a more extensive audience. Through years of painstaking labor, they constructed an assessment tool that would become the most popular psychological instrument in the world for the general population.

While the two women closely followed Jung's ideas, they added a fourth dichotomy to their measurement, Judging–Perceiving, which identifies how a person orients to the outside world. With the Judging attitude, an individual prefers a planned, organized, and structured approach; with the Perceiving attitude, one favors an open-ended, flexible, and spontaneous method. Thus, the Myers-Briggs Type Indicator (MBTI) instrument reports individual results for four dichotomous scales: (1) Extraversion (E)–Introversion (I); (2) Sensing (S)–Intuition (N); (3) Thinking (T)–Feeling (F); and (4) Judging (J)–Perceiving (P). After answering a series of questions (with each question related to a single polarity), a participant receives scores that indicate on which side of each dichotomy he prefers to operate, along with the clarity of that preference—ranging from slight, to moderate, to clear, to very clear. The clarity index reveals how much energy a person tends to invest in that preference: a small amount, a moderate amount, or a very significant amount. Descriptive material then helps the person understand how he might employ these preferences in life situations. In addition, when the scores from the four scales are brought together, they identify an individual's psychological type, of which there are sixteen possibilities. The information contained in type profiles delivers further data to assist in the pursuit of self-understanding and self-development.

The MBTI instrument has been widely embraced in the business, professional, and educational communities, as well as by individuals who seek deeper self-awareness or a greater knowledge about how other people function. The MBTI materials aid people in the refinement of communication, decision making, leadership, and team skills, and they furnish a potent resource for counseling, coaching, teaching, and training.

Particularly relevant for this author have been the applications for team leadership and small-group life. For thirty years, I have immersed myself in the study of group behavior, with psychological typology contributing an invaluable lens for the enterprise. In collaboration with the Center for Applications of Psychological Type (CAPT), an organization co-founded by Isabel Myers and Mary McCaulley, we developed the Klein Group Instrument for Effective Leadership and Participation in Teams (KGI) assessment. The intent was to create a new measurement that could stand alone as a team-building tool, but also complement the MBTI instrument, extending deeper the applications of typology into group activities. Despite the loftiness of these goals, we achieved them. While the KGI assessment is embedded in a powerful web of group behavior theories, offering an exciting new model to guide leadership and team development, the MBTI materials add insight into the psychological energies that can creatively inform these developmental processes. On the personal level, the KGI and MBTI assessments support the individuation process that increases leadership and group skills; on the team level, they promote the synergy that produces the highest collective performance.

In this chapter, data will be presented on psychological typology and its relationship to group behavior—grounded in years of research involving qualitative and quantitative analyses, as well as a broad review of the relevant literature (see *KGI® Manual*). Over the years, thousands of people have been trained with the two instruments, and hundreds interviewed about their learning experiences. The details demonstrate the rich relationship between typology and group life. Following this analysis, the succeeding chapters explore the ways that the KGI and MBTI measurements can be utilized in tandem for coaching and team building, with step-by-step procedures and case studies. As will be seen, the two measurements can combine in a dynamic skill-building experience.

Psychological Preferences:
Attitudes and Behaviors in Small Groups

To present this information in a clear, accessible manner, the most important group attitudes and behaviors for each dichotomy will be displayed in two parallel columns, demonstrating the contrasting tendencies of the two preferences. Then a more elaborate analysis will follow for each of the preferences, explaining underlying motivations and issues related to its effective application in small groups.

1. Extraversion–Introversion Dichotomy

Extraversion (E)	Introversion (I)
Active member in a group	Quieter member, hesitant in speaking up
Responds quickly in discussions	Reflects for a while, then responds
May need to slow down to let others speak	May need to be invited to speak
Shares personal information more easily	Reserved in sharing personal information

Extraversion

> By definition, Extraverts have a strong social orientation. When interviewed, they often say: to be in a group *means* you should participate. It's almost like an ethical imperative—one should be engaged in the discussion, active in the collective effort. However, the clarity of preference can be very influential. For an Extravert with a slight preference, participation may proceed in a more cautious manner, since the score indicates that while the person leans towards Extraversion, there is a significant, balancing Introverted energy. In general, though, Extraverts like to announce where they stand on the issues compared to other people in the group.

> Because of their external orientation, many Extraverts jump right into a discussion and consistently assert themselves. They respond quickly to the opportunity for conversation.

The down side is they may come across as domineering. Extraverts with a clear, or very clear preference, fall more easily into this category. They may need to reduce their verbal air time to give others a chance. They need to realize that when they become over-heated with enthusiasm, they can come across as "pushy" or "overbearing." A useful antidote to this impulse is to stop and invite quieter members to speak, thereby expanding the number of voices in the conversation. This can play to an Extravert's desire to have a lot of ideas in a discussion, with people bouncing ideas off one another, an activity that stimulates their thinking. It also helps the group, as a whole, to analyze a topic.

> When Extraverts participate, it makes them feel that they *really belong* in the group, a driving value for them. They want to do their share, so they feel connected to their teammates and to the enterprise. If an Extravert doesn't say something during a group discussion, the individual may later experience a sense of emptiness, a feeling of regret. The person may significantly ramp up his or her participation in the next team encounter to compensate.

> Prompted by their social orientation, Extraverts like to promote group unity and team spirit. They often take the initial step to introduce themselves to others and try to make friends in the group. They assume they will like people as they get to know them, establishing productive bonds. This optimistic expectation drives their outgoing approach. As part of this activity, they are willing to share a variety of personal information. The sharing of personal information aids in the building of interpersonal rapport and trust. These actions can inspire others to do the same, steps that build greater team cohesion.

> Many Extraverts are uncomfortable with silence in a group. When a lull occurs in a conversation, an Extravert may jump in with a comment or suggestion to fill the gap. The goal is to keep the conversational ball rolling. However, such quiet times present an opportunity to observe the group, to be

more alert to body language, and to evaluate the silent messages. When Extraverts learn to hone their observational and listening skills, it makes them stronger group players.

▸ For Extraverts, a critical goal is to see the group's plans effectively carried out. They like to take action, and they often devote a great deal of energy to this end. But part of their reasoning is that successful task execution provides a positive incentive for team members. Success makes people excited about working together again; it infuses optimism about future collaborations. These emotions help ignite synergy on a team, increasing people's excitement and commitment to the enterprise. Extraverts thrive on this energy and try to promote it.

Introversion

▸ People with the Introversion preference like to think deeply about the ideas expressed in a group discussion. Because of their reflective nature, they may carefully ponder a point before sharing it. As a result, when the timing is right, they can contribute very pertinent ideas to the conversation, related to task, interpersonal, and negotiation issues. They may offer astute arguments that are persuasive, influencing others. This can move them into a leadership role.

▸ On the other hand, because Introverts take more time to think about matters, they may have trouble keeping up with a fast-paced group conversation, causing them to feel disconnected and out of sync. By the time they are ready to articulate an idea, the issue may have already slipped into the team's rearview mirror. This makes it harder for them to share ideas, which, in turn, can undermine their feeling of effectiveness. This is a challenge that many Introverts struggle with in groups. They can feel self-conscious, out of rhythm, and become fearful of being judged as incompetent. In fact, many Introverts walk into groups anticipating this social awkwardness, an attitude that further inhibits them. To reduce this problem, it is valuable to start a group session by going around the table and having everyone share a point, so all members get into the conversation. This breaks the ice and involves Introverts in the flow of the conversation, making it easier for them to participate later.

▸ It is worthwhile to note that when an Introvert is silent for a long period of time, it becomes increasingly difficult for the individual to contribute to the group. The sense of belongingness fades as the sense of being marginalized increases. This is the way that a team can fragment—losing member participation and commitment, thereby reducing team cohesiveness and productivity. When Introverts are invited to speak, at the beginning of a session or during it, they can contribute relevant ideas. When others appreciate these ideas, Introverts feel respected and more integrated into the team. With a couple of experiences like that, Introverts often begin to contribute more on their own, without an invitation. Interestingly, as our research has shown, they can even become as talkative as Extraverts in that particular group context. Introverts with a slight preference, having significant counterbalancing Extraversion energy, usually move more swiftly in this direction and, sometimes, don't need an invitation at all.

▸ When Introverts make a commitment to build their social skills, learning to participate more artfully in group life, they can turn it to great effect, becoming high-quality leaders. But because their natural tendency is to turn inward, it takes a conscious effort, patience, and persistence to accomplish this goal.

▸ Because Introverts may remain silent in a group discussion, it can cause them to receive the more undesirable assignments when work is delegated for a project. They may not express their interests or volunteer for work that inspires them. As a result, they can inherit jobs that may feel meaningless, dampening their commitment to the work and reducing their efforts. This is another reason why it is important to make sure Introvert voices are heard—so their interests are recognized, and they receive assignments that motivate them to put forward their best efforts and contribute successfully to the group. As they increase their confidence and identification with the group, they will help a team utilize all of its personnel to best effect.

▸ Since Introverts like to "pick the right spot" for entering a group conversation, searching for a safe opportunity to make a successful contribution, they are usually effective group observers. They can be attuned to the messages communicated by facial expression, body language, and tone of voice. They can pick up on the undercurrents in group dynamics. When they share insights about these observations, they help a team become more aware of its group processes, providing the opportunity to make worthwhile adjustments. In this way, they can make productive contributions from a member's role, a valuable skill for both Introverts and Extraverts to cultivate.

▸ Sharing personal information at the appropriate time and in the appropriate dose helps group members get to know each other and builds team cohesion. For Extraverts, generally speaking, this is an easier proposition. Introverts tend to be more reserved in this regard. One way to help them is to conduct a team activity where people pair up with one other person to share some personal information, such as hobbies, travel experiences, or special interests. In this more private context, it is easier for Introverts to express themselves, opening them up to share with the group later on. Over time, when there is an atmosphere of mutual respect, the sharing may go to deeper levels, which can further strengthen interpersonal rapport.

2. Sensing–Intuition Dichotomy

Sensing (S)	Intuition (N)
Zooms in on practical details	Zooms out to the big picture
Likes a step-by-step system	Likes creative efficiency
Is precise with the facts	Envisions long-term possibilities
Clearly structures plans	Finds compromise and adapts plans

▸ People with a Sensing preference pay attention to the "here and now" and have a very practical orientation. They want to know how things work in the real world and what ideas are effective. In a group discussion they approach a task from this perspective, providing practical leadership. They tend to adopt a conservative approach, based on tried-and-true methods, grounded in proven results. On the flip side, this approach can make them resistant to innovation, doing things in new and different ways. If they don't see a clear, practical benefit from innovation, they find it irritating.

▸ Sensing types are capable time managers for a group, overseeing the time during a particular meeting or creating a timeline for a project. With their close attention to detail, they have a sharp awareness of how much time it takes to accomplish things and can assist the team in this regard, contributing to accurate task planning.

▸ Many Sensing types state that they enjoy working cooperatively in a group, but in a business-like manner. They will work diligently and systematically to accomplish team goals. They like to make sure the group is clear on the instructions before embarking on a task. They offer assistance in structuring the work, blocking it out in reasonable steps. They are clever in identifying the progression of activities and sub-steps that are necessary to accomplish larger goals.

▸ Being precise with details is a signature characteristic of people with a Sensing preference. They exhibit patience in examining the details, making sure things are exactly right. This makes them excellent with quality control for a team project. They can minutely assess if the work is in order or if there are defects that need correction.

▸ However, like Introverts, Sensing types can feel out of sync in a group. When teammates fire off a burst of ideas, skipping from thought to thought, they can find the experience disorienting. They prefer a slower, more deliberate approach. Intuitive types, who can move rapidly between abstract ideas, making spontaneous associations along the way, can lose Sensing types in the process. This can be a real source of tension in a group. Intuitive types need to slow down and spell things out in greater detail, in order for Sensing types to see the progression of ideas and stay in the discussion. Sensing types will certainly ask detailed questions about things they see as important in the enterprise. Intuitive types need to be patient and respect this process.

Intuition

> Because they like to look at the "big picture," people with a preference for Intuition can provide visionary leadership for a team. They can spot trends, future directions, and new opportunities as they survey the landscape in which the team is operating. They can readily envision future possibilities. Articulating these ideas to their teammates, they can be thought provoking, as well as inspirational. Bold and enthusiastic, they like to paint the canvas with big, sweeping strokes, trying to excite people's imaginations.

> People with an Intuition preference display a vivid interest in future possibilities. But as they express their vision, they must be sure to explain the steps in their reasoning, the ideas that led them to the vision, so others comprehend the logic behind their plan. This makes their case more compelling and it will help others to get on board with the strategy. Sharing the underlying reasoning is essential. Plus, this gives the team as a whole the basis for formulating the fine details of the plan, which will produce a stronger venture that all can buy into.

> When it comes to collaborating on a group project, many people with an Intuition preference express the philosophy that the obvious answer isn't always the best answer. Unlike their Sensing counterparts, they prefer an innovative approach that brings the spark of originality to the project. This

impulse is channeled advantageously when they bring their creativity to make the task effort more efficient. What innovations will save time, effort, or money? How can a better product be made? Insights from Intuitive members can be the basis for experiments that refine team performance and achieve stronger results.

> The Intuition type's ability to recognize connections among disparate ideas can impact negotiations, particularly the construction of win-win agreements. The win-win approach seeks accords that benefit all members. Such agreements build team unity and boost morale. Intuitive types have a knack for identifying the middle ground that brings together people's interests in this way. When they do, it makes people feel included, which can increase their commitment to the work. This is an area where Intuitive types can contribute to high team performance.

> As a group labors on a project, there are adjustments that can be made to the plan to improve performance. Intuitive types often notice where adjustments can be inserted, helping to strike an agreement to modify the plan. Such modifications along the way help to produce better outcomes. When Intuitive types pay attention to these opportunities, they can deploy their skills in a very productive manner.

> While people with Intuition bring creativity and vision to a team, they may also have a tendency to become rigid and defensive when others don't buy in. The boldness and the conviction that give them the courage to express new ideas can turn into stubbornness and hard headedness. This is when this type needs to use those negotiation skills to strike a compromise. If a compromise can't be reached, the individual needs to be careful not to become resentful and withdraw from the team; rather, he must calm down and continue to be a contributing member. As he well knows, there will be other opportunities in the future.

3. Thinking–Feeling Dichotomy

Thinking (T)	Feeling (F)
Focuses on problem solving	Shows concern for team atmosphere
Is logical in approach to the task	Pays attention to members' feelings
Is brief and concise when speaking	Enjoys sociable conversation
Gives objective feedback	Likes to show appreciation
Argues for point of view	Seeks to maintain team harmony

Thinking

- When participating in a group, many with a Thinking preference say they are motivated by a simple principle: you are in the group to contribute ideas. The mission is to share ideas, solve problems, and complete the task. As a result, these types want to stir up interest in a topic, so others will start thinking about it and express their viewpoints. The team can then move forward with problem solving. Thinking types take a lead role in attacking a task and getting it done.

- Thinking types like to consider others' views on a topic to understand why they think the way they do. They weigh the evidence that other people present in support of their positions. Towards this end, Thinking types will ask teammates to explain their reasoning. They wish to understand the logic behind their views and determine the strength of the logic. The goal is to find the best ideas and determine the best structure for the plan.

- People with a Thinking preference try to speak concisely, so that others can hear them clearly and comprehend their ideas. They like focused, precise communication, which is effective in the execution of a task. They usually disdain long-winded, repetitive talk. They also tend to dislike the social conversation that meanders off task. While social talk may be valuable for creating a constructive team atmosphere, Thinking types may appear impatient and brusque in response to it. However, when they learn that social talk can build team cohesion, ultimately resulting in better task outcomes, they become more tolerant and will participate to some degree.

- In the give-and-take of group debates, Thinking types can appear thick-skinned. They often express the attitude: if you reject my idea, it's okay, because you are simply rejecting some possibility, not me as a person. During the sharing of ideas, people often disagree, as they weigh the strengths and weaknesses of various points. In the potential combativeness of this exchange, Thinking types tend not to take it personally, and they do not worry about being accepted by other members. They prefer to be respected for their ideas and the objectivity of their analysis. They like to argue for their point of view, aiming to make the most persuasive case. In giving feedback to others, they seek to be objective, but sometimes can be too blunt in the process. In this regard, they can easily overlook the sensitivity of Feeling types, who can take these matters personally. This difference in perspective can cause tensions within a group.

- Many with a Thinking preference consider attention to feelings in a group to be counterproductive. They often say that feelings will only tell people why they want something and can obscure an objective analysis of the task. Focusing on feelings, in their opinion, clouds logical reasoning. Therefore, they can remain detached from the feeling currents in a group, seeming impersonal and distant. This can put them at odds with Feeling types, who value the emotional expression that builds interpersonal relations on a team. When Thinking types become aware that attention to feelings can benefit team productivity, motivating people to higher quality work, they can become more open in this regard. As they integrate an awareness of emotional issues, they can evolve into more versatile leaders.

Feeling

• While many with a Thinking preference believe that attention to feelings will limit a person's performance in a group, those with a Feeling preference tend to hold an opposite view. For them, sharing personal perspectives in a group (i.e., people's feelings, values, and individual stories) is critical for building interpersonal rapport. This is essential for developing a sense of camaraderie and establishing a team spirit. Therefore, they enjoy spending time with other members in social conversation, getting to know them better. For Feeling types, being in a group means building up social relations and nurturing a team spirit, which is necessary to foster a cohesive team effort and the resultant synergy.

• According to many with a Feeling preference, zeroing in on the positive feelings in the group generates positive energy for the task. When individuals demonstrate excitement for the work, it can energize others, reverberating throughout the entire team. Feeling types often say that when no enthusiasm is being expressed, they find it harder to function and get the job done. They feed off positive energy and like to stir up enthusiasm among the members. However, they need to be careful that they don't let their excitement distract them from looking at the details of a project in a thoughtful, systematic, and logical way.

• Feeling types like to express appreciation to other members for their contributions to the team. The intent is to support and encourage others, to increase teammates' self-esteem. This breeds positive feelings in the group. Feeling types see appreciation and praise as important reinforcement, strengthening people's social identities and motivating them to actively participate in the team.

• A large number of Feeling types express a keen awareness of what it is like to be an outsider in a group, to be an outcast. They personally know the pain of this situation, which leaves an indelible memory. Consequently, they are driven by a desire to prevent other members from feeling like outsiders, wanting them to feel that they belong. To accomplish this, many Feeling types will reach out to someone who has been emotionally bruised in a group debate, showing that person sympathy and trying to get that person back into the fold. With a demonstration of personal support, they seek to keep the other person from feeling greater isolation and potentially becoming alienated from the team. They may express this support in the actual group setting, but also in one-on-one conversations outside of the group. In this way, they work hard to maintain team harmony and keep everyone involved in a constructive fashion.

• Many Feeling types state that they pay close attention when other group members express emotions, so they can identify what people value and care about. With this information, Feeling types try to be cautious about what they say, to avoid hurting their teammates' feelings. Also, when others express passionate enthusiasms, Feeling types often take note and look for ways to help members harness those energies for the group, such as assigning roles or duties that enable people to channel their passions for the collective good.

4. Judging–Perceiving Dichotomy

Judging (J)	**Perceiving (P)**
Establishes goals	Collects information
Likes fixed plans	Likes flexible plans
Moves the task along	Wants to have fun doing the task
Focuses on results/ conclusion	Focuses on options/ adaptation

Judging

• In a group setting, people with a Judging attitude usually focus on several things: the planning process, decision making, and task implementation. They like to work in an organized fashion, often taking a leadership role in helping a group define the goals, structure the work, and execute the plan. They prefer a fixed plan and enjoy driving the plan to conclusion.

- While Judging types concentrate on steering tasks to completion, they need to resist the temptation to push work through too quickly, without sufficient participation from others. Fast-track execution without appropriate member participation can lead to sloppy outcomes. A team then needs to go back to clean up the mistakes, which takes more time in the long run. Being patient on the front end of a job, with proper analysis and member inclusion, is the better path to competent work.

- When they recognize these concerns, many Judging types have adjusted their style to be more proficient group facilitators. For these individuals, the following approach is preferred: seek input from other members on how to do the task, help structure a collective plan, and then guide the group in a direction that people find agreeable. Since a group involves a number of people, this is a sound approach to achieve quality results in an efficient way. It reflects an intelligent method of facilitation, one that every person can embrace to create a more realistic and thoughtful leadership style.

- One skill that Judging types often refine to be more capable group members is perspective taking. They pay attention to others' views in order to understand practical ideas that will aid the cause. They also gain insights into people's motivations for the project. Always, the goal is to delegate responsibilities to the right people who can complete the work in a superior manner. By paying closer attention to others' interests, Judging types can match the right person with the right role, making the venture more organized and more profitable.

- In general, Judging types take a serious approach to the task, cultivating a focused, reasonable, and thorough method for the work. They can become frustrated when other members do not share their dedication and seriousness. They need to be patient and flexible in these situations, finding ways to constructively engage wayward members without alienating them.

Perceiving

- Perceiving types like a group with an open, flexible approach to completing a task. They value a team that can work towards a goal but is free about how it might get there. They like to gather a lot of information and examine the task from multiple angles. They want to take their time to discuss a range of strategies. The learning that takes place in the exploration of ideas is just as important to them as reaching the final goal. For them, there is no need to be compulsive about getting to the objective. When you are compulsive, you put on blinders and may overlook valuable information.

- For many Perceiving types, a critical objective for group work is to have fun. Accordingly, they like to express humor during a meeting, keeping the mood light, upbeat. A heavily structured, overly serious group atmosphere can stifle them. They'd prefer to brainstorm, generate a lot of ideas, and enjoy the fruits of a creative process. In this regard, they may clash with Judging types who tend to have a more structured, solemn style.

- Because they like to be flexible, Perceiving types tend to keep an open mind about almost everything that goes on in a group. They are very adaptable. One significant application of their philosophy is a willingness to express acceptance when other members make mistakes during the group's collaboration. Sometimes, mistakes can mean a real setback, and the perpetrator feels embarrassed, dejected, and publically humbled. Often, a Perceiving type is the individual to express forgiveness within the group. This can produce healing for the team. Anyone can make a mistake, and in such a situation, it is crucial to show support and then move forward in a positive direction while learning from the error. In this stressful context, a Perceiving type can demonstrate leadership on the interpersonal level, refocusing the effort and restoring team unity.

- In a similar vein, many Perceiving types state that in a group context they are willing to acknowledge to teammates when they make a mistake. Instead of covering up the error, they prefer to be honest and admit it. They believe that such communication encourages adaptability in the team by identifying a mistake, correcting it, and learning from it. This prevents a group from going in a wrong direction for a prolonged period of time, unaware of a critical error. Honest, open communication is paramount if a team wants to flourish, and this approach supports healthy communication.

- The real nemesis of Perceiving types is group deadlines. Favoring an open-ended approach and wanting to be unrestrained by structure, they can have trouble finishing work on time. They can remain "in process" with the task, without their deliverables. To address this issue, many admit that it's worthwhile to have Judging types set up a timeline to meet deadlines, as long as it is negotiated up front, in a fair way, and allows for some flexibility during the journey.

The above descriptions provide central information about how people with different personality preferences tend to operate in small groups. All individuals bring certain skill sets to group events. They benefit by refining established skills and by adding new ones that broaden their approach and expand their capabilities. To take skill acquisition to the next level, people can employ the KGI materials along with their type information to stretch their social performance. Since the KGI model presents the best ideas on team leadership and group dynamics, it is the perfect vehicle to create a more flexible, powerful skill package for small groups. In the next chapter, the connection between the Klein Group Instrument and Myers-Briggs Type Indicator assessments is diagramed, serving as the foundation for an integrated approach to personal coaching and team building. ✖

CHAPTER 19

Klein Group Instrument® and
Myers-Briggs Type Indicator® Connections

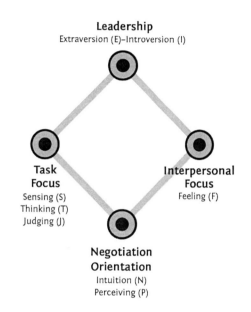

Leadership
Extraversion (E)–Introversion (I)

**Task
Focus**
Sensing (S)
Thinking (T)
Judging (J)

**Interpersonal
Focus**
Feeling (F)

**Negotiation
Orientation**
Intuition (N)
Perceiving (P)

The above diagram displays the primary relationships between the Klein Group Instrument major scales and Myers-Briggs Type Indicator psychological preferences. The diagram is drawn from a correlation study conducted with over a thousand people who took both measurements, as well as from qualitative research data compiled from four hundred participant interviews. The model illustrates the most relevant links between the instruments, which serve as a point of departure for counseling and training practices that will promote impressive leadership and social development.

For the KGI Leadership scale, the Extraversion–Introversion dichotomy has a clear association. Most notable is the connection with the Extraversion attitude, since people with this preference

are inclined to self-expression, action, and collaboration. They usually flourish in a small-group setting, where they articulate their ideas and step up to facilitate the event. However, for a leader to be most effective, a person should also be a good listener and a keen observer of the reactions and behaviors of other members. One must be able to listen as well as speak, and to observe as well as facilitate. Introverts have the disposition to listen and observe in groups, so they can pick the most comfortable spots to enter a discussion. This is an asset. An individual who establishes the right balance between Extraversion and Introversion can create the most influential leadership style, with the ability to voice ideas that connect with the concerns of other members.

Regarding the Task Focus scale, the preferences of Sensing, Thinking, and Judging have vital associations. People with a Sensing function like to bring a practical perspective to the task assignment, while Thinking types want to contribute problem-solving skills, and Judging types wish to share their knack for organization. The essential interests of each of these preferences converge in a natural way in a task undertaking.

For the Interpersonal Focus scale, the preference of Feeling has a distinct connection. People with this preference want to foster a positive emotional atmosphere on a team because constructive emotions motivate people to do their best work. They have a desire for warmth, affiliation, and harmony; as a result, they pay close attention to other members' feelings, usually responding with consideration and support.

With respect to Negotiation Orientation, individuals with a Perceiving attitude like to examine issues from a variety of angles, to consider a range of options. Consequently, they often invite others into a conversation to hear their opinions and expand the possible choices. This promotes perspective taking and inclusion. People with an Intuition preference utilize their ability to see connections between different ideas; they discern links among various members' interests and assist a team in finding win-win agreements. They can identify the middle ground that will unify a group in its collective effort.

As can be seen, there are compelling connections between the psychological preferences and the components of small-group life identified in the KGI system. People with different personality preferences instinctively concentrate on certain aspects of a group activity, and the Klein Group Instrument assessment brings these patterns into sharper focus. The KGI model enables people to add new skills in these favored areas, so they can expand and refine that participation. The model then encourages people to move on and develop their neglected group behaviors and their opposite personality preferences. Since the model shows how diverse group activities are integrated into a purposeful whole, it challenges individuals to acquire a broad array of skills that make them well-rounded players, providing a dynamic pathway for social development.

This is why the KGI–MBTI method can have such a transformational impact, opening people's eyes to group life in a new way and allowing them to adjust attitudes and behaviors in a more informed manner. They learn to employ existing preferences with greater precision, and they learn to build up neglected preferences and skills. This pattern of development connects directly to the individuation process of Carl Jung and the self-actualization model of Abraham Maslow, emphasizing thoughtful development that inspires people to grow in fulfilling directions; it also supports the expansion of social skills in ways that align with the ideas of Alfred Adler.

A clear example of how this works can be seen in the interplay of the KGI Task Focus and Interpersonal Focus scales and the MBTI Thinking–Feeling dichotomy. As mentioned in Chapter 2, the task and interpersonal sides of group life form opposite poles, representing opposite concerns. A person with a Thinking preference usually concentrates on the task side, while someone with a Feeling preference normally gravitates towards the interpersonal. Both have a commitment to their respective interests, and may even judge the other side as misguided. Thinking types may view Feeling types as fuzzy with analysis, too loose with the facts, while Feeling types may see Thinking types as cold and uncaring, not in touch with people issues. In both cases, it can be hard to appreciate the other side, let alone develop skills related to that perspective.

Our examination of group dynamics, however, makes it apparent that effective management of both the task and the interpersonal components is crucial for creating a high-performing team. A capable leader, or group member, needs to be alert and nurture both sides. Pointing out this fact gets the attention of Thinking types and Feeling types, prompting them to reevaluate their point of view. It helps them become aware of the narrowness of being one-sided in a group setting and challenges them to be open to the opposite preference, to build opposite skills which will give them greater versatility. By obtaining skills in both areas, they can become better group facilitators, responding more flexibly to task and interpersonal concerns, thereby stirring superior team performance. What proves additionally valuable is that when they make these adjustments to become stronger team leaders, the skills carry over into a range of other social interactions. They generalize the techniques and apply them in a variety of contexts, including intimate relationships, family life, and friendships, leading to more expansive social individuation.

During years of research with the KGI–MBTI training model, we observed a large number of people who increased their skills in exactly this way, acquiring a new vision of group dynamics and obtaining new skills that made them more ambidextrous leaders. As a result, they became more socially balanced individuals in teams and in other contexts as well; they constructed a refined social self that raised their self-confidence, self-esteem, and sense of self-efficacy.

In the next chapter, the methodology for applying this model in coaching and counseling sessions is explained. ✄

CHAPTER 20

Coaching and Counseling with the KGI® and MTBI® Assessments

Applied in tandem, the Klein Group Instrument and Myers-Briggs Type Indicator assessments provide a system that enables individuals to become accomplished team leaders and small-group members. The combination deepens self-understanding, the understanding of others, and the understanding of fundamental group dynamics, introducing a reflective practice that creates a polished social performance. The research demonstrates that people who acquire new skills in five KGI subscale areas can significantly

alter their group behavior, tapping more fully their potential for leadership and social connection. They can become impact players—people who not only elevate their own performance, but who raise the performance of those around them. This chapter outlines the procedure for working one-on-one with clients using this method, a system that professionals will be able to apply in a wide variety of contexts.

To begin, a summary of the steps in the process will be introduced to orient the reader, followed by a more detailed explanation of each item.

1. Arrange for the client to take the instruments. When the results are in hand, the consultation can proceed.

2. Begin with an overview of the goals of the KGI–MBTI training process, namely, the development of a range of new leadership and group skills that can be applied to a variety of group contexts.

3. Explain to the client the structure of the MBTI measurement, with the four dichotomies that contain eight preferences. The preferences reflect the ways that energy can move through the personality; explain the typical behaviors for the eight preferences. Mention the clarity index for each preference, with slight, moderate, clear, and very clear designations. Point out how the four scores are combined to create sixteen types.

4. Have the client read his or her individual MBTI profile. Do the results seem accurate to the client? Why or why not?

5. Inspect the clarity of preference for each dichotomy, determining if the client has a slight, moderate, clear, or very clear score.

6. Identify the highest score among the four scales, the one that is the most regularly used. This is often the most influential preference with respect to group behavior.

7. Present an overview of the KGI model, explaining the diamond design, the major scales and subscales, the composite graphs, and the feedback system with growth statements.

8. Have the client read through his or her KGI® Individual Profile. Do the scores seem accurate to the client? Why or why not?

9. Review the composite graphs on the last page.

10. How do the MBTI preferences express themselves in the KGI composite graph results? For example, the client has a clear Thinking preference and high scores in the KGI Task Analysis and Task Implementation subscales.

11. How does the strongest MBTI preference express itself in the KGI composite graph scores? How does it influence the direction of the client's group behavior?

12. Utilize the KGI Inter-Subscale Combinations (ISC) to expand the analysis and evaluate which subscales to focus on for skill building.

13. Identify the specific subscales for skill acquisition.

14. For the top two subscale choices, select appropriate behaviors to practice from the "Behaviors That May Help You Grow" in those sections of the KGI® Individual Profile.

15. What MBTI preferences, or opposite preferences, will be involved in this skill building effort?

16. Analyze the group settings where the client will be practicing the new skills. Based on these contexts, what adjustments to the skill-building strategies might be necessary?

17. Have the client practice two new skills for a number of weeks.

18. Review the skill practice with the client. What things went well? What didn't go well? What adjustments could improve performance? How was the experience

of building skills with an opposite preference or preferences?

19. What additional skills can be added to the practice?

20. Have the client continue the practice of new skills.

21. Repeat the skill-building procedure until five new skills have been gained across multiple subscales. (This can take a number of months.)

22. Reflect with the client on how the new skills can be applied in multiple group contexts, including family life and in the most personal one-on-one relationship.

Each of these points will now be examined in greater detail to describe the process more fully.

1. *Arrange for the client to take the instruments.*

   ▸ The Klein Group Instrument is administered through the Center for Applications of Psychological Type website (CAPT.org). The coach can set up a professional account and send the administration to the client, or have the client go online and take the assessment herself (see Chapter 7). If a coach is an MBTI-certified practitioner, that instrument can be administered personally. Alternatively, the client can take the instrument online.

2. *Begin with an overview of the goals of the KGI–MBTI training process, namely, the development of a range of new leadership and group skills.*

   ▸ The purpose is to execute a step-by-step process to expand the client's team leadership and group membership behaviors.

   ▸ The KGI model focuses on essential functions in small groups. Utilizing the KGI® Individual Profile, the client identifies and then practices specific techniques to improve performance in these aspects of group life.

   ▸ The MBTI instrument provides insights into one's personal psychology, which supports the development of the new behaviors. In this way, the two measurements are integrated in the method. The MBTI data also offer insights into the patterns of other people's group behavior, which is useful for facilitating any small group.

- The client will learn a reflective model of skill development that over time can lead to a very considerable increase in leadership and group expertise. The model can transform a person's entire approach to small-group life and to social relations in general.

3. *Explain to the client the structure of the MBTI measurement, with the four dichotomies that contain eight preferences. The preferences reflect the ways that energy can move through the personality; explain the typical behaviors for the eight preferences. Mention the clarity index for each preference, with slight, moderate, clear, and very clear designations. Point out how the four scores are combined to create sixteen types.*

- The Myers-Briggs Type Indicator instrument is a well-established psychological assessment, one with which the client may already be familiar. Ask if the client has taken the instrument before and, if so, does the client remember the basic elements of the model?

- Introduce (or reintroduce) the client to the MBTI system, explaining the four dichotomies

and the focus of each of the related preferences. It is beneficial to provide a client with the handout *Words to Help Understanding of Type Concepts* that contains descriptors for each of the eight preferences; this strengthens comprehension of the material. The handout is available from CAPT.

- Explain clarity of preference: how the clarity of one's preference reflects how regularly one tends to exercise that preference and how much one may access the opposite preference in the dichotomy. The clarity index goes from slight, to moderate, to clear, to very clear. A person with a slight preference is more likely to use both sides of the dichotomy at different times, fairly equally, while the more a person moves out the scale towards very clear, the more consistently the individual tends to utilize just that one preference.

- Explain how the four scale scores combine to define one's psychological type, with sixteen type possibilities: ESTJ, ESFJ, ENFJ, ENTJ, ESTP, ESFP, ENFP, ENTP, ISTJ, ISFJ, INFJ, INTJ, ISTP, ISFP, INFP, INTP.

There is a personality profile for each of these types.

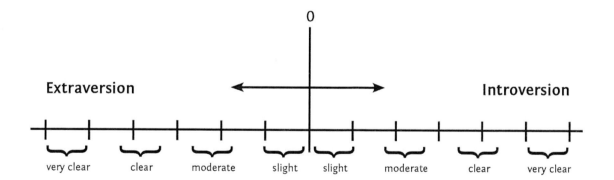

0

Extraversion ← → Introversion

very clear | clear | moderate | slight | slight | moderate | clear | very clear

4. *Have the client read his or her individual MBTI profile.*

- Have the client read through his or her personal MBTI results. Allow time for the client to reflect on the accuracy of the results. If the client has examined the personal MBTI results in advance of this session, then just proceed to the next point.

Do the results seem accurate to the client? Why or why not?

- If the client has taken the instrument before, how do the current results compare to previous results? Are they the same, or have there been changes? If there are changes, what factors, in the client's opinion, caused the differences? This part of the discussion can raise issues that will be relevant for later skill building. For example, a client with a preference for Introversion has already made efforts to be more expressive in groups, moving the individual in the direction of Extraversion. This indicates the client's willingness to try to build up an opposite preference.

▸ In general, the goal is to assess "goodness of fit," how precisely the MBTI descriptive material connects to the client's sense of how she tends to act. Many times, when a client doesn't believe that a particular scale score is correct, it's because the client indicated a "slight" preference in answering questions for that particular dichotomy, selecting behaviors related to both sides and therefore striking something of a balance. Reflect with the client on the contexts in which she likes to deploy the different, opposite behaviors. This will be useful information later when deciding strategies for new skill development, based on the client's established tendencies.

▸ When a client has a "slight" score for one, two, or more dichotomies, the client may feel that the type description is not accurate. In this case, it is worthwhile to present the handout *Descriptions of the Sixteen Types*. It contains short, one-paragraph descriptions of all sixteen types and is available from CAPT. For each "slight" score, have the client substitute the opposite preference letter from that dichotomy in the individual's four-letter type result and look at the description for this new outcome. Ask the client which of the two descriptions is most accurate. This offers a client the flexibility to examine and compare multiple descriptions. Whatever item(s) the client selects, discuss the factors that determined the choice. Again, this will be valuable information for constructing a grounded, accurate plan for skill development later on.

5. *Inspect the clarity of preference for each dichotomy, determining if the client has a slight, moderate, clear, or very clear score.*

▸ People with a moderate, clear, or very clear preference usually find the descriptive data more accurate, because they regularly act from the preference. However, it is worthwhile to ask if there are any ways the individual might act out of preference in a group setting because *there can always be some variations*, according to a person's particular background and experience. Understanding such variations can help the consultant customize the skill-building plan for the client. For people with a slight score, as previously noted, discuss the precise contexts where the preference applies.

6. *Identify the highest score among the four scales, the one that is the most regularly used. This is often the most influential preference with respect to group behavior.*

▸ The Myers-Briggs system provides a method to determine the dominant function among Sensing–Intuition and Thinking–Feeling preferences. However, our research suggests that among the eight preferences, the one with the highest clarity index often exerts a very important influence on group behavior. For example, if Introversion is the highest score, a person will tend to be reserved in most aspects of group life; or, if Judging is the highest score, the person is usually very active in organizing the group's efforts. The strongest score may well be from the Sensing-Intuition or Thinking–Feeling dichotomies. In any event, the score with the most regular usage often exerts a potent influence on group behavior. So it is worthwhile to discuss this issue with a client and assess how it plays out.

7. *Present an overview of the KGI model, explaining the diamond design, the major scales and subscales, the composite graphs, and the feedback system with growth statements.*

(To assist a consultant in preparing for this session, see Appendix: The Basic Script for Introducing the Klein Group Instrument Assessment.)

- Start by introducing the diamond design of the KGI model. Define the major scales and their interrelationships depicted around the diamond. Then describe the subscales of each major scale. The one-sentence descriptors for the subscales create a clear picture, and the information in the paragraph-long descriptions will fill out the concepts. (This information is found in Chapters 2 and 3.)
- Describe the sequence of information in a major scale section of the KGI® Individual Profile: the graph with a visual display of performance; the general statement about the person's pattern of action in that domain; and, for each of the subscales, the detailed information about strengths, areas of challenge, and behaviors that will help the client grow, i.e., growth statements. (This information is explained in Chapter 9.)
- Emphasize the pivotal role of the growth statements, since they guide practical skill development with the instrument. The individual profile contains 15-20 such statements.
- Mention the composite graphs at the end of the profile, which provide a visual summary of the client's overall performance. Explain how the Composite Major Scale Graph enables the client to identify the area that receives the greatest amount of personal energy and the one that receives the least. These represent two important benchmarks for assessing performance.
- Introduce the Individual Composite Subscale Graph, containing the sequence of all subscale scores. This graph provides a perfect tool to assess the client's group behavior, showing the levels of involvement in the skill domains. **It will be the centerpiece for interpreting the client's performance and making decisions on how to improve.**

8. Have the client read through his or her KGI® Individual Profile.

- The client may have received the personal report prior to this meeting and previously reviewed the results. If so, move on to the next step. If not, allow ample time for the client to examine, in a systematic manner, the information in the report.

Do the scores seem accurate to the client? Why or why not?

- As with the MBTI results, it is necessary to assess the "goodness of fit" of the KGI scores. From the client's point-of-view, how accurate are the scores? What are key strengths? Significant challenges?
- Ask the client to share the reasoning behind his or her evaluation. For scale scores that seem inaccurate, invite the client to share examples from recent group behavior (over the last several months) that demonstrate a different pattern of performance.
- For a subscale score that the client views as inaccurate, it can be worthwhile to integrate that domain into a skill building strategy in the near future. For example, if a person states that the Initiative score is lower than expected, create an opportunity, early on, to apply Initiative skills and assess how things proceed. This offers an opportunity for a realistic assessment of the skill area.

9. Review the composite graphs on the last page.

- It is time for a more comprehensive assessment of the client's behavior by examining the composite graphs at the conclusion of the profile. The levels of energy investment across the various domains can be evaluated.
- For the Individual Composite Major Scale Graph, what is the highest scale score, and what is the lowest? These indicate where the most and least amounts of energy are being invested and offer initial markers about how the client operates in groups. The highest reflects the area that naturally draws client interest and is the most comfortable area for participation. The lowest score attracts less interest. It may be an area that is somewhat or completely avoided. Invite the client to respond to this general assessment of his group behavior.
- For the Individual Composite Subscale Graph, what subscales fall in the High section? Medium? Low? What elements stand out for the client in this graph? What behaviors are

most comfortable? What are moderately comfortable? What are uncomfortable and, perhaps, neglected? (Information to assist the reader in assessing these elements is located in Chapter 10.)

10. *How do the MBTI preferences express themselves in the KGI composite graph results?*

▸ At this point, the influence of the psychological preferences on the client's group behavior is examined in detail. The diagram of the KGI diamond model and MBTI preferences introduced in Chapter 19 frames the discussion. Using that diagram as a reference, how do the client's MBTI preferences match up with the pattern of group behaviors indicated by the Individual Composite Subscale Graph?

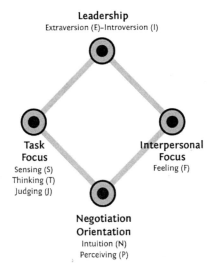

Leadership
Extraversion (E)–Introversion (I)

Task Focus
Sensing (S)
Thinking (T)
Judging (J)

Interpersonal Focus
Feeling (F)

Negotiation Orientation
Intuition (N)
Perceiving (P)

▸ When a client has moderate, clear, or very clear scores for certain preferences, they generally match up with the graph results as predicted by the KGI–MBTI diamond diagram. For example: a clear Thinking preference would tend to produce correspondingly high scores in Task Analysis and Task Implementation, but lower scores in Positive Group Affiliation and Feeling Orientation. A clear Feeling preference would tend to produce the opposite KGI results.

▸ If the moderate, clear, or very clear MBTI scores do not correspond to the KGI scores in appropriate ways, investigate the reasons for the discrepancy. Because of past experiences in groups, people may develop skills that involve their opposite preferences, and

they can become quite proficient and comfortable with the use of these skills. This can become apparent from the KGI results. This situation opens the door for a consultant to explore, in a very thoughtful way, how a client operates in groups, and what adaptations the client has made to broaden the skill base, working with a range of MBTI preferences.

▸ When a client has slight scores for particular MBTI preferences, it is much more likely that there will be perceived discrepancies with the predicted pattern in the KGI/MBTI diamond diagram. Since a client with a slight score tends to employ actions from both sides of the dichotomy, this tends to translate into similar skill diversity in groups. Again, this is an opportunity for a consultant to examine the client's thinking, motivations, and skill development in very specific ways as she examines the Individual Composite Subscale Graph.

▸ In discussing the KGI–MBTI connections, it is always important to identify where the client has utilized opposite preferences to gain group skills. For a person with a slight preference, this may happen rather easily. For someone with moderate, clear, or very clear preferences, the challenge is increasingly difficult. In any event, when someone uses opposite preferences, it expands the person's skill arsenal in critical ways. The KGI and MBTI models seek to direct people to build up their neglected group skills and opposite personality preferences to become multifaceted performers. When a client has achieved this in some previous circumstance, he will be able to build on this experience if he is made more conscious of the value of these actions.

11. *How does the clearest MBTI preference express itself in the KGI composite graph scores? How does it influence the direction of the client's group performance?*

▸ Target the MBTI preference with the highest clarity index score. Reflect with the client about how the energy in this preference is expressed in the composite graphs, affecting the major scales and their subscales. The strongest preference will often drive the group performance. Examine how this may be happening for the client. For example, a very clear Extraversion score can lead to high scores across the KGI Leadership section, especially in the Assertiveness subscale.

▸ Conversely, the preference opposite the clearest contains the least amount of energy, making it a much more challenging area to build skills. Ask the client about her or his reaction to working with this preference. What attitudes about this preference may hold the client back from using it? (For example, does the client see the employment of this preference as "a waste of time"?) Discuss the group situations in which it might be profitable. Examine points in Chapter 18: Psychological Type and Group Behavior to see some of the benefits for deploying it.

12. *Utilize the KGI Inter-Subscale Combinations to expand the analysis and evaluate which subscales to focus on for skill building.*

▸ Examine the client's subscale scores through the lens of the Inter-Subscale Combinations. Based on these relationships, what areas would be most advantageous to target for skill building? Reflect with the client on these options. (Complete information on the ISC system is found in Chapter 10.)

The Inter-Subscale Combinations are:

1. **Assertiveness** with **Perspective Taking**
   This pairing enables a person to strike a balance between speaking and listening, in order to cultivate a more competent leadership and membership style.

2. **Group Facilitation** with **Task Focus** and **Interpersonal Focus Subscales**
   This combination allows a client to refine group facilitation across the two primary dimensions of group life: task and interpersonal.

3. **Initiative** with **Negotiation Orientation**, **Task Focus**, and **Interpersonal Focus Subscales**

This sequence permits a participant to evolve into a vital team leader by integrating a battery of indispensable skills.

4. **Constructive Negotiation Approach** with **Positive Group Affiliation**
   This pair targets factors that spark synergy in a team, propelling a group to its highest level of performance.

5. **Task Analysis** with **Task Implementation**
   This set allows one to achieve a better balance between the complementary skills in a task enterprise, leading to higher quality outcomes.

6. **Positive Group Affiliation** with **Feeling Orientation**
   This combination enables a client to inspire team spirit through the effective management of emotional issues within the group.

13. ***Identify the specific subscale areas for skill building.***

▸ Select the most important subscales for skill development. Prioritize a list of five subscale areas for the skill-building agenda.

14. ***For the top two subscale choices, select appropriate behaviors to practice from the Behaviors That May Help You Grow sections of the KGI® Individual Profile.***

▸ For each of the two subscale domains, go into the profile and examine the *Behaviors That May Help You Grow* suggestions.

▸ Discuss with the client which of the growth statements would be most valuable to pursue.

▸ In selecting skills from a number of subscale areas, consider how these skills may blend together to expand performance in the most beneficial ways. For example, blending skills from the Task Focus and Interpersonal Focus subscales will increase flexibility in group facilitation, allowing a client to move more smoothly between the two to promote superior team performance.

15. ***Which MBTI preferences, or opposite preferences, will be involved in this skill building effort?***

▸ Evaluate with the client how the psychological energies from the MBTI system will be involved with the skill-building process. At times, it may mean the use of established preferences. Since the client is comfortable with these preferences, she may readily apply them. But the goal is to use the preferences with more conscious awareness. How can these energies be employed to best effect with the skill building? For instance, how can an Extravert channel that social energy in an even more capable way?

▸ Utilizing existing preferences in a more sophisticated manner does present issues. For example, an individual with a clear score for Thinking may need to throttle down a devotion to Task Analysis, which, if it gets carried away, can produce paralysis by analysis—prolonged analysis of a subject beyond what is needed. This can waste time and slow down the completion of the task so that the team has trouble meeting a deadline.

▸ When the client implements an opposite preference, there are a number of challenges to address. By definition, an opposite preference tends to be neglected by the client (to varying degrees). The person doesn't enjoy these actions and may outright avoid them. It is important to discuss the client's attitudes and feelings in this regard, to evaluate how much resistance may exist. A person with a clear preference for Introversion may feel a lot of anxiety about embracing Extraversion to work on KGI Assertiveness or Initiative. The individual may feel a great deal of hesitation. It's necessary to assess such issues in order to construct an appropriate strategy for skill development. When there is a lot of resistance, then a consultant needs to identify small, even very small, baby steps to get the client to take action. By taking small steps and starting to see some results, the client will gain confidence. Over time, the client will be open to taking larger strides. The experience of taking this approach can produce deep learning. Despite resistance and fear of failure, the client becomes aware that moving in small steps and with persistence garners results. The client begins to feel, "I can do it," which builds a whole new level of confidence and encourages a willingness to take on bigger challenges.

▸ It should be noted that this KGI–MBTI design has proven to be an excellent approach to get people to develop their opposite preferences. Given that people want to improve their social skills, the approach introduces clear applications connected to their opposite preferences, offering significant payoffs in leadership development. In KGI coaching situations Introverts have embraced Extraversion to become more productive leaders. Thinking types have embraced Feeling, and Feeling types have embraced Thinking to become better group facilitators. The system provides a very practical incentive that inspires people to work with opposite preferences in pursuit of social growth. In this practice, people gain valuable insights and experiences that are part of the individuation process. Not only do they acquire new skills for the here and now, but they also acquire a growth mindset that can have continuing benefit in their future development.

▸ When advising clients on the use of opposite preferences, several points should be addressed.

(1) Explain in a clear, logical way the benefit of this effort, concentrating on the acquisition of relevant group skills.

(2) Acknowledge the challenge of mastering the skills that have been previously neglected. It takes more determination to overcome previous resistance and hesitation.

(3) Devise reasonable steps for experimenting with opposite preferences. Taking small steps, particularly at the beginning, is the right way to go.

(4) Help the client to envision success. Too often, the development of opposite skills is burdened by negative thinking. Clients may dwell on personal inadequacies and expect weak or poor outcomes. Negative thinking can be a significant problem; it needs to be countered by positive thinking, positive self-talk, and hopeful expectations, which sustain

a desire to keep practicing. A person should envision the effective execution of the skill that will bring desired outcomes.

> *The importance of positive self-talk.* Too many people defeat themselves with negative self-talk, saying things like: "I can't really do this" "I am not good at this" or "What if I mess up and people think I am incompetent?" undermining conviction and effort.

In this enterprise, it is critical to create a positive self-talk mantra:

"I am going to jump in and try this new skill. I will take action and learn from it. Even if it is not exactly right the first time, I will make adjustments and get it right. It will be excellent to acquire this new skill."

KGI research has shown that people get *real traction with a new skill on the third attempt*. The first attempt may work decently, the second may go better, but the third attempt can be the charm. A person usually achieves much greater competence and self-confidence at that moment. This is an important concept for the client to understand, helping the individual to be patient and to persist—critical ingredients for self-improvement.

> *The importance of envisioning success.* For any individual, trying out new skills in areas that were previously neglected poses a real challenge. A person can be hampered by imagining feeble outcomes and bad reactions from others. Like negative self-talk, a creeping, negative vision will have a detrimental effect.

Clients need to create a constructive mental image: a vision of taking a positive action that will benefit the team. Other people will appreciate this contribution and will have positive reactions. The individual will become more effective socially, which will feel satisfying. Ask a client to envision these situations. It will strengthen motivation to apply the new skills, bearing in mind that many participants over the years have been very pleasantly surprised by the positive reactions from teammates in response to their efforts. Their experiences teach us about the value of having positive expectations.

16. *Analyze the group settings where the client will be practicing the new skills. Based on these contexts, what adjustments to the skill-building strategies might be in order?*

> Invite the client to explain the specific group contexts where he or she will practice the new skills. Is the individual working with a group of peers or in a group with bosses? What are the typical group assignments? What factors may inhibit or support the effort to acquire new skills? In response to these factors, how might the skill-building strategies be modified to increase the probability of success? What are the specific situations that will be most advantageous to try the new skills? Analyze the contexts and timing for attempting the skill(s), to fine-tune the strategies and increase the probability of success.

> Employ psychological typology with this analysis. What are the personality preferences of other group members? Are there a lot of Extraverts in the group? Or many Introverts? Are there many Sensing, Intuitive, Thinking, Feeling, Judging, or Perceiving types? If the distribution of type preferences in the group leans in a certain direction, how might this impact the client's strategy? What might be appropriate adjustments?

> In one-on-one encounters with other group members, the client wants to consider the potential type preferences of the colleague. Drawing on type knowledge, the client can make adjustments that will improve communication, developing a more precise approach. For example, with KGI Perspective Taking, being aware of how an ESTJ takes in information and makes decisions compared to an INFP will enable the client to make adjustments to enhance the practice of Perspective Taking. If the client can temporarily employ opposite preferences to strengthen communication in such an encounter, he will have employed a tremendous tool. As a client masters this way of assessing others and adjusting interpersonal strategies, the client becomes more flexible in dealing with a wide range of people, increasing his ability to influence and lead.

17. *Have the client practice two new skills for a number of weeks.*

> ‣ The client must now begin the practice of actual skills. **It is absolutely necessary to take action.** Only by practically applying the new strategies will the client make them his and integrate them into a long-term leadership pattern.

> ‣ There are a few things to do in final preparation for the practice. First, make sure the client has clear, practical steps in mind about what should be done. If he is venturing into very new territory (which is often the case), make sure the steps are reasonable. If a client tries to do too much too soon, it can become overwhelming. For example, a very reserved Introvert may practice Assertiveness by making one or two comments in a designated meeting; then see what transpires, and how it feels. If things go well, the client will gain a feeling of success, making it easier to expand the effort, building it up more over time. If things don't go so well, the client should make a suitable adjustment in strategy and try again.

> ‣ Second, remind the client that it is necessary to make at least **three attempts** with a new skill. The third attempt is often the tipping point. An initial attempt may only partially succeed, but with some adjustment, it may go much better. The goal of three attempts encourages persistence. Third, to further encourage persistence, suggest the client review his skill goals regularly and keep them in the forefront of his mind. By keeping goals before his eyes, the individual maintains a focus that makes him ready and able to practice, strengthening the effort.

18. *Review the skill practice with the client. What things went well? What didn't go well? What adjustments could improve performance? What was the experience of building skills with an opposite preference or preferences?*

> ‣ This is an opportunity to aid the client in establishing a reflective practice, one of the cornerstones of this method. A reflective practitioner assesses personal actions and refines them to become a more effective

player. As a client masters this approach over time, it opens up an ongoing growth process, helping her to realize systematically a greater portion of her potential.

> ‣ First, discuss with the client any successes with the skill building. Praise the effort. Ask what helped the attempt to succeed—attitude, effort, or adjustments in a particular context. Whatever contributed to success will be useful to revisit with future skill building.

> ‣ Second, evaluate where efforts may have fallen short. Why so? Importantly, what adjustments could be made to transform the situation into a success? Did the client make repeated efforts with the skill building, as previously suggested? Were there three attempts? Assess the client's approach. Reinforce the idea of repeated attempts and the refinement of practice.

> ‣ What did the client learn from his attempts to employ an opposite preference? What was the level of difficulty in working with the preference? What attitudes and actions helped the client press forward with the skill building? What insights did the client gain about developing this side of his personality? How did the client feel when successes occurred? What insights could make the practice easier next time? Certainly, as a client sees that an opposite preference can be used successfully in group contexts and be developed with persistence, this will build confidence, increasing motivation to work on other opposite preferences in the future.

19. *What additional skills can be added to the practice?*

> ‣ Review the original list of subscales selected for development. What new ones can be added for the next round? What new behaviors will balance, or expand, the initial skills from the first round? What MBTI preferences will be involved this time around? As before, discuss particular strategies based on the use of opposite preferences, and evaluate the group situations where the skills will be applied.

20. *Have the client continue the practice of new skills.*

- The client should apply the same approach as before, with consistent practice and adjustment of strategies along the way. The client should continue to apply the reflective practitioner method, promoting self-awareness and self-development, cultivating that growth mindset.

- In the first phase of the skill building with the KGI–MBTI method, the client may experience a surge, with an initial burst of effort and positive results. As time goes on, however, it can be easy to lapse back into old group habits. This is why a coaching process is so instrumental: the client has someone to report to, prompting the client to keep working to achieve positive results in order to share them with the coach. The consultant should pay attention to the elements that enable the client to succeed and reinforce them, while also helping the client to overcome challenges with flexible problem solving.

21. *Repeat the skill-building procedure for new skills across five subscale domains.*

- For optimal results, the consultant should direct a client in a skill-acquisition process that involves five different KGI subscales. That level of development produces a fluid leadership style, one that creates real versatility for managing diverse group events. It also challenges the client to acquire skills with several MBTI opposite preferences, broadening the client's personality. As noted in Chapter 5, a very significant transformation can take place. By attaining this level of skill expansion, a client can develop a new social identity, based on the ability to be a capable leader who interacts successfully with others. The client becomes well-equipped to manage a wide variety of small-group situations. As a result, the client's whole attitude about group life and social relations can change in a very positive way. The consultant is able to guide the client to a new point of view and a greater degree of self-confidence.

- The client also acquires a deeper appreciation for self-development. This method raises awareness about the opportunities for personal growth when one sets clear behavioral objectives, implements a reflective practice, and makes smart adjustments along the way. Through this process, a client attains a higher level of self-actualization and individuation. Since self-development should be a lifelong process, the client is now better equipped for this journey.

These points explain the method for coaching with the KGI and MBTI assessments, a model that can be utilized in business, sport, organizational, educational, professional, and religious settings—wherever people wish to expand their leadership and group skills. In the next chapter, case studies illustrate how this method was implemented in a number of these contexts. ✄

CHAPTER 21

Coaching Case Studies with the KGI® and MTBI® Assessments

The case studies presented in this chapter demonstrate how professionals have applied the KGI–MBTI model in real world settings, assisting clients in achieving positive results with their leadership development. The examples are drawn from the business world, the non-profit sector, and a university sport team, revealing how the approach can empower people in any circumstance.

Financial Services Director

Norman served as Director of Property Investment for a major financial services corporation. He participated in a steering committee with five other directors in his division, and he had eleven employees reporting directly to him. As he conceived it, his primary role was like that of a point guard on a basketball team—he needed to distribute the ball to the right people (give proper assignments to the right staff) in order to lead his team to victory.

His Myers-Briggs Type Indicator results revealed that he was an ESTJ, with a slight score for Extraversion, a slight score with Sensing, a moderate score with Thinking, and a moderate score with Judging. When asked to evaluate the results, he stated that they fit him well, but declared that the Thinking function was most influential, the one on which he most depended. With respect to the Klein Group Instrument, his strongest scores were Assertiveness and Perspective Taking, both in the high range. There

was a cluster of other subscales with medium scores that appeared ripe for development: Group Facilitation, Initiative, Task Analysis, Task Implementation, Positive Group Affiliation, and Feeling Orientation. Reviewing the results, he stated they reflected his pattern of group performance.

Though Assertiveness and Perspective Taking represented his strongest assets, the consultant felt that Norman could refine his approach with them. Assertiveness stood close to the mid-point in the High section, which could easily slip into overuse. A growth statement for that subscale advised a selective employment of the skill, counseling Norman to pick his spots for speaking up. This was a worthwhile adjustment to consider. One way to channel the energy, suggested the consultant, was to ask more questions in group discussions, as recommended by a growth statement in Perspective Taking. Combining Assertiveness with Perspective Taking in this way would assist Norman in obtaining a better understanding of the thinking processes of his direct reports. With this information, he could be more precise in assigning duties to his employees, matching the assignments more exactly with their interests, and thereby promoting higher performance. In addition, he would be able to balance his use of Extraversion and Introversion, establishing more equilibrium between speaking and listening. Given his slight score on the Extraversion scale, indicating a reasonable amount of Introverted energy at his disposal, this would be a prudent play, providing him with greater flexibility in using skills from both sides of the dichotomy. Norman appreciated the logic of this integrated strategy.

For the Group Facilitation subscale, the consultant thought Norman should link it to the Task Focus area. The idea of utilizing more probe questions would be a part of this process. Norman could use questioning to gather people's thoughts about task plans. He could also get members to bounce ideas off each other, so they could stretch their thinking about the strategies. Following a Group Facilitation growth statement, he could then help the group rank the best options to pursue. Noting Norman's Judging preference, the consultant advocated a strategy adopted by many with this preference: make sure you hear everyone's opinions first; then hash out the plan together (finding the middle ground) and check with everyone as you finalize the design, making sure all members are on board.

This strategy would inspire a systematic, thorough facilitation, and it could also improve his efforts with Task Analysis, which displayed a score in the middle of the Medium section. He could also use probing questions with Task Implementation, investigating people's ideas about adjustments that would strengthen the plan as they went along. Norman appreciated how this strategy perfected his facilitation skills, while allowing him to refine his dominant Thinking preference in the process.

Finally, for the first round of practice, there was the issue of Initiative, which drives the effort for leadership development. At the moment, Norman declared that he felt so overloaded with responsibilities it seemed he was working twenty-three hours a day. The consultant recognized his stress level and didn't want to ignore it. Still, there might be a small leadership opportunity that

would be appropriate. As the Initiative growth statement proposed, Norman should stay alert for a situation to put his best skills on display. The consultant declared that they could approach it with the psychological concept of "Flow" (Csikszentmihalyi 2002). Norman could be alert for a leadership opportunity that had great interest, a reasonable level of challenge and, crucially, a reasonable time commitment so it wouldn't burn him out. Also, they wanted something that would provide excellent visibility in the organization. With these guidelines in mind, Norman would, very judiciously, watch out for such an opportunity. In six weeks, he and the consultant would talk again and evaluate his progress.

At the next meeting, Norman reported a number of positive experiences. In general, he said he was more "mindful" in group contexts. He observed group interactions in a new way, more aware of his pattern of involvement and, also, the patterns of other members. He had gotten a grip on his Assertiveness, deploying it with more judgment. He now interjected more questions during meetings about the "whys" and "hows" of what people were doing with their tasks, becoming more rigorous with Task Analysis. He tried to encourage a forum for ideas, which, in turn, energized his own Thinking preference. He'd likewise used the questioning strategy with Task Implementation. For example, when a technology problem emerged on one project, he immediately posed a lot of questions, clarified key points, and helped the team brainstorm adjustments that got it back on track in a timely way. The team expressed satisfaction about the way he managed the situation. Norman declared that he not only employed Perspective Taking to greater advantage in formal meetings, he also employed it with greater effect informally. Walking down a hallway with a direct report after a meeting, he asked further questions to explore the employee's perspective. They were able to tweak the team strategy a bit more, right then and there.

With a smile on his face, Norman announced that he'd also found a way to build on the Initiative subscale. He had executed a ten-minute presentation for two hundred people about customer service, sporting the title: "Every Interaction Counts." When the chance appeared for the presentation, he recognized that it matched their criteria, so he grabbed it. For the assignment, he wrote a short statement that was clear, practical, and motivational. It challenged his communication skills, forcing him to sharpen his ideas into a distinctive message. The presentation had been a success. Afterwards, he had a stimulating discussion with the group of directors in his division about the points he'd made, opening up a thoughtful dialogue about customer service.

The consultant stated how impressed he was with Norman's efforts. The client had taken on various challenges and done superior work, particularly with his short presentation for the division, which met their tight specifications. He added that Norman had refined the use of his Thinking and Judging preferences in a very productive way. Norman answered that he enjoyed experimenting with new skills, loved seeing positive results, and looked forward to the next round.

The consultant suggested they examine the KGI Interpersonal Focus domain. He pointed out there was a special relationship among the subscales that would play to Norman's advantage: the Positive Group Affiliation subscale connected to the Constructive Negotiation Approach subscale. The two reverberated off one another; they were one of the Inter-Subscale Combinations in the KGI system. With a high score for Constructive Negotiation Approach, Norman already sought to obtain win-win agreements, something that lifted team morale. If he increased his efforts with Positive Group Affiliation, he would further enhance team spirit, making people even more disposed to pursue win-win. He could get a double benefit from this endeavor.

Norman liked the suggestion, especially the way that working on group affiliation would augment his established interest in win-win. The consultant then mentioned that Feeling Orientation should also be in the mix. Feelings in a group send signals, messages about when people are unhappy and when they are enthusiastic. Paying attention to feelings and addressing them promptly helps to keep a team on track. That would be critical part of this new strategy. As a growth statement in Feeling Orientation indicated, he could listen to people's feelings about issues and pay attention to their motivations. He could then tap these motiva-

tions to solve problems and to delegate task assignments. This would help Norman be the effective point guard that he had been talking about, but it would require the use of an opposite MBTI preference, Feeling. He needed to redirect some of his attention to watch out for emotional issues.

This new agenda, said the consultant, would enable Norman to round out his leadership skills in a substantial way. He would evolve into a much more flexible, ambidextrous leader. Norman said he would give it try. For the next six weeks, he would have the opportunity to practice.

When the two conversed again, Norman had impressive things to share. With his direct reports, he had introduced "team breaks" every couple of weeks. Members picked up a snack, walked outside together, and had a conversation. The goal was simply to talk, work related or not. Laughing, Norman said people now got to hear everyone's weekend plans. But by this means the participants became better acquainted, and everyone became more approachable. For Norman, the exchange deepened his awareness of his employees, expanding his understanding of their interests and concerns. As team spirit became stronger, office communication improved as information circulated more fluidly among members.

He then took it another step, asking the veteran members on the team to reach out more to the newer people. Since everyone was better acquainted, this became an easier proposition. He enlisted senior people to mentor rookies—to share knowledge, to help with problem solving, to extend any necessary support. This effort generated more camaraderie on the team. It also put in motion his plan to build more leadership skills in the group. During this phase, he informed subordinates about principles from the KGI system, giving them insights into group dynamics and leadership development.

Norman announced that he'd also taken an assignment to supervise a troubled team in his division, as another leadership initiative. The team had tumbled into dysfunction. Members were very competitive with each other, resentful of anyone's successes, and even sabotaged each other's efforts. Consequently, they had difficulty completing their assignments. When his superiors searched for a troubleshooter to manage the team, Norman stepped up, feeling grounded in his new knowledge of group dynamics. In their first meeting, he encountered a rigid group of people, a bunch of robots around a table just going through the motions.

He met one-on-one with each member. Applying Feeling Orientation skills, Norman paid attention to the feelings in the room. People felt slighted, disregarded, disrespected. Everyone had grievances. As he listened patiently, he realized that just his listening and personal attention seemed to bring some relief. Many negative emotions had been bottled up for some time; people were happy to vent and consider the situation with an outside party. As he listened and asked questions, he paid attention to any spark flying in a positive direction. He looked for some interest, some excitement, some ambition by which an individual might become engaged in a constructive way with the group. When he completed the sessions, he had harvested indispensable information about people's experiences and the group's history. Now the aim was to restore respect, collegiality and, over time, trust. It would not be easy but restoring these elements could return the team to healthy functioning.

At a subsequent team meeting, Norman shared a story about a troubled team he was on early in his career. Things got toxic: people wasted their time with infighting, and team meetings became something to dread. He hated it. He found that people enjoy work when teammates get along, when the group immerses itself in absorbing projects, and when people find satisfying ways to contribute. They all needed to bury the hatchets, restore mutual respect, and improve their communication. Most basically, people needed to talk to each other. He invited everyone to an informal social event after hours.

At the gathering, there was obvious social stiffness, but slowly, people started to loosen up. Norman cultivated his relationships with individual members. Through these associations, he encouraged people to move in more constructive directions, advising them to identify tasks that attracted them and to undertake those tasks. Sometimes he cited things that people had said in the interview sessions about their interests, urging them along those paths. Bit by bit, things improved. He observed firsthand how pivotal social relations are for a group. He recognized that reestablishing positive rapport can be a slow, deliberate process, but absolutely necessary for the restoration of a team.

Norman made remarkable strides in his leadership development. When he reflected with the consultant about their collaboration, he stated that their partnership had gotten his mental wheels turning, challenging him to think in new ways. The KGI model altered how he viewed group interactions, alerting him to important issues he'd previously neglected. The model taught him how to diversify his skills, how to apply different strategies at appropriate times, and how to be an effective leader in a wider array of contexts. What he loved was the broad application of the skills: in his direct reports' team, in the directors' team, and in the unsettled team. He felt more confident in any team, something that inspired him to take on the assignment with the disaffected group.

Regarding the MBTI skills, he had struck a better balance between Extraversion and Introversion, definitely improving his ability to respond to others in group settings. He utilized the Intuitive function to think creatively about how to apply new skills, and he refined the use of his Thinking function in the Task Focus domain. Significantly, he'd started employing his Feeling function with real benefit. This was the toughest challenge, but once he saw the value of the preference, he pushed forward. It turned out to be exactly the right item for working with that alienated team. Seeing the worth of Feeling for managing social relations, he would continue to refine it and round out his leadership performance. It taught him not to just drive a task forward, but to be a person, too, someone who pays attention to others' feelings.

Non-Profit Organization Junior Executive

Alicia was the Director of Community Relations for a regional office of a national non-profit organization. She also served as the Assistant Youth Director at her church. In her mid-thirties, her ambition was to nurture her leadership abilities, obtain additional skills, and climb to positions of higher authority, thereby advancing her career.

With her MBTI results, she had a moderate score for Introversion, a moderate result for Intuition, a moderate score for Feeling, and a clear result for Judging, making her an INFJ. She believed that the scores were accurate, but declared that the Judging preference remained her strongest quality. Whenever she took action, she always tried to be extremely organized, which was her most distinctive trait. With the KGI scores, she agreed that Assertiveness, Initiative, and Feeling Orientation were the weakest aspects of her performance, all landing in the low-Medium section of the graph. The other scores seemed correct, but she stated that she wished to polish her skills with Group Facilitation, Constructive Negotiation Approach, and Task Analysis, results that fell in the middle-to-high medium range.

Right away, Alicia spotlighted a basic challenge that she faced at work. With her potent Judging attitude, she was an excellent "closer," someone who completed tasks in a timely manner, always meeting deadlines. Once she acquired this reputation, coworkers tended to exploit her, dropping work on her at the last minute, knowing she'd stay up all night, if need be, to get it done. Given her preference for Feeling, she'd take on these late assignments to please people, having trouble saying "no." She'd throw herself into overdrive, finish the tasks, but then feel utterly exhausted afterwards. In addition, she felt stressed as she plowed through to completion, fearful about making mistakes with key information. She hated that, and she really wanted to change this pattern.

The consultant explained that the Assertiveness subscale could be a real asset in this situation. She needed to define appropriate boundaries with people, not just let them dump work on her at the last second. She needed to speak up for herself. A growth statement from this subscale talked about being able to raise issues and identify problems in a discussion. Alicia needed to clarify the problems it caused her when she took on these tardy assignments; she needed to be right up front with people. She didn't have to simply acquiesce. Certainly, there might be times, said the consultant, when it would be appropriate to take on such an assignment, but she needed to determine that. One thing that would help would be the application of an opposite preference, Thinking.

Stepping back from her desire to please, she should realistically assess: Is this feasible for me to do? How much time and effort will it take? How important is it? Assessing these points, she could determine the smart way to handle the request. She could also be honest about her needs in the situation, the need to not give up chunks of free time and physically wear herself out. While Alicia had to shift to an opposite preference, something that can be uncomfortable, it would be the appropriate way to evaluate the situation, define her rights, and get others to be more considerate.

The consultant said that utilizing another opposite preference, Sensing, would also be profitable. It would help her pay attention to details and slow down her activity. When she dashed to conclude the work, her Intuitive preference might be involved, with its drive to move hurriedly through a project. By being patient, by proceeding in an unhurried way, she could reduce some of the stress. She could pay attention to her body, take deep breaths, and try to relax. If she paced herself in a Sensing manner, she could better control the situation. The Sensing function also connected to a growth statement from Task Analysis, suggesting that she examine all of the available information in a more thorough way when she managed an assignment. So Alicia decided to consciously experiment with the Sensing and Thinking preferences for the next six weeks, at which point she would update the consultant on her progress.

When she reported back, Alicia announced that she was proud of herself: she'd become more self-aware, and she was "different." In dealing with colleagues, she set her boundaries on several occasions, turning down requests to hurriedly complete late work. She presented her case logically and diplomatically. The situations resolved themselves in a reasonable way, with the benefit that she didn't get trapped by a request. She stated that she felt more authentic and more confident in herself as a person. The consultant congratulated her on these successes.

The application of the Sensing and Thinking functions also paid off in another way. She had been placed in charge of a team that prepared the budgets for next year. Of course, this meant organizing a terrific amount of details. Recognizing the challenge, she shifted into her "Sensing zone," as she called it. She slowed down the pace and patiently sorted through the financial figures. At certain moments, she said that deploying this opposite preference was challenging, as she struggled to calm herself when she became edgy with this form of work. But she knew the importance of the task and stuck with it, piloting the project to a competent conclusion. Her persistence with this practice and seeing positive outcomes built up her confidence.

Then there was a new challenge. When her boss reviewed the budgets, she concluded that Alicia had made a substantial mistake. In the past, Alicia said, she would have been more intimidated, anxious about a confrontation with the boss. But she kept her poise at the meeting and patiently reviewed the documents. Sure enough, the boss had made the mistake! Alicia's information was correct. Consequently, everyone in the organization acquired a greater respect for her work. Alicia declared that this was so different from how she'd faced such challenges prior to the coaching. Before, she would've been more fearful, quick to doubt herself, knowing her tendency to fly over details. By consciously applying the Sensing and Thinking preferences, she had a greater faith that she had executed the task properly and that knowledge brought some relief. The resolution of the conflict showed her the value of these preferences.

Alicia noted that it wasn't just at work that things were different but also at home. Reducing the job pressures had allowed her to act differently with her husband. Previously, she'd walk into her house at the end of the day, burdened by irritations, and start venting to her husband to release the stress. She'd erupt with emotional outbursts. Now, being in a calmer place, she changed that practice. Arriving home, she started by asking her husband about his day, what things were on his mind, paying attention to his issues. Grateful for the consideration, he responded in kind. Together, they rebalanced their communication pattern, creating a healthier dialogue, correcting a problem that had been vexing them for quite a while.

At church, she coordinated the production of

a play for the youth group. Instead of taking on too much, as she often did, she reflected on how she could delegate responsibilities to orchestrate a real team effort. Thinking logically and practically, she considered who would be the best people to take on various assignments. She approached different parishioners about the matter. At a meeting, they organized the assignments, with people sewing costumes, constructing decorations, and assisting with rehearsals. As a growth statement from her Group Facilitation subscale suggested, she built relationships with members, assessing their various interests and talents, and drew on these to mobilize the effort. Following a very entertaining youth-group performance, everyone praised her organization of the event. Alicia was thrilled at the way her leadership skill building flowed into other aspects of her life, with her husband and with her religious community.

For the next round, Alicia announced the goal of establishing better rapport with her boss. After an analysis of the boss's patterns of behavior, the consultant and Alicia posited that Sarah was an ENFP. Both ladies shared preferences for Intuition and Feeling, a favorable overlap. The consultant suggested that Alicia employ a growth statement from Perspective Taking, targeting the use of questions to investigate the deeper levels of feeling and experience of her boss. She could also employ Feeling Orientation, to pay attention to Sarah's motivations and interests regarding future work assignments. With these particulars, Alicia could respond in an informed way to the boss's interests. She could look for opportunities to get involved in Sarah's plans in a win-win fashion, so both would benefit. The consultant added that Alicia should pay attention to ways she could step up and showcase her talents more broadly, integrating an Initiative subscale concept. As part of this practice, he noted that she should try to balance Extraversion with Introversion, blending her speaking and listening skills in a more harmonious manner. This could really enhance her leadership development. After six weeks, they would check back to see what had transpired.

At the next appointment, Alicia reported some exciting news. Her first item didn't relate directly to their established plan, but she felt compelled to share it. It turned out that she had been sent to a national conference in Atlanta. In a large ballroom, with a sea of people from across the country, administrators randomly assigned participants to each table. They then asked the audience to brainstorm ideas for innovative programs that would serve a range of needy populations. Her table contained a diverse mix of representatives from many states, all strangers to one another. Seizing the opportunity, Alicia asked if she could be the one to facilitate the activity and her tablemates consented. Following her Group Facilitation growth statements, she got everyone into the discussion, helping the group rank its strategies and best options. In the process, she praised members' efforts, emphasizing the "we" aspect of the collaboration. Later, when all tables submitted their results, the administrators announced that her table had done the best job, coming up with an expansive list of creative, practical ideas! Proud of their achievement, her teammates complimented her on her smooth facilitation style. As Alicia recounted this exhilarating experience, she beamed with pleasure. Her coach applauded the effort, saying that it was particularly impressive for an Introvert to step up and embrace such an opportunity.

Then Alicia addressed her sessions with her boss, Sarah. By asking questions and by listening closely to Sarah's opinions, Alicia got in tune with her vision. Alicia extended some of the ideas with imaginative suggestions and identified places where she could contribute. Sarah appreciated Alicia's creativity and enthusiasm. Later, Sarah rewarded her with a plum assignment: she would coordinate a major fundraiser for the region, a drive that would purchase school supplies for homeless and underprivileged children. Given her deep love of young people, Alicia had found exactly the right mission, a match for her Feeling values. But she declared that networking with such a sizable community, on so many levels, would require all of the Extraversion she could muster!

In this context, with such a worthwhile mission, replied the consultant, Alicia had a tremendous incentive to rise to the occasion—she would find the energy she needed. He added that ideas from the Constructive Negotiation Approach subscale would be an advantage in this enterprise. Constructing win-win proposals when she

reached out to various constituencies would increase their buy-in. She should keep that in mind. After a moment, she replied that generating a lot of publicity for their contributions would be one of the first points in a negotiation. Clever ideas had already started percolating in her mind. In another six weeks, they would check in to see how the project worked out.

At the next session, Alicia was delighted to explain what transpired. With her project group, they designed an inspiring media campaign for the fundraiser, entitled "Load the Bus." A big yellow school bus, with the campaign logo emblazoned on the side, traveled around the community, picking up actual school supplies and financial contributions from businesses and organizations. She'd signed up twenty-three companies, plus a range of professional groups and community agencies. Local newspapers and television stations covered the campaign, doing press shoots with the bus parked outside a company's office and the employees gathered around. The project ignited an enormous amount of goodwill, besides generating a busload of school materials for the children. The project had been an outstanding success. Along the way, she received wonderful feedback about her social networking, which made her more and more comfortable with the Extraversion preference.

Then she delivered the *coup de grace*. Her boss, Sarah, declared that over the recent months she'd seen such impressive development in her subordinate that Alicia had outgrown her job. Her current skill level surpassed the requirements of her present position. A committed mentor, Sarah said that she would assist Alicia in finding a higher-level position in their organization, or in another non-profit in the region. Sarah was now dedicating herself to helping Alicia reach her full potential.

Alicia felt ecstatic, having advanced towards her professional goals much sooner than she could have imagined. She expressed her appreciation for the KGI–MBTI model, which raised her awareness about how she was functioning, enlightened her about alternative strategies, and inspired her to expand her skills. The experience had given her a new self-confidence. As her confidence grew, she said that she had become more willing to challenge herself, to stretch her comfort zone, and to discover how much she could accomplish. The results amazed her. A key asset, she acknowledged, was an improved ability to listen to others, to absorb their concerns, and to respond to them thoughtfully. This was evident with Sarah, with her husband, and in Atlanta. Concentrating on her leadership development had been invaluable for her, enriching her life across the board.

University Football Team Captain

Malik was one of the defensive captains on the university football team, the leader of the cornerbacks' position group. Starting in the preseason, he began to meet with an executive coach to hone his leadership skills, so he would be better prepared to help the team achieve a winning season. With a major in Business Management, he also had an eye to the future; he envisioned using these skills later to establish a flourishing business career.

His MBTI score indicated he was an INTJ, with a slight preference for Introversion, a moderate result for Intuition, a moderate preference for Thinking, and a slight leaning towards Judging. According to Malik, these results seemed accurate, with Thinking being his foremost preference. Concerning his KGI results, his lowest score was for Assertiveness, in the low-Medium section. The highest was Task Analysis, soaring all the way to the top of the graph, seriously above the Task Implementation score, which hovered just above the line in the low-High section.

His Group Facilitation and Initiative results fell in solid areas, low-High and high-Medium, respectively. But the KGI® Individual Profile revealed an underlying challenge as a leader— Malik felt uncomfortable in the spotlight, concerned that people would negatively judge him. He acknowledged this was true, and it would be a challenge to overcome. He stated that all of the KGI areas just identified would be worthy of attention. He added that he also wanted to refine skills with Positive Group Affiliation and Feeling Orientation, which he believed could help him build greater cohesion with his position group.

A quiet, reserved man, Malik said he looked up to professional football players who were humble, not show-offs, and worked hard at their craft. He liked those who responded to adversity, who stepped up when things got tough. Regarding his own Assertiveness score, in the low-Medium zone, he said that when he came up with good ideas, ones that would help the team, he would express them. At those moments, he became assertive. It was agreed that this coaching process would provide him with many worthwhile ideas to share, with the aim that he would become a more confident communicator. One thing that would help him reduce his fear of being judged would be taking the time to really arrange in his mind what he wanted to say, and declaring it in a clear, focused, steady manner. With that approach, he could be more confident about his statements. His Introversion attitude would assist him with the reflection, but he needed to tap Extraversion to express himself more often and become increasingly comfortable in taking that risk.

In addition, he could combine Assertiveness with Perspective Taking, asking questions of his position players to gain a broader understanding of their thinking. For example, he could inquire about how they read offensive formations, and what adjustments they could make, as defensive players, to thwart certain plays. Also, they could refine their way of communicating in actual games, so they could adjust quickly when the opposition did something surprising. Given his strong score for Perspective Taking, he could employ that asset and introduce more questions, thereby boosting his Assertiveness.

In assessing game situations with teammates, his very high Task Analysis score could lead him to overanalyze various issues. He should watch out for an inclination to overuse the skill. It was suggested that he keep in mind Task Implementation, to keep the analysis connected with actual play execution. His group should discuss different techniques but practice them shortly thereafter and analyze what worked best to get the job done. This would strike a better balance in the task area and would be more efficient. Drawing on the Sensing function would help him maintain an immediate, realistic focus. If he facilitated the position group's efforts in this fashion, they could achieve better results.

Armed with these ideas, Malik began his application of new leadership skills. After several weeks, he returned to report on his progress. Right off, he announced that he had started asking more questions of all of his players, in warm ups, in practices, and in position group meetings. This propelled him into an active leadership role, talking to people, exchanging ideas, and helping the members consider how to coordinate their efforts. In position meetings, he consciously drew upon Extraversion energy, stepping briskly to the podium, keeping the discussion moving, and making sure every player participated in the conversation. He felt satisfaction about the way the quiet players were sharing points and being heard. He could see they were getting more comfortable with their teammates. When he asked people questions, he found he could process their ideas fairly easily, based on all of his experience, and could often impart helpful ideas. He also invited others to make suggestions. As a result, his facilitation of meetings had been going smoothly.

Also, during practices and actual games, his group refined their communication for executing defensive adjustments. When an opponent moved into a certain offensive formation, the players talked in coded terminology, making sure all defensive backs were alerted, then switching into appropriate positions. They made the terminology clear and easy to grasp, not ambiguous or confusing in any way. Their clever system helped them consistently carry out their assignments, which contributed to the team's winning the first three games of the season. Malik was pleased with the results they had been getting so far.

The leadership coach congratulated him on his successful efforts. He asked Malik what other factors might disrupt proper execution on the field. The captain replied that being nervous, feeling the pressure, and becoming uptight would inhibit performance. The coach suggested that he could employ Feeling Orientation to watch for body language signals, or ask questions about how players were feeling in order to monitor when stress was building up. He could then calm people down so they could maintain proper concentration. The aim was to stay in touch with his guys and keep everyone in a stable emotional state, which could, hopefully, reduce errors. Malik agreed that such tactics would be worthwhile. The coach also advised him to clearly praise people's strong play, or other efforts that showed commitment, such as dedication to hard physical conditioning. When a captain praises these efforts, it shows players that the leader is paying attention, aware of them, ready to support quality effort. That builds up their confidence and their feeling of connection to the group. Such gestures would foster the Positive Group Affiliation that Malik wanted to achieve.

Both the Feeling Orientation and Positive Group Affiliation actions, added the coach, required the use of the Feeling function, an opposite preference for Malik. For a person with a Thinking orientation, this presented a real challenge since feelings often went overlooked. But attention to feelings would be indispensable for expanding his skills.

Malik said he would give it a try. He acknowledged that he needed to get feelings more on his radar screen because he recognized they played an important role in football and in groups in general.

"Are there opportunities for you to praise and encourage other players, besides those who are in your position group?" asked the coach.

"With another captain, I lead all of the players in stretching before our joint weight lifting, which we call Team Lifts."

"There you go. When you're leading the stretching, you should watch for the people who are putting in a solid effort and speak up with a good word. Encourage players to be consistent and work hard. The more you practice giving praise, the more natural it will be for you."

"Okay," said Malik, "I'll go for it."

In a few weeks the captain of the cornerbacks returned to provide an update. The team had continued to win, sustaining an undefeated season, so a certain excitement charged the air.

Malik stated that he now watched people's emotional reactions more closely. He zeroed in on how players responded to different situations. If someone made an obvious error and started to show signs of getting down, with a drooping head and slumped shoulders, he made a point of going over and sharing a word of encouragement. Since a lot of his guys were quiet men, he really needed to observe their actions and read what was going on so he could respond appropriately. Likewise, he paid attention to their successes in making plays and was quick to voice praise. Through this process, he began to see more clearly in what situations, and in what formations, people performed their best. The goal was to put people in the right situations so they could succeed. He had started to get a better feel for that and communicated those thoughts to the coaches.

Malik also shared that he had become more active in speaking to all sorts of players during stretching and Team Lifts, trying to solicit a hearty effort from everyone. He was building rapport with more guys, which felt rewarding, and the team seemed to be growing closer as the weeks went by, maintaining their winning streak.

The leadership coach commended Malik on the excellent job he was doing. He asked him about his comfort level in adopting more Extraversion and Feeling in his leadership style, those opposite preferences. Was it getting easier, more comfortable for him?

Malik replied that it was getting more comfortable. At first, he had to push himself to take action, telling himself they were the right strategies, that it would help the team. He plunged ahead. Then he saw how the players responded to his actions, how they appreciated his encouragement and support. In turn, his position people, and the team as a whole, started playing even better. They were getting results. That really motivated him. Seeing they were on the right track, he kept following the instructions, and it became like second nature to take these actions. Now, when he saw someone pushing hard in calisthenics, he spoke up immediately with a compliment, not even thinking about it.

"That is how you integrate new skills into your regular leadership style," replied the coach. He told him to be aware of the process, so Malik could continue to build on it in the future. In a conscious way he could select and integrate other skills in this manner.

Then the coach asked Malik about any other issues he might be facing as they moved into the last phase of the season.

The captain said there was the issue of maintaining motivation with his third and fourth string position players. As deep back-ups, they didn't get

much, if any, playing time. The junior varsity games, where they did get a chance to play, were now over.

"In what ways," said the coach, "do you think you can mentor them? Keep them actively involved?"

After reflecting for a moment, Malik replied that he could share some things from his own experience. He could tell them about his first year with the team when an injury put him on the sideline, preventing him from showcasing his skills. What he found was that it was important to do the "mental reps," to study game film and rehearse in his mind making the right plays. He did the same thing on the sideline as he watched other players. By displaying dedication in these ways, he had demonstrated to the coaches and teammates that he was "mentally in the game," that he was continuing to learn despite the physical limitation. Malik said he could encourage his men to do the same thing, to cultivate that work ethic. He recognized now that was part of what had landed him in the captain's role later in his career.

The coach said this was an intelligent approach. In fact, as opportunities arose on the sideline in coming weeks, Malik could actively prompt his men to think in these ways, giving them pointers to reinforce them.

Malik nodded in agreement.

Finally, the coach pointed out the need for the captains on offense and defense to spend some extra time with players from the opposite side of the ball to deepen team unity. If they fashioned a truly cohesive squad, it would give everyone the best chance for an undefeated season. Without batting an eye, Malik said he would do his part. Since he had already done some of that outreach while leading the stretching before Team Lifts, he felt comfortable stepping up to execute that plan.

The team completed an undefeated season, winning the conference championship, as Malik made some outstanding contributions on the field. He had a couple of key interceptions, and he coordinated his backfield people in an astute and savvy way. Even more, he built such a rapport with so many players that he became an influential leader. He facilitated position meetings, led conditioning events, and spent time on the sideline with players from every aspect of the team—not just his skill group or other defensive players, but with offensive players as well. He imparted thoughtful insights and sometimes injected a little humor to keep his teammates loose. Just like the professional players he admired, he did it in a low-key, non-flashy way, steadily perfecting the craft of leadership. In the end, whenever you mentioned his name to any of the other captains, they spoke glowingly about Malik's contributions to the championship season. They said that he really stretched himself in every way to help the team secure victory.

These cases exhibit some of the ways that the KGI–MBTI method can elevate people's leadership performance, propelling them to new levels of success. The three studies reflect an experience that many have had with this method. In the next chapter, a series of composite subscales graphs, with talking points for people with different personality types, will assist professionals in applying this system with their own clientele, so those individuals can obtain similar rewarding outcomes. ✕

CHAPTER 22

KGI® and MTBI® Individual Graphs with Talking Points

With practice, professionals can master the techniques for interpreting the Klein Group Instrument and Myers-Briggs Type Indicator results. The model's straightforward structure makes the task easier than with many other instruments and approaches. Employing the KGI Individual Composite Subscale Graph and the clarity indexes for the MBTI preferences, a coach and client examine the patterns of group activity. They select subscales to address and choose growth statements that identify behaviors to practice.

How will the client draw on existing preferences in the enterprise? Will it require the use of opposite preferences? Or, as is often the case, some combination of both? How can the psychological energies of the preferences be best channeled for skill development? As a client develops a battery of new skills, including the use of underdeveloped opposite preferences, substantial growth takes place. When a client acquires skills in five different KGI subscale domains, a remarkable transformation can occur, related to leadership performance and overall social behavior. Along the way, the client's self-esteem and self-confidence increase, strengthening the growth process.

To aid professionals in the application of the model, thirty-two cases are provided in this chapter, with KGI and MBTI results, and five talking points to guide an analysis. For each of the sixteen MBTI types, there are two cases, displaying distinct differences, which highlight the individuality of

each person within this framework. While two people may possess the same type score, they can operate very differently in groups, based on their past experiences and social development. This is precisely what KGI data depict—the uniqueness of each person's pattern of group behavior. A consultant can then customize an intervention to meet the exact needs of the client. The pattern of skill development will have a unique fingerprint.

The examples offer insights into the interpretive method, which includes the use of Inter-Subscale Combinations. These examples present points that professionals can employ with their clients. Matching their clients' results with those of the case studies, they can adapt a range of ideas for their clients' situations. As they experiment with the method, they will gain greater competence and become more artful, mastering a process that produces multiskilled, highly capable leaders and group members.

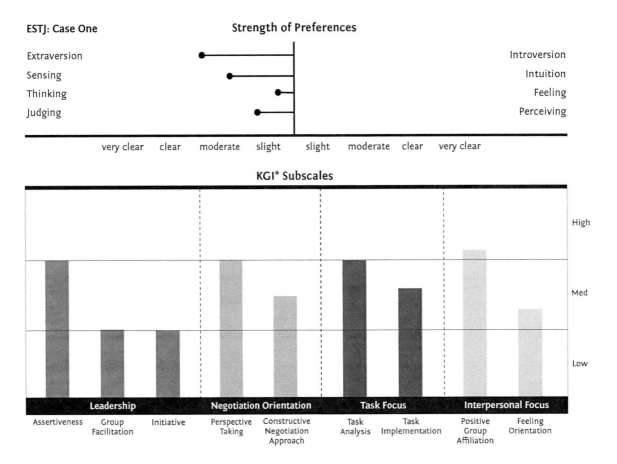

ESTJ: Case One

Strength of Preferences

	very clear	clear	moderate	slight	slight	moderate	clear	very clear	
Extraversion									Introversion
Sensing									Intuition
Thinking									Feeling
Judging									Perceiving

KGI® Subscales

Leadership			Negotiation Orientation		Task Focus		Interpersonal Focus	
Assertiveness	Group Facilitation	Initiative	Perspective Taking	Constructive Negotiation Approach	Task Analysis	Task Implementation	Positive Group Affiliation	Feeling Orientation

Note: The feedback points are designed as if a consultant is speaking directly to a client.

1. **Task Analysis with Task Implementation:** Invest more energy in Task Implementation. Concentrate on moving the work along, assisting the team in making adjustments to get the best results. Given the higher Task Analysis score, there may be a tendency to overanalyze a task. Be alert to this and take action sooner. Bring the Judging preference to bear in organizing the action, the Thinking function for making key adjustments, and Sensing for monitoring the details.

2. **Constructive Negotiation Approach:** With the information you gather through Perspective Taking, scrutinize the data for win-win options that will bring some benefit to every member. Such agreements help to cement team unity. Exercise the Perceiving attitude to look at a broad range of issues, and the Intuitive function to scan for connections between different people's interests.

3. **Positive Group Affiliation with Feeling Orientation:** Observe people's responses during group discussions, noting their positive and negative reactions. The positive energy can be directed towards appropriate work assignments; negative energy needs to be addressed before it disrupts the team. Exercise the Introversion attitude and Sensing function to observe closely what is going on, and the Feeling function to manage the emotional currents. The constructive management of emotions supports the maintenance of a positive team spirit.

4. **Group Facilitation:** Step up and invite other members into the discussion. Get everyone contributing ideas on negotiation, task, and interpersonal issues. Be the straw that stirs the drink. Employ Extraversion and Perceiving to engage others and gather a range of ideas, Thinking to help set priorities, and Judging to organize the effort.

5. **Initiative:** Seize an opportunity to be a point person for your team. Select a project that is meaningful for you. Make the commitment to develop rapport with other members and to create a unified group effort. Cultivate the Feeling preference to sustain interpersonal rapport, and call in the Thinking and Judging preferences to navigate task issues.

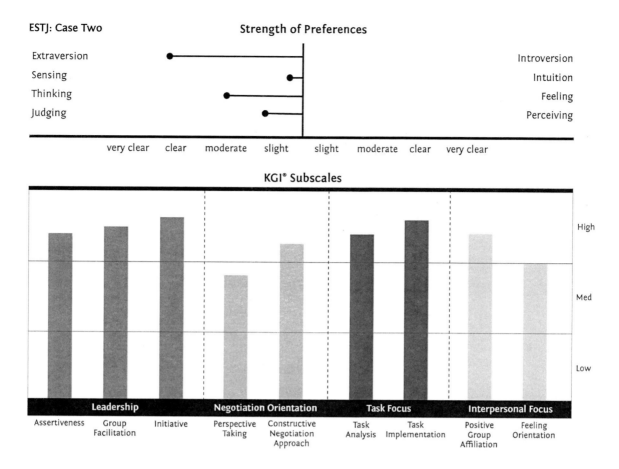

ESTJ: Case Two

Strength of Preferences

	very clear	clear	moderate	slight	slight	moderate	clear	very clear	
Extraversion		●							Introversion
Sensing				●					Intuition
Thinking			●						Feeling
Judging				●					Perceiving

KGI® Subscales

Leadership			Negotiation Orientation		Task Focus		Interpersonal Focus	
Assertiveness	Group Facilitation	Initiative	Perspective Taking	Constructive Negotiation Approach	Task Analysis	Task Implementation	Positive Group Affiliation	Feeling Orientation

1. **Assertiveness with Perspective Taking:** Investigate others' positions more thoroughly. Ask questions, assuming that you need to know more about their interests, perspectives, and concerns. Listen closely to what they say, and put yourself in their shoes to understand where they are coming from. This will provide substantial information for constructing win-win agreements in the group. Draw on Introversion to listen carefully and Feeling to experience the values that inform their positions.

2. **Feeling Orientation:** Scan members' expressions and body language to observe their emotional reactions to what's happening in the group. If people show signs of disinterest or withdrawing from the group, investigate their motivations. Try to get them back into the fold. Apply the Introversion attitude and Sensing function to observe the reactions, and the Feeling function to assess the emotions and then respond accordingly.

3. **Initiative:** Be more discriminating in assuming leadership roles. The score indicates you may take on too much, which may result in overload and burn out. Don't spread yourself too thin, which will reduce the quality of your work. Choose the most significant assignments that give you the most benefit for the effort. Cultivate your Thinking and Intuition preferences to identify the best options. Utilize Introversion to consider the most valuable path for you personally.

4. **Group Facilitation:** When you facilitate, make sure everyone is involved, especially people who may tend to be more reserved. Encourage people to get better acquainted in order to build more team cohesiveness. Take advantage of your Extraversion attitude to orchestrate broad interaction; the Perceiving attitude can assist with this process, too. Bring in the Intuition function to consider innovative ways to organize group activities that will stimulate deep thinking about the issues.

5. **Constructive Negotiation Approach with Positive Group Affiliation:** These two subscales are interconnected. As a team constructs win-win agreements, it boosts team spirit, and as morale rises, it produces greater incentive to seek win-win. Your scores for these subscales are strong, but developing more skills with Intuition will help you strike win-win accords, and utilization of the Feeling preference can enrich your efforts to build team spirit.

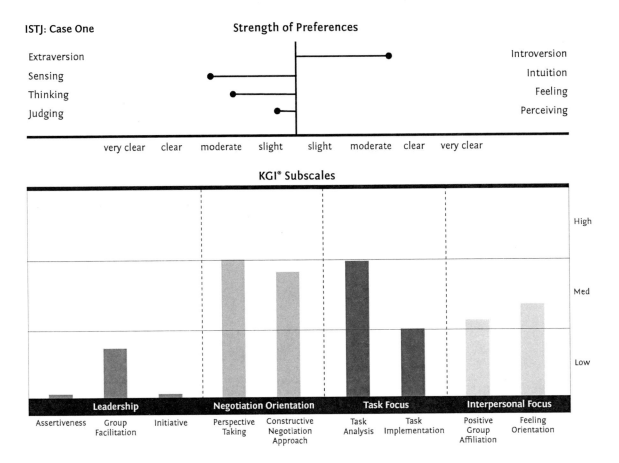

Strength of Preferences

	very clear	clear	moderate	slight	slight	moderate	clear	very clear	
Extraversion									Introversion
Sensing									Intuition
Thinking									Feeling
Judging									Perceiving

KGI® Subscales

Leadership — Assertiveness, Group Facilitation, Initiative
Negotiation Orientation — Perspective Taking, Constructive Negotiation Approach
Task Focus — Task Analysis, Task Implementation
Interpersonal Focus — Positive Group Affiliation, Feeling Orientation

1. **Assertiveness:** Jump into the conversation more often, particularly during negotiations and task analyses, your strength areas. Share your best ideas. Other members will appreciate your worthwhile contributions. Employ the Extraversion attitude to be more conversational, and the Thinking function to share practical ideas.

2. **Group Facilitation and Negotiation Orientation:** Become more involved in helping the team strike win-win agreements during negotiations. Invite people to share perspectives on issues, and bring together their different interests into a coherent design. Utilize Extraversion to take on a leadership role, Perceiving to hear from a range of people, and Intuition to put the pieces together for a win-win approach.

3. **Task Analysis with Task Implementation:** Become more involved with putting the task plan into operation. Take on specific responsibilities related to your interests and talent sets. Communicate regularly with other members, seeking ways to make the process more efficient. Based on your Task Analysis score, you lean in the analytic direction, perhaps too much. Balance your analysis with increased engagement in the implementation phase. Exercise skills with Sensing to pay attention to the details, with Thinking to make tactical refinements, and with Judging to bring the work to successful closure.

4. **Positive Group Affiliation:** Take time to talk to, and get to know, other members. This will add depth to your Perspective Taking, enabling you to better understand people's views, and it will help you to build bonds that will make you feel a part of the team. Expend Extraversion energy to reach out, and Feeling energy to establish interpersonal connections.

5. **Initiative:** Search for an opportunity to lead the team in a small project, or part of a project. Be willing to dive in and take on the responsibility. Direct the team in constructive ways—inviting everyone to participate, brokering win-win agreements, and guiding task execution to a solid outcome. Draw on Extraversion to take the helm, Intuition to construct joint accords, and Judging to guide the project to its destination.

ISTJ: Case Two

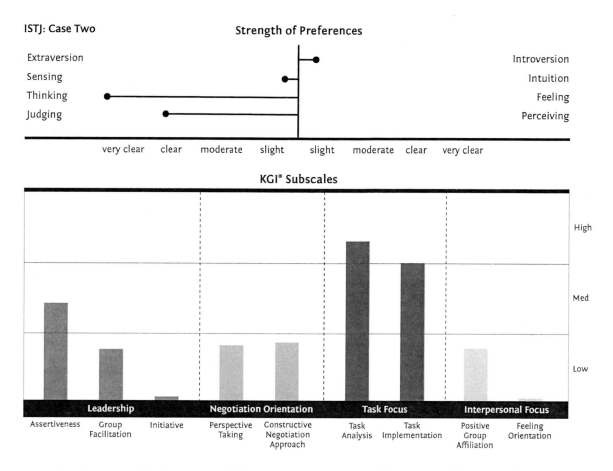

Strength of Preferences

	very clear	clear	moderate	slight	slight	moderate	clear	very clear	
Extraversion					●				Introversion
Sensing				●					Intuition
Thinking	●								Feeling
Judging		●							Perceiving

KGI® Subscales

Leadership: Assertiveness, Group Facilitation, Initiative

Negotiation Orientation: Perspective Taking, Constructive Negotiation Approach

Task Focus: Task Analysis, Task Implementation

Interpersonal Focus: Positive Group Affiliation, Feeling Orientation

1. **Assertiveness with Perspective Taking:** Increase your participation by asking questions of other members to assess their ideas, interests, and values. Share your ideas and concerns, too. Practice the Extraversion attitude to pursue a more active role, the Perceiving attitude to look at a range of perspectives, and Thinking to express your ideas.

2. **Group Facilitation with Task Focus:** There is an excellent opportunity to rise up in a leadership role by facilitating the task effort. Bring others into the discussion and examine the task enterprise in detail. Employ the Extraversion attitude to be more vocal, and the Thinking and Judging preferences to get the work done in a most competent way.

3. **Feeling Orientation:** Study other members' facial expressions and body language to assess their reactions, positive and negative. Paying close attention to these reactions will strengthen your Perspective Taking, enabling you to engage others more thoughtfully. Use Introversion to hone your observation skills, Sensing to notice physical details, and the Feeling function to consider the emotional content.

4. **Positive Group Affiliation:** Take the time to become better acquainted with other team members. Talk to them in various situations. As you build rapport, communication will become easier when you collaborate on tasks. Employ Extraversion to reach out to others, and the Feeling function to develop relationships.

5. **Initiative:** Take a leadership role with a project, or part of a project—one that interests you. Invite participation from other members. Look for the mutual ground where members' concerns come together. Use Extraversion to be more vocal, Intuition to find the connections between different people's positions, Thinking to guide the task, and Judging to direct the efforts to positive conclusions.

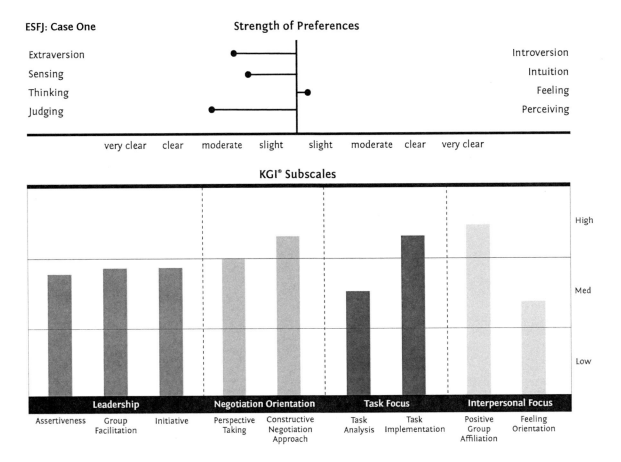

Strength of Preferences

Extraversion							Introversion
Sensing							Intuition
Thinking							Feeling
Judging							Perceiving

very clear　clear　moderate　slight　slight　moderate　clear　very clear

KGI® Subscales

Leadership			Negotiation Orientation		Task Focus		Interpersonal Focus	
Assertiveness	Group Facilitation	Initiative	Perspective Taking	Constructive Negotiation Approach	Task Analysis	Task Implementation	Positive Group Affiliation	Feeling Orientation

1. **Assertiveness and Feeling Orientation:** Express your feelings and values about the issues under discussion. Let people know where you stand and what things excite you, what part of the work you most want to be involved in. Use your Extraversion preference to speak up and your Feeling preference to provide the content.

2. **Group Facilitation and Negotiation Orientation:** Ask questions to better understand group members' concerns regarding the task. With Perspective Taking, listen for their underlying interests. Identify key points to help find the middle ground for win-win agreements, using Constructive Negotiation Approach. Employ Introversion to listen closely and Intuition to discover the middle ground.

3. **Task Analysis with Task Implementation:** Be careful about a tendency to push forward with Task Implementation before there is enough forethought and planning. Your Judging function may be prompting you to move forward too quickly.

Be patient. Invite other members to share their strategies about how to design the task plan. Help the team fashion the best overall strategy. Draw on Perceiving to look at a variety of options, and the Thinking preference to consider the best data. Then use your Judging preference to move into strong action.

4. **Positive Group Affiliation:** Take an active role in establishing a team spirit. Reach out to other members and build constructive relationships. In team meetings, promote positive communication and mutual respect. Be a role model. Employ your Extraversion and Feeling preferences in these practices.

5. **Initiative:** Identify a group project where you can take the lead role, putting the other new skills into practice. Make sure to keep others involved. Apply Extraversion to step up, Feeling to stay connected to people, Thinking to coordinate the task, and Judging for overall organization.

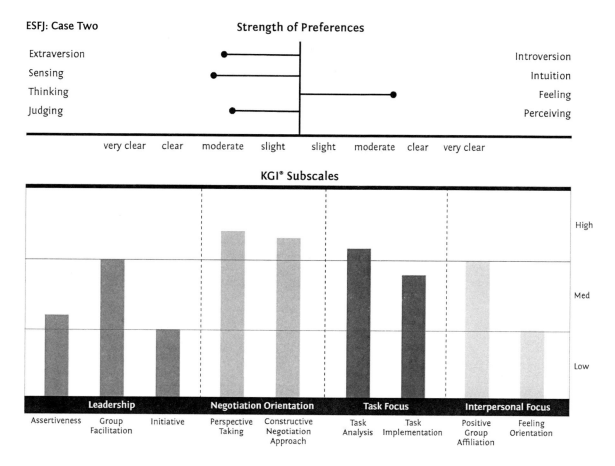

ESFJ: Case Two

Strength of Preferences

	very clear	clear	moderate	slight		slight	moderate	clear	very clear
Extraversion									Introversion
Sensing									Intuition
Thinking									Feeling
Judging									Perceiving

KGI® Subscales

Leadership — Assertiveness, Group Facilitation, Initiative

Negotiation Orientation — Perspective Taking, Constructive Negotiation Approach

Task Focus — Task Analysis, Task Implementation

Interpersonal Focus — Positive Group Affiliation, Feeling Orientation

1. **Assertiveness with Perspective Taking:** Speak up and share your opinions. You are listening to others to understand their positions—express your reactions to what you are hearing. Present your perspective so others know where you stand. Employ your Extraversion attitude to make your voice heard, and the Thinking preference to articulate your ideas in a clear, direct, accessible way.

2. **Task Analysis with Task Implementation:** The results indicate that you lean more in the direction of analysis. Build up your performance in Task Implementation. As the team executes its strategy, help the group monitor the effort and move the work along. Apply the Sensing function to watch the details, the Thinking function to evaluate performance, and the Judging attitude to keep things well organized.

3. **Positive Group Affiliation with Feeling Orientation:** Results show substantial attention to team spirit, but there's a need for more awareness with Feeling Orientation. This can enhance efforts in Positive Group Affiliation. Listen and watch for what inspires people; also, note what turns them off. Help people pursue their enthusiasms, and address problems when they arise. This will sustain

a positive atmosphere that fosters high productivity. Utilize the Introversion attitude to listen and observe, and the Feeling function to respond to other members in a considerate, personal way.

4. **Group Facilitation and Negotiation Orientation:** The negotiation scores demonstrate strength. But performance can be augmented by use of the Perceiving function to look at a broader array of member concerns, and the Intuitive function to consider more connections among these concerns to strike win-win agreements. If you employ these preferences more consciously, your facilitation of negotiations can be even more effective.

5. **Initiative:** Assume a key leadership role for a team project. Employ your skills in negotiation to facilitate win-win agreements that build team cohesion. Engage everyone in the task enterprise, delegating assignments, wherever possible, based on people's interests and enthusiasms. Employ the Intuitive and Perceiving preferences to design win-win agreements, the Feeling function to maintain positive morale, and the Thinking function to manage the task in a logical way.

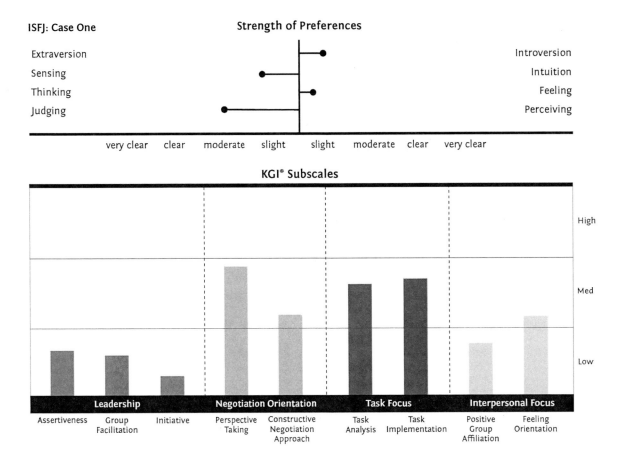

Strength of Preferences

	very clear	clear	moderate	slight	slight	moderate	clear	very clear	
Extraversion									Introversion
Sensing									Intuition
Thinking									Feeling
Judging									Perceiving

KGI® Subscales

Leadership — Assertiveness, Group Facilitation, Initiative
Negotiation Orientation — Perspective Taking, Constructive Negotiation Approach
Task Focus — Task Analysis, Task Implementation
Interpersonal Focus — Positive Group Affiliation, Feeling Orientation

1. **Assertiveness with Perspective Taking:** You pay attention to others' concerns in the group, but you should state your ideas more frequently in discussions. Explain your positions on various issues. With perceptions you gain from PT, reply to others' concerns. Work with Extraversion to jump into the conversation and the Sensing function to explain your positions in detail.

2. **Group Facilitation with Task Focus:** Become active in helping the group advance the task effort. Present your ideas about task strategies and invite others to do the same. Help select the best approach. Stay involved during implementation to assist the group in achieving high quality outcomes. Exercise Extraversion to become more involved, Thinking to evaluate the task, and Judging to help organize the undertaking.

3. **Constructive Negotiation Approach:** Exploit your insights from Perspective Taking to formulate mutually beneficial agreements for the group.

Assess where different member concerns overlap, so joint accords can be struck. Polish your Feeling function by tuning in to others' perspectives more empathically, and develop Intuition to see where different positions can blend into a common accord.

4. **Positive Group Affiliation:** Spend some time with other group members to get better acquainted. As you become more familiar with each other, establishing a greater comfort level, your communication will become smoother. Draw on Extraversion to be more socially active and the Feeling function to nourish interpersonal rapport.

5. **Initiative:** Be willing to take a prominent role in a significant group project. Bring your negotiation and task skills into play. Get all members into the conversation. Build a positive team atmosphere. Use Extraversion to step up, Feeling to build a positive atmosphere, and Judging to shape the group's efforts.

ISFJ: Case Two

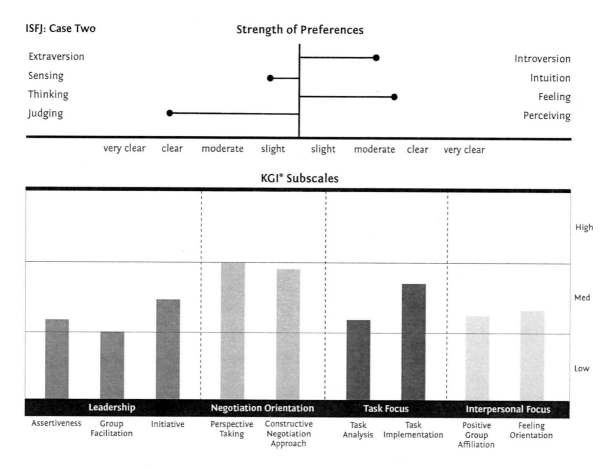

Strength of Preferences

	very clear	clear	moderate	slight	slight	moderate	clear	very clear
Extraversion							Introversion	
Sensing							Intuition	
Thinking							Feeling	
Judging							Perceiving	

KGI® Subscales

Leadership			Negotiation Orientation		Task Focus		Interpersonal Focus	
Assertiveness	Group Facilitation	Initiative	Perspective Taking	Constructive Negotiation Approach	Task Analysis	Task Implementation	Positive Group Affiliation	Feeling Orientation

1. **Assertiveness with Perspective Taking:** Articulate your positions for the group, explaining the facts that back them up. Ask probe questions about other members' positions and get clearer about their ideas. Help team members play off each other's ideas to forge the best strategies. Cultivate Extraversion to participate more actively in group discussions and Sensing to express details in a clear, succinct manner.

2. **Group Facilitation with Negotiation Orientation:** Take a leadership role in conducting a negotiation process with the group. Draw on your skills with Perspective Taking to obtain vital information on people's interests, then search for the connections that can bring people together in agreements that benefit everyone. Turn to Extraversion for the social energy, Feeling for perspective taking, and Intuition to sew together creative agreements.

3. **Task Analysis:** Study how members with strong analytical skills evaluate a task. How do they dissect a project? Pay attention to the details of their approach and start to consider tasks along the same lines. Deploy your Introversion to closely observe others' tactics, Sensing to evaluate the

details, and the Thinking function to logically approach the task.

4. **Constructive Negotiation Approach with Positive Group Affiliation:** The Constructive Negotiation Orientation score indicates your intention to design agreements that unite the team and benefit all members. Positive Group Affiliation aligns with this aim, creating a team spirit where members bond with each other and want to help. Channel energy from CNA towards Positive Group Affiliation to build it up, which, in turn, will profit CNA. Exert the Extraversion preference to reach out to others, use the Feeling function to raise team spirit, and Intuition to find the middle ground that creates mutual benefit.

5. **Feeling Orientation:** Check out other members' emotional reactions that are expressed facially or in other body language. Watch for signs of interest and excitement and then assist the group in delegating work that will direct this energy productively. If there are signs of anger or irritation, help the group respond promptly in order to restore harmony. Bring to bear your Introversion to observe others, Sensing to note the physical details, and Feeling to detect the emotional content.

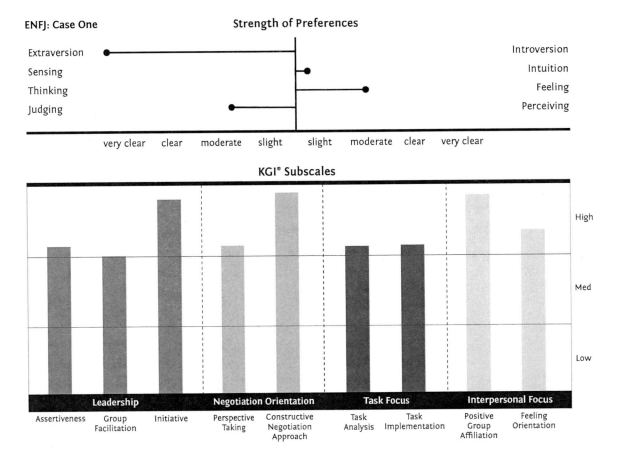

Strength of Preferences

KGI® Subscales

1. **Initiative:** Your level of Initiative appears too high. You may take on too much, and you may become so dominant in the group that other members' knowledge and skills are not being utilized in the most productive ways. The very clear Extraversion score seems to be fueling this pattern. It would be helpful to develop skills with observing and listening (Introversion) in order to sit back and thoughtfully pick your spots to be active. Assess others members' abilities and look to integrate them into the group's work.

2. **Group Facilitation with Task Focus:** There is an opportunity to refine your facilitation skills in the Task Focus domain. With Task Analysis, exercise the Perceiving attitude to stimulate a broad discussion that examines the task from many angles. Then draw on the Judging preference to help structure and execute the plan. Invite ideas from everyone, so all voices are heard and all members are involved.

3. **Constructive Negotiation Approach:** The amount of energy you are pouring into this area could be reduced. While constructing win-win agreements is a major goal, there is a point where such extreme enthusiasm can create blindness to situations where these agreements won't work. The combination of very clear Extraversion and moderate Feeling can be feeding this eagerness. Step back and take a more objective stance. Use observation (Introversion) and objective analysis (Thinking) to assess the situation, making sure that an authentic win-win agreement is possible in the particular context.

4. **Positive Group Affiliation:** This is another sector that could be toned down. Your ardor in this sphere may create too much socializing, too much interpersonal conversation. This can distract people from the task, potentially causing resentments. Strike more balance between your attention to the social atmosphere and to the task assignment. Use the Thinking function to watch for excessive emotion in this regard and to keep an eye on the task concerns. Use the Judging function to pay more attention to the task enterprise.

5. **Task Analysis with Task Implementation:** While these scores are strong, there is an opportunity to refine your approach to upgrade your performance. With Task Analysis, develop skills with the Sensing function to look more closely at the details in the situation and then consider the strategic possibilities using your Intuition preference. Also, employ Thinking to evaluate adjustments to the plan when implementing it, which will make the plan more efficient and successful.

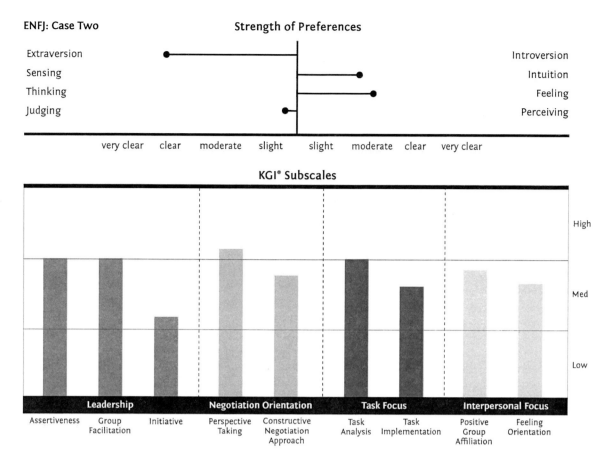

Strength of Preferences

Extraversion							Introversion
Sensing							Intuition
Thinking							Feeling
Judging							Perceiving

very clear · clear · moderate · slight · slight · moderate · clear · very clear

KGI® Subscales

Leadership			Negotiation Orientation		Task Focus		Interpersonal Focus	
Assertiveness	Group Facilitation	Initiative	Perspective Taking	Constructive Negotiation Approach	Task Analysis	Task Implementation	Positive Group Affiliation	Feeling Orientation

1. Constructive Negotiation Approach: Drawing on insights you obtain about other members' interests and concerns (through your use of Perspective Taking), put more effort into creating win-win agreements for the team. Employ the Intuition preference to see connections between different members' interests and identify the common ground.

2. Task Analysis with Task Implementation: There is an inclination to attend to analysis more than implementation. Balance the two elements by building up the implementation side. As the team works to carry out a project plan, facilitate open communication along the way. Invite members to share information about how the work is going, monitor the progress, and make any necessary adjustments to secure successful outcomes. Your Extraversion can support this communication, but pay attention to small details (Sensing), new problem-solving (Thinking), and ways to make the effort more efficient (Judging).

3. Group Facilitation with Positive Group Affiliation: Work to improve the social atmosphere on the team. Encourage members to become better acquainted. Facilitate an activity where members share personal information and develop more rapport. Employ your preferences for Extraversion and Feeling.

4. Feeling Orientation: Reflect on your feeling reactions during group events (Introversion) to pick up on the emotional currents in the situation. Be willing to share, in a reasonable way, these reactions. Refine the use of your Feeling function in the process.

5. Initiative: Step up to be the point person for a team project. Foster an open exchange of ideas on task strategy and create opportunities for people to make constructive contributions to the effort. Use your Extraversion to engage people, the Thinking preference to assess the best strategies, and the Judging attitude to organize the enterprise.

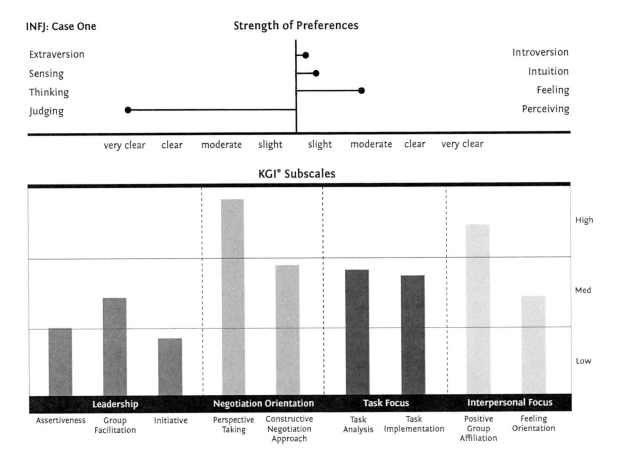

Strength of Preferences

Extraversion		Introversion
Sensing		Intuition
Thinking		Feeling
Judging		Perceiving

very clear · clear · moderate · slight · slight · moderate · clear · very clear

KGI® Subscales

Leadership: Assertiveness · Group Facilitation · Initiative

Negotiation Orientation: Perspective Taking · Constructive Negotiation Approach

Task Focus: Task Analysis · Task Implementation

Interpersonal Focus: Positive Group Affiliation · Feeling Orientation

1. **Assertiveness with Perspective Taking:** With such a high Perspective Taking score, you have a tendency to put everyone else's concerns above your own and to take a back seat. Reduce some of the PT energy, transfer it into Assertiveness, and put forward your own opinions. Let your voice be heard. Challenge yourself to use the Extraversion attitude in a conscious, intentional way and the Feeling function to share your values and concerns.

2. **Group Facilitation and Negotiation Orientation:** Given your skills in negotiation, it's a smart place to assist the group. Invite people to share their positions, probe to obtain greater detail, and promote the construction of win-win agreements. Adopt an Extraversion attitude in this context, use the Perceiving preference to gather a wide range of points, and bring your Intuitive function to bear to identify the patterns for win-win decisions.

3. **Positive Group Affiliation with Feeling Orientation:** Become more attuned to other members' emotional reactions. By becoming more aware, you can expand your Perspective Taking and also help the team manage emotional issues.

Through the constructive management of emotions, a team can enlarge Positive Group Affiliation, an area of high interest for you. Use Introversion and Sensing to observe closely, your Feeling preference to interpret what is happening, and Judging to organize a more productive team environment.

4. **Task Analysis with Task Implementation:** The scores in the Task Focus domain are very solid, but they could be enhanced by a greater use of the Thinking function. Watch others who have that function and notice how they evaluate a task and then execute it. Imitate their strategies and build up your thinking.

5. **Initiative:** Pursue an opportunity to be a group leader where you can exercise your diverse skills in negotiation, task, and interpersonal relations. You have an array of skills, but they need greater exposure. As you try out a leadership role, be sure to engage other members. Mobilize Extraversion to be more vocal, Intuition and Thinking to plan creatively, and Judging to keep the group's efforts well organized.

INFJ: Case Two

Strength of Preferences

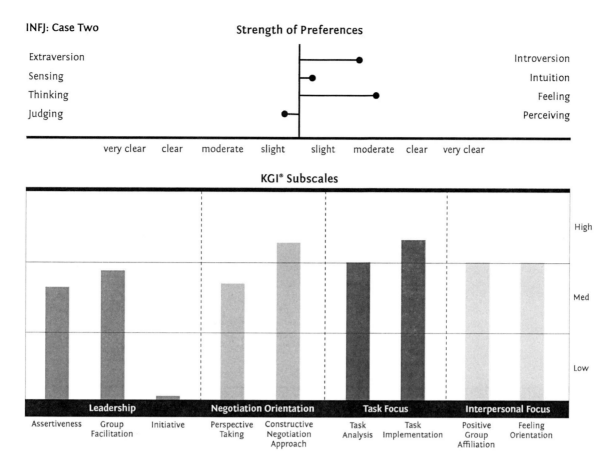

Extraversion	●———	Introversion
Sensing	●—	Intuition
Thinking	———●	Feeling
Judging	●—	Perceiving

very clear   clear   moderate   slight   slight   moderate   clear   very clear

KGI® Subscales

	Leadership			Negotiation Orientation		Task Focus		Interpersonal Focus	
	Assertiveness	Group Facilitation	Initiative	Perspective Taking	Constructive Negotiation Approach	Task Analysis	Task Implementation	Positive Group Affiliation	Feeling Orientation

1. **Assertiveness:** Express your ideas more often in the group. Utilize some Extraversion energy to speak up, Thinking energy to push forward ideas, and the Feeling function to share your own values.

2. **Perspective Taking and Constructive Negotiation Approach:** You have a strong impulse to design win-win agreements with a team. But Perspective Taking, which supports your ability to construct such agreements, needs greater development. Ask probe questions to get a deeper understanding of other members' interests, concerns, and values. Use Extraversion to ask more questions, the Perceiving preference to examine a broader range of issues, and the Feeling preference to see things from others' perspectives.

3. **Group Facilitation with Interpersonal Focus:** Profit from your skills in the Interpersonal Focus realm. Help facilitate rapport-building conversation in the group. Become involved in casual conversation before and after meetings to get better acquainted with others, fostering group cohesion. Bring into play the Extraversion attitude, the Feeling function, and the Judging attitude to reach out and champion group harmony.

4. **Task Analysis with Task Implementation:** Be more patient with Task Analysis, so you can evaluate in greater detail the problems and opportunities with a task project. View the task from multiple angles, considering the various options to construct the best strategy. The score with Task Implementation indicates a slight tendency to jump into action before fully examining the task. Check that impulse and make sure the strategy is sound. Apply the Sensing function to be patient with details, Perceiving to examine an array of issues, and the Thinking preference to reflect more fully on the options.

5. **Initiative:** You have a series of skills in negotiation, task, and interpersonal relations. Try out a leadership role so you can put these skills on display. Seek opportunities to take on leadership responsibilities. To start, it can be a shared leadership position, a joint effort with another colleague. Then, take the plunge with a solo assignment. Use Extraversion to step into the spotlight, Thinking to deal with the task, Feeling to manage the people, and Judging for overall organization.

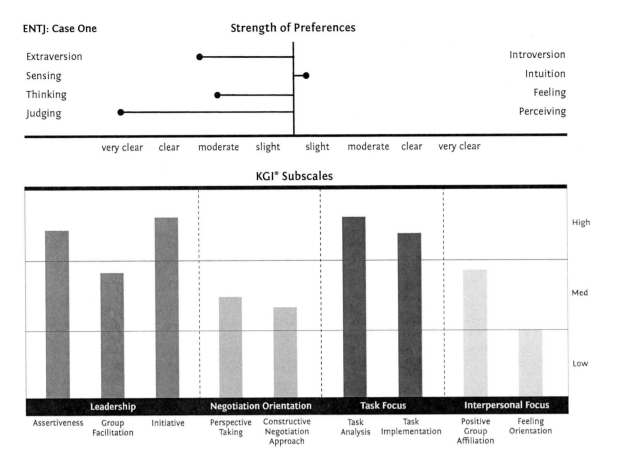

ENTJ: Case One

Strength of Preferences

	very clear	clear	moderate	slight	slight	moderate	clear	very clear	
Extraversion									Introversion
Sensing									Intuition
Thinking									Feeling
Judging									Perceiving

KGI® Subscales

Leadership: Assertiveness, Group Facilitation, Initiative

Negotiation Orientation: Perspective Taking, Constructive Negotiation Approach

Task Focus: Task Analysis, Task Implementation

Interpersonal Focus: Positive Group Affiliation, Feeling Orientation

1. **Group Facilitation with Interpersonal Focus:** You possess skills for facilitating a team in the Task Focus domain. The challenge is to become a better facilitator with Interpersonal Focus. To support the effort, it's necessary to develop more skills with the Feeling preference. Pay attention to other group members' enthusiasms, interests, and values. Look for ways to delegate work based on their interests, channeling that energy into practical contributions for the team. Take time to build interpersonal relations that enhance Positive Group Affiliation.

2. **Assertiveness with Perspective Taking:** Direct some of the Assertiveness energy towards asking other people questions. Investigate their positions and get them more engaged in the discussion. Use Introversion skills to listen closely and Feeling to see things from their perspectives. This can provide insights about how to address people's concerns to create a more cohesive team, plus it can reveal worthwhile ideas related to the task effort.

3. **Constructive Negotiation Approach:** Utilize your Intuition skills more consciously to create win-win agreements in the group. Explore associations between various members' interests to find the common ground where all members can benefit from an accord. This inspires greater member com-

mitment to the work and increases team cohesion. Building skills with the Perceiving preference will assist you in looking at a wider range of options in a negotiation.

4. **Task Analysis:** The score indicates that you may tend to overanalyze a task, hunting for the "perfect" plan and brainstorming too many possibilities. When a team overanalyzes the task, it can lose valuable time in the process. You may need to reel in your Intuition and Thinking preferences if you are getting carried away with the analysis. Use the Sensing function to be more practical and grounded with analysis, and the Judging preference to conclude when a reasonable solution is found.

5. **Initiative:** Given this high score, you may take on too many leadership responsibilities. In the long run, this can be exhausting and reduce the quality of your work. Be selective in choosing leadership roles, selecting the ones that are most personally relevant and that offer the best opportunities to advance your career. It would also be beneficial to look for opportunities to share leadership responsibilities with other members. Encourage others to get involved to create more team collaboration on projects. Instead of having everyone dependent on your initiative, you can foster theirs, which can boost the overall enter-

prise. Employ your Introversion attitude to self-reflect on what matters most to you, and the Intuition function to assess which leadership roles will have the most long-term benefits for your career.

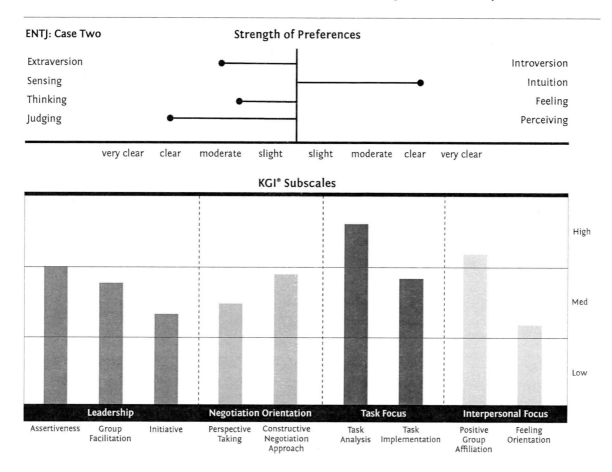

ENTJ: Case Two — Strength of Preferences

Extraversion								Introversion
Sensing								Intuition
Thinking								Feeling
Judging								Perceiving

very clear — clear — moderate — slight — slight — moderate — clear — very clear

KGI® Subscales

Leadership			Negotiation Orientation		Task Focus		Interpersonal Focus	
Assertiveness	Group Facilitation	Initiative	Perspective Taking	Constructive Negotiation Approach	Task Analysis	Task Implementation	Positive Group Affiliation	Feeling Orientation

1. **Positive Group Affiliation with Feeling Orientation:** Pay attention to team members' reactions—their facial expressions and body language—to see what excites them and what turns them off. Gain insight into what affects teammates by developing more observation skills (Introversion), attention to physical detail (Sensing), and awareness of emotions (Feeling). This information can assist in the creation of a positive atmosphere on a team, Positive Group Affiliation, which is an established interest area.

2. **Perspective Taking with Constructive Negotiation Approach:** Sound out other members on their views, interests, and motivations. Ask probe questions to get greater detail and listen closely to their responses. Combine asking questions (Extraversion) with close listening (Introversion). Use this information to construct win-win agreements, drawing on Intuition to find the middle ground to reach accords.

3. **Task Analysis with Task Implementation:** Reduce some of your emphasis on analysis. You may become too enthralled with all of the possibilities in a strategy to the point of excess. Draw on your Judging preference to move to Task Implementation sooner. Use your Thinking preference to fine-tune the task strategy as you implement it. Ultimately, this will save you, and the team, significant time, which gets wasted with overanalysis.

4. **Group Facilitation with Task Focus and Interpersonal Focus:** By making the adjustments described above for Task Focus and Interpersonal Focus, you will be better positioned to facilitate the group's efforts. Maintain awareness of both domains, drawing on appropriate Thinking and Feeling skills, and strike a balance between the two as you facilitate. This will promote high team performance.

5. **Initiative:** Be willing to step into a lead role for a team project. Facilitate a real team effort, keeping all members involved, and delegating responsibilities according to people's clear skills and interests. Draw on energies from Extraversion and Judging, supported by that opposite Feeling function.

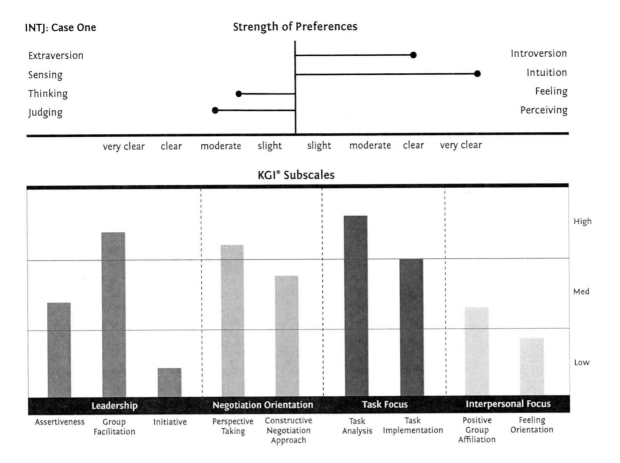

Strength of Preferences

	very clear	clear	moderate	slight		slight	moderate	clear	very clear	
Extraversion										Introversion
Sensing										Intuition
Thinking										Feeling
Judging										Perceiving

KGI® Subscales

1. **Assertiveness with Perspective Taking:** As you listen to other members' positions, employing your skills with Perspective Taking, reply to their statements. Counter with your own opinions and invite feedback about them. You can also make proposals for win-win agreements that will bring people together around their common interests. Bring into play Extraversion energy to make your voice heard and use the Intuitive function to find associations among ideas that create win-win accords.

2. **Task Analysis with Task Implementation:** Take care not to overanalyze task issues during the planning stage. Your score indicates a leaning in that direction. Be cautious about prolonged theoretical debate; move more directly into taking action, implementing the plan. Use your Thinking function to be aware of this issue and address it, and bring forward the Judging attitude to organize the effort efficiently.

3. **Constructive Negotiation Approach with Positive Group Affiliation:** You have a significant desire to create win-win accords in the group, which connects with creating Positive Group Affiliation. Win-win boosts team morale.

Conversely, doing more to build up PGA will instill a greater team desire for win-win. Knowing this, you can channel some of your CNA energy into PGA, thereby expanding your group skills in a substantial way. Tap into the Extraversion attitude to find more social energy and the Feeling function to get more in tune with the emotions in the group.

4. **Feeling Orientation:** Pay attention to people's emotional reactions in the group, both positive and negative. This will enrich your Perspective Taking. Help to direct member emotions in constructive ways, which will aid your efforts with Positive Group Affiliation. Use Introversion to be a good observer, the Sensing function to stay in touch with here-and-now behaviors, and Feeling to perceive emotional currents within the group.

5. **Initiative:** Avail yourself of the opportunity to be the lead person for a team project. Take advantage of your task skills to advance the group's work and your talent with negotiation to pursue mutually satisfying agreements. Make your abilities more visible in a leadership role. Draw on Extraversion to take action, Thinking to manage the task, and Judging to organize the effort.

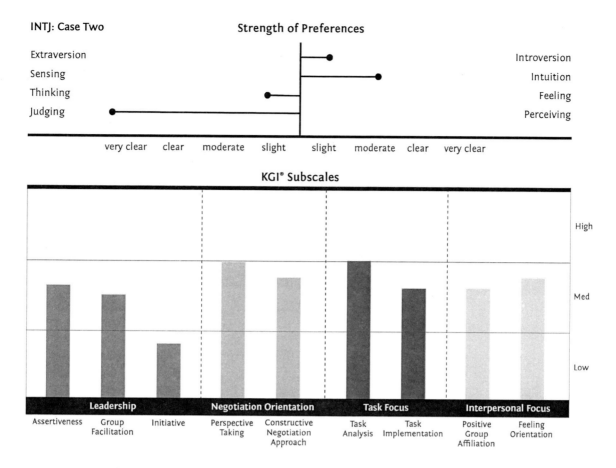

INTJ: Case Two

Strength of Preferences

	very clear	clear	moderate	slight		slight	moderate	clear	very clear
Extraversion									Introversion
Sensing									Intuition
Thinking									Feeling
Judging									Perceiving

KGI® Subscales

	High
	Med
	Low

Leadership — Assertiveness, Group Facilitation, Initiative

Negotiation Orientation — Perspective Taking, Constructive Negotiation Approach

Task Focus — Task Analysis, Task Implementation

Interpersonal Focus — Positive Group Affiliation, Feeling Orientation

1. **Group Facilitation and Negotiation Orientation:** Rise up and assist the group with its negotiations. Take advantage of your skills in Perspective Taking and guide the team in carving out win-win solutions for both task and interpersonal issues. Activate Extraversion energy to take a leadership role, Perceiving to look at a range of member issues, and Intuition to identify the links between different interests that can unify the team.

2. **Task Analysis with Task Implementation:** Generate more balance between the TA and TI elements. There is a slight bias towards analysis, which may cause you to overthink the task issues. Put the task plan into action sooner, monitor initial results, and modify the strategy as you proceed. Rely on the Sensing function to scrutinize the details, Thinking to assess the proper adjustments, and Judging to navigate the project to conclusion.

3. **Assertiveness:** Express your point of view more often in group conversations. You listen and observe others, but should also react to their ideas and express your own creative thoughts. Based on your scores here, you are attuned to many issues in the group. Have the confidence to speak up and be more of a contributor. Plug into untapped Extraversion energy in this regard.

4. **Positive Group Affiliation:** Encourage the group to take some time to become more familiar with each other. Do some rapport-building activities. You can take a leadership role to spur the group forward. Mobilize some Extraversion energy to lead the group and the Feeling function to enhance interpersonal relations.

5. **Initiative:** Do not be timid—step up into a primary leadership role with the team. Let others see your range of skills as you lead a project. Bring people together to attack the task and guide it to successful conclusion. Utilize Extraversion to step up and Judging to organize the team in the enterprise.

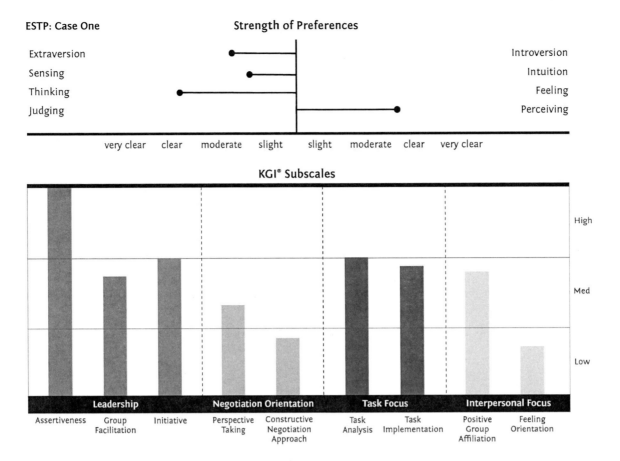

ESTP: Case One

Strength of Preferences

	very clear	clear	moderate	slight	slight	moderate	clear	very clear	
Extraversion									Introversion
Sensing									Intuition
Thinking									Feeling
Judging									Perceiving

KGI® Subscales

Leadership: Assertiveness, Group Facilitation, Initiative

Negotiation Orientation: Perspective Taking, Constructive Negotiation Approach

Task Focus: Task Analysis, Task Implementation

Interpersonal Focus: Positive Group Affiliation, Feeling Orientation

1. **Assertiveness with Perspective Taking:** Dial down your Assertiveness, which may come across to others as overbearing. Channel some of this energy into asking questions and investigating others' concerns. Listen closely to their reactions and refine your position based on their ideas. Initiate more give-and-take and be open to moving in new directions with your analysis. Learn to sit back and listen more (Introversion skills) to balance your participation style. Employ your Thinking function to stretch your analysis.

2. **Group Facilitation with Task Focus:** Take action to assist the group in the task effort. Get members to contribute ideas for task analysis; examine the project from different angles and identify the best strategies. As the plan moves into action, foster broad communication so the members stay on the same page and achieve strong outcomes. Take advantage of Extraversion and Thinking to keep the ideas flowing and draw on Judging energy to organize the team in the most efficient ways.

3. **Constructive Negotiation Approach with Positive Group Affiliation:** You pay attention to group morale with Positive Group Affiliation.

Fashioning win-win agreements in Constructive Negotiation Approach would help enhance group morale since the two play off each other. During group negotiations, deploy your skill with the Sensing preference to look closely at details, and then experiment with the Intuition preference to search for connections that will identify the middle ground for win-win. Using these preferences in combination can bring high-quality outcomes.

4. **Feeling Orientation:** Pay more attention to the emotional currents in the group. Notice other members' emotional reactions through facial expressions and physical gestures. Whether these go in positive or negative directions will tell you important things about how the group is operating. Begin to engage the Feeling preference to become aware of these issues.

5. **Initiative:** Your efforts to take on significant leadership roles will be embellished by improving your skills in Negotiation Orientation and Interpersonal Focus. You will become more flexible and well-rounded, better able to ignite synergy on a team. Learning to utilize Intuition and Feeling more astutely will be integral to this process.

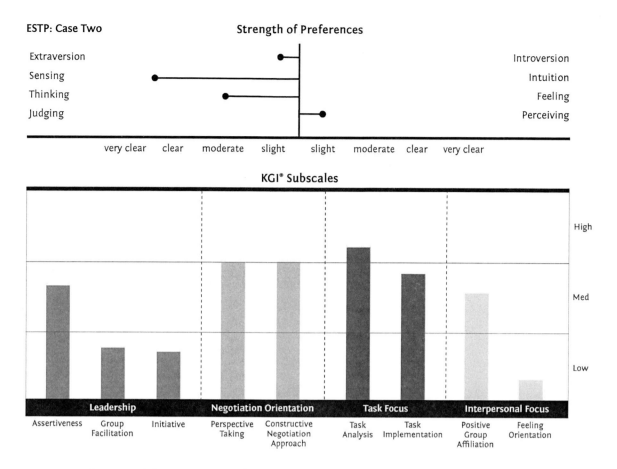

ESTP: Case Two

Strength of Preferences

	very clear	clear	moderate	slight	slight	moderate	clear	very clear
Extraversion					●			Introversion
Sensing		●						Intuition
Thinking			●					Feeling
Judging					●			Perceiving

KGI® Subscales

Leadership · Assertiveness · Group Facilitation · Initiative

Negotiation Orientation · Perspective Taking · Constructive Negotiation Approach

Task Focus · Task Analysis · Task Implementation

Interpersonal Focus · Positive Group Affiliation · Feeling Orientation

1. **Assertiveness with Perspective Taking:** During discussions, as you gain perspective on others' ideas and concerns, share your own thoughts on the subject. Articulate points of agreement and points on which you differ, becoming more involved. Use your Extraversion and Thinking preferences to increase your involvement.

2. **Feeling Orientation:** Learn to tune in to the emotional currents in the group; begin by watching emotional reactions of others, their facial expressions and body language, and pick up on the positive and negative trends. Insights you obtain will deepen Perspective Taking. Use the Introversion and Sensing preferences to observe closely and develop the Feeling preference to attune to the emotional content.

3. **Group Facilitation:** Step into a leadership role to help the group advance its work, particularly with respect to negotiation and task, your strongest skill areas. Put these strengths on display, sharing your sound ideas. Also, get others into the conversation—solicit their ideas and, together, fashion appropriate group strategies. Utilize your Extraversion and Thinking, but also draw on the Perceiving attitude to look at range

of ideas. Use Intuition energy to strike creative agreements and develop innovative task strategies.

4. **Task Implementation:** There is an opportunity to further refine your efforts in this domain. As your group implements a plan, assist the team in maintaining smooth communication. Make sure people stay on the same page and make creative adjustments as appropriate. Utilize your Extraversion energy to stay active, Intuition to nurture creative ideas, and the Judging attitude to coordinate planning and activities in an efficient manner.

5. **Initiative:** Take advantage of a chance to be the group leader for a project. In this capacity, build up Positive Group Affiliation with the team. Set aside some time when people can get to know each other and increase rapport. Create a comfort zone that is inclusive and supportive. Then facilitate the work using Constructive Negotiation Approach and a spirited Task Focus. Apply the Feeling function to establish a positive atmosphere and your Perceiving attitude to elicit a wide array of ideas from people. With Intuition, identify the common ground that makes for strong agreements.

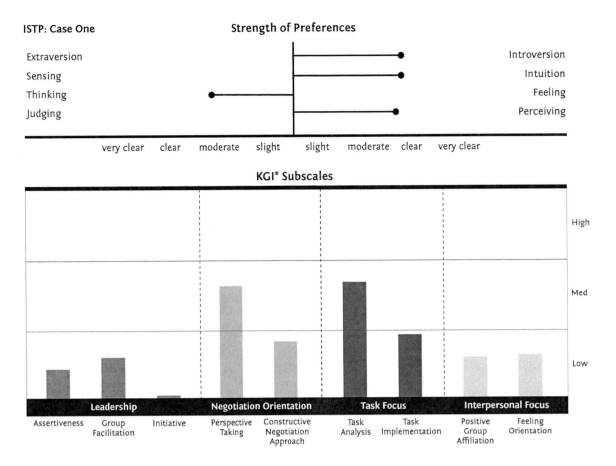

Strength of Preferences

	very clear	clear	moderate	slight	slight	moderate	clear	very clear	
Extraversion							●		Introversion
Sensing						●			Intuition
Thinking		●							Feeling
Judging						●			Perceiving

KGI® Subscales

1. **Assertiveness with Perspective Taking:** Participate more in group discussions. As you listen to others' concerns, utilizing your Perspective Taking skills, raise your own issues to join in the conversation. Share your opinions during the analysis of the task, which is a strength area for you. Pull on your Thinking preference for sound task ideas and begin to tap into some Extraversion energy to express them.

2. **Group Facilitation with Task Analysis:** Invite others to share their ideas about possible task strategies. Offer your own suggestions. Instigate a dialogue in which you build on each other's ideas, moving to a higher level of analysis. Capitalize on your Thinking function for the analysis, but embrace Extraversion to speak up and the Judging attitude to organize the effort.

3. **Constructive Negotiation Approach:** With the insights you gain about others' views and interests during group discussions, try to assemble win-win agreements where everyone receives some benefit from the decision. Exercise the Sensing function to acquire details about others'

interests but then branch out into Intuition to consider possible connections between different people's positions, helping to find the middle ground that builds consensus.

4. **Positive Group Affiliation:** Take time to get acquainted with the other team members. Talk with them before, after, or outside of meetings. Get to know who they are, what they care about, what engages them. As you develop some rapport, it can increase your comfort level and grease the wheels of collaboration. Apply some Extraversion energy to reach out and some Feeling energy to build relationships.

5. **Initiative:** Take advantage of small opportunities to assume a leadership role in certain phases of a group project. Be responsible for some part of the work that has attraction for you, and begin to practice your new group skills. As you achieve some initial success in this fashion, you can eventually take on more responsibilities. Tap Extroversion energy to get more involved, Feeling energy to respond constructively to others, and Judging energy to organize the activity.

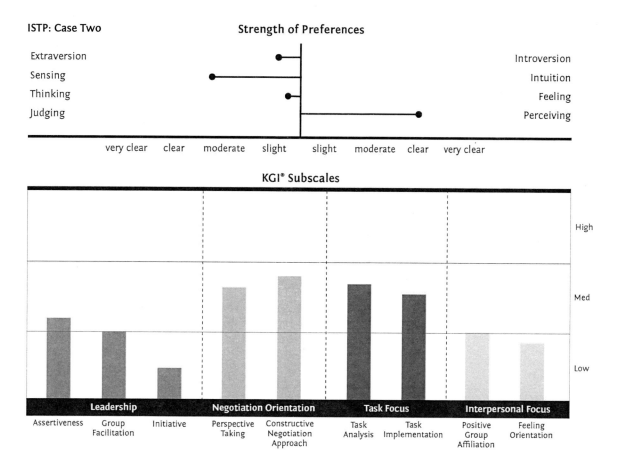

Strength of Preferences

	very clear	clear	moderate	slight	slight	moderate	clear	very clear	
Extraversion				●					Introversion
Sensing		●							Intuition
Thinking				●					Feeling
Judging							●		Perceiving

KGI® Subscales

Leadership: Assertiveness, Group Facilitation, Initiative

Negotiation Orientation: Perspective Taking, Constructive Negotiation Approach

Task Focus: Task Analysis, Task Implementation

Interpersonal Focus: Positive Group Affiliation, Feeling Orientation

1. **Assertiveness:** Voice your thoughts during task discussions and negotiations. Share ideas about how to get the job done. Convey your vision for how the team can formulate win-win agreements in Constructive Negotiation Approach. Utilize Extraversion energy to speak up, Thinking energy for the task discussion, and cultivate the Intuition preference to assist you in discovering the common ground for joint agreements.

2. **Group Facilitation:** Help expedite the group's efforts in the negotiation sector. Solicit the ideas, interests, and concerns of other members. Then help the group structure win-win agreements so everyone will get benefit from the team's efforts. Turn to the Perceiving attitude to solicit a wide range of opinions, the Feeling function to get a deeper understanding of people's interests, and the Intuition function to discover pertinent connections for win-win decisions.

3. **Positive Group Affiliation:** Get more personally acquainted with other members. Casual conversation can happen at almost any time and will help build rapport, making formal task collabora-tion easier. Utilize Extraversion energy to interact with people and the Feeling function to nurture positive regard.

4. **Feeling Orientation:** Watch other members' facial expressions and body language to assess their reactions to what is being said. When do they positively perk up? When do they withdraw and shut down? Assess how people react to your words and those of others. Take advantage of the Introversion attitude to observe others closely, the Sensing function to watch the details, and increase the Feeling function to be aware of the emotional patterns.

5. **Initiative:** Undertake a leadership role in some team project or part of a project. Bring people into the discussion, listen closely to their positions, and pursue mutual agreements that will help the group bond. Generate a thorough task analysis and assign responsibilities based on people's interests. Pull on Extraversion and Thinking energy to logically move the work along, and Judging energy to bring it to a firm conclusion.

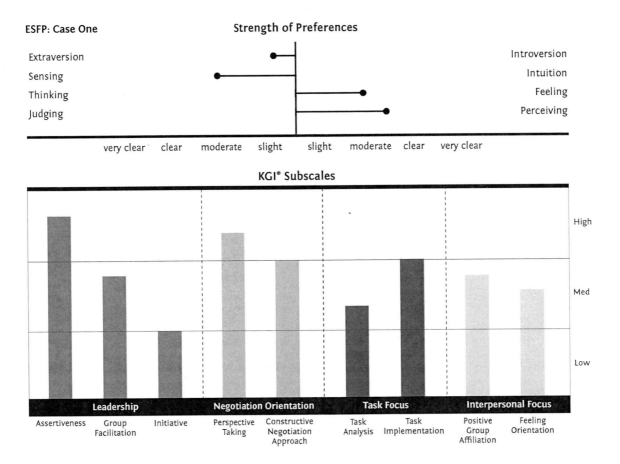

Strength of Preferences

	very clear	clear	moderate	slight	slight	moderate	clear	very clear	
Extraversion				●					Introversion
Sensing			●						Intuition
Thinking						●			Feeling
Judging							●		Perceiving

KGI® Subscales

Leadership: Assertiveness, Group Facilitation, Initiative

Negotiation Orientation: Perspective Taking, Constructive Negotiation Approach

Task Focus: Task Analysis, Task Implementation

Interpersonal Focus: Positive Group Affiliation, Feeling Orientation

1. **Assertiveness with Perspective Taking:** Tone down the use of Assertiveness. Direct some of this energy towards Perspective Taking by asking questions to assess other members' interests. Sit back, listen, and observe more, tapping into Introverted energy, thereby blending the use of Extraversion and Introversion.

2. **Group Facilitation with Positive Group Affiliation:** Take a role in facilitating team-building activities with the group, helping the group acquire more of a team spirit. This will draw on your Extraversion and Feeling preferences and strengthen the team's Positive Group Affiliation.

3. **Task Analysis with Task Implementation:** Observe how other members who are strong in TA dissect problems for the group. Adopt some of their methods of analysis, building up the Thinking function and acquiring a more systematic approach to evaluating a task. Be patient. The Task Implementation score indicates that you may rush to complete a task without enough calm analysis.

4. **Feeling Orientation:** Be willing to share your feelings in a group; be willing to model for others openness to emotional expression. Invite others to share their feelings, especially when you see facial expressions or body language indicating significant reactions. Help the group expand communication in this area. Draw on energies from Extraversion, Sensing, and Feeling to assist you in this process.

5. **Initiative:** Look for an opportunity to step up into a lead role on some task project. Use your skills with Perspective Taking and Constructive Negotiation Approach to pursue win-win agreements. Get everyone involved in strategy development and task execution. Use the Perceiving attitude to consider a wide range of strategy options. Experiment with the opposite preferences of Intuition (being open to creative ideas within the group) and Judging (organizing the group's efforts in efficient ways).

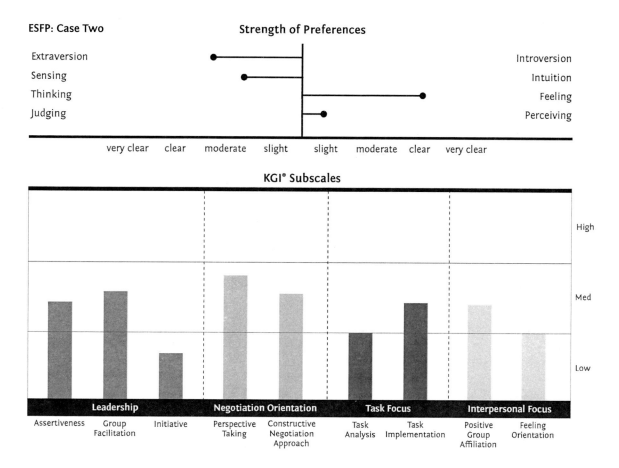

ESFP: Case Two

Strength of Preferences

	very clear	clear	moderate	slight	slight	moderate	clear	very clear
Extraversion			●					Introversion
Sensing				●				Intuition
Thinking							●	Feeling
Judging					●			Perceiving

KGI® Subscales

	Leadership			Negotiation Orientation		Task Focus		Interpersonal Focus	
	Assertiveness	Group Facilitation	Initiative	Perspective Taking	Constructive Negotiation Approach	Task Analysis	Task Implementation	Positive Group Affiliation	Feeling Orientation

1. **Assertiveness:** Speak up and express your ideas more, then invite others to react to them. Share your reactions to their feedback. Employ Extraversion to express yourself and Thinking to discuss a variety of ideas.

2. **Task Analysis with Task Implementation:** Listen to how people with skills in task analysis assess a project. See how they attack problems. As you recognize their techniques, be alert for opportunities where you can share ideas in a similar manner. Take advantage of opportunities to become more involved with the execution of a plan, helping to move the work along. Draw on Introversion (listening and observing), Thinking (contributing ideas) and Judging (helping to complete the task).

3. **Feeling Orientation:** Study people's facial expressions, body language, and tone of voice to assess their emotional reactions. When people are enthusiastic, seek to understand the source of their interests; when they become negative, look for the cause of the trouble. Try to help the team manage emotions in constructive ways. Refine the use of your Extraversion, Sensing and Feeling preferences in these ways.

4. **Group Facilitation and Negotiation Orientation:** Employ your skills with Perspective Taking and Constructive Negotiation Approach to assist the team in pursuing win-win agreements. Be proactive in fashioning a mutually supportive environment where people encourage and help one another. Draw on energy from Extraversion, Feeling, and an opposite preference, Intuition (to find the middle ground for win-win agreements).

5. **Initiative:** Seek an opportunity to be the leader for a group project. Select something that has meaning for you and then pick up the reins. After you have strengthened your skills with Task Analysis and Feeling Orientation, you will be in a solid position to aid the team in balancing task and interpersonal concerns. Tap into energy from Extraversion, Intuition (creating a team vision for the task), Thinking (task execution) and Feeling (interpersonal relations).

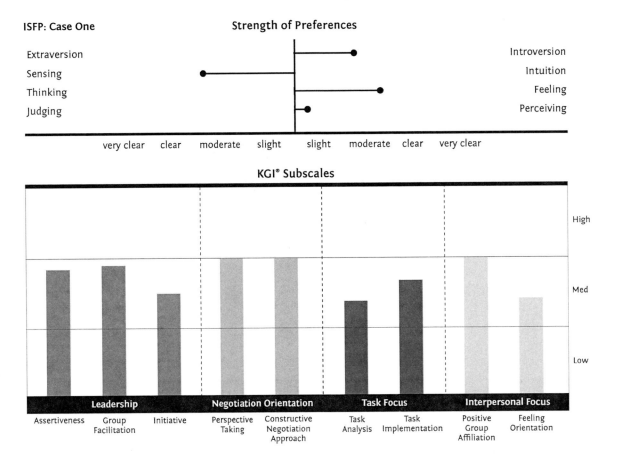

Strength of Preferences

Extraversion		Introversion
Sensing		Intuition
Thinking		Feeling
Judging		Perceiving

very clear · clear · moderate · slight · slight · moderate · clear · very clear

KGI® Subscales

Leadership	Negotiation Orientation	Task Focus	Interpersonal Focus
Assertiveness · Group Facilitation · Initiative	Perspective Taking · Constructive Negotiation Approach	Task Analysis · Task Implementation	Positive Group Affiliation · Feeling Orientation

1. **Group Facilitation and Negotiation Orientation:** Lend more of a hand in facilitating negotiations in the group. Help forge win-win agreements that benefit all members and solidify team unity. Exploit your skills in Perspective Taking and Constructive Negotiation Approach to their fullest extent; put them on display to advance the team. Bring into service Extraversion to speak up, the Feeling function to grasp members' deeper concerns, and Intuition to search for common ground among different members' concerns.

2. **Task Analysis:** Discern how members with analytical skills evaluate the task and present persuasive plans. Adopt some of their tactics, which will enhance your own analytical abilities. Use the Introversion attitude to observe closely how other members operate and the Thinking preference to structure logical arguments about task strategies.

3. **Task Implementation:** Take a more active role in forwarding the task effort. As the team implements its agenda, monitor the progress, help to promote clear communication among members, and look for ways to make the effort more efficient. Exercise Extraversion to promote the flow of conversation, Thinking to analyze the team's approach, and Judging to assist in organizing the project.

4. **Positive Group Affiliation with Feeling Orientation:** You can support your interest in Positive Group Affiliation by paying closer attention to the feeling reactions of other members. Watch for the expression of positive and negative emotions, and be alert for ways to manage those emotions to keep the team on a good track. Use Introversion to watch for emotional reactions, Feeling to assess the emotional content, and the Judging attitude to bring order to the situation.

5. **Initiative:** Take up the challenge of leading a group project. Capitalize on your skills with negotiation and Positive Group Affiliation to establish team unity. Get everyone contributing ideas and committed to the task. Mobilize Extraversion to increase your level of participation, Feeling to guide the team in bonding, and Judging to coordinate the efforts with the task.

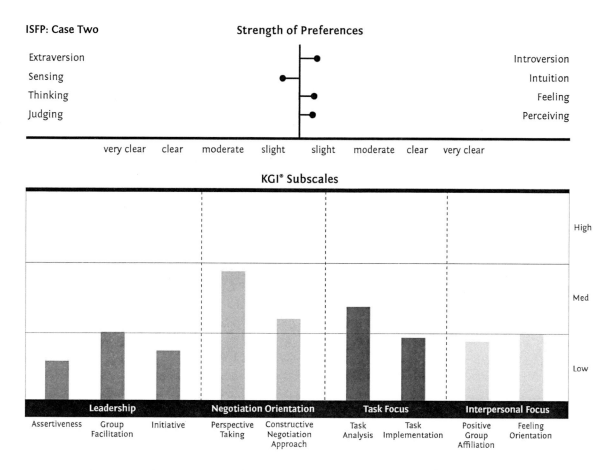

ISFP: Case Two

Strength of Preferences

Extraversion	Introversion
Sensing	Intuition
Thinking	Feeling
Judging	Perceiving

very clear   clear   moderate   slight   slight   moderate   clear   very clear

KGI® Subscales

High

Med

Low

Leadership			Negotiation Orientation		Task Focus		Interpersonal Focus	
Assertiveness	Group Facilitation	Initiative	Perspective Taking	Constructive Negotiation Approach	Task Analysis	Task Implementation	Positive Group Affiliation	Feeling Orientation

1. **Assertiveness with Perspective Taking:** Throw your hat into the ring: share your ideas and get more into the flow of team discussions. As you listen to others' opinions, express whether you agree or disagree, or where you might propose to view an issue at a fresh angle. Help the team expand the conversation. Draw on Extraversion energy to raise your voice; use your Thinking preference to express the ideas that are the most relevant for you.

2. **Constructive Negotiation Approach:** Profit by the insights you gain from Perspective Taking and assist the group in fashioning win-win agreements. Help the team find the middle ground that builds team cohesion and motivates members to do their best work. Utilize Introversion and Perceiving to listen to a range of member concerns, and then employ Intuition to examine the connections between their different interests.

3. **Positive Group Affiliation:** Spend time talking with other team members before and after meetings. Break the ice with Extraversion to speak up, and employ your Feeling function to build bridges with others.

4. **Feeling Orientation:** Become more attuned to other members' emotional reactions during discussions, which will deepen your Perspective Taking and increase your awareness of people's concerns and issues. Exercise Introversion to observe the group, Sensing to pick up physical cues, and Feeling to identify the emotional undercurrents.

5. **Group Facilitation with Negotiation Orientation:** Aid the team in its negotiations. Invite others to share their perspectives on various issues, including how to solve the task. Present your own ideas. Construct joint accords that bring group members together. Utilize Extraversion to be more expressive, Intuition to find mutual agreements, and Judging to help organize the team.

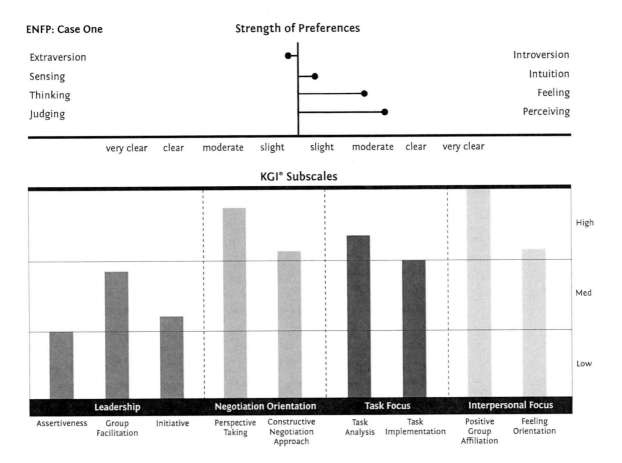

Strength of Preferences

	very clear	clear	moderate	slight	slight	moderate	clear	very clear	
Extraversion				•					Introversion
Sensing				•					Intuition
Thinking						•			Feeling
Judging						•			Perceiving

KGI® Subscales

Leadership — Assertiveness, Group Facilitation, Initiative
Negotiation Orientation — Perspective Taking, Constructive Negotiation Approach
Task Focus — Task Analysis, Task Implementation
Interpersonal Focus — Positive Group Affiliation, Feeling Orientation

1. **Assertiveness with Perspective Taking:** Express your own ideas more often in the group. As you listen to others' opinions (with Perspective Taking), see where your views connect and then present them. Invite others to respond to your ideas. Build up your slight Extraversion preference with more active participation.

2. **Constructive Negotiation Approach with Positive Group Affiliation:** Reduce some of your focus on Positive Group Affiliation. While it is important, you appear to be concentrating on it too much, which can put too much emphasis on socializing. Constructive Negotiation Approach is closely related to PGA. As you promote win-win agreements, it increases a positive atmosphere on the team. Channel some of the PGA energy towards CNA. Utilize the Intuitive function to find connections between members' interests to create mutually satisfying decisions.

3. **Group Facilitation with Task Focus and Interpersonal Focus:** Step up and take more of a leadership role to assist the group in its work. Two areas to address: help the group pay attention to emotional issues in the Feeling Orientation domain (utilizing your Feeling function), and

coordinate the task efforts in Task Implementation (building up skills with the Judging preference). With the latter, you display substantial ability already, and this could be a natural way to refine your skills while also developing the opposite attitude, Judging.

4. **Feeling Orientation:** Pay attention to members' enthusiasms and interests related to various aspects of the work. Help the team delegate task assignments based on member interests. Use Introversion to listen closely to others, Sensing to watch their body language, and Extraversion to express reactions that assist the group in operating more effectively.

5. **Initiative:** Pursue an opportunity for a lead role with a group project. Bring together your skills in the negotiation, task, and interpersonal domains to build a cohesive team effort. Work on your Thinking function to analyze the task thoroughly and implement the plan successfully. Use the Judging function to organize the effort in an efficient way. The Feeling function will aid you in staying in touch with the people issues as the project proceeds.

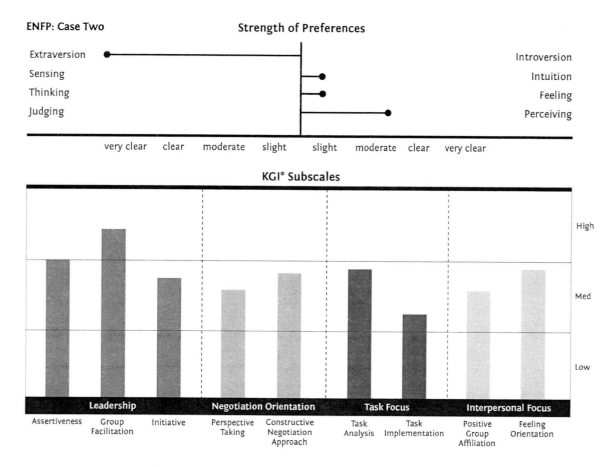

ENFP: Case Two

Strength of Preferences

| | | very clear | clear | moderate | slight | slight | moderate | clear | very clear |

Extraversion — Introversion
Sensing — Intuition
Thinking — Feeling
Judging — Perceiving

KGI® Subscales

High

Med

Low

Leadership — **Negotiation Orientation** — **Task Focus** — **Interpersonal Focus**

Assertiveness | Group Facilitation | Initiative | Perspective Taking | Constructive Negotiation Approach | Task Analysis | Task Implementation | Positive Group Affiliation | Feeling Orientation

1. **Assertiveness with Perspective Taking:** Use Assertiveness to ask more questions. Invite others to share ideas and then investigate their positions. Listen closely to their views. This will strengthen your Perspective Taking and yield valuable data for negotiations, task efforts, and building interpersonal relations. Develop listening skills with the use of Introversion, and collect a broad array of information by cultivating your Perceiving preference.

2. **Group Facilitation with Positive Group Affiliation:** Help the group conduct activities that promote interpersonal sharing, so members develop more rapport and team spirit. Consciously apply your skills with Extraversion and Feeling to accomplish this goal.

3. **Task Analysis with Task Implementation:** Acquire more skills in the implementation domain, helping the team put a plan into action and achieving a successful conclusion. The higher Task Analysis score indicates a greater leaning towards analysis, but raising the implementation side will balance your performance, producing more exceptional task outcomes. Grow skills with the

Thinking preference to monitor progress with a project and with the Judging attitude to organize the work more efficiently.

4. **Initiative:** Find an opportunity to lead a large project. Bring to bear your skills with Constructive Negotiation Approach to orchestrate win-win agreements, which will solidify team unity and inspire a strong task effort. Employ the Intuitive preference to define the common ground for these agreements, the Feeling preference to stay in touch with the people and sustain morale, and the Judging preference to attend to the organizational issues.

5. **Feeling Orientation:** Exploit your abilities with the Feeling preference to understand more deeply others' emotions and perspectives. Tune into physical gestures that express emotion (using the Sensing preference) and, as is reasonable, investigate what is going on with people. With your Extraversion and Feeling preferences, make emotional issues more discussable in the group.

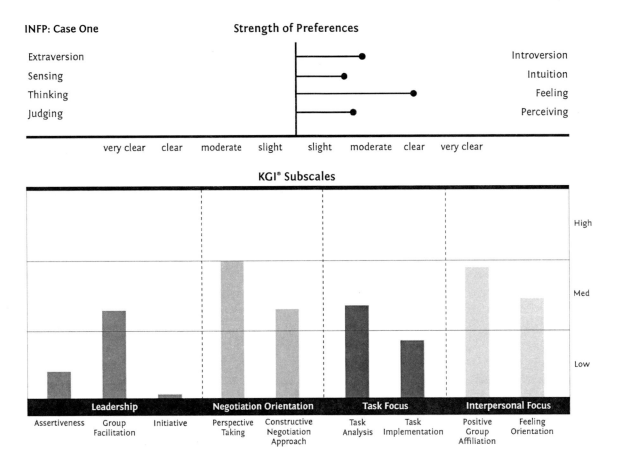

Strength of Preferences

Extraversion		Introversion
Sensing		Intuition
Thinking		Feeling
Judging		Perceiving

very clear · clear · moderate · slight · slight · moderate · clear · very clear

KGI® Subscales

Leadership · Negotiation Orientation · Task Focus · Interpersonal Focus

Assertiveness · Group Facilitation · Initiative · Perspective Taking · Constructive Negotiation Approach · Task Analysis · Task Implementation · Positive Group Affiliation · Feeling Orientation

High · Med · Low

1. Assertiveness with Perspective Taking: Through Perspective Taking, you have a keen awareness of other members' interests, concerns, and values. In response, express your own opinions about where you agree or disagree with others. Use this approach as a means to participate more in group discussions. Embrace Extraversion energy to raise your voice and Thinking to articulate your ideas.

2. Group Facilitation and Negotiation Orientation: Assist the group in formulating win-win agreements that will make the team more cohesive and productive. Draw on insights from Perspective Taking to forge joint decisions that benefit everyone. Think creatively to find points of connection among different members' positions, so you can bring them together. Exercise the Feeling preference to get in others' shoes and understand their points of view, the Intuition preference to identify where different positions can come together, and Extraversion to lead the group.

3. Task Analysis: Observe how members with strong skills in analysis dissect task problems and solve them. Let them be your role models. Practice Sensing (looking closely at facts), Perceiving (examining a broad range of issues), and Thinking (logically structuring the effort).

4. Task Implementation: Become more involved in the team's efforts to put plans into action. Communicate ideas on how to get the project moving and aid the team in making the adjustments that will improve the effort. Tap into Thinking and Judging energies for this endeavor.

5. Initiative: Pursue the opportunity to lead part or all of a group project. Pick something that really interests you and that will bring your best skills forward. Make sure to pull the other members in, building on their ideas and interests so they are on board with the effort. Use your skills with Negotiation Orientation and Interpersonal Focus. Exercise Extraversion energy to take action, Feeling to engage others, and Judging to organize the project.

INFP: Case Two

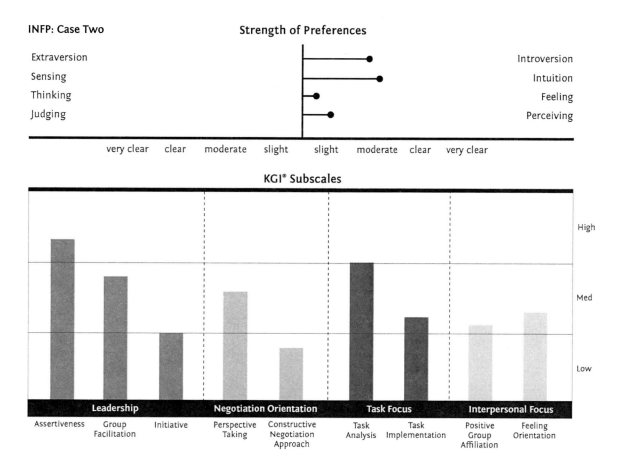

Strength of Preferences

	very clear	clear	moderate	slight	slight	moderate	clear	very clear
Extraversion						Introversion		
Sensing							Intuition	
Thinking				Feeling				
Judging				Perceiving				

KGI® Subscales

Leadership: Assertiveness, Group Facilitation, Initiative
Negotiation Orientation: Perspective Taking, Constructive Negotiation Approach
Task Focus: Task Analysis, Task Implementation
Interpersonal Focus: Positive Group Affiliation, Feeling Orientation

1. **Assertiveness with Perspective Taking:** Employ your Assertiveness to ask more questions of others, to probe their views and positions. What do they think of your statements? What are their concerns? Put your Feeling function to work to look at things from their side, expanding your Perspective Taking. Use the Perceiving attitude to examine many angles, which will expand how you see the situation. Draw on Introversion to listen closely.

2. **Constructive Negotiation Approach:** Capitalizing on the information obtained from your enhanced Perspective Taking, try to fashion win-win agreements so all members gain. This will increase team unity and member commitment to the work. Your preference for Intuition enables you to see connections between differing positions—consciously use that to create win-win situations. Bring the Perceiving attitude into the mix, considering a wide range of possibilities.

3. **Task Analysis with Task Implementation:** Be careful not to overanalyze a task. You can get caught in the excitement of analysis, neglecting the need for direct action. Move more quickly to implement a plan and develop skills in that direction. Bring to bear the Judging attitude to organize the effort and the Thinking function to assess progress and make adjustments as the work rolls along.

4. **Positive Group Affiliation:** Take time to get more acquainted with other team members, conversing with them before or after meetings, or on other occasions. Get to know their interests and hobbies to see if there are areas of mutual enthusiasm. Be willing to employ Extraversion to extend yourself socially and Feeling to construct interpersonal bridges.

5. **Initiative:** Find the right team project or part of a project to take on a leadership role. Choose a situation that has significance for you, something for which you have passion. But get everyone else involved—solicit ideas, do joint problem solving, and delegate responsibilities to people with appropriate interests. Summon Extraversion to interact more, Sensing to monitor details, Feeling to create a positive social atmosphere, and Judging to organize the venture.

Strength of Preferences

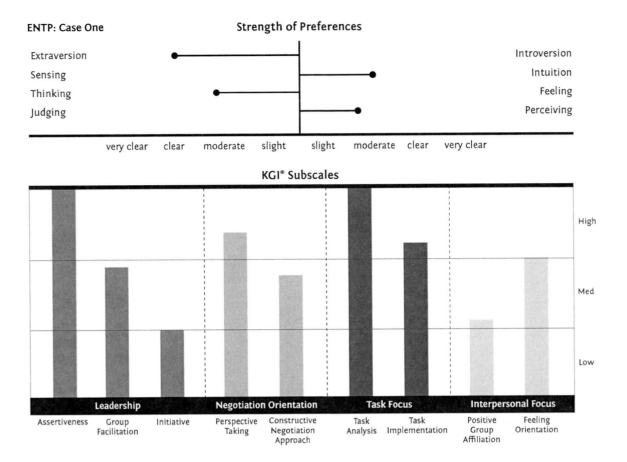

KGI® Subscales

1. **Assertiveness:** Sit back, listen, and observe more. Watch how other members interact with each other to get more of a feel for the group atmosphere. Your current level of assertiveness can come across as domineering, undermining your leadership effectiveness. Pick your spots to contribute and raise issues that are the most important for you. Develop the Introversion skills of observing and listening to balance your strong Extraversion.

2. **Group Facilitation with Task Focus:** Put more energy into facilitating the team's efforts in the task area. Invite members to share their ideas to analyze the project, promoting a dialogue about strategy. Include your ideas, but engage others in the process. Beware of a tendency to overanalyze the topic. Keep the discussion focused, with everyone contributing, and move it forward at a reasonable pace. Use the Thinking preference but build new skills with the opposite attitude of Judging, keeping everyone's eyes on the target and organizing the effort in an efficient manner.

3. **Positive Group Affiliation:** Take strides to get to know other group members. Before or after meetings, take time to talk with them. As you develop relationships, it becomes easier to communicate and

collaborate. Use existing skills with Extraversion to start conversations, but employ Introversion to listen closely. Also, cultivate the Feeling preference to understand others' motivations and concerns, developing a positive mutual regard.

4. **Constructive Negotiation Approach:** Work more consciously to help the group construct win-win agreements during negotiations. Drawing on insights about other members' positions gained through Perspective Taking, help the team define common interests that bring them together and unify them. This will inspire greater commitment to the work and higher quality outcomes. Apply skills from the Perceiving preference to examine everyone's ideas, and from Intuition to see connections between these points.

5. **Initiative:** Seek an opportunity to be the main leader for a project. Be sure to pay attention to the people issues—bringing everyone into discussions, fashioning win-win agreements, and maintaining a positive team atmosphere. Keep the task enterprise focused and timely. Use skills with Extraversion to facilitate the effort, with Feeling to pay attention to team atmosphere, and with Judging to organize the project efficiently.

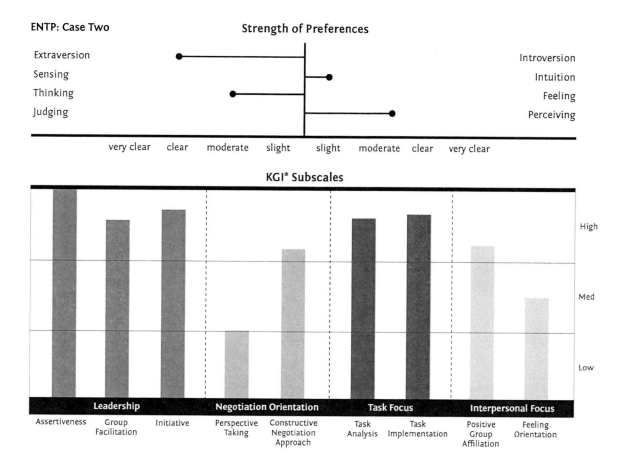

Strength of Preferences

	very clear	clear	moderate	slight	slight	moderate	clear	very clear	
Extraversion									Introversion
Sensing									Intuition
Thinking									Feeling
Judging									Perceiving

KGI® Subscales

Leadership | Negotiation Orientation | Task Focus | Interpersonal Focus

Assertiveness, Group Facilitation, Initiative, Perspective Taking, Constructive Negotiation Approach, Task Analysis, Task Implementation, Positive Group Affiliation, Feeling Orientation

1. **Assertiveness:** Throttle down the amount of Assertiveness, which, at the current level, may be seen by other group members as overbearing. Listen to and watch how other members interact to get a better feel for their personalities and how the group is operating. Selectively pick your times to enter the conversation, making points that are most critical for you. Remember that when you frequently express many ideas, people listen less closely and may even turn you off. Practice skills with Introversion to listen and observe more.

2. **Perspective Taking:** Channel some of your Assertiveness energy into asking questions of other members to hear their perspectives on the issues. Really listen to others' statements and mirror back to them what you heard to check for clarity in the communication. If there is any confusion, ask probing questions to gain accuracy. Put yourself in their shoes to obtain a deeper understanding of their views. Deploy skills with Extraversion to engage other members, Introversion to listen closely, and the Feeling function to get a better grasp of people's interests and motivations.

3. **Group Facilitation:** Take advantage of your facilitation energy to get everyone involved in the group's activities. Make it a real team effort. Note

that with all of your leadership energy, you may assume too much responsibility so that others just sit back and become passive. Get people invested in actions to help the team. From insights you have gained from Perspective Taking, delegate responsibilities to members according to their interests so they will put more effort into their tasks. Draw on your Intuition function to creatively manage the team, and work on skills with Judging to organize the enterprise.

4. **Positive Group Affiliation with Feeling Orientation:** Pay attention to people's facial expressions and body language to assess their reactions. Be willing to ask people how they are feeling and to express your own feelings. This will keep you connected with the team and provide worthwhile information to pursue Positive Group Affiliation. Employ skills from the Sensing function to observe physical reactions, skills from the Feeling function to address emotional issues, and skills from Extraversion to promote a positive environment on the team.

5. **Initiative:** Be more selective in taking on leadership roles for group projects. Your score indicates that you may take on too much and become overloaded, which is not only stressful but can lead to poor outcomes when you are stretched too thin.

Part of the answer is to get others involved so they can share some of the leadership responsibilities, distributing the pressures and providing mutual support systems. Use Introversion to reflect on your own best choices for leadership positions and the Thinking preference to create realistic strategies for shared leadership.

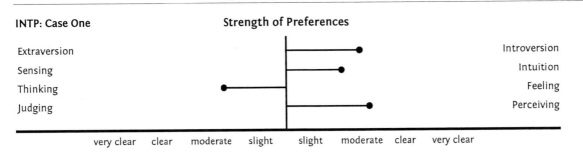

INTP: Case One

Strength of Preferences

	very clear	clear	moderate	slight	slight	moderate	clear	very clear	
Extraversion									Introversion
Sensing									Intuition
Thinking									Feeling
Judging									Perceiving

KGI® Subscales

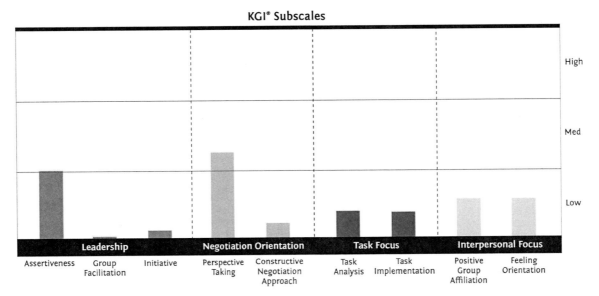

| Leadership | | | Negotiation Orientation | | Task Focus | | Interpersonal Focus | |
| Assertiveness | Group Facilitation | Initiative | Perspective Taking | Constructive Negotiation Approach | Task Analysis | Task Implementation | Positive Group Affiliation | Feeling Orientation |

1. **Assertiveness with Perspective Taking:** Express your opinions more often during discussions. Invite others to share their ideas to create more of a dialogue. Investigate task issues from multiple angles to construct strong strategies. Adopt Extraversion to speak up and the Thinking function to contribute a variety of ideas.

2. **Group Facilitation and Negotiation Orientation:** Promote conversation in the Negotiation Orientation sector. Utilize your attraction to Perspective Taking to probe people's positions and uncover their deeper concerns. Then try to find connections between different members' concerns to establish the common ground for win-win agreements. Your Intuition preference is the right tool for finding the middle ground, so apply it accordingly. Use Extraversion energy to get involved and the Perceiving attitude to assess a range of concerns.

3. **Feeling Orientation:** Scrutinize group members' facial expressions, body language, and voice intonations. Assess their reactions to issues: what draws them in, what turns them off. Use this infor-

mation to evaluate potential buy-in as you propose agreements in a negotiation. Exercise the Sensing function to watch physical gestures, and the Feeling function to attune to the emotional cues.

4. **Task Analysis with Task Implementation:** Study how members who are strong in Task Focus present ideas and organize the group. How do they analyze the task and devise plans of action? How do they delegate assignments, promote coordinated team effort? Notice their techniques and begin to imitate them. Exploit your Introversion to watch others' behaviors, Thinking to gauge their approaches, and the Judging attitude to assist in organizing the team.

5. **Initiative:** After you expand your skills in the above areas, take advantage of an opportunity to lead a team in an appropriate project. Choose something in which you'd really like to invest energy. Take the risk and plunge in, but remember to engage the members, prompting them to share ideas and become actively involved. Employ Extraversion to assume an active role and engage others, and Judging to organize the effort.

INTP: Case Two

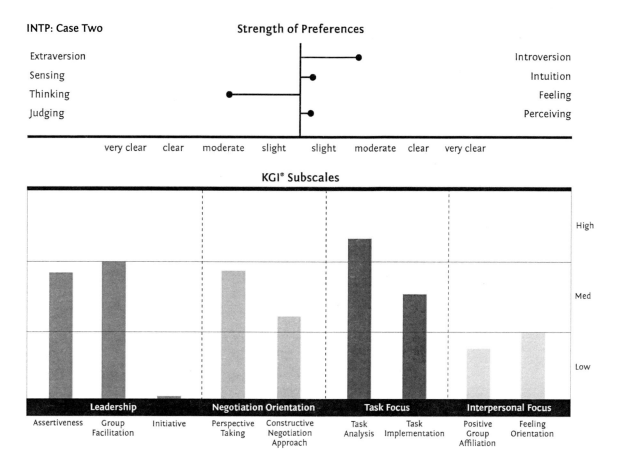

1. **Constructive Negotiation Approach:** Take advantage of the insights gained from Perspective Taking with regard to team members' interests, concerns, and values. Locate the common ground, places where people's interests can come together in win-win agreements. Exert your Perceiving attitude to scan the various concerns, your Intuition to see vital connections among the points, and apply Extraversion to speak up and facilitate this discussion.

2. **Task Analysis with Task Implementation:** Beware of overdoing Task Analysis. The results indicate that you may spend too much time contemplating a strategy, overanalyzing it, and then waiting too long to take action. When a plan is implemented, help monitor the progress in order to guide the effort to successful completion. Deploy Extraversion to actively participate in this process, Thinking to assess plan execution, and the Judging attitude to advance it to conclusion.

3. **Positive Group Affiliation:** Take time to get more acquainted with other group members. Partake in small talk and build informal relationships. This will increase camaraderie. Exercise Extraversion to talk more often with people and the Feeling function to establish deeper rapport.

4. **Feeling Orientation:** Assess people's emotional reactions during discussions; notice what disturbs people and what encourages or inspires them. Use this information to better understand their motivations and interests. Use Introversion to observe other members, Sensing to tune into the physical details, and Feeling to pick up on the emotional content.

5. **Initiative:** Find an opportunity to take a leadership role with part of a project. Share leadership responsibilities and put some of your new group skills into practice, particularly with negotiation and task. Start to climb the stairs towards greater leadership roles. Bring to bear Extraversion, Thinking, and Judging.

These cases reflect the wide variety of results that can occur when the KGI and MBTI tools are combined in the individual coaching process. As seen, there can be significant variation in the way that people with the same type preference operate in small groups. The method identifies these variations, which allows a professional to deliver very exact, personalized guidance for the cultivation of new skills. The method customizes a plan for each client's particular needs.

Continuing in a similar vein, a consultant can also customize a plan for a team, based on its specific ways of operating. In the next chapter, the KGI–MBTI model for team building is presented, opening up another avenue to promote growth and development. ✕

CHAPTER 23

Method for Team Building with the KGI® and MTBI® Assessments

When the Klein Group Instrument® and Myers-Briggs Type Indicator® assessments join in a team-building procedure, individuals can enter into a sophisticated analysis of personal and team issues. They identify new directions for their leadership development, and design new strategies for their team's interactive processes. With psychological typology in the equation, they examine the underlying energies that are affecting both areas, finding ways to channel the energies effectively and efficiently. Every individual has an opportunity

for social growth, while members fortify their joint efforts. Collaborating on two fronts, they create a powerful learning dynamic that ignites the synergy which will foster the highest productivity.

The KGI–MBTI method can be applied to a newly formed team (where people are not well acquainted) or to a seasoned, established unit. In either case, a group becomes a learning team. The system puts people on the same page with a shared vision, allowing them to work together to refine their communication, task performance, and social relations.

The team-building model has been developed in two distinct contexts: first, in business, professional, organizational, and sport settings, connected with personnel training; second, in academic classrooms, related to university instruction of undergraduate and graduate students. With this second design, the method can also be adapted for high school classrooms.

Since the two team-building approaches have special features, they will be introduced sepa-

rately. To start, a general design is described for business, professional, organizational, and sport training, a procedure that can be applied flexibly in these arenas. In the next chapter, the academic design is presented, describing the approach an instructor would pursue with students. Both methods will be illustrated with case studies in Chapter 25.

General Design for Team Building

A consultant or trainer can apply this method with a group consisting of three to ten members, though some may be slightly larger. The following procedure would be suitable for an established team, often the norm in a consulting intervention. At the conclusion, alterations to the design will be discussed for working with a newly formed team. In either case, the consultant would *pre-arrange* for testing with the KGI assessment.

Important note: When implementing this approach, *a consultant must register participants in*

a team format to administer the KGI assessment.
This is essential to obtain the KGI® Group Profile, which anonymously merges individual scores for the report. (See Chapter 7 directions for organizing a KGI® Group Profile.)

For the Myers-Briggs Type Indicator assessment, participants may obtain results online through the MBTI Online website. If the consultant is a certified MBTI practitioner, the individual may coordinate administration of the instrument.

The training also utilizes two one-page handouts: *Words to Help Understanding of Type Concepts* (descriptors for the eight MBTI preferences), and *Descriptions of the Sixteen Types* (one-paragraph descriptions of the types). These can be purchased from CAPT.org.

Team-Building Process

1. *Members take the instruments and receive individual KGI and MBTI results.*

- Since the KGI assessment is administered online, a consultant sends the participants their personal results electronically prior to the first training session. Group members review their scores and examine the *KGI® User's Guide* accompanying the profile. The latter orients participants to the principal ideas addressed in the training. Members are able to print a copy of their profile and bring it to the opening event.

- If participants take the MBTI assessment online, they will bring their results to the first session. If the consultant is a certified MBTI practitioner, he or she may personally administer the instrument beforehand and then distribute the results at the opening session.

2. *A brief outline of the training program.*

- The program proceeds in these steps (with time estimates for the activities):

A. An opening session to make introductions, review program goals, and present the Klein Group Instrument and Myers-Briggs Type Indicator models (60–90 minutes).

B. A coaching session with each member to evaluate the individual's KGI and MBTI results and set an agenda for personal skill building (90 minutes each).

C. A group session to explore collective MBTI results and KGI® Group Profile results, in order to establish team strategies to improve performance. This may include setting up mentoring relationships within the group so people can assist one another in their personal skill-building efforts (60–90 minutes).

D. A follow-up group session to assess team progress and update the strategies (60–90 minutes, usually four to six weeks later.)

E. Follow-up individual sessions, as appropriate. These can be conducted over the phone, or in person, scheduled around the second team meeting (45–60 minutes a session).

F. It is worth noting that follow-up sessions have sometimes included working with a pair of team members, to assist them in improving their specific working relationship. According to the team's needs, a consultant can be flexible in arranging such sessions.

Scheduling: The consultant should have the above elements in mind when negotiating a schedule with an organization. For a group with five members, items A–C would require two days of training. Follow-up sessions would be arranged for the amount of time indicated. It is possible for a consultant to schedule additional follow-up sessions, beyond what is indicated, as appropriate for a particular circumstance.

3. *The opening session with the entire team. (Approximate time: 60–90 minutes.)*

Initial Phase
- Start with basic introductions, so everyone becomes acquainted.
- The consultant reviews the goals for the training:

A. The aim is to establish a learning team. Every member will acquire new leadership and group skills, and people will support one another in this quest. Together, members will also evaluate their interactive processes and refine their efforts to become a high-performing team.

B. Each member will build leadership and group skills by taking advantage of the KGI and MBTI individual results. There will be one-on-one coaching sessions to assist people in this process.

C. Following the one-on-one meetings, the members will receive, via e-mail, the team's KGI® Group Profile. (Providing hard copies is also an option.) Members should review the collective results, and there will be a group meeting to assess the report.

D. As a group, members will establish goals to enhance their teamwork, setting an agenda to improve particular processes.

E. There will be follow-up sessions to evaluate the members' and the group's progress in achieving the designated goals.

F. At this point, it is necessary to review some basic ethical guidelines.

In this enterprise, it is important to establish an atmosphere of mutual respect, trust, and support. The individual profiles are the property of the individual respondents. Members have the right to select what information they want to share. When there is an atmosphere of trust, people tend to be more open with sharing their data, which benefits the team. But information shared in the group must stay within the group, unless some other agreement is made with the participants' free consent.

Myers-Briggs Type Indicator® Phase

▸ To begin, it is important to ask, "How many people have taken the MBTI tool in the past?" Usually, the number ranges from some to all of the members. This question helps the consultant assess background knowledge, which influences how to pace and focus the material. For first-time people, it is necessary to move in a slow, clear, and methodical fashion. For a group with previous experience, it is possible to move more quickly in reviewing familiar material.

▸ The consultant presents the Myers-Briggs Type Indicator information, starting with a review of the following concepts:

A. The MBTI instrument seeks to identify positive personality preferences that all people possess. It is not meant to negatively categorize anyone in any way. It provides an opportunity for people to better understand themselves, to understand others, and to develop their talents. Based on the ideas of well-known psychologist Carl Jung, the model demonstrates how psychic energy flows in different directions in the personality, with people preferring certain paths over others. Working with Jung's ideas, the mother-daughter team of Katherine Briggs and Isabel Myers constructed the Myers-Briggs Type Indicator assessment to bring the benefit of his typology to a broader audience.

B. Introduce the design of the MBTI model, the four dichotomies with the eight preferences: Extraversion (E)—Introversion (I); Sensing (S)—Intuition (N); Thinking (T)—Feeling (F); Judging (J)—Perceiving (P).

C. Identify the characteristics of each of the eight preferences. (The handout *Words to Help Understanding of Type Concepts* can be introduced at this stage of the presentation.)

D. Explain that the clarity of preference reflects how regularly one tends to exercise that preference and to what extent one may access the opposite preference in the dichotomy. A person with a slight preference is more likely to use both sides of the dichotomy at different times, fairly equally, while the more a person's preference moves out to the moderate, clear, and very clear categories, the more consistently the individual tends to utilize that one preference.

E. Describe how the scores on the four dichotomies combine to create one's psychological type, with sixteen different possibilities: ESTJ, ESFJ, ENFJ, ENTJ, ESTP, ESFP, ENFP, ENTP, ISTJ, ISFJ, INFJ, INTJ, ISTP, ISFP, INFP, INTP.

▸ If participants have not already received their MBTI results electronically, the

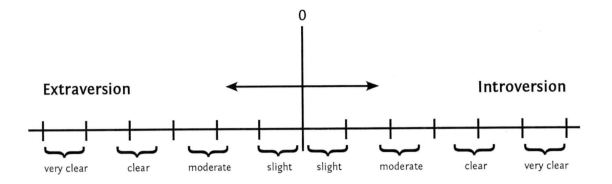

0

Extraversion ← → Introversion

very clear   clear   moderate   slight   slight   moderate   clear   very clear

consultant should then pass out the MBTI materials and have members read their information. (This occurs when a consultant administers a paper-and-pencil version and scores the materials.)

F. Questions to pose after members have reviewed their results:

 • How many people feel their results fit well to very well? (This invites people to validate the accuracy of their results.)

 • For those who don't feel there's a good fit, ask: why not? Often this relates to a slight score on a particular dichotomy, which produces some ambiguity because the respondent's score falls into a zone where behaviors from both preferences are used in a somewhat balanced way. In this case, a member may conclude that the description of one preference does not adequately address other meaningful behaviors used from the opposite prefer-ence, leading to the feeling that the profile is not an exact fit. That issue should be explained. If an individual has more than one slight preference among the four dichotomies, the problem is compounded.

G. This is an appropriate moment to distribute the handout *Descriptions of the Sixteen Types.* When a participant has a slight score with Sensing, for example, as part of an ISTJ result, the client can now look at the description for INTJ, to see if that is a better

fit. For any slight score(s), a participant may use this adjustment, which allows an individ-ual to make a personal decision about which type is the best fit.

H. For people who have taken the instrument before, ask: how do these results compare to previous administrations? For some, they are exactly the same. For others, there may be differences. When significant differences occur, analyze the person's work and social experiences during the period between administrations. See how an individual adapted to outside circumstances. Since people adjust to their environments, changes in social situations, or job responsibilities, can cause a person to redirect psychological energies and respond differently to the assessment questions. It is also worthwhile to ask, does an individual believe there are other forces that induced a shift in preference(s)?

 • This is where the handout *Words to Help Understanding of Type Concepts* can be very helpful. Reviewing the handout, ask participants to examine each preference and put a plus (+) next to words that seem very appropriate and a minus (-) next to ones that don't fit. This allows the participants to assess, in detail, behaviors that are most personally active, enabling them to make a more grounded assess-ment of the material.

I. Inform participants that in this skill-building model, there will be opportunities to utilize and refine existing MBTI preferences, as well as chances to explore, practice, and gain comfort with opposite preferences. Through this experience, members will increase their social competencies and become well-rounded leaders and group participants, expanding the social aspect of their personalities. This process connects to Carl Jung's concept of individuation, in which people broaden their talents to more fully realize their potential.

Klein Group Instrument® Phase

(To assist a consultant in preparing for this phase, see Appendix: The Basic Script for Introducing the Klein Group Instrument® Assessment.)

‣ The consultant should now present KGI information in this sequence:

A. Explain that the Klein Group Instrument assessment is designed to assist people in expanding their team leadership and group skills. These skills have widespread application. They are relevant not only for interpersonal and small-group contexts in businesses, professions, organizations, sport teams, and religious communities, but in other social situations, such as relations with a significant other and in family life. So there can be tremendous benefit from this training.

B. The KGI assessment is constructed so it can complement the MBTI assessment for both individual and team development.

C. Introduce the KGI diamond model, with its four major scales, and include a brief description of each scale. (Utilize the one-line descriptors in Chapter 2 and related ideas from the paragraph descriptions in Chapter 3.)

D. Explain the points, listed next, that clarify how the KGI design targets basic team functions, making it a potent team-building model.

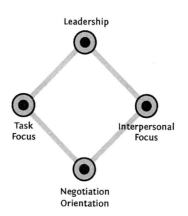

Leadership: Every group needs a leader (or leaders) to step up and guide the group in its efforts. This is an essential principle for effective small-group operations.

Task Focus: The KGI model targets task-oriented teams. It is not about informal, Saturday-night social gatherings, but about group situations where there is a task to complete.

Interpersonal Focus: Since people in a group need to collaborate to get work done, there is always the matter of interpersonal relations—how members get along—which affects the quality of the effort and the final outcome.

Negotiation Orientation: Negotiation addresses concerns with task planning and task execution as well as interpersonal issues that arise. Accordingly, negotiation energy moves towards both the task and interpersonal areas of group life.

‣ Mention Robert Bales' theory about the tension between task and interpersonal concerns: as you focus on one, you take your eyes off the other. The team needs to attend to both. There is a back and forth rhythm in how a group moves between these elements, which the KGI helps the team manage. Negotiation assists in addressing this tension and in maintaining team harmony (see Chapter 2).

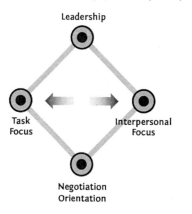

E. Mention the research on what causes synergy in a team: Inclusion (addressed by the win-win approach in Negotiation Orientation) and Social Awareness (attended to by Interpersonal Focus). This is visually expressed in the diagram below. So the KGI model is right on target in fostering skills that lead to individual development and team synergy, propelling a group to a lofty level of performance (see Chapter 4).

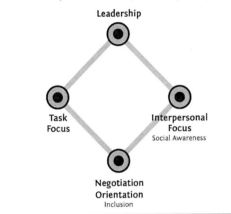

F. Present the KGI subscales with the short definitions (utilize the one-line descriptors from Chapter 3, with the paragraph-long descriptions to provide expanded explanations as needed). These define the essential skill-building areas of the instrument.

G. Describe the design of the KGI® Individual Profile, which is divided into four sections based on the four major scales: Leadership, Negotiation Orientation, Task Focus, and Interpersonal Focus.

▸ Mention that each subsection opens with a graph displaying the levels of performance for the main scale and its related subscales, using a low, medium, and high standard. The graph levels reflect how often a person tends to use skills in each category. For Low, a person tends to use a skill 0–49% of the time; Medium 50–74% of the time; High 75–100% of the time.

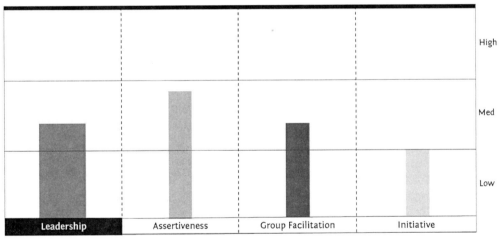

*Represents a composite score for all the subscales of the **Leadership** scale

▸ Explain that the section then introduces a statement describing the respondent's basic orientation in this area of group activity. The statement corresponds to the score in the first column in the graph, in this case, the composite Leadership score. The statement is calibrated to a low, medium, or high result.

▸ Following this information, for each of the subscale areas there are statements about what the person *enjoys* doing in that area of group life, things that might be *challenging*, and suggestions for *growing specific new skills*.

H. Explain the dynamic growth orientation of the instrument: it supports skill acquisition in essential areas of group life, enabling people to become more proficient leaders and group members. The skills generalize to a wide variety of contexts, really boosting a person's overall social competence.

I. Show pictures of the composite graphs at the end of the KGI® Individual Profile: one displays the major scales in a sequence and the other the subscales scores in a row. The former allows the participant to see the "big picture" of performance; the latter enables the individual to define a very precise plan for obtaining new leadership and group skills. Zero in on the composite subscale graph.

Your KGI® Subscales

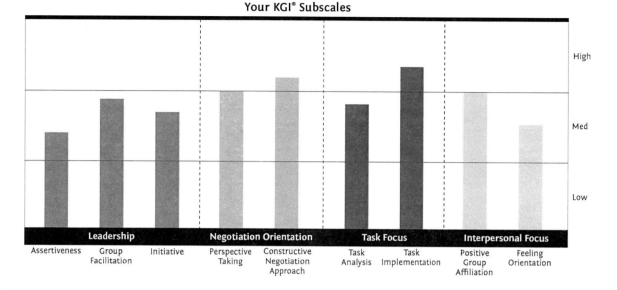

Important: Since the KGI subscales target the core areas of group activity, it is worthwhile for an individual to balance efforts across all of the domains in order to be an effective, all-round performer. When outfitted with a complete set of these skills, an individual is well-equipped to be a potent leader and group member, someone who can promote synergy in a team, i.e., top performance.

J. Briefly mention that all of the individual scores will be combined anonymously to produce the KGI® Group Profile, something the team will investigate later in this training process.

K. Present the KGI diamond model showing the correlations with the MBTI preferences, the key connections between the assessments. (The data have been calculated through quantitative and qualitative analyses. See the information in Chapter 19.)

- Explain that the MBTI preferences naturally express themselves in ways that relate to the KGI scales and subscales. This allows a person to assess how psychological energies flow in one's group behaviors. It permits the construction of a plan to build new group skills

using existing preferences and also opposite preferences.

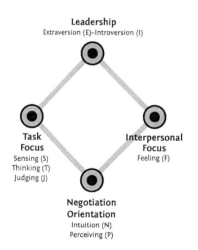

L. Show a slide that presents a person's MBTI preference scores on top and KGI composite subscale graph on the bottom. Describe how individual KGI subscale results can be evaluated according to the MBTI preferences. (In the next graph, we see how the individual's ESTJ preferences produce strength in the KGI Leadership subscales of Assertiveness and Initiative and in the KGI Task Focus domain. Most notably, the Negotiation Orientation and Interpersonal Focus sectors are underdeveloped. To acquire skills in these areas, the individual would be aided by building up the opposite MBTI preferences of Intuition, Feeling and Perceiving. This skill acquisition would also enable the person to be more effective in the Group Facilitation area.)

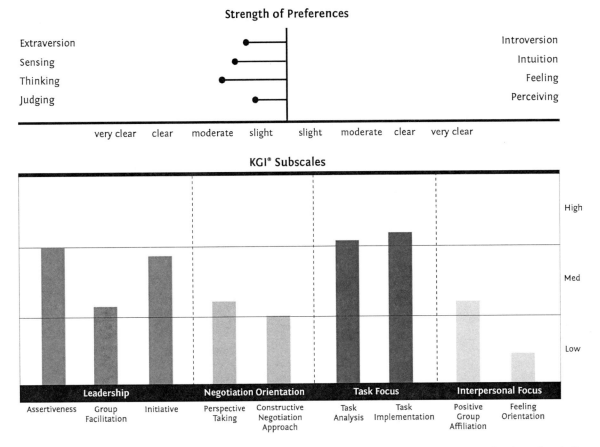

Strength of Preferences

Extraversion	Introversion
Sensing	Intuition
Thinking	Feeling
Judging	Perceiving

very clear   clear   moderate   slight   slight   moderate   clear   very clear

KGI® Subscales

High

Med

Low

| Leadership | Negotiation Orientation | Task Focus | Interpersonal Focus |

Assertiveness   Group Facilitation   Initiative   Perspective Taking   Constructive Negotiation Approach   Task Analysis   Task Implementation   Positive Group Affiliation   Feeling Orientation

M. Explain to the participants the steps for individual skill building with the KGI and MBTI instruments, as follows:

▸ Identify your key strengths in the various KGI subscale domains.

▸ Assess which areas are problematic for you.

▸ What new skills will be the *most valuable, most meaningful for you* to develop in order to expand your leadership and group behaviors? Where do you want to be in the future with respect to your group skills? Identify your vision and then pick subscale areas to work on.

▸ From the selected subscale areas in the KGI® Individual Profile, identify growth statements to implement. Prioritize these new skills and establish a learning agenda.

▸ Experiment with one or two new skills in appropriate group settings.

▸ Continue to practice and refine the skills until they become more comfortable and more integrated into your style. Usually, practicing a skill on *at least three occasions* will solidify it.

▸ Develop a relationship with a colleague who can give you feedback about these efforts. It is valuable to get outside, objective feedback about your performance from someone you can trust.

▸ As you master certain new skills, select additional ones that will help you further expand your competence as a leader and group member. Seek to become more fully functioning in these pivotal areas of group life. If you obtain new skills in *five different KGI subscales*, you can significantly transform your leadership and social style.

- Your MBTI preferences provide insights into psychological energies that can be utilized to build your group skills. Both your existing preferences and your opposite preferences come into play with this skill building. Existing preferences allow you to enlarge established strengths and refine their applications; the opposite preferences help you acquire new skills in undeveloped areas that broaden your range of activity and really balance your performance.

- Respond to any questions the members have about the model and the two instruments. Mention that the next step will be to conduct individual sessions with members to help them design their personal plans for skill building.

4. Conduct individual coaching sessions with the various team members (90 minutes per session).

- The consultant will meet with each member, coaching the individual according to the KGI and MBTI design described in Chapter 20.

- The consultant will help an individual construct a plan to work on specific skills to promote the individual's social development.

- During the coaching session, obtain detailed information about the person's perspective on the current team:

  A. With respect to the team, what issues and concerns stand out for the client?

  B. How does the individual get along with other team members? Identify positive relationships and difficult ones.

  C. What larger organizational issues may be affecting how the member participates in this group?

- This information provides insights into the interactive dynamics within the team and assists a consultant in tailoring strategies for the individual's needs. By confidentially discussing these issues with all of the group members, the consultant gains a comprehensive knowledge about the issues impacting the team. This knowledge is invaluable for setting appropriate agendas for individual

members as well as for selecting the most effective strategies for the team as a whole.

- By the end of the session, the particular client's skill-building agenda will be set.

5. The team session with the KGI® Group Profile and MBTI® data.

- In advance of this meeting, all members receive an electronic copy of their KGI® Group Profile for review. A paper copy can also be passed out in advance of the session. Since it is a substantial document, give participants ample time prior to the meeting to look it over.

- By this point, people have become very acquainted with the KGI® and MBTI models from the presentation, coaching sessions, and their review of the team's KGI® Group Profile.

- Tell the members that they will now investigate how the method can help them refine the group's collective processes. Like an individual working on specific behaviors, the team can adjust particular group processes to elevate its performance.

Myers-Briggs Type Indicator® Phase

- Start by having the members share their type preferences. They should mention what they believe are the most significant aspects of their personal results, e.g., most accurate points regarding interests and behaviors, and anything that appears questionable. If the members are well acquainted, it's possible to have other members give a person feedback about items that appear questionable. Based on what they've observed of the individual's behavior, do they agree or disagree with the individual's assessment of the MBTI data?

- Construct with the group a type table: a sixteen square grid showing the distribution of the members' MBTI scores.

  A. With respect to the eight preferences, which ones have the most representation?

  B. Ask the participants: how do you think these preferences influence how the group approaches leadership, task execution, negotiations, and interpersonal relations?

Example: If Thinking types are in the majority, does the group attack the task logically but overlook interpersonal considerations? The type data can identify meaningful trends.

C. Which of the eight preferences is underrepresented or missing? How does this create blind spots in the ways the group may handle leadership opportunities, task execution, negotiations, and interpersonal relations?

▸ As the team moves on to the KGI graph materials, it will consider how to utilize members' MBTI preferences most productively. The MBTI information alerts the group to strength areas where many people have certain preferences and weaker areas where few people or no one has a specific preference. The KGI data will enable the team to assess these issues in greater detail by presenting collective results on essential aspects of group life. The group can then evaluate how various members may take leadership roles, based on their preferences and group skills, to guide the team in more constructive directions. A lone Feeling type, for example, may be designated to help raise group awareness about overlooked emotional issues, enabling the team to deal with those issues more constructively.

Klein Group Instrument® Phase

▸ The consultant now brings the KGI® Group Profile into the discussion, proceeding in the following manner:

A. An overview of the KGI® Group Profile. Begin with a description of the components of the profile and the information they contain.

　1. The **Introduction**, which presents the diamond model and spells out the goal of forging a learning team.

　2. **Communication and Confidentiality.** This segment establishes ethical guidelines for the sharing of personal results as part of a team-building process.

3 **Team Results: the Composite Graphs.** The section contains the Group Composite Major Scale Graph and the Group Composite Subscale Graph, with points about how to interpret each of them, so members can assess their collective performance.

4. **Action Steps.** This component outlines the steps for choosing subscale categories to address, finding suggestions to improve the team's interactive processes in the appropriate subscale sections of the report, implementing those strategies, and pursuing an ongoing developmental process that will make the group a high-performing team.

5. **The Four Major Scale Sections.** The team receives feedback along the four major domains (Leadership, Negotiation, Task, and Interpersonal). Each section includes a graph that identifies the range of member scores for the major scale and its subscales, a team assessment statement for that area, and suggestions on how to improve group performance in each of the subscale categories. This design is similar to the sequence of information in the KGI® Individual Profile.

6. **One-Sentence Descriptions of the KGI Major Scales and Their Subscales.** On the last page of the profile are brief descriptors of the scales and subscales, providing an easy reference for the essential ideas in the KGI skill-building system.

B. The consultant will now move into an analysis of the *Group Composite Subscale Graph*, guiding members in the evaluation of their collective performance. This graph allows a group to proceed in the most efficient, focused manner. It should be noted that the KGI® Group Profile also contains the Group Composite Major Scale Graph, which presents a "big picture" of team performance. A consultant may find it useful to reference the major scale graph in certain situations; however, this is discretionary and not absolutely required. On the columns of

Graph Analysis

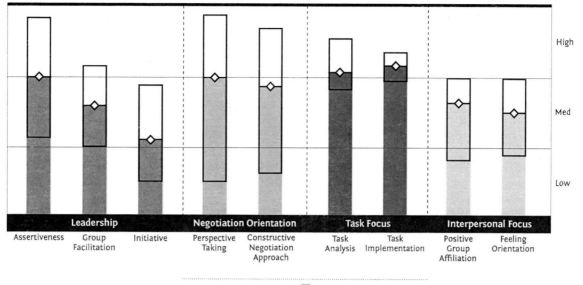

Assertiveness	Group Facilitation	Initiative	Perspective Taking	Constructive Negotiation Approach	Task Analysis	Task Implementation	Positive Group Affiliation	Feeling Orientation
Leadership			**Negotiation Orientation**		**Task Focus**		**Interpersonal Focus**	

—◇— Group Average   ☐ Range of Individual scores

the subscale graph are rectangular boxes depicting the range of member scores. Explain to the group how to interpret these results (see Chapter 15 about graph interpretation).

› Here are discussion points the consultant can introduce:

1. In surveying the sweep of the graph, what insights do the members gain about how they invest their energies across the various domains?

2. In the opinion of the members, do the top scores seem like the team's greatest strengths? Do people see these skill areas actively in use when they work on a task?

3. Are any of the top subscales being overused to the team's detriment?

4. For example, Task Implementation has the highest result, with a tight cluster of member scores. Everyone seems to have a similar focus. Because of this circumstance, do members tend to push a task to completion a little too quickly? Do they need to pay a bit more attention to Task Analysis to maintain the most effective balance between the two?

Overuse of a skill area can be as much of a problem as underuse. The team will want to examine this issue and see if it wants to use certain skills more selectively.

5. How does the team evaluate the lowest scores in the graph? Do they seem accurate as areas of low performance? Which domains, in the team's opinion, need the most attention? Why?

C. Draw on the Inter-Subscale Combinations (ISC) to assess the graph. What relationships among the subscales would be beneficial for the team to address?

› The ISC groupings with relevant questions for a team:

1. **Assertiveness** with **Perspective Taking**. How is the team balancing the management of speaking and listening in its discussions? What might be adjusted?

2. **Group Facilitation** with **Task Focus** and **Interpersonal Focus Subscales**. How is the team managing the pivotal task and interpersonal operations? How might the team facilitate these differently, for greater effectiveness?

3. **Initiative** with **Negotiation Orientation**, **Task Focus**, and **Interpersonal Focus Subscales**. Where do people have substantial skills in these areas? How might members share leadership roles, based on strong skill sets, to make the team more productive in these different domains?

4. **Constructive Negotiation Approach** with **Positive Group Affiliation**. How does the team balance its energy investment in these two sectors? Since they are related, how might the team adjust its actions to maximize this connection? The interplay of these two subscales helps to create synergy on the team, producing excellent performance.

5. **Task Analysis** with **Task Implementation**. Which item has a higher score? Does the team lean too much in one direction? How can members strike a better balance between these two task operations?

6. **Positive Group Affiliation** with **Feeling Orientation**. Is the group neglecting either one, or both? How can the group build stronger team spirit and attend to feelings more effectively?

Based on the above graph, if the team created better balance between Constructive Negotiation Approach and Positive Group Affiliation, it could generate greater synergy in the team and really upgrade performance. Members can consciously work to elevate PGA and bring it more in line with Constructive Negotiation Approach, thereby enlivening the atmosphere and creating greater team cohesion.

The Group Composite Subscale Graph also allows the group to examine the precise pattern of the team's performance in a subscale area by looking at the range of member scores in the rectangular box on the particular column. If there is a wide distribution, such as with Perspective Taking on the graph, then some members have stronger skills while others are less developed. People with stronger skills can become leaders in helping the group refine its efforts in that domain. They can also offer mentoring tips to groupmates who are trying to build skills in this area. If there is a tight cluster of scores, particularly in a Medium or Low section of the graph, the team as a whole might benefit from some form of group training to acquire new skills.

D. How does the team want to balance its performance across the subscale domains? What areas should be strengthened to enhance overall performance?

- Given the graph data, what are two or three specific subscales to target for improvement?

Once the specific subscales have been selected, the team should look into those particular sections of the KGI® Group Profile, reviewing the group process suggestions.

- Which process suggestions appear to be most worthwhile to implement?

- How would the team want to prioritize the suggestions? Which will be first? Second?

- How should suggestions be modified in some way for the team's specific needs?

E. How will the MBTI preferences play a role: the effective use of well-established preferences in support of this effort, or the development of underused preferences to help the process?

F. How can the team assign responsibilities in the most effective ways?

- Are there opportunities for members to share leadership?

- How will the team delegate responsibilities to appropriate people?

- Where can members mentor one another to support individual skill building within the parameters of refining the team's processes?

G. What will be the timeline for implementing an action plan with the new processes?

6. *Discuss the appropriate time to follow up with the team.*

- Allow the team adequate time to practice its new skills. The consultant should check in, usually four to six weeks later, to evaluate progress.

- The consultant can then help the team further modify its strategies, expand the skill building, and provide additional coaching for the members.

- The consultant wants to train members in a reflective practice, so that they will experiment with new skills, assess results, and make adjustments to increase their effectiveness. As certain goals are reached, people can select additional skills to work on and really strengthen individual and team performance. As members refine an array of personal skills and group processes, they will establish a flexible, more dynamic way of operating, which will, in turn, vault the team to a significantly higher level of performance.

- In the follow-up session, the consultant will be able to determine with the group what further work would be appropriate to schedule. Phone sessions with individual members are one item to consider. Discuss any other support that will advance the learning process.

Adjustments for consulting with a newly formed team

For a brand new team, the initial phases of this method would be the same. Administration of instruments and the first phase of the training remain intact. However, a consultant would approach the individual coaching sessions, and the team session with the KGI® Group Profile somewhat differently. Here are appropriate modifications:

Coaching Session

When members do not have a shared history, it is beneficial during one-on-one counseling to focus more attention on an individual's general experience in small groups. This deepens a consultant's understanding of the client's patterns of behavior and will guide the skill-building process in a realistic way. (Even with an established team, exploring some of this history would be appropriate, but a coach needs to explore thoroughly the current group context. That would remain the key priority.)

The consultant should ask the client to provide clear illustrations of how he or she behaves in various group situations. These experiences should be considered in relation to specific KGI scores, for example, a high Assertiveness score, or conversely a low Assertiveness score. Invite the client to describe meaningful variations in performance, i.e., acting differently based on changing group contexts.

- The consultant should pursue the following questions:

  A. What particular small-group situations tend to be most productive for the client? Why?

  B. What particular group situations are most difficult? Why?

  C. What concerns does the client have with this new group assignment?

Team Session with the MBTI® Data and KGI® Group Profile

Since the group is newly constituted, a fundamental aim is to create a situation where members become better acquainted, feel comfortable, and start to pull together as a team. The intent is to establish an atmosphere of mutual acceptance and respect, creating a forum where members can share ideas, values, and concerns in an open manner. The MBTI and KGI tools provide data that supports mutual understanding and team strategizing. *By employing this information, a team can accelerate its development, nurturing communication around central issues of group performance.*

- A consultant would start with the Myers-Briggs Type Indicator material, but be sure to take a bit more time, so people can become more familiar with each other. Invite members to identify their personality types. People can share a few comments about what they think are their most significant scores.

- The consultant can then introduce a type table, illustrating the distribution of the MBTI personality types for the group. With its sixteen squares, the table provides a visual reference for how the team's different personalities are distributed. As before, review the proportion of Extraverts to Introverts, Sensing to Intuitive types, Thinking to Feeling types, and Judging to Perceiving types. How do the scores cluster? How diverse are they? Again, take more time to help a newly formed team get a clear picture of its situation.

A. Where are the team's strengths based on the distribution of preferences? Example: There is a significant number of Intuitive types who bring skills with future planning, innovation, and vision.

B. Where are the team's soft spots, where certain preferences are under-represented or missing entirely? Example: There are no Sensing types, so detailed, practical analysis may lag in discussions.

C. What adjustments can the team make to manage its strengths and challenges in ways that will maintain a balanced, effective performance? Example: There is one Thinking type, who will need to take a leadership role in ensuring the groupconducts a thorough task analysis when devising a strategy.

This part of the discussion will help the team better understand the skills that members possess, and it sets a baseline for how the team can maximize its strengths and adjust for its deficiencies.

  ‣ The consultant helps the team scrutinize the Klein Group Instrument information, focusing on the Group Composite Subscale Graph, assessing the top scores and the range of medium and low scores. Since the members haven't spent significant time together, the consultant emphasizes the dilemmas associated with the lower scores and the problems of overusing the top scores. This will orient the team to essential concerns to address. Together, members can reflect on the issues, fashioning some initial strategies.

    How would the team like to balance its performance given this landscape? For a team without a history, this information inspires a thoughtful analysis, as a group evaluates its tendencies and establishes a plan to promote sound collaboration.

  ‣ The consultant facilitates the discussion, presenting information to help the members consider options, showing how different subscales can be linked for maximum benefit using the Inter-Subscale Combinations. (Example: Positive Group Affiliation and

Feeling Orientation can be developed in tandem to establish a positive team spirit with proper attention to the emotional issues.)

  ‣ The consultant assists in the examination of the range of member's scores, using these data to expand the strategies. The information can help with assigning members responsibilities for certain tasks and organizing mentoring support where appropriate. For a new team, this will help with the construction of a more enlightened plan right away.

After the team selects subscales to work on, members turn to the body of the report to examine specific suggestions to strengthen their performance. Each subscale section contains a menu of options in this regard. The consultant helps the group think through the best alternatives, and the ways that the suggestions might be adjusted for particular group needs.

  ‣ With a newly formed team, the consultant will be more proactive in describing various issues and options for the group. A veteran team, often, will spontaneously interpret results that connect with their direct experiences, introducing examples from their shared background to illustrate issues and then delving into problem solving. Their hands-on experiences have tremendous practical benefit. A newly constructed team lacks this resource, so, accordingly, the discussion turns more speculative, with the consultant helping to fill in gaps, offering various interpretations, and taking a greater facilitative role to aid the team in finding its bearings. Bit by bit, the team comes together, defining strategies to explore. The actual practice of new strategies will help the group solidify its identity as a team.

    Checklist of things to attend to with a new group:

    1. Help create an atmosphere of mutual respect and acceptance.

    2. Conduct an ice-breaking activity that will help members get acquainted.

    3. Foster an open discussion so the team members understand each other's views.

4. Use Perspective Taking and Constructive Negotiation Approach to work on consensus building. Help members think in terms of win-win solutions.

5. Assess the range of members' scores in subscale areas to organize an appropriate delegation of responsibilities and, as appropriate, mentoring relationships. Promote the building of personal bonds in the enterprise, which will increase team cohesion.

With this adjusted approach, a consultant can address more precisely a new group's needs. The group will then be able to advance in a more coordinated manner, accelerating its development into an effective team. It will have a head start in its pursuit of high performance.

In the next chapter, another feature of the KGI–MBTI team-building method will be explained, the application for an academic classroom.

CHAPTER 24

KGI®–MTBI® Training in the Academic Classroom

At the university level, the KGI–MBTI method has been integrated into undergraduate courses (Organizational Behavior, Leadership and Team Skills) and graduate courses (Foundations of Leadership (MBA), Team Leadership (MBA), Sport Leadership, Administrative Skills and Mentoring). In these classes all of the students obtained new leadership and group skills, sometimes with remarkable changes in attitude and behavior. The benefits of training in an academic setting are the opportunity to work

with participants for a longer period of time and the chance to monitor more closely their skill acquisition. In the end students are empowered as team leaders and group members, equipped for their future positions in business, the professions, and diverse organizations.

Because KGI and MBTI materials are clear, accessible, and easy to work with, the educational model outlined below is applicable to high school classrooms as well. Students need to be able to self-reflect and attend to social interactions in a focused way. Once they reach the age of fourteen, they have the cognitive capacity to acquire these skills. So the design is adaptable for grades 9–12, but it applies most optimally to upper-class students, those in the junior and senior years, who, as a rule, have more social maturity.

In today's world, students are often over-loaded with technological equipment: smart

phones, tablets, laptops, etc. While they tap out messages to friends around the world, they can be remote to the people sitting right next to them. In general, it seems that social skills have eroded; many students lack perspective-taking ability, emotional intelligence, and social awareness. Interestingly, the KGI–MBTI model has proven to be an effective antidote to this condition, challenging students to look around, see others more clearly, and interact with them in constructive ways. Students have learned to be supportive teammates and engaging leaders, harnessing the KGI concepts and applying them with powerful results. It is to be hoped that more professors and teachers will embrace this method of social development. After all, the students are the future leaders and group members upon whom the world depends, and this design can instill the practical skills they need.

Skill-Building Process

Since the academic schedule affords months to work with the model, the pace of training can be slower and more deliberate than in formal organizational settings. Students have ample time to absorb ideas and plenty of opportunity to practice skills. After assigning students to teams, the instructor introduces a variety of tasks so students can develop a battery of skills. They write reflection papers about their experiences, cultivating a self-reflective practice that offers lifelong benefit. Critically, they develop a growth mindset, learning how to nurture their talents in a persistent, ongoing way, something that is always a valuable objective in the educational process.

‣ Here is an outline of the elements in this training procedure:

> **A. Introduction to the Myers-Briggs Type Indicator Model**—an examination of the MBTI system, including personal results.

> **B. Introduction to the Klein Group Instrument Model**—an exploration of the KGI system, including personal results, along with an analysis of how the KGI and MBTI assessments intersect in this skill-building process.

> **C. Personal Plan for Skill Building**—a paper assignment identifying the student's goals for acquiring leadership and group skills with the KGI–MBTI method.

> **D. Group Activities**—a series of group exercises enabling students to practice their new skills while they work together to develop a high-performing team.

> **E. Reflection Papers**—a number of assignments allowing students to examine their skill-building experiences and refine them in order to ascend to higher levels of social effectiveness.

‣ These components will now be explained in detail to provide a complete picture of this training approach.

A. Introduction to the Myers-Briggs Type Indicator® Model

‣ The instructor begins by having students take the MBTI measurement and recording their scores. The next step is to evaluate the results and assign teams.

‣ With awareness of the variety of scores in the class, the instructor should **assign the students to groups of four or five members**. The eight different preferences should be represented in each group, along with appropriate gender and ethnic diversity. The aim is to create a situation where students must respond to people with different personality preferences, challenging them to adapt to different styles and to forge an effective team from scratch. Wherever possible, people who are well acquainted should be put in separate groups. The team assignments must be made prior to the MBTI presentation to the class.

Suggested resources for training: Employ the handouts *Words to Help Understanding of the Type Concepts* (descriptors for the eight personality preferences) and *Descriptions of the Sixteen Types* (one-paragraph descriptions of the types), which can be obtained from CAPT.org.

‣ In the first session, the instructor should do a focused presentation (approximate time: 50 minutes) to orient students to the MBTI material, including the following points:

1. The MBTI instrument seeks to identify positive preferences that all people possess. It's not meant to negatively categorize anyone in any way. The material provides an opportunity for people to better understand themselves, understand others, and find ways to collaborate more effectively in groups.

2. Introduce the four dichotomies with the eight preferences: Extraversion (E)–Introversion (I); Sensing (S)–Intuition (N); Thinking (T)–Feeling (F); Judging (J)–Perceiving (P). Describe how psychological energy flows in these polarities, with people tending to prefer one side more than the other.

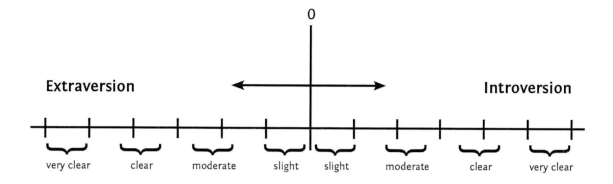

3. Identify the basic characteristics for each of the eight preferences. (The instructor can introduce the handout *Words to Help Understanding of Type Concepts*.)

4. Explain clarity of preference: the degree of preference reflects how regularly one tends to exercise that preference and reveals how much one may access the opposite preference in the dichotomy. A person with a slight preference is more likely to use both sides of the dichotomy at different times, fairly equally, while the more a preference moves towards moderate, clear, and very clear, the more consistently the individual tends to utilize just that one preference.

5. Describe how the scores on the four dichotomies combine to create one's psychological type, with sixteen different possibilities: ESTJ, ESFJ, ENFJ, ENTJ, ESTP, ESFP, ENFP, ENTP, ISTJ, ISFJ, INFJ, INTJ, ISTP, ISFP, INFP, INTP.

6. The instructor should then invite the students to review their individual MBTI results. Students should assess what information they agree with and what they don't find accurate.

> ‣ Pose this question: How many people feel that their results fit them well to very well? Participants can respond by raising their hands, providing a quick visual tally of their self-appraisal. Often a very solid majority of the class raise their hands.

7. For those who don't feel there is a good fit, discuss the following points. A lack of fit may relate to a "slight" score on a particular dichotomy, which produces ambiguity because the score falls right near the borderline of the two preferences. When responding to questions for that dichotomy, the person's answers reflected both sides at an almost equal rate, creating something of a balance. As a result, the student finds that descriptors addressing just one preference may not include meaningful behaviors she uses from the opposite preference, making it feel like the profile is not a precise fit. If an individual has more than one slight preference, it compounds the problem. In such cases, flip the letter in that dichotomy to its opposite, with the other letters remaining the same, and read the short description of that type. (Introduce the handout *Descriptions of the Sixteen Types* for this purpose.) The other description may feel more precise to the student. Or, examine the words for that particular dichotomy on the handout *Words to Help Understanding of Type Concepts* and determine which points seem most accurate from each side. That can help clarify the situation. In any case, it is valuable to talk individually with students who don't believe that there is a good fit and assess their thinking on the matter.

8. Another issue can be that students are unaware of how they actually behave. This can likewise produce confusion when they evaluate the accuracy of their results. It's productive to have students consult with

someone in the class who knows them well to see if that person agrees with the scores. This can also be done with someone outside of class. Such an exchange can open up a student's perspective, causing a reassessment of results, and clarification about how one actually behaves. It may also raise further questions, which can be productive if it stimulates curiosity and prompts a student to investigate additional type material, such as in an Internet search.

9. For students who have taken the instrument before: how do these results compare to previous scores? For some, they're exactly the same. For others, there may be some differences. With differences, discuss the person's social experiences during the interim to see how he may have adapted to particular circumstances. Since individuals adapt to their environments, these adjustments, for a significant period of time, cause a person to redirect certain psychological energies and respond differently to the assessment. If an Introverted student has had more social contacts, for example, it can incline the individual more towards Extraversion. Also, ask if a student believes that there are other forces that may have caused a shift in preference(s).

10. Put the students into their teams and let them share their results. Have the students describe their thoughts on their personal results: points they agree with and potential issues. Based on their psychological preferences, the students should explain how they like to operate in small groups. What behaviors do the students prefer? What behaviors do they tend to avoid? This will help the members get acquainted and set a baseline for future work.

B. *Introduction to the Klein Group Instrument® Model*

- The instructor will now have the students take the KGI assessment. If the instructor wishes simply to utilize the KGI® Individual Profile with this training, the students may go to the CAPT.org website, register themselves, and take the instrument. Each student will receive a personal report plus the *KGI® User's Guide*, which presents comprehensive information about the profile and its applications. Students can print out their profiles and bring them to class for the training. The instructor should make a copy of each student's Individual Composite Subscale Graph to keep on file for consultations with the student.

Important note: If the instructor wishes to include the KGI® Group Profile as part of this program, he or she must register the participants into a team format for administering the assessment. Group registration is necessary to obtain the KGI® Group Profile, which anonymously aggregates the individual scores for the report. The instructor must list the email addresses of the participants in a team cluster. Members will then receive an electronic prompt to take the instrument. To organize the groups in this way, the instructor will need to collect email addresses in advance and load them into the system. For assistance, contact the Center for Applications of Psychological Type at 800.777.CAPT. The cost for each KGI administration plus the cost for a group profile should be considered in advance and managed accordingly.

- Using this system, the instructor can monitor the following processes:

    1. Checking when students have taken the KGI measurement, with the ability to send an email reminder when people don't follow through in a timely fashion.

    2. Sending out the KGI® Individual Profiles to participants when the timing is right, or printing hard copies to deliver in class.

    3. Directing the website to construct the KGI® Group Profile when all members have completed the instrument.

    4. Emailing the students a copy of their KGI® Group Profile at the appropriate time, or printing hard copies to distribute in class.

- The instructor would begin the actual training (approximate time: 50 minutes) by introducing the following points: (To assist an instructor in preparing for this session, see Appendix: The Basic Script for

Introducing the Klein Group Instrument®
Assessment.)

1. Explain that the Klein Group Instrument assessment is designed to assist people in expanding their team leadership and group skills. It was constructed to complement the MBTI assessment for personal and team development. Not only does it help individuals acquire new social skills, it also enables teams to ignite the synergy that inspires top performance.

2. Introduce the diamond model, with the four major scales, and include a brief description of each scale. (Utilize the one-line descriptors and other relevant ideas from the paragraph descriptions in Chapters 2 and 3.) The scales identify the basic activities in small-group life; explain how the elements interconnect.

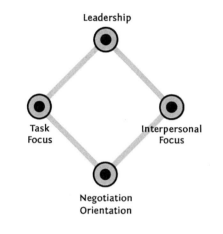

Leadership

Task Focus

Interpersonal Focus

Negotiation Orientation

3. Describe the nine subscales (utilize the one-line descriptors and relevant ideas from the paragraph descriptions in Chapter 3). The subscales define the fundamental skill-building areas of the instrument.

› **Leadership subscales:** Assertiveness, Group Facilitation, and Initiative.

› **Negotiation Orientation subscales:** Perspective Taking and Constructive Negotiation Approach.

› **Task Focus subscales:** Task Analysis and Task Implementation.

› **Interpersonal Focus:** Positive Group Affiliation and Feeling Orientation.

4. Explain the design of the KGI® Individual Profile, which is divided into four main segments, according to the major scales: Leadership, Negotiation Orientation, Task Focus, and Interpersonal Focus.

› At the start of each major segment, there is a graph displaying the respondent's frequency of performance for the main scale and the respective subscales. The graph has Low, Medium, and High sections, allowing for a rapid visual assessment of one's behavior in this sector. For Low, the respondent uses these skills 0–49% of the time, for Medium 50–74%, and for High 75–100%.

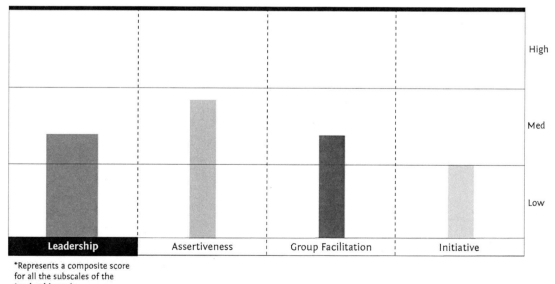

| Leadership | Assertiveness | Group Facilitation | Initiative |

High

Med

Low

*Represents a composite score for all the subscales of the **Leadership** scale

- The section then introduces a statement describing the respondent's basic orientation in this area of group activity. The statement corresponds to the score in the first column in the graph, in this case, the composite Leadership score. The statement is calibrated to a low, medium, or high result.

- For each subscale in this domain, there are statements about what an individual enjoys doing in this area, what might be difficult or challenging, and suggestions for developing specific new skills.

- Emphasize the critical growth orientation of the instrument: to support skill acquisition in essential aspects of team leadership and small-group life. The suggestions for developing new skills

in each subscale category fuel this enterprise.

- For every KGI® Individual Profile, there will be 15 to 20 growth statements among all of the subscale categories. These enable an individual to acquire a wide range of skills, making one a well-rounded team player.

- Show pictures of the composite graphs at the end of the KGI® Individual Profile, one displays the major scales in a sequence and the other the subscales scores in a row. The former allows the participant to see the "big picture" of performance; the latter enables the individual to devise a very precise plan for obtaining new leadership and group skills. Zero in on the composite subscale graph.

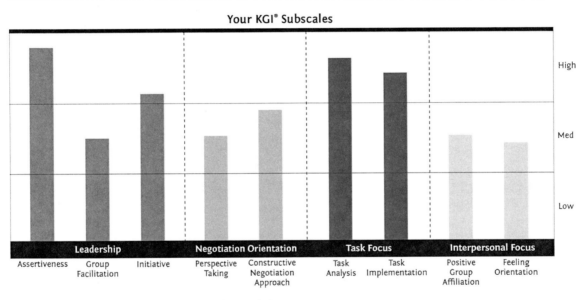

Your KGI® Subscales

- Point out the highs (strengths) and the lower areas (challenges) in the results, according to the columns on the graph. The goal is to balance efforts across the various domains in order to be an effective, all-round performer. When outfitted with a complete set of these skills, an individual is well-equipped to be a potent leader and group member, someone who can promote synergy in a team, i.e., top performance.

5. Mention the Inter-Subscale Combinations (ISC) to expand the interpretation of the graph results.

- **Assertiveness** with **Perspective Taking**: creating an appropriate balance between speaking and listening skills.

- **Group Facilitation** with **Task Focus** and **Interpersonal Focus Subscales**: refining facilitation skills across the two primary sectors of group life— task and interpersonal.

- **Initiative** with **Negotiation Orientation, Task Focus,** and **Interpersonal Focus Subscales:** building a flexible leadership style by integrating skills from these vital areas.

- **Constructive Negotiation Approach** with **Positive Group Affiliation:** perfecting skills that will promote synergy on the team, resulting in high-quality group outcomes.

- **Task Analysis** with **Task Implementation:** achieving a better balance between these complementary skills in the task arena.

- **Positive Group Affiliation** with **Feeling Orientation:** nurturing team spirit through the effective management of emotional issues within the team.

6. Explain the KGI and MBTI connections. Present the KGI diamond model and the correlations with the MBTI preferences, illustrating the interconnection of the instruments. (The data have been calculated through quantitative and qualitative analyses—see Chapter 19.)

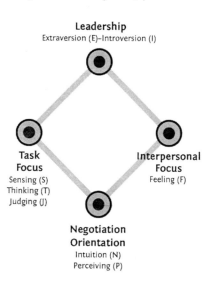

Leadership
Extraversion (E)–Introversion (I)

Task Focus
Sensing (S)
Thinking (T)
Judging (J)

Interpersonal Focus
Feeling (F)

Negotiation Orientation
Intuition (N)
Perceiving (P)

- Discuss how the MBTI preferences naturally express themselves in certain ways in groups. The overlay of the MBTI preferences on the KGI diamond demonstrates this pattern. The diagram helps people to see how psychological energies flow in their group behaviors, which will be an asset for building new skills that utilize existing preferences and also opposite preferences.

- An existing preference allows us to channel current energy in a more conscious, intentional way to enlarge our skills.

- An opposite preference requires building skills in an even more deliberate, painstaking way in order to strengthen a less developed area. It often requires challenging ourselves to do what we don't enjoy in order to activate our undeveloped potential and to gain new insights. As we gain mastery with the opposite preferences there can be a tremendous spurt in social growth along with the skill development.

7. Show slides that present a person's MBTI preference scores on top and KGI composite subscale graph on the bottom. Describe how individual KGI subscale results can be evaluated according to the MBTI preferences.

- For the Introverted individual on the next page, we see underdeveloped leadership skills, but also assets in the areas of Perspective Taking and Positive Group Affiliation. There are solid, moderate scores in several subscale areas. How can the person cultivate more Extraversion to become a better leader? How can the individual employ the assets of Intuition, Feeling, and Judging most effectively in this process? How can the individual employ opposite MBTI preferences to balance out performance across the other KGI subscale dimensions?

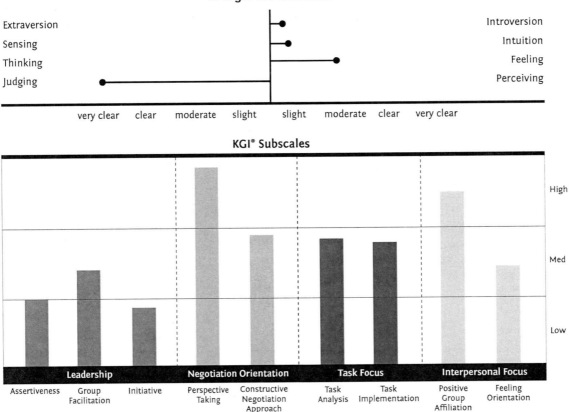

Strength of Preferences

	very clear	clear	moderate	slight	slight	moderate	clear	very clear	
Extraversion									Introversion
Sensing									Intuition
Thinking									Feeling
Judging									Perceiving

KGI® Subscales

Leadership: Assertiveness, Group Facilitation, Initiative

Negotiation Orientation: Perspective Taking, Constructive Negotiation Approach

Task Focus: Task Analysis, Task Implementation

Interpersonal Focus: Positive Group Affiliation, Feeling Orientation

8. Describe the procedure for skill building with the KGI and MBTI results.

▸ Explain to the students the following steps:

A. Identify your key strengths in the various KGI domains.

B. Assess which areas are problematic for you.

C. What new skills will be *most valuable, most meaningful for you* to develop in order to expand your leadership and group behaviors? Where do you want to be in the future with respect to your group skills? Identify your vision and then pick subscales to work on.

D. From the selected subscale areas in the KGI® Individual Profile, identify growth statements to implement. Prioritize these new skills and establish a learning agenda.

E. Your MBTI preferences provide insights into psychological energies that can be utilized to build your group skills. Both your existing prefer-ences and your opposite preferences will come into play with this skill building. Existing preferences allow you to enlarge established strengths and refine their applications; the opposite preferences help you acquire new skills in undeveloped areas that broaden your range of activity and really balance your performance. How do the MBTI preferences connect with the skill areas you have chosen to work on?

F. Experiment with one or two new skills in your in-class group and other, relevant group settings (this can include school clubs and sport teams).

G. Continue to practice and refine the skills until they become more comfortable and more integrated into your style. Usually, practicing a skill on *at least three occasions* will solidify it.

H. Develop a relationship with a classmate who can give you feedback about these efforts. When it is given in a sincere way that is meant to be helpful, objective feedback about your performance is very useful. It will help you refine your leadership techniques.

I. As you master certain new skills, select additional ones that will help you to further expand your competence as a leader and group member. Seek to become multiskilled in these key areas of group life.

If the instructor plans to use the KGI® Group Profile in the training, mention that in addition to the individual skill development, the team will also work on refining its group processes.

Briefly mention that all of the individual scores can be combined anonymously to produce the KGI® Group Profile, which the team will investigate later. (Mention that no one is personally identified in these results.)

C. *Personal Plan for Skill Building*

• This assignment requires a student to design a personal action plan, based on specific growth statements, which will guide his or her initial skill building in the class. The specifications for the paper:

1. This paper identifies your plan for developing two specific leadership or group skills based on your KGI Individual Profile. You will be developing skills based on the Behaviors that May Help You Grow in the subscale sections. You will work on these new skills in your in-class team, as well as in outside groups when opportunities present themselves.

• This paper will be one to two pages in length.

2. Start with the first KGI subscale and growth statement you wish to work on. Name the specific KGI subscale and then state the growth statement verbatim.
Example: Assertiveness. Raise questions about issues under discussion, especially about problem areas that you see. Solicit input from others and help the group analyze the topic.

3. Explain briefly why you chose to work on this growth statement.

4. Describe how your MBTI preferences or opposite preferences can be involved in this skill building process.
Example: I have a preference for Introversion and I will need to draw on Extraversion energy to build my Assertiveness skill.

5. Identify a second KGI subscale and growth statement you wish to work on. As before, name the KGI subscale and then state the growth statement verbatim.

6. Explain briefly why you chose this growth statement.

7. Describe how your MBTI preferences or opposite preferences can be involved in this skill building process.

• The students will submit the paper to the instructor, who will evaluate the clarity and precision of the design and provide appropriate feedback so each student has a sound plan for skill building.

D. *Group Activities*

1. Sharing Personal Goals with the Team (approximate time: 20–30 minutes).

• Students will share with teammates their goals for skill building. Mention to the students the need to respect teammates' personal goals and that this information is confidential, for use in this classroom only, unless people grant special permission.

Guidelines to establish: allow individuals to select the specific information that they feel comfortable sharing with other members. These decisions need to be respected. It should be noted that such respect can, over time, encourage members to be freer and more open in sharing information. Also, information shared in the group must stay within the group, unless some other agreement is made with the participants' free consent.

▸ Discussion questions for students:

A. How can members support one another in this pursuit of new skills? Where do certain members already have skills which others will be working on? What pointers can be shared?

B. How can two members working on similar skills share experiences as they go along and encourage each other in the process?

2. Team-Building Exercise (approximate time: 45 minutes).

Give the groups a team-building exercise to help them become better acquainted and practice problem solving.

▸ The *Lost at Sea* exercise can be an excellent option to help the teams work together in a problem-solving activity. (This can be found on the Internet.) Or another activity can be selected.

▸ Have the students complete the task in class and process the results.

▸ Allow team members to reflect on how they functioned as a team during the activity and how members may have begun to practice some of their new skills.

3. A Subject-Matter Activity (approximate time: 30–50 minutes).

In a subsequent class, provide students with an activity that is subject-matter related. The activity should fit into one class period, with an opportunity for the students again to reflect on their teamwork after the activity concludes.

▸ This enables students to collaborate on course content while they refine leadership and group skills. For example, it could be the analysis of characters in a short story for an English class or an article on leadership for a Business Management class.

▸ Such collaboration expands cognitive functioning. When a cluster of people share and build ideas, the thinking process of everyone is enhanced. That is part of what creates synergy in teams.

▸ The activity also allows students to refine their group processing abilities. Following the activity, the team can reflect on how it performed.

▸ With regard to group collaboration, what did the members do well? How can they build on those successes next time?

▸ What things did not go so well? What adjustments will help the team to perform better next time?

4. Research Project with a Class Presentation (multiple-day assignment).

▸ It is now possible to expand the challenge of a team assignment, having members collaborate in more elaborate ways. This can be a research project with a solid content focus, in which members collect various data and combine the information to make a PowerPoint® presentation for the whole class.

▸ Members should seek ways to integrate their interests and skills so they can be an effective team, raising their efforts to the next level, thereby constructing a strong set of material. The instructor will provide class time on different days so students can work on the project. Students will also need to conduct research on their own outside of class.

▸ During the actual presentation, all members need to be speakers, participating in an equal way. This enables students to practice another leadership skill—effective public speaking.

▸ The project will receive a team grade. The presentation will be evaluated on its clarity, organization, and thoughtfulness.

5. Project with the KGI® Group Profile (an alternative option for the research project).

If an instructor is using the KGI® Group Profile with the training, this is the right time to introduce it. The teams can now work on a project to assess their KGI team results and identify strategies to improve their interactive processes, which will include a PowerPoint presentation.

> - The faculty member would first introduce the KGI materials in the following manner:

An overview of the KGI® Group Profile: begin with a description of the components of the profile and the information they contain.

> - The **Introduction**, which presents the diamond model and spells out the goal of forging a learning team.

> - **Communication and Confidentiality**. This segment establishes ethical guidelines for the sharing of personal results as part of a team-building process.

> - **Team Results: the Composite Graphs**. The section contains the Composite Major Scale Graph and the Group

Composite Subscale Graph, with points about how to interpret each of them, so members can assess their collective performance.

> - **Action Steps.** This component outlines the steps for choosing subscale categories to address, finding suggestions to improve the team's interactive processes in the appropriate subscale sections of the report, implementing those strategies, and pursuing an ongoing developmental process that will make the group a high-performing team.

> - **The Four Major Scale Sections.** The team receives feedback across the four major domains (Leadership, Negotiation, Task, and Interpersonal). Each section includes a graph that identifies the range of member scores for the major scale and its subscales, a team assessment statement for that area, and suggestions on how to improve group

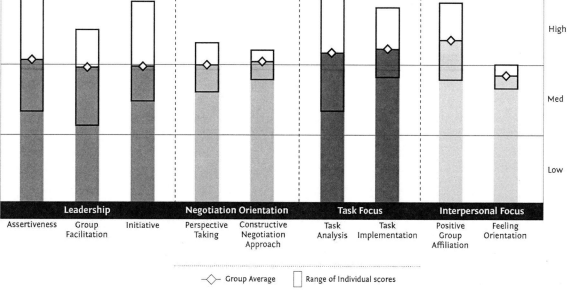

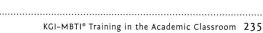

performance in each of the subscale categories. This design is similar to the sequence of information in the KGI® Individual Profile, but with a group focus.

> **One-Sentence Descriptions of the KGI Major Scales and Their Subscales.**
> On the last page of the profile are brief descriptors of all of the scales and subscales, providing an easy reference for the essential ideas in the KGI skill-building system.

• The instructor would then speak to the students about the analysis of the *Group Composite Subscale Graph* from the KGI® Group Profile, showing them how they can evaluate their collective performance. (See example on previous page.)

> • The Group Composite Subscale Graph depicts all of the subscale columns in a row, but with the range of member scores indicated on each column. Explain how the black rectangular box indicates the highest member score at the top and the lowest at the bottom. The diamond line indicates the average score for the team. Explain that the smaller area in the rectangle, above or below the diamond line, contains the larger number of member scores (see Chapter 15 about graph interpretation).

> • How might the team want to balance its performance across the subscale domains? What areas should be elevated to improve overall performance?

• In what areas is there such a wide disparity of scores that people with strong scores can mentor those with softer scores?

• What *two subscales* areas would be most useful for the team to address?

Important: In training students for the analysis of the Group Composite Subscale Graph, it has been discovered that keeping the evaluation to a simple examination, without the use of the more elaborate Inter-Subscale Combinations, has worked best. The goal is to provide a basic experience of a team development process for the students.

Once specific subscales have been selected, the team should look into those particular sections of the KGI® Group Profile and review the group process suggestions.

• Which suggestions appear to be the most worthwhile to implement?

• How would the team prioritize the suggestions? Which will be first? Second?

• Are there opportunities for members to share leadership? How will the team delegate responsibilities to appropriate people?

Each team is now given the assignment of designing a presentation about how it intends to refine its group processes. The specifics for this team project are as follows:

• Each team will review its KGI® Group Profile to assess its performance and decide on strategies to strengthen teamwork. Based on these goals, each team will organize a PowerPoint presentation that will include the following material: The first slide will show the Group Composite Subscale Graph with the nine subscales. The team will analyze its investment of energy across the various subscales and reflect about how it can adjust its performance to increase group effectiveness. In evaluating particular subscales, it will address the range of member scores and how that affects team strategies. The group should address five subscale areas and analyze the issues in reasonable detail.

• The second slide will list the two subscales that are the team's top priorities to work on.

- The third slide will identify the first of the two subscales and state the group process suggestion that has been chosen for application. The members will explain how they will implement it.
- The fourth slide will identify the second of the two subscales and state the group process suggestion that has been chosen for application. Again, the team will explain how they will implement it.

All members need to speak in the presentation, participating at an equal level. There will be a team grade. The presentation will be evaluated on its clarity, organization, and thoughtfulness.

6. Other Group Activities (approximate time: variable).

- The instructor will subsequently introduce other types of activities that enable the students to continue to practice their skills. It is possible to include physical team-building activities, such as Tower Building and Ring Toss. Students develop group strategies to master games that present hands-on challenges. These activities bring a fresh angle to the training, which helps to energize the students. Using the KGI subscales of Task Analysis and Task Implementation, the instructor can organize an effective evaluation of how the groups operated during these activities.

- Another effective tactic is to introduce focused readings on leadership or group topics and have teams take turns doing class presentations on the material. A team must decide on the most critical ideas in the article, put the ideas up on the board, and teach the class about the information. The team must also create discussion questions to facilitate meaningful class engagement with the material. All team members must be active leaders during the session. This approach enables students to further refine their public speaking skills. They also refine group facilitation techniques as they orchestrate a substantive class discussion. These sessions will expand everyone's thinking about relevant leadership and group issues.

E. Reflection Papers

When students reflect on and write about their skill-building efforts, it strengthens the learning process. By articulating what went well, what didn't, and what adjustments can be made to refine performance, the participants develop a reflective practice that will not only help them in the present but will be a useful tool in the future as they continue to build new group skills.

After the students have participated in several group activities, they can write an initial reflection paper about their experiences with practicing new leadership and membership skills.

1. An outline of directions for the first reflection paper:

- What new KGI behavior went well? Describe in detail not only what you did but also the group's responses to your actions.

- What behavior was difficult to practice? Describe what happened. How do you propose to modify your approach to make it more successful?

- Assess the skill building according to your MBTI preferences. Explain how one of your current preferences was helpful in building a new skill. Be specific and explain fully. Describe how one of your opposite preferences influenced the situation. Again, be specific and explain in detail.

- What insights have you gained so far about the process of building leadership and group skills?

- This assignment should be 3–4 pages in length.

After students complete this first assignment, they can think about expanding their practice by selecting other skills to work on from different KGI subscales. Subscale growth statements will identify specific behaviors to implement. *In particular, they should now select items that will necessitate the use of their MBTI opposite preferences.* This will add greater challenge to the enterprise, enabling students to become more flexible leaders and group participants.

Once they have selected the new skills, students will apply them in ongoing classroom group activities. Students should again be encouraged to expand their practice by using the skills in outside situations, too.

After an appropriate period of time, the students will write a second reflection paper about their experiences in developing additional group skills. This paper will put more emphasis on working with opposite MBTI preferences, and balancing the use of skills in the MBTI dichotomies.

2. An outline of directions for the second reflection paper:

- Identify your four MBTI preferences (ex., ENTP). Identify the clarity index for each one; the preference is slight, moderate, clear, or very clear. Then define your four opposite preferences (ex., ISFJ).
- Select one of the four MBTI dichotomies: Extraversion—Introversion; Sensing—Intuition; Thinking—Feeling; or Judging—Perceiving.

    A. What have you done to balance skills in this dichotomy? How have you worked with your opposite preference? What has gone well? What has not gone well? Explain in reasonable detail.

    B. What insights have you gained from your experience that will guide you in creating more balance in the future? Be specific in explaining behaviors you would like to obtain and why.

- How did this MBTI skill-building connect to your efforts to develop group skills with the KGI model? Identify specific KGI subscales that were involved. How did your efforts with the MBTI model enhance your work with the KGI skills?

- Select a second dichotomy from the MBTI system.

    A. What have you done to balance your skills in this area? How have you worked with your opposite preference? What has gone well? What has not gone well? Explain in reasonable detail.

    B. What insights have you gained from your experience that will guide you in creating more balance in the future? Be specific in explaining behaviors you would like to obtain and why.

- How did this MBTI skill building connect to your efforts to develop group skills with the KGI model? Identify specific KGI subscales that were involved. How did your efforts with the MBTI model enhance your work with the KGI skills?

- This paper assignment should be 4–5 pages in length.

The second paper encourages students to approach skill-building from a different angle, promoting an alternate perspective and expanding their reflective practice. The goal is to help students acquire skills in articulating their personal experiences, reflecting on their practice, and making adjustments that promote personal growth.

- The assignment provides an instructor with insight into a student's thinking process and potential for behavioral change. The instructor can offer precise feedback about the student's efforts, establishing a serious dialogue to advance the student's growth.

If the instructor integrated the KGI® Group Profile into the training, it is possible to introduce a reflection paper that would specifically address that endeavor, adding another dimension to the analytical process. In this paper, the student evaluates the team's experiences in adjusting its collective processes.

3. An outline of directions for the third reflection paper:

- Identify a KGI subscale and the group process suggestion that your team decided to work on.
- As the group applied the suggestion, what went well? What did not go well? What further adjustments would enhance its effectiveness?
- In what ways did the MBTI preferences and opposite preferences play a role in this effort? Explain in reasonable detail.
- Identify the second KGI subscale and the group process suggestion that your team decided to work on.
- As the group applied the suggestion, what went well? What did not go well? What further adjustments would enhance its effectiveness?
- In what ways did the MBTI preferences and opposite preferences play a role in this effort? Explain in reasonable detail.
- What insights did you gain about the team-building process from this experience? What issues are important to focus on as you try to make a group a high-performing unit? Explain your reasoning.

With this last® paper, students reflect on pertinent group-dynamics issues, related to guiding a team toward high performance. For developing leaders, this is an invaluable perspective, one that will help them become impact players, individuals who can lead teams in productive and rewarding directions.

In academic settings, the KGI–MBTI training model has been very effective, enlightening students in business, engineering, education, psychology, social work, criminal justice, and other disciplines. Team skills are essential in all of these occupations, so the usefulness of the material is apparent and, as a result, students have been seriously motivated to put in the effort to acquire new skills.

The student empowerment that comes from the KGI–MBTI training is exciting. The method enriches the students' social interactions in the classroom, provides them with skills they can apply in outside group situations, and prepares them for their future careers. Consequently, the model helps students elevate their social performance on multiple levels.

In the next chapter, case studies demonstrate how the KGI–MBTI team-building approach has raised performance in a variety of settings: sport, professional, and the academic classroom. ✶

CHAPTER 25

Team-Building Case Studies with the KGI®–MTBI® Assessments

Football Team: Winning a Championship

The Western New England University Golden Bears finished the 2014 football season with an 8–2 record, losing the conference championship to the Massachusetts Institute of Technology. From that disappointment, Head Coach Keith Emery and I identified an opportunity to create a cutting-edge approach to team building that would produce better results. Coach Emery appointed me as an assistant coach, a new "Leadership Coach," who would work with the captains' group to expand their

leadership skills with the ultimate aim of raising the performance of the entire team. Utilizing this innovative strategy, the 2015 team produced a 10-0 regular season record, the first undefeated season in program history, winning the New England Athletic Conference championship. In the NCAA Division III Coaches' Poll, the Golden Bears were ranked number 19 in the nation. The following account explains how the Klein Group Instrument and Myers-Briggs Type Indicator method for team building contributed to that success.

The band of captains consisted of nine players, a "One Captain," the overall leader of the team, plus eight position captains who headed the various specialty groups: quarterbacks, running backs, receivers, offensive line, defensive line, linebackers, cornerbacks, and safeties. This corps of veteran players included six seniors and three juniors, students who represented a range of academic disciplines—business, engineering, psychology,

and criminal justice. Given their professional aspirations, we recognized this was an excellent opportunity to train them in leadership skills that would benefit the team during the season but would also prepare them to be capable leaders in their future careers. Driven by the combined "present and future benefit," the captains were motivated individuals whose work ethic was exemplary, producing impressive personal development and, by extension, exceptional team results.

The challenge facing these young men was summed up by one captain in preseason: "For three years you are a follower on the team, and then you are selected to be a captain. You aren't sure exactly what to do. As a strong player, you know you should be a role model with your performance in practice and on the field on Saturdays. You know you can be a leader in that way. But there is so much more to being a really effective leader. You need to get a clear vision about what is necessary, and the skills you need to acquire to be an impact guy."

The KGI diamond turned out to be the perfect model to orient the captains to essential leadership skills that would enhance the team's performance, allowing them to guide the other players in the right directions. With this knowledge, they could create the synergy that would elevate the position groups' and the entire team's levels of play.

The design for the leadership coaching and the team-building process assumed the following structure. For each captain, there would be three individual coaching sessions, targeting personal strategies based on the KGI and MBTI results—one consultation in the preseason, one at midseason, and one in the last phase of the campaign. These sessions incorporated the method used with executive coaching in businesses and professions, featuring skill acquisition in the KGI subscale domains and utilization of preferred and opposite MBTI preferences. In addition, there would be "Captains' Meetings" on alternate weeks during the season, where the athletes would discuss issues in their position groups and devise strategies to improve performance. Likewise, they would develop strategies for the team as a whole. With this enterprise, data from the KGI® Group Profile would inform the planning.

The composite MBTI score for the captains' group was ENTP. There were 7 Extraverts and 2 Introverts, 6 Intuitive types and 3 Sensing types, 6 Thinking types and 3 Feeling types, and 5 Perceiving types and 4 Judging types.

In the individual sessions, all members received suggestions for balancing their specific Assertiveness and Perspective Taking results and ideas for perfecting their Group Facilitation and Initiative. There were also refinements for negotiation, task, and interpersonal relations. Depending on their particular psychological preferences, certain skill areas involved the use of existing preferences while others demanded the utilization of opposite preferences. The expectation was that all captains would strive to become multifaceted leaders during the course of the season, acquiring a range of skills along the KGI spectrum and expanding their employment of MBTI preferences. During coaching sessions, individuals would report on their progress, identifying where they employed the new skills, reflecting on further adjustments, and then selecting additional skills to practice.

During the first captains' team meeting in the preseason, we examined the Group Composite Subscale Graph from the KGI® Group Profile.

We noted the top subscale score: Task Analysis. Given the group's overall preferences for Intuition

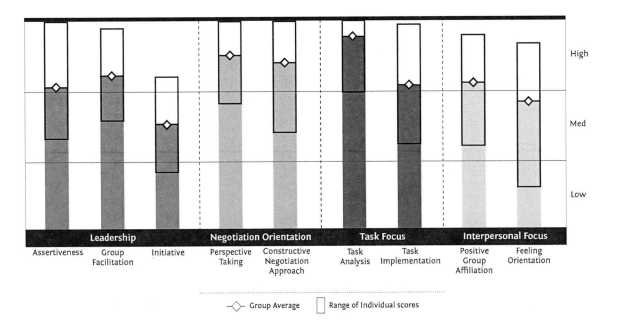

and Thinking, this made perfect sense. Team members naturally generated creative ideas for the task endeavor, which was excellent, yet there were also potential liabilities. We didn't want to spend too much time on abstract ideas or ones that looked narrowly at the job at hand. We wanted to apply creative thinking in a broader way, examining team spirit, the feelings of teammates, and how to negotiate in constructive ways. We agreed this would be our approach. We also acknowledged the group strengths in Perspective Taking and Constructive Negotiation Approach, definite resources as we worked together to strengthen the position groups and the entire team.

As we began to investigate the lowest scores, I took the reins, directing attention to the Task Implementation result, which languished as the fourth-lowest score. From my experience, I knew a subscale in that position might display a critical softness for a team. In this situation, that appeared to be the case. While Task Implementation always plays an important role in any group effort, it is particularly critical on a football team. The offense, defense, and special teams enter a game with precisely calculated strategies and then execute the plans, making necessary adjustments along the way. The members of the captains' unit oversee this activity for each position group. In the heat of a game, this presents a formidable challenge. If the captains' group could target this aspect of their work and fine-tune it, there would be positive consequences. With the first official game just ten days away, the time was ripe for attention to this subscale.

Referencing the process suggestions in the Task Implementation section of the KGI® Group Profile, we discussed the following questions:

- What are the best ways to systematically evaluate our task execution?

- How can we communicate most clearly the adjustments that need to be made during a game?

- How do we give feedback to people who make mistakes? How do we give feedback that is supportive and doesn't tear someone down?

- What are different ways we can recognize teammates who carry out assignments

capably, to give them a motivational boost?

At the end of the discussion, we felt we'd advanced our work in a meaningful way: we'd outlined ideas in response to each of these topics. Paying attention to the MBTI data, we noticed that the composite preference for the group was Perceiving. For this exercise, we talked about consciously drawing on Judging energy, which would help with organizing our efforts in a smoother, more efficient manner.

Not wanting to overload everyone, we decided to address only these ideas in the first phase of our collaboration. In the next meeting we would place other subscales on the list.

The captains practiced their new skills from the individual sessions and our ideas on Task Implementation. The team won its first two games, so we were off to a solid start.

At the next meeting, we tackled the group's lowest subscale score, Initiative, and the third lowest, Assertiveness. With the former, we examined the range of player scores, which ran from low-High down to the Low section. I asked the players with the stronger scores to share a few thoughts about their motivations for stepping up as leaders and insights they had gained about the process. A key idea was reinforced: it wasn't about waiting for ideal circumstances to take on a leadership role, it was about the willingness to plunge in and learn as you went along. You couldn't worry about being perfect, you had to take risks. Since every captain had identified certain leadership goals, they knew what to pursue. This discussion bolstered their motivation to push ahead.

We connected these ideas to the Assertiveness subscale. Captains needed to make their voices heard, they couldn't be passive observers. Generally speaking, everyone had some skills in this domain. However, to become better leaders, they needed to be even more proactive, triggering conversations with their players in the weight room or during stretching, as well as in practices and during actual games. Part of the strategy was to ask more questions, combining Assertiveness with Perspective Taking, so they could obtain knowledge about what teammates were thinking and feeling. That information would aid in developing strategies and building positive morale. It was especially important to start discussions with quiet players and new players, so they would feel more a part of their units and of the team as a whole. The captains had to reach out and make things happen.

From this conversation, the captains pursued a joint mission—to establish strong lines of communication across all of the subdivisions in the squad.

At the start of the next session, we invited the captains to share an issue they had encountered in their position groups. One captain mentioned that some players had gripes about not getting enough playing time, an opportunity they felt they deserved, and their complaints soured the atmosphere. In a similar vein, another mentioned the issue of a starter who had been benched due to poor play and now suffered from plummeting morale. Together, we brainstormed strategies for dealing with these issues. During the peer sharing, people played off each other's ideas and thrashed out specific tactics, assisting one another in the refinement of their leadership thinking.

The discussion evolved into an analysis of Feeling Orientation, the next subscale on our KGI list. We reflected together on the necessity of staying attuned to emotional issues that emerged in the position groups and the team at large. For a majority of the men, who were Thinking types, this posed a substantial challenge.

By inclination, they tended to avoid feeling issues, wanting to side-step them. The day's discussion, however, highlighted the need for dealing with emotions in order to help individuals and the group to remain on an even keel. We talked about watching people's body language and facial expressions to pick up on the feeling vibe underneath. Then it was a matter, once again, of Assertiveness, of asking questions and making the feelings discussable. From Feeling Orientation process suggestions, we added these points:

- Listen respectfully.
- Avoid judgments.
- Get clear about the sources of the problem. Get specific details.
- Try to problem solve. Refocus the teammate in a positive way.

We acknowledged that, as a group, like it or not, everyone had to develop the Feeling preference in order to be an effective leader. Everyone had to step up to manage emotional issues.

During this phase, we had additional one-on-one sessions to support each player with the struggles of skill development. To their credit, everyone accepted the challenges and tried to practice the new skills. Extraverts and Introverts adjusted their speaking and listening skills, Thinking types tried to attune themselves to emotional issues, Feeling types tried to use more logical analysis. With persistence and thoughtful adjustments, the men made strides in acquiring skills, employing the opposite psychological preferences as part of the package. In our coaching sessions, we talked about the particular problems the men faced in their situations. We discussed modifications to improve strategies, and there was praise for successes. Taking it one, clear, conscious step at a time, everyone marched forward.

Part of what made these changes possible was that we were seeing results; the team kept on winning, maintaining an undefeated record. Everyone recognized that something special was happening, and it motivated the captains and the other players to stretch themselves and push their growth edge. This positive momentum encouraged people to do the difficult, to strive to master formidable skills, and in the process, the captains matured as leaders and the team gained greater cohesion.

In the last phase of the campaign, we sought to really strengthen team unity. The team would face its toughest opponents. To have the best chance to win out, we needed to be a very tight-knit group, a squad of players who would play for each other, sacrifice for each other, and fight for each other. A deep camaraderie would count for a lot.

At the captains' meeting, we discussed the atmosphere on the team. As the players described it, the team was confident yet cautious. While they felt that our team was as good as, or better than, any of the challengers on the schedule, they knew unexpected things could happen: a fumble, an interception, a special team miscue, some error that could turn a game and cause defeat. With that notion, a fear factor had crept in. No one wanted to be the guy who made the mistake that cost everyone the perfect season. Even some of the coaches acknowledged they were anxious about making a bad play call, putting players in the wrong positions, something that could lead to disaster. Such thinking can cramp minds and bodies, making it harder to be loose and responsive, the ingredients that produce success on the field.

The antidote seemed to be with Positive Group Affiliation. All season long we had fought to establish a culture of respect, dignity, brotherhood, and mutual support. The band of captains had done a great job in reaching out to all of the members of the position groups to instill these values. Leading by example, they showed they were not cliquish stars, but regular men who treated other players as equals and befriended the quietest people and the rookies. Everyone saw what they were doing, and it galvanized the team. We aimed to deepen those ties. We wanted to strengthen the regard and friendship in the position groups. We also wanted to build more bridges between offensive and defensive players, because this division can divide a team. During the week, they practiced strenuously against each other to be game ready. Such regular, hardnosed combat can produce festering animosities. We now wanted offensive and defensive captains to mingle more with players from the opposite side, displaying that we were one team, no matter what the specialties, no matter how fierce the practices. The aim was to build more trust, so the players would know that if they did make a mistake, someone else would be there to step up and fight to make a play that would pull the game out. Everyone would be looking out for one another.

On the last day of the regular season, the undefeated Golden Bears played their toughest conference rival, a team with one loss. According to conference rules, there would be no co-champion. Based on the tie-breakers, the team that emerged victorious in the game would win the title.

In the fourth quarter, the score was tied 21–21, and it evolved into a defensive struggle, neither team willing to concede a drive that would be decisive. It appeared the game would be settled in overtime. With a little over a minute to go, our opponent had possession deep in its own territory.

On a running play, there was a ferocious collision; two of the Western New England defensive captains, in a co-tackle, slammed into each other. The helmet of one struck his teammate squarely on the elbow.

As the star outside linebacker stood up, his arm had gone completely numb, dangling at his side. Dazed, he turned to trot off the field. But his teammates blocked him. He was a tremendous player, part of the soul of the defense. They implored him not to leave with a minute left. As we had talked about so often, they asked him to reach down to find something more.

Emboldened by his teammates' words, he decided to stay.

On the next play, the quarterback rolled out and threw the ball. The linebacker with the numb arm cut in front of the receiver and made an incredible interception, just before going out of bounds. In his four-year career, it was the only interception he ever made.

The play electrified his teammates and the fans. The offense bounded onto the field. The quarterback captain and the running backs captain alternated carries and in three plays covered the distance and punched the ball into the end zone— for the win and for the championship.

Fortunately, our linebacker only had a stinger, a short-term nerve response, but his courage had inspired the team. Two of the offensive captains then seized the initiative. It was the beauty of shared leadership. As we had been saying all season, the fate of the team would rest on the shoulders of the captains and their leadership abilities.

Medical Practice

A medical specialty practice hired a consultant to conduct a team-building intervention with the clinical and administrative support staff, a group that consisted of five people: a nurse practitioner, a licensed practical nurse, a program manager, an administrative assistant, and an information technology specialist who presided over an elaborate record keeping system. These professionals backed up two physicians in the office.

Because of its high-quality services, it was a booming practice, treating hundreds of patients a week. At times the stresses could really mount, putting pressure on communication and interpersonal relations, and precipitating tensions in the staff. Recently, staff frictions had seriously escalated, affecting the workplace. So the consultant was brought in to administer the Klein Group Instrument and Myers-Briggs Type Indicator method to address these issues and forge a smoother-functioning team.

The intervention included an opening presentation, one-on-one individual sessions, and team meetings to refine the group processes. The dominant MBTI score for the staff was INTJ. There were 3 Introverts and 2 Extraverts, 3 Intuitive types and 2 Sensing types, 3 Thinking types and 2 Feeling types, and 4 Judging types and 1 Perceiving type.

In the one-on-one sessions, the consultant evaluated the personal scores from the KGI and MBTI measurements, assisting staff members in identifying the skill areas that would enhance their communication, their interpersonal techniques, and expand their leadership abilities. This included discussion about how their preferred psychological preferences and their opposite preferences could play a role in the enterprise. The consultant also

interviewed each member about his or her perspective on the team and the issues confronting the medical office.

It became clear that all members took pride in their first-rate practice. Everyone was intent on delivering quality care for every patient. But the stream of patients pouring through the door could feel overwhelming. There was pressure to manage a sea of details—for each diagnosis and treatment, for each follow up, and for the tide of information required for insurance purposes. To handle the situation, members maintained a strict task focus to keep the system rolling; everyone sought to stay in lock step. Still, there were times when mistakes occurred, communication misfired, and personal tensions flared. As a result, teamwork broke down and resentments would start to fester. A central goal was to create stronger interpersonal bonds, so that staff would support each other in managing these stresses and sustain high-caliber performance.

At the first team meeting, the consultant and staff examined the Group Composite Subscale Graph from their profile.

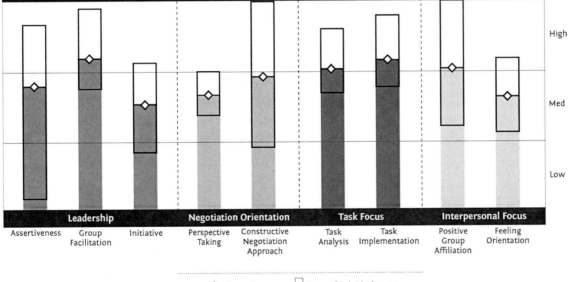

In the High section of the graph resided three important subscales: Group Facilitation, Task Implementation, and Positive Group Affiliation. The consultant pointed out that for a team with an Introversion leaning, the Group Facilitation score in the top spot was surprising, but also very beneficial. As seen in the distribution of member

scores for this subscale, everyone felt comfortable stepping up to be a facilitator as the situation might require. This gave the team flexibility, with all of the players able to take a lead role at times, which aided the office in managing the crowd of patients filling the waiting room.

Given the group's Judging preference and the

fast-paced environment, the consultant noted that the high Task Implementation score made sense. People were poised to move the work right along, which was all to the good. The Positive Group Affiliation result reflected the members' desire to have a positive atmosphere in the office. Yet, with all the pressures, a cheerful mood wasn't something that would just happen. People had to consciously focus on it and nurture it. With an overall Introversion leaning, they should cultivate some Extraversion. If they made the effort to increase interpersonal rapport, it would aid the team in sustaining satisfying morale.

To start, the consultant suggested they make Group Facilitation an even stronger asset, which would require building up the Assertiveness and Perspective Taking domains. These represented two softer scores in the team's results, but they could enhance facilitation in a relevant way. Whenever anyone facilitated an interaction, it would be important to make sure that all voices were heard and enough questions were asked so that all concerns were explored. This would apply to interactions with patients as well as with staff. While it could require a bit more time, it would ensure that enough information was collected so that sound decisions were made. These techniques paved the way for productive facilitation, and they would certainly support the goal of offering excellent care. Significantly, this approach would help reduce mistakes. With some perseverance, he assured everyone, they would learn to do it more precisely and efficiently, so the time issue would be reduced.

As the staff reviewed the graph, strengthening these softer areas made sense to them, especially in support of their most preferred domain, Group Facilitation.

They talked about implementing these ideas in staff meetings. Digging into the KGI® Group Profile, they studied the process suggestions. With Assertiveness, they noticed from the result that a few members might dominate a meeting, while one or two others might not say much at all. The more dominant people needed to be patient, pulling back at times to make sure quieter people could share. The quieter people needed to make more of an effort to join in the conversation. Everyone needed to air their thoughts. With

Perspective Taking, they recognized they could ask more questions to get further details, to probe people's reasoning and concerns, and deepen the conversation. Whoever facilitated a discussion wanted to pay attention to these dynamics and put the strategies into action in a respectful manner.

The consultant declared this expanded conversation would benefit the Task Analysis area. By broadening the discussion, people could assess task issues from more angles, examine additional points, and generate more creative solutions. They would be better able to tap into each other's thinking and insights, fortifying Task Analysis and moving it more into line with their sturdy Task Implementation, thereby raising overall task performance. Given the serious emphasis on task execution in their office, this would be a real advantage.

People around the group nodded in agreement. They liked the way the strategies interconnected and brought multiple advantages. They now had an agenda to pursue in the coming weeks.

When the consultant followed up for the next round, group members had made progress. They practiced the new skills and saw improvements with communication and problem solving. There was one notable exception, related to the interactions of the information technology specialist and the program manager. They experienced a communication conflict and were at odds with each other.

The consultant spoke to each one personally. The IT specialist had an ENTP score. In his previous coaching session, he declared that he hated dull routine; in fact, he'd left his previous position with another medical group when the job deteriorated in that direction. What he enjoyed was riding a creative edge, finding and customizing new software that would be more successful in the office. He liked to really burrow into new technology, master it, and then train everyone in the applications. He now admitted that this pursuit had distracted him, so he missed a deadline and overlooked some details for record keeping. He stated that this caused the dispute with the program manager. He regretted the mistakes, but felt the manager made too big a deal out of it. In the larger scheme of things, he contributed a lot to the practice by keeping it abreast of cutting-edge technology. These were small lapses that should not be a major problem.

The program manager, on the other hand, possessed an ISTJ score. While the office might be action-packed, she stated that she thrived on it, finding it rewarding to maintain a smooth-running operation. This required oversight of a considerable amount of data. With regard to the IT specialist, she recently discovered missing information in some records. When she contacted him about what had happened, he simply said, "I don't know" and seemed nonchalant about the situation. She would have much preferred hearing, "I will investigate the matter." His attitude irritated her, reflecting the mindset that he was being interrupted about little things when he had more important things to do. Details related to records were significant, and she felt he needed to take the time to stay on top of them. And with other projects she assigned him, he was often late—this wasn't the first time he'd fallen behind and thus made it hard to keep business flowing in the office. She had asked questions, trying to grasp his perspective, but there were moments when his attitude simply annoyed and exasperated her. She hadn't brought this issue up previously because she thought the training process would straighten it out without it becoming some awkward, contentious issue. But now she felt that was a mistake.

The consultant set up a session with the two of them to analyze the predicament. He started out by informing them that their psychological typologies provided insights into the issues at hand. This would be an intelligent way to approach the discussion. Regarding the four MBTI dichotomies, they had opposite preferences for three of them, something that would make collaboration more difficult. Earlier in the training, he had explained how people with opposite preferences address situations differently. For example, Sensing types like to pay attention to details, while Intuitive types are interested in creativity and the big picture. With the Judging attitude, there is a concern with schedules and task completion, contrasted to the Perceiving attitude, which is more open-ended and tends to have difficulty in meeting deadlines. These points helped to explain the conflict between the two employees. The consultant pointed out that typology allows team members to evaluate behavior in a way that moves beyond "personality flaws" and directs the conversation constructively, so they can gain insights and solve problems together.

The two parties listened attentively and appeared receptive to the approach. The consultant went on to say that the KGI subscales of Perspective Taking and Constructive Negotiation Approach supplied additional ideas that would aid in this process. The goal was to deepen their mutual understanding and find a middle ground. They needed to construct a win-win accord, one that would be mutually agreeable.

With that understanding in place, they began to explore the current issues. The consultant invited the program manager to share her perspective about what was needed to maintain an efficient office. She spoke about the tight management of details and the execution of tasks in a timely manner. In her opinion, these were indispensable requirements for an effective office and they required close attention.

The consultant then invited the IT specialist to share his thoughts. He said he respected what she said, but from his vantage point, the integration of top-end software helped to achieve these goals. It made the control of data more organized, and it helped to get work done more quickly. Personally, he liked the creative challenge of discovering and adapting such software; it was part of what made his job meaningful.

The consultant said he would like each person to reflect on the other's concerns. How could they respond to each other in realistic ways that would have mutual benefit and improve performance in the office? In practical terms, how could they balance the Sensing and Intuition, and the Judging and Perceiving interests?

Together, they hashed out an agreement. The IT staffer would spend more time with information management, making sure things were complete and submitted on time, according to the day-to-day needs of the practice. In general, he would tighten up his time management so that other people who depended on him were not losing time. This included participation in special projects that emerged in the clinic. The program manager agreed to provide certain funds so he could explore new technologies. She didn't mind when he spent time on innovative interests, as long as it didn't interfere with meeting daily responsibilities. With creative pursuits, however, she wanted him to concentrate on those that would have a relevant, immediate impact for the practice. That would make his creative work truly purposeful.

In conclusion, they agreed to follow through on these points and provide feedback to one another to refine their agreement.

Afterwards, the consultant assisted the staff in improving their collective situation. He suggested they look at Constructive Negotiation Approach and Positive Group Affiliation. These two subscales play off each other, reinforcing a positive social energy that contributes to high team performance. The staff already possessed a firm asset with Positive Group Affiliation. What they needed to do was channel some of that existing energy towards Constructive Negotiation Approach. By more consciously constructing win-win agreements, they could further improve team morale, intensifying team spirit. This would help people deal with stress because they would be more comfortable in turning to each other for support, based on a feeling they were really working together to solve problems.

As they examined some of the process suggestions from their KGI® Group Profile, they agreed they could have an after-hours social event to relax together and get better acquainted. With respect to negotiations, people could try to be more flexible in modifying their positions to find common ground, keeping the idea of win-win in the foreground.

From the MBTI perspective, the consultant mentioned that building up the social side would require the use of Extraversion, which could be done strategically. Some focused, interpersonal time would be a plus, but they could experiment with it and see what worked best for everyone. During negotiations, they should remember to draw upon their overall Intuition preference, with its inclination to find connections between different people's interests. They should consciously apply that energy in an advantageous way.

When the consultant contacted the staff for the final time, there had been substantial improvements. The IT specialist had been creating a daily "to-do list," prioritizing the day's activities so he could stay on top of his responsibilities. This helped him maintain the necessary focus. During conversations with the office manager, he jotted down detailed notes, enabling him to execute the desired tasks more promptly. These efforts made the office manager more comfortable with him. She felt their communication, across the board, had significantly improved. As a reward, she provided funds so that he could attend a national software convention in Los Angeles. On her side, she investigated staff members' concerns in greater depth, asking more questions and trying to learn more about their perspectives. She consciously sought to construct win-win agreements, having witnessed the difference it could make for maintaining healthy morale and encouraging enthusiastic effort. Integrating the KGI Feeling Orientation subscale, she also made strides with paying attention to body language and facial expressions that conveyed emotional reactions. Becoming more alert to these signs, she responded to emerging issues in a prompt way, which enabled her to nip problems in the bud before they became really disruptive.

The whole staff had joined together for an ice cream social, a light-hearted, fun time, in stark contrast to the serious mood that generally pervaded the office. The event provided a pleasant antidote to the regular routine—people relaxed, mingled, and talked about things in a leisurely manner. Everyone agreed they should have events like this more often. They found it made communication easier in the days that followed. In general, people became more aware of the different personality styles on the team. They could adjust their approach according to people's preferences, making the interactions more effective. They also learned strategies about how to facilitate capably and negotiate in ways that strengthened their teamwork. Implementing these new ideas, they felt they became a more cohesive, resilient team, which, in turn, created a more positive atmosphere in the office.

University Leadership Course

The undergraduate course, Leadership and Team Skills, employs the Klein Group Instrument and Myers-Briggs Type Indicator approach to train students in successful small-group participation. Students learn how to read group dynamics, how to become capable leaders and members, and how to spark synergy in teams. Every student is assigned to an in-class group (with 5 members) that serves as a laboratory for exploring new skills and for shaping a high-performing unit. Together, they tackle a range of assignments, including decision-making tasks, hands-on physical activities, and the examination of business and professional case studies. With the cases, they evaluate personalities and team dynamics and articulate strategies to steer a group to higher ground. In the latter part of the semester, they conduct an interview with a community leader and make a major presentation to the class about their subject.

Using the MBTI and KGI measurements as a framework, they identify the subject's preferences and favored team tactics, and decipher the leader's group philosophy. Through the series of presentations, the class examines a variety of leadership approaches.

To illustrate the individual and team processes in this course, a group from a recent semester will serve as an example. Having a collective type preference of ESTP, the team consisted of 3 Extraverts and 2 Introverts, 3 Sensing types and 2 Intuitive types, 3 Thinking types and 2 Feeling types, and 4 Perceiving types and 1 Judging type. It included two women, a recent African immigrant to the United States and a Hispanic-American, along with three men of Caucasian-American background. They represented majors in History, Health Science, Mechanical Engineering, Psychology, and Business Management.

At the start of the semester, the students took the KGI and MBTI assessments. After a lecture on the designs of the measurements and how to interpret the scores, they wrote a short paper outlining a personal development plan. They targeted two KGI subscales and the related growth statements, describing how their MBTI preferences and opposite preferences would be involved in their practice of new skills.

Following the assignment, the students were placed in their semester-long team. They began with a get-acquainted, introductory activity. Later, they shared their MBTI results and their KGI skill-building objectives. Reflecting on their objectives, they discussed ways to assist one another in skill acquisition during the term, with the aim of becoming a learning team. The next week they performed a group decision-making exercise, so they could get a better feel for each member's values and interactive style.

In the ensuing class, the team received its KGI® Group Profile. Members had to analyze the data and consider how to improve their group processes. At the end of this activity, they met with the instructor to discuss their plan.

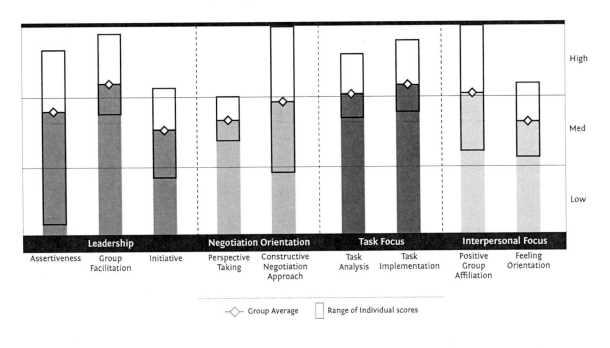

The students identified several objectives. While the team, overall, had solid scores with Assertiveness and Perspective Taking, it was clear from the subscale graph that not everyone was active in these domains. As they collaborated, they wanted to make sure everyone participated and that all perspectives were considered. All members would seek to balance their Extraversion and Introversion energies in constructive ways.

With Group Facilitation and Initiative, they wanted to ensure that every member had an opportunity to take a leadership role in some activity as the semester progressed. They would rotate the leadership role, based on people's skill goals and the nature of the activity. In this endeavor, they would pay attention to the application of the Thinking and Feeling functions related to Task Focus and Interpersonal Focus issues.

For Constructive Negotiation Approach, they wanted to consciously construct win-win agreements whenever possible. Members with the Intuition preference would take an active role in pointing out ways to bring different interests together for joint agreements. Members with the Sensing preference would study these actions to learn practical techniques.

As the group became involved in assorted team activities in the next phase of the semester, the instructor noticed that different members posed questions to their groupmates to secure broad participation. Initially, the Extraverts took the lead, but, over time, the Introverts also asked more questions and facilitated the group. For one exercise, when members had to do a short presentation for the whole class, they demonstrated careful organization in the way they coordinated their performance, with every member authentically and equally participating. Each person also received feedback about his or her presentation style, related to tone of voice, pace, eye contact, and physical posture, so people could refine those aspects of their leadership skills.

For the interview assignment, the team had to speak with the Dean of the College of Pharmacy, and the group quickly mobilized for the mission. Interestingly, an Introvert with a Feeling preference took a lead role in designing a number of questions that would investigate leadership topics in a logical and detailed way. Another Introvert

took a proactive role in contacting the dean's office, coordinating the event so it would be convenient for everyone's schedule. When the day arrived for the interview, members later disclosed they had felt nervous. Before the meeting, an ESTJ member gave the team a pep talk, praising various members' efforts with the preparation; the speech raised morale and shored up their confidence. They went on to conduct an energetic investigation of the dean's leadership experiences.

When the day arrived to set the schedule for the class presentations, the team volunteered to be first. Out of all the groups, it demonstrated the most motivation, happy to be placed in the initial slot. The members diligently practiced their presentation, and when they stepped to the front of the room, they delivered a fluid, thoughtful discussion of their subject's leadership style, an analysis grounded in sturdy detail. Each member played an appropriate role. Impressively, their presentation styles were markedly improved. They had helped each other perfect the tone of voice, pace, eye contact, and physical gestures, drawing on feedback received earlier in the semester. It turned out to be a superb performance, one that set a high bar for the groups that followed.

At the end of the semester, the students wrote a final paper about how they personally employed their new skills in an outside-of-class group situation. The team members related the following stories.

One of the young women served on the Board of Directors for the Alternative Spring Break Program, which arranges community service projects in locations across the country for students who want to dedicate spring vacation to helping others. At the start of the semester, she had been a very shy, reserved person, but the course had enabled her to blossom socially. As she and several board members constructed student teams to travel to the various sites, she rose up and assumed a much more active role. Since she had been such a reserved person at the beginning of the term, her colleagues were surprised by this transformation. She stated that the experience of being valued by her group in the course allowed her to gain confidence, prompting her to take on more of a leadership role with her committee.

In a similar vein, she wrote that on short

notice, she had been asked to address a fundraising dinner for church groups that had resettled her family in the area. In the past, she noted, such a request would have made her faint. But armed with skills from our class, she agreed to do the presentation. Watching her pace and enunciation, and adding a couple of jokes to relax the audience, she made the evening a great success. She was thrilled by her performance.

The other young lady had been involved in a group research project in another course during the term. She and her groupmates were strangers to each other. Applying strategies from the leadership class, she stepped up to facilitate the group's efforts. With a respectful manner, she coordinated the project, guiding it to a triumphant conclusion. When everyone received a strong final grade, her teammates, with sincere appreciation, praised her leadership abilities.

One of the young men was captain of the lacrosse team at the university. He had a Thinking preference. Not being one to pay attention to others' feelings, he decided to work on the KGI Feeling Orientation subscale. At team practices, he said, there could be a lot of yelling when people made mistakes, which, at times, became peppered with obscenities. In this atmosphere he noticed how certain players, particularly the younger ones, got down on themselves. With heads drooping, their concentration and effort started to flag. As captain, he changed the approach. He began to speak with a calm voice, talking to other players with consideration, simply pointing out, in a logical way, the proper technique adjustment. He found this reduced the negative emotions, and other players began to imitate his style. Team members began to connect with each other in productive ways, which later translated into greater success in actual games.

Another gentleman was the Command Sergeant Major for the ROTC program at the university. With Sensing, Thinking, and Judging preferences, he admitted that it was not his style to praise other people's efforts. A hardnosed, buttoned-down guy, he focused on the bottom line and demanded effort. He noticed that many cadets, particularly the younger ones, became nervous and uncomfortable in his presence. From his experience in the leadership class, he saw the value of praise as it related to Group Facilitation and strong Task Implementation. At a training event conducted at a military base, he had the entire battalion, one hundred cadets, in formation before him. Changing his approach, he called to the front ten of the younger cadets who had been performing above and beyond expectations. He recognized their efforts to the whole battalion. He found that this action raised their spirits to an incredible level. By the expressions on the young cadets' faces, he could see that it meant the world to them. The next day he observed that every cadet was moving with more energy and purpose in the hope of receiving similar recognition.

The last fellow received an internship in the mayor's office during the semester. An Introvert with a Feeling preference, he recognized the need to improve his KGI Task Focus skills, requiring the exercise of more Sensing and Thinking energies. To practice the skills, he accepted the assignment of coordinating a university presentation by the mayor. Investigating how such events were arranged on campus, he did all of the advance organization. When his supervisor reviewed the plan, she was pleased with the thoroughness of his effort, stating that he had covered every required point without any direction from her. In the end, he made a significant contribution to a noteworthy event.

From these stories, it's clear how classroom skill building transfers to outside activities and can provide a real sense of accomplishment. Such achievement spurs a legitimate feeling of self-confidence, a vital ingredient for ongoing leadership development. As a result, the students are well prepared to take on future leadership roles as they forge ahead into their business and professional careers.

In the next chapter, KGI Group Composite Subscale Graphs are introduced, representing sixteen teams, each with a different dominant MBTI type preference. They offer talking points that will guide professionals in the application of the KGI–MBTI team-building method. ✄

CHAPTER 26

KGI® and MTBI® Group Graphs with Talking Points

To aid professionals in team-building interventions with the Klein Group Instrument and Myers-Briggs Type Indicator assessments, the following examples present the talking points that a consultant may use in the evaluation of group results. These cases demonstrate ways to interpret graph data and construct strategies to expand team-work. Once a consultant and a team agree on particular subscales for skill building, they can refer to those sections of the KGI® Group Profile to select process suggestions

to direct improvement. With regard to the MBTI results, the talking points include suggestions about how the existing team preferences and the opposite preferences may be employed most profitably.

The examples portray the diverse manner in which teams may operate, influenced by their dominant personality style. In each instance, the MBTI score is the composite score for the group, displaying the dominant preference for each of the four dichotomies based on the combination of member scores. All sixteen personality types are

represented, offering benchmarks for dealing with any team with a particular dominant pattern. Each group consisted of five members, an optimal size for small-group work. The KGI segment relies on the Group Composite Subscale Graph, the central element in the group profile, providing rich material for a focused yet intricate analysis. As before, the Inter-Subscale Combinations system is integrated into the discussion at appropriate times.

continued on next page >

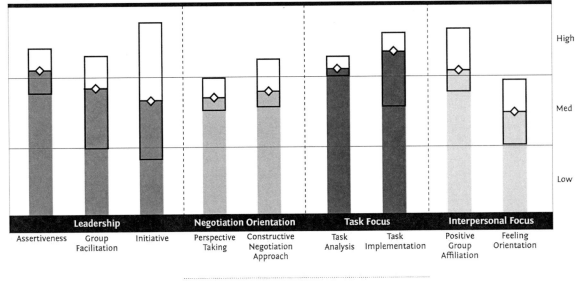

High

Med

Low

| Leadership | Negotiation Orientation | Task Focus | Interpersonal Focus |

Assertiveness | Group Facilitation | Initiative | Perspective Taking | Constructive Negotiation Approach | Task Analysis | Task Implementation | Positive Group Affiliation | Feeling Orientation

◇— Group Average   ☐ Range of Individual scores

1. **Assertiveness** with **Perspective Taking:** There is a substantial amount of Assertiveness energy on the team. The challenge is to make sure everyone gets air time and no one is left out. A worthwhile approach is to expand questioning in the group, inviting everyone to participate. This will also enhance Perspective Taking, as people learn more about each other's positions. The most active members should take a leadership role in helping the team strike a better balance between these two operations. Members can use the Introversion attitude to listen more closely to one another.

2. **Constructive Negotiation Approach** with **Positive Group Affiliation:** The team has solid social energy, expressed in its Positive Group Affiliation score. It should channel some of that energy towards Constructive Negotiation Approach, making a more conscious effort to find win-win agreements, which will boost the social spirit on the team. The Intuitive function can assist in finding the middle ground among different members' positions to construct win-win accords. This will increase team cohesion, resulting in a more unified effort on tasks.

3. **Group Facilitation:** In areas where members have demonstrated skills—task, interpersonal, or negotiation—the group should provide them with opportunities to facilitate the work. Capitalize on their expertise and support leadership development, which will enhance the group's ability to

manage a variety of projects. The Perceiving attitude would help with finding new, flexible approaches for managing leadership on the team.

4. **Feeling Orientation:** There is untapped potential here. The team would do well to pay more attention to the emotional reactions of the members. When does anger or irritation, for example, disrupt someone's participation, resulting in the group losing that person's relevant input? When does someone's passion for a certain piece of the work go unrecognized and, consequently, unharnessed? By applying the Feeling function, members can stay attuned to these emotional currents and respond to them more effectively.

5. **Initiative:** There are some members who have not developed this leadership skill to a meaningful degree. Those who have, most likely dominate group activities. The team should aid members in taking reasonable leadership roles in appropriate aspects of the work. Use Introversion to listen to members' interests and enthusiasms, Intuition to creatively shape leadership options for them, and Judging to organize the efforts.

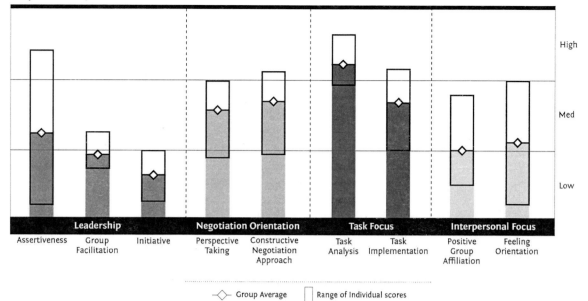

High

Med

Low

| Leadership | | | Negotiation Orientation | | Task Focus | | Interpersonal Focus | |

Assertiveness | Group Facilitation | Initiative | Perspective Taking | Constructive Negotiation Approach | Task Analysis | Task Implementation | Positive Group Affiliation | Feeling Orientation

◇ Group Average   ☐ Range of Individual scores

1. **Assertiveness** with **Perspective Taking:** Some members may dominate a discussion, while others may say nothing at all. Everyone needs to make their thoughts known during discussions to create an authentic team dialogue. With regard to Perspective Taking, members with higher scores in this domain should be role models, inviting others to share their thoughts. Balance the use of Extraversion for speaking up and Introversion for listening. The Perceiving attitude would also be relevant, creating a desire to hear more ideas, perspectives, and strategy options.

2. **Positive Group Affiliation:** Members could benefit from rapport-building activities that stimulate a sense of team spirit. Certain members have skills in this area, based on the graph result. Using Extraversion and the Feeling function, which incline people to value each other, the skilled members can provide leadership by introducing exercises that would help members become better acquainted, thereby strengthening team cohesion. As team cohesion increases, productivity goes up as well.

3. **Group Facilitation:** Which members have skills in Interpersonal Focus? Which members have skills with Task Focus or Negotiation Orientation? Members with skills in these areas can support the team by facilitating these segments of group discussions. Sensing, Intuition, Thinking, and Feeling preferences can all be utilized at particular

times, as needed, to examine details, create a vision, employ logic, or establish interpersonal rapport.

4. **Feeling Orientation:** The group would profit from training in the recognition and management of feelings during team meetings. For many members, this is a repressed area. It is important to recognize that emotions impact people's motivations: positive ones increase effort, while negative ones decrease it, affecting participation on the team. Creating a more constructive climate for dealing with emotions would, in the end, enhance mutual understanding and aid productivity. The development of the Feeling function would be part of the process, as would refining the use of Sensing to pay attention to body language and facial expressions that communicate emotions when people work together.

5. **Initiative:** No one appears to be excited about stepping into a leadership role on the team. This is an opportunity for group learning as members experiment with leadership actions and support each other in the acquisition of new skills. The team can be a mini-laboratory where people try out new roles and receive feedback about how to refine their performance. Members need to deploy Extraversion to take action, Thinking to match their talents with appropriate projects, and Judging to organize the efforts in beneficial ways.

Graph Three: ESFJ

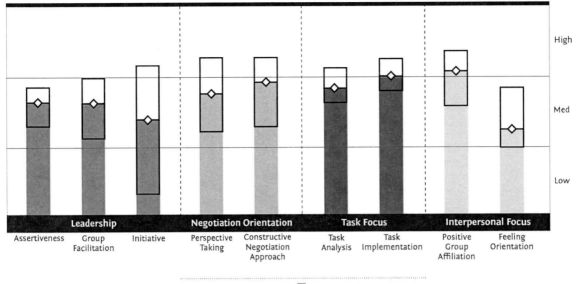

Leadership			Negotiation Orientation		Task Focus		Interpersonal Focus	
Assertiveness	Group Facilitation	Initiative	Perspective Taking	Constructive Negotiation Approach	Task Analysis	Task Implementation	Positive Group Affiliation	Feeling Orientation

—◇— Group Average   ▢ Range of Individual scores

1. **Assertiveness:** Members with higher scores in this area should invite quieter members to share their opinions. Be sure to get everyone into the discussions. The more people express their opinions and feel part of the group, the more they will speak up on their own over time, without the need for prompting. Members can harness Extraversion to express their opinions, Thinking to articulate ideas concisely and logically, and Sensing to relate relevant details that support their positions. This will foster a thoughtful dialogue on the team.

2. **Perspective Taking and Constructive Negotiation Approach:** Members shouldn't assume they know each other's interests and concerns. They should assume they don't know enough and investigate further to expand their PT. Employ the Sensing function to learn more details and Introversion to listen closely. This information will strengthen efforts to find common ground with Constructive Negotiation Approach. The Intuitive function can assist here, enabling members to find connections among the various interests to construct win-win agreements.

3. **Group Facilitation with Interpersonal Focus:** Despite an overall preference for Feeling, the team's lowest result is for Feeling Orientation. It has the right tools—Extraversion, Sensing, and Feeling—to pay attention to emotional issues in the here and now, make the issues discussable, and manage the team's emotional life to greater advantage. The team needs to do more to cultivate the

FO domain. This will help instill more openness and rapport, supporting the effort to build a team spirit with Positive Group Affiliation.

4. **Task Analysis with Task Implementation:** Members with skills in TA should model for the team effective analytical techniques. Others can follow suit and acquire more competence. The team should look at assorted problems, opportunities, and solutions for the task, drawing on the Perceiving function to consider the issues broadly. Then the Thinking function can help assess the most logical paths to pursue. With TI, the group has an admirable tendency to move work forward to completion. But does it jump the gun—pushing a job forward without completely thinking through the strategy? The lower Task Analysis score indicates this possibility. The team should be patient in developing a plan, which can enhance the quality of the final outcome.

5. **Initiative:** The group may rely on the drive of one or two members to lead the team in its work. This fails to capitalize on the full leadership potential of the team. Forge an atmosphere that encourages initiative. Allow members to think creatively about a project and give them some reign to pursue their ideas. Encourage people to take more leadership when their knowledge and their skills are pertinent to the work at hand. Deploy the Thinking function to identify people's gifts, and use the Judging attitude to organize opportunities so the gifts can be put into play.

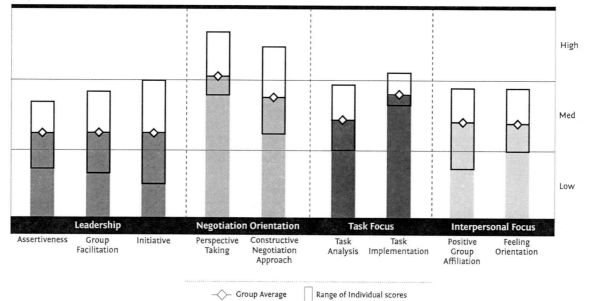

Leadership | Negotiation Orientation | Task Focus | Interpersonal Focus

Assertiveness | Group Facilitation | Initiative | Perspective Taking | Constructive Negotiation Approach | Task Analysis | Task Implementation | Positive Group Affiliation | Feeling Orientation

High / Med / Low

◇— Group Average   ☐ Range of Individual scores

1. Assertiveness with **Perspective Taking:** Team members are paying attention to one another's ideas, interests, and values. But are members too deferential, so that people are reluctant to share differing opinions and speak their minds? More members need to speak up, making their ideas and interests known. Broaden the use of the Extraversion attitude so that everyone contributes, along with the Thinking function to express thoughtful ideas. Introverts have many valuable ideas, but they need to state them and expand the dialogue within the group.

2. Group Facilitation: Members need to step up when they have relevant knowledge and skills for a project and help facilitate the effort. Members can facilitate according to their particular expertise, for example, with Task Analysis or Positive Group Affiliation. They should tap Extraversion energy to rise up and the Judging attitude to organize things in an appropriate manner.

3. Constructive Negotiation Approach with **Positive Group Affiliation:** The group's performance can be enhanced in a couple of ways. The Intuition function helps identify connections between different members' positions, which aids in constructing win-win agreements for CNA. Draw on Intuition energy. Also, nurture Positive Group Affiliation. As members get more acquainted with each other and more comfortable, they become more inclined to pursue win-

win arrangements. The group has Feeling energy, important for building relationships, but it needs Extraversion to express it and bring people together in a more personal manner.

4. Task Analysis with **Task Implementation:** As a group, the members form a tight unit with everyone focusing on implementation issues. This is a real strength. But the quality of task outcomes could be enhanced by improving Task Analysis. Consider more ideas about how to do a task, examining the topic from multiple angles. The Perceiving attitude relishes fresh perspectives, as does Intuition. The Thinking function can help evaluate the pros and cons of specific new strategies. Experiment with these preferences. With better strategies, the team could take its performance to the next level.

5. Initiative: One or two members may dominate this sector, while others take little or no leadership actions. Create opportunities for all members to take on leadership roles, perhaps with small initiatives at first. Help teammates build skills and confidence. The Extraversion, Thinking, and Judging preferences will support this venture; members can encourage each other to utilize these preferences more intentionally.

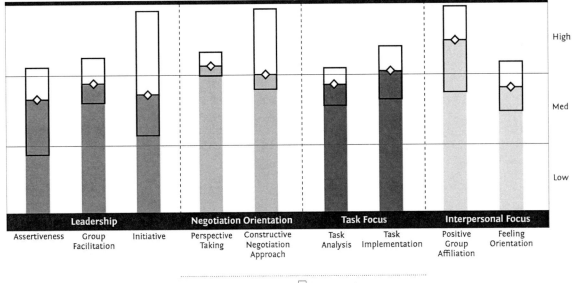

| | Group Average | | Range of Individual scores |

1. **Assertiveness** with **Perspective Taking:** While group members have a solid commitment to listening to each other and understanding one another's perspectives, does the atmosphere become too deferential? Are people reluctant to express differing opinions? Encourage the employment of Extraversion to get all members speaking up, so people hear their concerns. Perhaps some Thinking energy, with its boldness of expression, would be beneficial. Find a balance between speaking and listening that establishes a quality team dialogue.

2. **Initiative:** The group is not mining the leadership potential of a number of members. A clear challenge is to find ways to share leadership on projects. Identify the strengths of the more reticent members and provide them with the chance to use those skills in a lead role. Encourage and support one another in leadership activities. More prominent leaders can mentor the new leaders. Help all members enlist Extraversion energy, along with the Judging attitude, to step up, organize, and lead at appropriate times.

3. **Task Analysis:** The team needs to be more patient in analyzing a task in order to establish a sound plan. The Perceiving attitude would promote the examination of a broader range of issues, so the team can consider more strategy options. The Thinking function would then assist in selecting the best ones. Given the team's

commitment to Task Implementation, improving the analysis side could really benefit overall task performance.

4. **Constructive Negotiation Approach** with **Positive Group Affiliation:** Members like to create a positive social atmosphere on the team. Harness that energy for constructing more win-win agreements, which will further boost morale. Engage the Feeling function so people look out for each other's interests, and draw on Intuition to find connections among those interests that will produce popular agreements.

5. **Feeling Orientation:** There is reasonable alertness to emotional issues on the team, but the team could exploit this resource to better advantage. There may be a tendency to shy away from dealing with negative issues because the team gives so much attention to being cordial with Positive Group Affiliation. Utilize Introversion to listen closely to others' issues and Sensing to watch the body language that may reveal unstated feelings. Be willing to make negative emotions discussable.

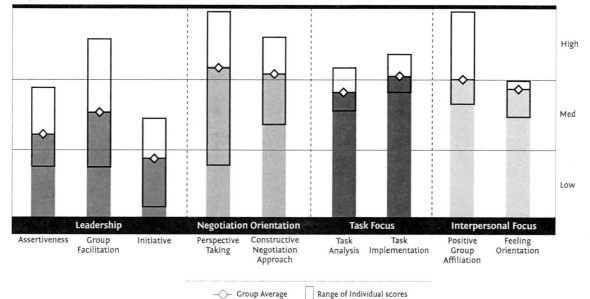

Leadership: Assertiveness, Group Facilitation, Initiative

Negotiation Orientation: Perspective Taking, Constructive Negotiation Approach

Task Focus: Task Analysis, Task Implementation

Interpersonal Focus: Positive Group Affiliation, Feeling Orientation

High / Med / Low

◇— Group Average   ☐ Range of Individual scores

1. Assertiveness with Perspective Taking: The team should work to create better balance between speaking skills (Assertiveness) and listening skills (Perspective Taking). This will raise the quality of conversation during team discussions. Encourage members to speak up and share ideas during a meeting, then others can ask probe questions to get a deeper grasp of their views. This provides substantive data for devising win-win accords with Constructive Negotiation Approach. Practice Extraversion for more self-expression, Thinking to articulate clear ideas, and Intuition to elucidate visions for effective collaboration.

2. Positive Group Affiliation: The team could structure some short activities to help people become more familiar with each other. With a strong leaning towards PGA, the members could build on this inclination and establish even greater team cohesion. Using Extraversion, people can explain their interests and motivations. As they get better acquainted, members will be inspired to fashion more win-win agreements, further boosting morale.

3. Task Analysis with Task Implementation: The team is doing a solid job with Task Analysis but could expand the effort by using the Perceiving attitude to survey a broader array of issues, and the Thinking function to build a sturdy, logical plan. With its Judging attitude, the team likes to move the work along, as seen in Task

Implementation. But it needs to cultivate more patience when designing the plan. Bringing analysis and implementation into better balance will increase the quality of the team's work.

4. Group Facilitation with Negotiation Orientation, Task Focus, and Interpersonal Focus: The team has many talented people and could enhance its performance by creating more shared leadership opportunities. Based on people's skill sets with negotiation, task, and interpersonal, give members opportunities to facilitate the group in these areas, developing their leadership potential. People with skills in Group Facilitation can mentor their teammates.

5. Initiative: Similar to the suggestions for Group Facilitation above, investigate how to divvy up assignments according to people's talents to assign larger leadership roles. Members can contribute to specific aspects of a project, helping facilitate in that area; later, they can take on more responsibility to guide an entire project. The team can sequence the skill building in this way, allowing members to expand their leadership capabilities. Practicing Extraversion is a key, along with other preferences as they apply to different components of the group's work.

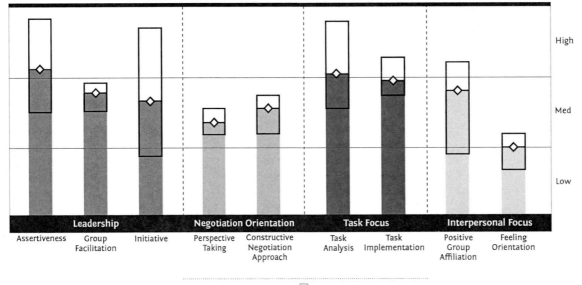

1. **Assertiveness**: The team exhibits significant verbal energy with this score. One goal is to make the group's discussion balanced and inclusive. The team could establish a time limit for a speaker in order to keep the conversation moving. It's important to prevent the competition for air time from becoming so intense that it produces a negative atmosphere for the team. The team needs to channel its Extraversion in a productive manner.

2. **Perspective Taking**: Members should ask more questions of one another and listen closely to the ideas being expressed, developing patient listening by using the Introversion attitude. Also, participants can apply the Perceiving attitude with its curiosity and its openness. As members gain more perspective and mutual understanding, it will enhance their efforts with Constructive Negotiation Approach, the fashioning of win-win agreements.

3. **Feeling Orientation**: How does the team manage feeling issues? When someone becomes upset, stemming from a conflict in a discussion, does the team just ignore it? Members need to pay attention to their teammates' emotional reactions. When negative feelings erupt in the

room, people need to address and reduce them. When people express enthusiasms, the group needs to channel that energy into productive work. The team can develop skills with the Feeling preference to acquire greater competence in recognizing and regulating emotional issues.

4. **Task Implementation**: The team has a solid score, but refining the performance would enhance productivity. The team should focus on improving communication when executing a task and providing supportive help as the project progresses. Drawing on the team's Judging preference would enable members to better organize the effort. Also, use the Sensing function to pay attention to critical details and communicate information about them in a timely way.

5. **Initiative**: Design ways to share leadership for different aspects of a single project or in a series of projects. According to people's expertise, give them appropriate leadership roles and allow them to lead in satisfying, skill-expanding ways. This will boost morale and increase the quality of task outcomes. The Thinking preference will help to determine the proper assignments and the Judging preference with organizing the enterprise.

Graph Eight: INTJ

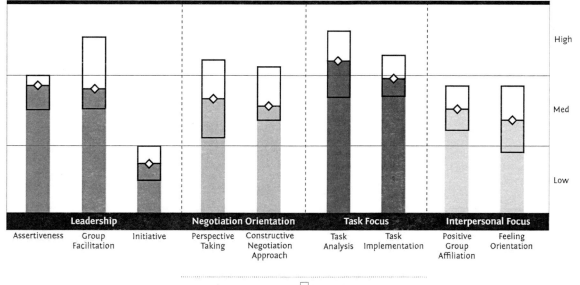

Leadership: Assertiveness, Group Facilitation, Initiative

Negotiation Orientation: Perspective Taking, Constructive Negotiation Approach

Task Focus: Task Analysis, Task Implementation

Interpersonal Focus: Positive Group Affiliation, Feeling Orientation

—◇— Group Average ☐ Range of Individual scores

1. **Assertiveness** with **Perspective Taking:** Make certain that all members are in the conversation. Don't just rely on the most assertive members to guide the group. Participants should take time to investigate their teammates' positions, to probe underlying interests and to get inside each other's shoes to really comprehend people's concerns. This would create a real dialogue on the team and could propel performance to the next level. Draw on Extraversion to speak up and Introversion to become more thoughtful listeners.

2. **Constructive Negotiation Approach:** Applying what is learned through Perspective Taking, members can craft more win-win agreements. They need to include everyone in the effort, seeking points of intersection among the various interests to establish common ground. Intuition will assist in finding the intersections, so consciously use that function for this purpose. Also, employ the Sensing function to look closely at the details.

3. **Positive Group Affiliation** with **Feeling Orientation:** If members develop greater interpersonal rapport, it will expand the lines of communication and increase productivity. Participants need to deploy Extraversion to converse more, taking time go get to know each other. They can use Feeling to build up the interpersonal relations, but the group has a problem—there is significant repression of the Feeling function. The team presses forward with task issues and ignores the

undercurrent of emotions. Members can apply Sensing energy to watch teammates' body language and Feeling to interpret emotional currents, positive and negative. If the team builds up personal relations and manages emotions more constructively, it will really enhance its overall performance.

4. **Group Facilitation:** The group should design opportunities for various members to take turns facilitating different aspects of its meetings or projects. Identify people's strengths in Task Analysis, Task Implementation, or Constructive Negotiation Approach, and give them the reins to guide the team when those skills apply. At some point, allow everyone to take a turn. This could infuse new energy into the team. The group would profit by employing Extraversion so all members share ideas and Perceiving so that a broad range of options are considered.

5. **Initiative:** It seems that no one wants to take on a prime leadership role, yet there appears to be a lot of talent in Assertiveness, Group Facilitation, and other skill areas. The group should address this issue and be willing to learn what work excites people? Where do they have a vision that could be worthwhile? Identify substantial leadership opportunities and help people embrace them. Use Thinking and Intuition to come up with creative ideas for leadership, and other preferences to support specific skill building.

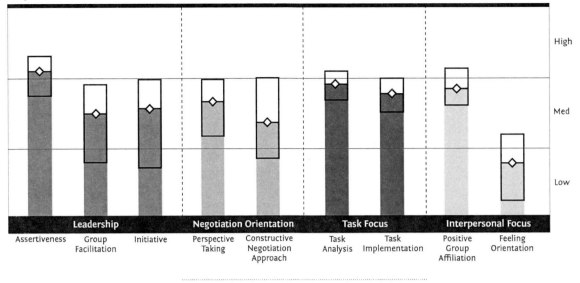

High

Med

Low

| Leadership | | | Negotiation Orientation | | Task Focus | | Interpersonal Focus | |

Assertiveness · Group Facilitation · Initiative · Perspective Taking · Constructive Negotiation Approach · Task Analysis · Task Implementation · Positive Group Affiliation · Feeling Orientation

◇ Group Average   ☐ Range of Individual scores

1. Assertiveness with **Perspective Taking:** If members are going to work well together, they need to have a sense of where their teammates are coming from, what motivates them, and what interests them. Drawing on the strong Assertiveness energy, members should make a point of asking each other more questions, probing more deeply one another's interests. Exercising the Introversion attitude would be beneficial, to listen closely and gauge others' concerns. If the team balanced Assertiveness (speaking) and Perspective Taking (listening) more effectively in discussions, it could create more dynamic collaboration among the members.

2. Task Analysis with **Task Implementation:** While all members seem engaged in analysis, there appears to be less involvement with implementation. Bringing these areas into greater balance would benefit the team. With implementation, maintain fluid communication so everyone is in the conversation and ready to perform actions that ensure high quality results. Bring to bear the Judging attitude to provide better organization and a sharper focus on completing the work.

3. Constructive Negotiation Approach with **Positive Group Affiliation:** The group should take advantage of its enthusiasm for Positive Group Affiliation (creating team spirit) and transfer some of that energy to Constructive Negotiation

Approach. The two are interconnected. When a team successfully pursues win-win agreements, it lifts morale, increasing team spirit. Recognizing this connection, the team can pay attention to both elements, enhancing team cohesion and elevating task productivity. For CNA, the Perceiving attitude will help to review a wide range of possibilities, while Intuition will assist in locating the middle ground among competing interests to find agreements.

4. Feeling Orientation: This is a repressed area. Members don't pay much attention to others' emotional reactions. Doing so, however, could pay dividends, enabling the team to deal more constructively with negative emotions and to harness positive emotions for greater benefit. Cultivating the Feeling function will be valuable for recognizing the various emotions. Also, apply the Extraversion attitude to make emotions discussable. When the team hits a wall with no energy to get the work done, have a discussion about how people are feeling and find a remedy.

5. Initiative: The team may be relying on just a few people to carry the leadership load. It should create more opportunities for members to develop leadership skills. Divvy up assignments so more members can take leadership actions based on their best skills. This will provide the team with greater flexibility when taking on projects because more people will be capable of executive actions to help the team.

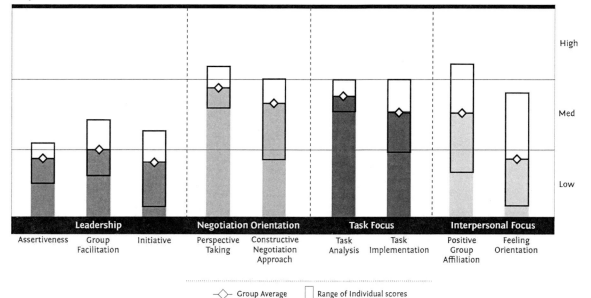

| | Leadership | | | Negotiation Orientation | | Task Focus | | Interpersonal Focus | |
| Assertiveness | Group Facilitation | Initiative | Perspective Taking | Constructive Negotiation Approach | Task Analysis | Task Implementation | Positive Group Affiliation | Feeling Orientation |

◇ Group Average   ☐ Range of Individual scores

1. **Assertiveness** with **Perspective Taking:** With so little Assertiveness energy, the group can have a problem generating meaningful discussion, but the team has the tools to break this pattern. A cornerstone of Assertiveness is sharing ideas and explaining your reasoning. The Thinking preference is concerned with expressing ideas and the Sensing function with providing the details to support your position. Members need to add some Extraversion to vocalize their ideas. Team members listen well, paying attention to teammates' concerns, but they need to step up and promote more active dialogue.

2. **Positive Group Affiliation:** Certain members seem to keep a distance from their teammates, simply focusing on the task and not generating any interpersonal rapport. Such social silence can be the enemy of high productivity. When members are better acquainted, they can collaborate more smoothly on a project. The team should take time to build up its social relations by utilizing two of its opposite preferences, Extraversion and Feeling, to establish more of a team spirit.

3. **Task Analysis** with **Task Implementation:** While all members get engaged in Task Analysis, the energy falls off for some people during the implementation phase. The group can improve its output by refining implementation. It should nurture consistent communication as the work proceeds. With Sensing, pay attention to the practical

details for completing the job; with Thinking, make necessary strategic adjustments. Use Extraversion to discuss these topics and Judging to coordinate the venture. This strategy would likely raise the team's productivity.

4. **Group Facilitation:** All members could benefit from facilitating some aspect of the group's work. In the Negotiation, Task, and Interpersonal areas, there are members with strong scores. Have these individuals facilitate in the appropriate area. Sharing leadership across these domains will benefit the entire team while helping individuals increase their leadership skills. Utilize Extraversion to become more active, and other preferences, as necessary, for specific job responsibilities.

5. **Initiative:** It appears that only one or two people are willing to assume a significant leadership role for the team—the rest are quietly sitting in a back seat. There is a real learning opportunity here. Address this situation directly and support each other in developing leadership skills. Each person can take a turn in leading a project. If there are problems, make them discussable and help one another solve them. Everyone will gain insights and experience. Employ the Thinking function to investigate how to be an effective leader and the Sensing function to maintain a practical focus. Draw on Intuition to experiment with creative approaches.

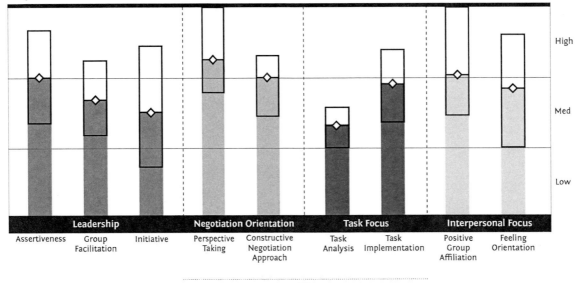

	Leadership			Negotiation Orientation		Task Focus		Interpersonal Focus	
Assertiveness	Group Facilitation	Initiative	Perspective Taking	Constructive Negotiation Approach	Task Analysis	Task Implementation	Positive Group Affiliation	Feeling Orientation

◇ Group Average ☐ Range of Individual scores

1. **Perspective Taking:** The team spends significant time investigating members' interests and concerns, which provides critical data for conducting negotiations and for sustaining a positive group atmosphere. But PT could also be applied to Task Analysis. Members could explore more fully one another's ideas related to task strategies, which would strengthen that process. Use Introversion to listen closely to teammates' ideas, and the Thinking function to design a sound plan.

2. **Task Implementation:** Members should draw on their social rapport to attack task execution. With consistent communication and interpersonal support, they can generate better task outcomes. The Sensing function will help people pay attention to the practical details and the Judging attitude with organizing the work in efficient ways. But they need to make sure they are patient with the Task Analysis phase of the project. If they develop a solid plan first, it will help to ensure the best results.

3. **Positive Group Affiliation** with **Feeling Orientation:** While the team displays solid attention to feelings, there is a significant disparity in this regard among the members. Some members are tuned out. People can take advantage of the Sensing preference to watch closely other members' facial expressions and body language. Get a read on physical clues that indicate emotional reactions, which can be negative (anger,

irritation) or positive (enthusiasm, excitement). Make this information discussable using the Extraversion preference and manage emotions in constructive ways. This will support a robust team spirit, which the team prizes.

4. **Group Facilitation:** Try a shared leadership approach: have two members manage the Task Focus effort—one with Task Analysis, the other with Task Implementation. Assign roles to members who have strong scores in the respective areas. Shoot for a higher level of analysis and more refined task execution. The leaders can provide each other with feedback, and other members can provide some, too. Use Intuition and Perceiving to find creative ways to improve the task endeavor, along with Judging to organize it effectively.

5. **Initiative:** The group may rely on just a few members to take leadership actions. But others could step up, too. There are untapped resources here. Identify members' skill sets and give them the chance to lead the group at appropriate times, building up their leadership muscles. This will give the team more leadership flexibility, which can be a real asset. Members can apply Thinking to find ways to put people in leadership roles and Judging to organize this effort for maximum productivity.

Graph Twelve: ISFP

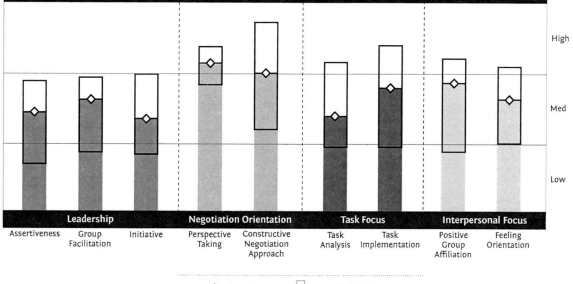

Leadership			**Negotiation Orientation**		**Task Focus**		**Interpersonal Focus**		
Assertiveness	Group Facilitation	Initiative	Perspective Taking	Constructive Negotiation Approach	Task Analysis	Task Implementation	Positive Group Affiliation	Feeling Orientation	

High
Med
Low

—◇— Group Average   ☐ Range of Individual scores

1. **Feeling Orientation:** Many members are aware of feeling issues during discussions. The team, as a whole, should then make these issues discussable. They can do this by adding Extraversion, so people talk about their observations. They can apply a considerable asset, the Feeling function, in a more conscious, collaborative way to manage the group's emotional life.

2. **Assertiveness** with **Perspective Taking:** The team should structure meetings so each person can share his or her concerns about important task issues. People can ask follow-up questions to obtain a deeper understanding of teammates' perspectives. The goal is to hear everyone's thoughts and to help people become more comfortable articulating their views. Exercise Extraversion to speak up more and the Perceiving attitude to consider a wide variety of opinions during a discussion.

3. **Task Analysis:** The group could strengthen its analysis by integrating the Thinking function more directly with its preferred Sensing and Perceiving. With Sensing, there is a practical attention to detail, and with Perceiving, the flexibility to review a range of options for task problems. By integrating Thinking into this pattern, it would help members assess probable consequences in pursuing certain choices and assist the team in logically structuring various strategies. There is at least one member with substantial skills in this area. That individual can be an important resource for the team, modeling techniques for systematic, logical evaluation of task issues. Others can adopt these methods and practice them, expanding their skill sets.

4. **Constructive Negotiation Approach** with **Positive Group Affiliation:** The team has a very positive interest in PGA, but there is a wide diversity of scores. Conducting some team-building activities so members become better acquainted could capitalize on this interest and further unify the team. Building higher morale would boost member motivation to contribute to group success, including the construction of win-win agreements. Consciously deploying Intuition energy to find the middle ground will assist the team with win-win negotiations, as people examine possible connections between their various interests.

5. **Initiative:** More members can take leadership actions for the team. Identify people's skill sets and then rotate leadership opportunities where their expertise would be most relevant. This will provide fresh energy for the team and will also arouse greater commitment to the work. People need to tap into Extraversion to rise up, Thinking to analyze the tasks and match people's skills, and Judging to stay organized when executing the strategies.

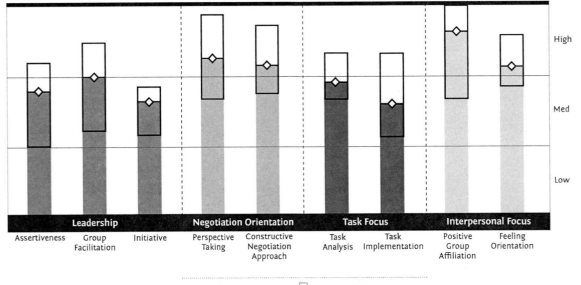

| Leadership | | | Negotiation Orientation | | Task Focus | | Interpersonal Focus | |
| Assertiveness | Group Facilitation | Initiative | Perspective Taking | Constructive Negotiation Approach | Task Analysis | Task Implementation | Positive Group Affiliation | Feeling Orientation |

◇ Group Average   ☐ Range of Individual scores

1. **Task Analysis** with **Task Implementation:** With TA, have members with higher scores lead the group, modeling appropriate analytical skills: the systematic evaluation of problems, resources, and opportunities related to addressing the task. Others can imitate these techniques to increase their skills. With TI, be sure to get everyone involved in the execution of the plan. There are a number of people who appear less engaged in this phase. Deploy the Thinking function to evaluate the task and the Judging attitude to better coordinate the implementation.

2. **Group Facilitation:** Take the measure of people's skills in the negotiation, task, and interpersonal spheres. Give people opportunities to lead the group in areas where they demonstrate high aptitude. Take advantage of their expertise and promote their leadership development. Draw on the Sensing and Thinking functions to assess the skill match-ups in a practical way, and the Judging attitude to organize opportunities for shared leadership.

3. **Assertiveness** with **Perspective Taking:** The team may be dominated by people with higher scores in Assertiveness. These members need to invite others to speak. Apply skills from Perspective Taking to investigate everyone's position and ensure all voices are heard. Members should balance the use of Extraversion (speaking) and Introversion (listening) to create a richer, more inclusive team discussion.

4. **Feeling Orientation:** The team has an important resource here. Employ it to best advantage. The team can establish a routine of checking in with members about how they are feeling about various issues, opening up a discussion about emotional reactions. By making people regularly aware of the feelings in the group, the team can direct this energy in the most productive ways and maintain high motivation. The team can consciously refine its use of established preferences for Extraversion and Feeling.

5. **Constructive Negotiation Approach:** Encourage all members to be proactive in suggesting options for win-win strategies. Members should be open to tossing out any ideas, playing and tinkering with them, making it a playful, creative enterprise. Participants can give free reign to the Intuition and Perceiving preferences and have fun in the process. People will look forward to coming to meetings and working with the team.

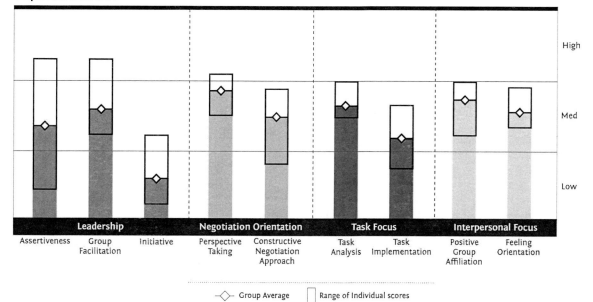

High

Med

Low

| Leadership | Negotiation Orientation | Task Focus | Interpersonal Focus |

| Assertiveness | Group Facilitation | Initiative | Perspective Taking | Constructive Negotiation Approach | Task Analysis | Task Implementation | Positive Group Affiliation | Feeling Orientation |

◇ Group Average   ☐ Range of Individual scores

1. **Constructive Negotiation Approach:** Get everyone involved in brokering win-win agreements that elevate group morale and promote a strong team effort. Members should spell out in detail their ideas and interests, applying the Sensing preference, and then employ the Intuitive preference to find connections between these ideas to strike mutually satisfying agreements. Utilize the data obtained from Perspective Taking to create win-win accords.

2. **Task Analysis** with **Task Implementation:** Both elements could use adjustments to make the group a more productive unit. Let members with the most skills in TA lead the discussion. They can formulate an analysis and then ask others for input, fine-tuning the strategy as everyone gets into the conversation. It's necessary for members to share their supporting evidence about why they think a strategy should be amended, making a logical argument that can persuade others. The Sensing and Thinking functions will support these actions. The team can identify initial steps with the strategy and begin the process of putting the ideas into action. As appropriate, the team can refine the strategy during implementation, using Intuition to make creative modifications.

3. **Assertiveness:** Make sure everyone gets into the conversation. At the start of a meeting, with the first topic, go around the table, inviting each person to share one or two points. People should include the reasons for their positions. Then have other members ask probe questions to get an even clearer picture. This can also be done with subsequent topics, helping everyone participate and establishing a bal-

ance between Assertiveness and Perspective Taking. Participants need to enlist the Extraversion attitude to speak up, Sensing to provide relevant details, and Thinking to share the reasoning.

4. **Positive Group Affiliation** with **Feeling Orientation:** The team should do more to nurture its interest in Interpersonal Focus. For PGA, members could introduce some team-building activities so they become better acquainted and develop more rapport. For FO, the team can pay more attention to emotional issues in the here and now, making these issues discussable. This will allow the team to manage the emotional climate more effectively. Introverted Feeling types perform best when there is a positive social atmosphere. Noting this fact, participants should become proactive in creating this environment, cultivating an Extraversion attitude along with the Feeling preference to reach out to one another and expand team spirit.

5. **Initiative:** The group has a hard time finding members who will take a top leadership role. This presents an opportunity for every member to ascend to that point position and help guide the team. Identify people's interests and encourage them to step up for an appropriate project. Members should support one another in these efforts. Discuss potent leadership tactics and assist teammates in developing and refining these techniques. Make it a group effort, a learning team. Draw on the Thinking function to identify pertinent leadership tactics, the Judging attitude to integrate new organizational skills, and the Extraversion attitude to make it happen.

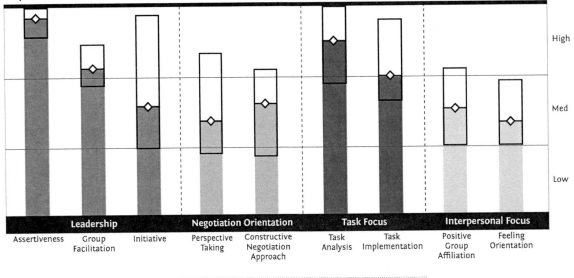

Graph Fifteen: ENTP

	Leadership			Negotiation Orientation		Task Focus		Interpersonal Focus	
Assertiveness	Group Facilitation	Initiative	Perspective Taking	Constructive Negotiation Approach	Task Analysis	Task Implementation	Positive Group Affiliation	Feeling Orientation

High / Med / Low

◇ Group Average   ☐ Range of Individual scores

1. **Assertiveness** with **Perspective Taking:** The group has an abundance of assertive energy, but the aim is to manage it well, to keep everyone in the discussion and not let it become a battle for air time. Members need to gain greater understanding of one another's interests, values, and concerns, which, in turn, can lead to a deeper level of collaboration. They need to ask questions and establish a real dialogue. Participants should exercise the curiosity ingrained in the Perceiving attitude to investigate others' positions, and Introversion to listen and observe more closely, enabling people to pick their opportunities to participate in beneficial ways.

2. **Task Implementation:** The team has great affinity for Task Analysis, but it could improve performance by elevating Task Implementation. It should pay more attention to this phase of the work. In particular, it can promote a communication process in which members regularly share ideas about how the work is progressing. Members should investigate ways to help one another with the various subtasks. Bring Sensing and Judging into the mix to pay closer attention to practical details and to better organize the effort.

3. **Constructive Negotiation Approach:** Members can create greater team cohesion by striving for win-win agreements. Searching for accords that

provide some benefit for all members will make everyone feel respected and included, motivating them to work harder. The group can more consciously employ Intuitive energy, which identifies the connections between members' views and establishes the common ground for agreements.

4. **Positive Group Affiliation:** While members may feel it is unnecessary to spend time building interpersonal relations, this, in fact, supports higher task performance. It is worthwhile to take some time to let members share stories about a recent success or a personal interest, enabling them to become better acquainted and thereby greasing the wheels for later task collaboration. Explore the Feeling function to build rapport and team spirit, and utilize existing Extraversion energy to enrich the social climate.

5. **Initiative:** The group would do well to distribute more leadership opportunities among the membership. It may be leaning on one or two people to guide the group, but there are latent leadership abilities in other members. Identify participants' special knowledge and expertise and give them the chance to lead the team in those areas, which will infuse new energy and support leadership development.

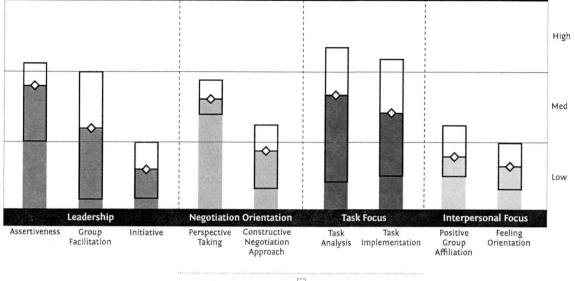

Leadership			Negotiation Orientation		Task Focus		Interpersonal Focus	
Assertiveness	Group Facilitation	Initiative	Perspective Taking	Constructive Negotiation Approach	Task Analysis	Task Implementation	Positive Group Affiliation	Feeling Orientation

◇ Group Average   ▢ Range of Individual scores

1. **Assertiveness** with **Perspective Taking**: Some members are definitely assertive, while some are quiet. Nevertheless, everyone needs to participate so the team can take full advantage of their knowledge. With PT, the team is clustered right in the middle of the medium area. There's a potential for the group to make this a more substantial asset. All members should ask questions, investigating one another's ideas and interests. This produces the data for creating effective task strategies and team agreements. The Extraversion attitude is necessary for people to speak up. Members can utilize Perceiving to stir their curiosity about other participants' positions and then make appropriate inquiries.

2. **Task Analysis** with **Task Implementation**: The team tends to prefer analyzing the task. With the Intuition and Thinking preferences, a lot of creative ideas can be bounced around. Does the team waste too much time in this activity? When the team achieves a solid strategy, it should move ahead with implementation. Make sure all members are involved in TA and TI activities. Draw on the Sensing function to maintain a practical focus and the Judging attitude to move the work towards completion.

3. **Constructive Negotiation Approach**: While the team gathers a reasonable amount of data through Perspective Taking, it doesn't use that information to structure win-win agreements.

Team cohesion could be enhanced by constructing accords in which everyone derives benefit, lifting morale. Employ Introversion to listen to each other, Sensing to identify critical details about what participants want, and then Intuition to find connections between the differing views. This will help the team identify opportunities for mutual gain. Finding win-win consensus will create greater member commitment to the work.

4. **Positive Group Affiliation** withs **Feeling Orientation**: The team should structure short activities that pair up members who aren't well acquainted. Invite them to talk about interests, hobbies, and travel experiences. Later, as they operate in the group, it will become easier for them to communicate and collaborate. In group discussions, pay attention to emotional reactions—what ideas excite members and what turns them off. In general, help participants get to know each other better. This will enhance their ability to collaborate. The Feeling function would assist members in creating a more positive team atmosphere.

5. **Initiative**: It appears that no one wishes to step up and lead the group. In fact, quite a few people seem to be shrinking from the prospect, given the cluster of scores at the bottom of the low column. There is a tremendous growth opportunity for all participants. Based on people's talents in the various subscale domains, distribute leadership opportunities, even small ones at first. Design

opportunities for shared leadership, partnering people in relevant ways to get the job done. Make it a leadership puzzle to be solved, putting the right members together at the right times. Make the undertaking a fun process, not an ordeal. Share feedback and help one another develop leadership skills. Use the Intuition (creativity), Thinking (analytical), and Perceiving (flexibility) preferences in a conscious way to advance this enterprise.

The above examples demonstrate how a consultant can weave KGI and MBTI concepts into multidimensional strategies that will spur high team productivity. The model has the ability to strengthen any team, by bringing psychological typology and group dynamics' elements into a fresh, creative application.

In the next chapter, to further expand a professional's repertoire, a series of activities are introduced which can be employed in workshops and training events to deepen participants' understanding of the model. ✖

CHAPTER 27

Training Activities

To support instructional practice with the Klein Group Instrument assessment, this chapter presents a series of training activities that will expand participants' comprehension of the material and help them to refine their strategies for skill development. These activities can be adapted to a variety of teaching and learning contexts. It should be noted that small-group discussions stretch members' thinking about ways to apply the information, encouraging participants to consider it from multiple angles based on different members' perspectives. Such dialogue promotes flexible thinking for shaping smart strategies in the pursuit of new leadership skills.

In a training context, there are fundamentally two types of situations: first, members do not generally work together and do not know each other very well; second, participants are part of a particular team that is seeking to improve its collaboration. Applications for both circumstances will be presented. In addition, there are exercises where the Myers-Briggs Type Indicator information is integrated into the training design.

Exercise 1: Role Model Analysis

GOAL: Participants reflect on leaders with whom they have worked who demonstrated strong skills in various KGI subscale domains. What patterns did they notice that might guide their own skill development?

SIZE: Two or three members per small group.

OVERALL TIME: 30–50 minutes.

DESIGN:

1. Invite the members to think about an experience with a leader who was strong in the Initiative subscale of the KGI system, one who brought energy to the team and really got things done.

2. What other skills, based on the KGI subscales (e.g. Positive Group Affiliation), did that leader demonstrate? How would you profile that leader's style, utilizing the KGI model?

3. What insights did people gain from the actions of this role model that might inform how they will conduct their own KGI skill building? What combinations of skills stand out as particularly beneficial?

4. Put people in pairs, or in groups of three, and let them share their thoughts about the above questions. Allow 15–20 minutes for the discussion.

5. In the large group, invite individuals to share their reflections. If the group isn't too large, have everyone share a few thoughts. If the group is sizeable, ask for a series of volunteers. Allow 20 minutes.

6. Analyze with the group how a leader may demonstrate great Initiative but also needs an array of KGI skills to do the job well.

Exercise 2: What Role Would I Play?

GOAL: Participants reflect on what role they might play in different small-group situations where their teammates have a variety of skills.

SIZE: Four or five members per small group.
TIME: 50–60 minutes.
DESIGN:

1. Examine group members' KGI results to assess their strengths and challenges in small-group settings. Place participants in groups of four or five members, in which there are a range of different KGI scores.

2. Ask members to share their KGI individual results.

3. Given the range of KGI skill sets on the team, how might the group organize its task efforts to best effect, maximizing the talents at hand?

A. What roles can different people play, based on their strengths?

B. Within the context of the group, how would members be able to learn new skills? How might they mentor each other to advance their skill development?

C. How can the members share leadership roles? Allow 15–20 minutes for the discussion.

4. Break up the original teams and assign people to a new team with different member scores. Repeat the exercise, analyzing how to build a productive team and how different roles would be distributed to various members. Allow 15–20 minutes for discussion.

5. In the large group, have the participants share insights about how they would adopt different roles in small groups, depending on the configuration of member scores. What strategies might they use to promote learning and growth?

6. In the discussion, analyze how, in work settings, we often are assigned to a range of different groups. In what kinds of small groups do people find themselves at work? What new strategies might people apply based on this exercise? Allow approximately 20–25 minutes for discussion.

Exercise 3: Designing Group Procedures to Create Team Synergy

GOAL: Participants devise a set of ground rules that would promote synergy on a team, guidelines that would move it towards maximum performance. Blending ideas from the nine KGI subscales, they fashion a list that attends to task, negotiation, and interpersonal issues in an optimal way. What things must a group emphasize to really succeed?

SIZE: Three, four, or five members per small group.
TIME: 60 minutes.
DESIGN:

1. Provide an overview of the activity: people will be assigned to teams in which they identify guidelines that the team will follow to incite high performance. Draw on ideas from the KGI subscales in the Task Focus, Interpersonal Focus, and Negotiation Orientation domains to construct the rules. What combination of ideas, in their view, would fuel optimal performance? Groups should identify 5 rules and will have 20–30 minutes for the activity. Afterwards, each team will present its list to the entire group, explaining its reasoning.

2. Divide the gathering into small groups of three, four, or five members each. Keep each group approximately the same size. Provide each team with news print and a magic marker.

3. At 15 minutes into the activity, check in with the groups about their progress. Allow another 10–15 minutes to complete the chart.

4. Have a representative from each small group present its list of rules, explaining why the team selected the points it did. What were their key priorities in establishing these rules? Allow 6–8 minutes per group.

5. After each group representative shares ideas, the facilitator will encourage the large group to compare and contrast different team results. What different philosophies are indicated? What ideas seem consistent among the groups? What appear to be the most essential strategies to focus on to produce synergy in a team?

6. As time allows, the facilitator can ask the participants how their own results on the KGI assessment influenced their strategies. Did they push for skill areas in which they were strong, or did they advocate, and value, areas in which they were moderate or even low? How do personal results influence what one believes works best for the team as a whole?

Exercise 4: Building KGI Skills with MBTI Opposite Preferences

GOAL: Participants will identify two new KGI skills to work on and articulate strategies about how to employ their MBTI opposite preferences to support this skill building. They will partner with a team member who has the opposite MBTI preferences, who will serve as mentor for this process.

SIZE: Two members per small group.

TIME: 50–60 minutes.

DESIGN:

1. Drawing on their KGI and MBTI personal results, ask members to select two specific growth statements from their KGI profile that would involve the use of their MBTI opposite preferences. Review the KGI–MBTI diamond, illustrating how the scales of the two assessments overlap, to inform their selections.

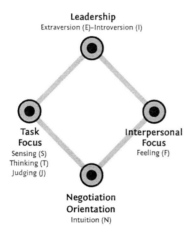

Leadership
Extraversion (E)-Introversion (I)

Task Focus
Sensing (S)
Thinking (T)
Judging (J)

Interpersonal Focus
Feeling (F)

Negotiation Orientation
Intuition (N)

2. Pair up the participants, setting up partners with opposite MBTI preferences, e.g., a person with ESTJ preferences works with an INFP. If it's not possible to find a four-letter opposite for all members, look for three opposite preferences, or two opposite preferences in the matchup. (The ideal is to have a partner with the opposite preferences for the two specific skills that are selected.)

3. For 10–15 minutes, ask one participant to share his/her KGI learning goals and the MBTI opposite preferences that would be involved in this skill building. Then have the partner provide insights about how the first person might proceed in cultivating skills with the opposite preferences. Since the partner, as a mentor, has preferences in these areas, she/he would identify motivations and techniques that would be beneficial. Share examples of positive results that have been obtained by using these preferences.

4. Since the use of a less-developed opposite preferences is challenging, the pair should outline a step-by-step approach for trying out the new techniques.

5. Have the pair reverse roles and then repeat the exercise for 10–15 minutes.

6. In a large group discussion have participants share their strategies. Together, participants can expand the analyses and articulate further suggestions. The discussion will run approximately 15–25 minutes.

Exercise 5: Creating Focused Goals for KGI Skill Building

GOAL: Participants construct concise goal statements for their KGI skill-building efforts. For two new skills, they will write goal statements that will clearly identify actions in specific groups that will demonstrate that the person is practicing and acquiring skills.

SIZE: Three or four members per small group.

TIME: 30–50 minutes.

DESIGN:

1. Provide an overview of the activity: people will write succinct goal statements for two new group behaviors chosen from their KGI results. For each, they will use a sentence or two. They will designate the group context in which they will work on the skill, how many times they will attempt the skill (example: Assertiveness—I will speak up two times in the weekly meeting) and what the content or quality of the participation will look like. With this goal statement as a measure, it should be easy to determine later if the person has practiced and acquired the skill or not.

2. Ask the participants to write their statements, giving 5–10 minutes for the exercise.

3. Put people into small groups of three or four members and have them share their results. Teammates should give feedback about the clarity and directness of the statements. Can other members clearly see the behavioral goals that are espoused? If not, they should help refine the statements. Provide 10–20 minutes.

4. In the large group, have members share their favorite goal from the exercise. Have them explain what helped them distill their vision in this activity. Raise the point that clear objectives set the stage for effective skill acquisition. Utilize 15 to 20 minutes for discussion, depending on size of the group.

Exercise 6: What I Can Contribute / Where I Want Mentoring

GOAL: Participants in an established team identify what they can best contribute to the team and, based on their KGI results, where they would like to be mentored for new skills.

SIZE: Complete team, up to 10 or 12 members.
TIME: 30–60 minutes.
DESIGN:

1. As a warm-up activity, have group members share a brief news item (one minute each) about something that went well during the past week. Create a positive atmosphere for communication.

2. Going around the horn again, each member will share the following information, grounded in their individual KGI results:

A. Here are specific skills I can contribute to the group.

B. Here are one or two skills that I wish to work on, and I would like mentoring suggestions on how to proceed most effectively.

3. Members can then make decisions on how to best employ various members' skills in the group, how to delegate responsibilities, and how to share leadership.

4. Members also discuss how they will help one another acquire new skills, by mentoring each other, sharing strategies, insights, and feedback. They will identify ways to create a learning team, where members support one another in the growth process.

5. This activity lends itself to a follow-up session where members evaluate how well they executed their strategies, and what adjustments would further advance the work.

Exercise 7: Establishing Strategic Priorities

GOAL: Participants in an established team identify their future strategic priorities and task objectives. How can the group develop into a high functioning team to achieve these priorities?

SIZE: Complete team, up to 10 or 12 members.
TIME: 60–90 minutes.
DESIGN:

1. Explain to the group that it will brainstorm its top strategic goals for the next year. What specific tasks will be involved to achieve these goals?

2. As the second part of the activity, members will draw on ideas from the KGI® Group Profile to identify ways they can enhance their group processes to achieve these goals. They select specific subscales to work on and, from those areas of the profile, choose specific group process suggestions to employ.

3. When the team concludes part one and two, it will consider how it performed during this activity. In what ways did members' participation reflect their KGI scores? What patterns emerged? What did they observe about team strengths and weaknesses?

4. Members can also examine their KGI® Individual Profiles to select some additional growth statements that would help them further enhance their performance. In what areas could they build new skills that would help their team achieve its goals?

Exercise 8: Reflecting on Connections between MBTI Preferences and Preferred Group Roles

GOAL: Participants identify connections between their MBTI preferences and their most preferred group roles, related to KGI subscale results.

SIZE: Two or three members per small group.
TIME: 30–50 minutes.
DESIGN:

1. After participants review their MBTI results, pass out the one-page handout with brief descriptors for each of the MBTI preferences (*Words to Help Understanding of Type Concepts* available from CAPT.org). Ask them to put a plus sign (+) next to

characteristics that fit, and double plus (++) next to ones they consider the most important.

2. Have them look over their KGI Individual Composite Subscale Graph, which illustrates their preferred ways of operating in small groups. What connections do they see? How do their MBTI preferences express themselves in group contexts?

3. Pair up members, or groups of three. Ask them to share information about the following questions:

A. What are my favorite roles on a team?

B. What are some other group roles I feel competent to play?

C. What tasks am I most enthusiastic about?

D. When, and in what ways, do I want to step up and lead the group?

E. How do my psychological energies, as identified by my MBTI preferences, express themselves in these group actions?

F. How can I employ my strengths in new ways to further enhance my performance?

4. As a large group, have members share the results from this discussion and provide one another with additional insights about these issues, i.e., the effective use of strength areas in small-group contexts. ✂

CHAPTER 28

Positive Social Psychology

Going forward, the Klein Group Instrument model can become the cornerstone for a new movement, namely, Positive Social Psychology. The intent is to promote the values of mutual respect, interpersonal understanding, social awareness, inclusiveness, and effective cooperation. When individuals and groups are motivated by these values, there is the greatest potential for high performance, the type of performance that achieves real excellence. There is also an opportunity to promote personal growth and

social development that will have long-lasting effects. In training people to be vigorous small-group leaders and team members, these values lay the foundation for the most creative and productive human interactions.

Every person is born with an innate capacity for social development, an ability to build skills that enable the individual to connect with other people in satisfying, enriching, and mutually enhancing ways. But this development needs to be cultivated in a thoughtful manner because it doesn't happen automatically; it requires training. The goal is to bring this potential alive, to operationalize it, providing people with the skills to make them socially successful. This doesn't mean that every individual needs to metamorphose into a highly animated Extravert, energetically working a crowd. The style of performance will vary according to the individual, customized to that person's developmental needs, but will always aim

at the constructive engagement of other people for fruitful collaboration.

The intent of the KGI model is to provide a clear pathway to the skill acquisition that generates growth and success for individuals and teams. The KGI diamond design offers a simple but potent structure to guide the process, enabling individuals to assess group situations more objectively, focusing on essential functions in group life while attending to the critical components that promote synergy in teams—social awareness and inclusiveness. Synergy occurs when member performance vaults to its highest level, yielding the sharpest thinking, the finest problem solving, and superior productivity. It is the true target for intelligent small-group effort. Ideally, the actions of leaders and members should direct a team towards the creation of synergy. What helps to unleash this energy are the humane values of being socially aware of others, respecting their dignity and talents, and establishing inclusiveness so that all can contribute to the enterprise. The KGI model raises consciousness about these issues and trains people to address them, introducing a logical system for the practice. As a result, the model instills optimism in group members, a confidence that they have the right tools to overcome their challenges and achieve superb outcomes.

Unfortunately, many children, adolescents, and young adults experience obstacles to their social development. In the rooms of their family homes, in the streets of their neighborhoods, and in the classrooms and playing fields of their schools, they experience callous treatment: coldness, disrespect, and rejection. To protect themselves, they erect barriers with negative attitudes, becoming mistrustful of others and pessimistic about the possibility of constructive collaboration. While participating in small groups, they can come to expect less of themselves, side-stepping responsibilities, and making excuses for lackluster performance. The treatment they receive puts a thorn in the side of their social development, something that can affect them for the rest of their lives, undermining the realization of their true potential. One of the goals of Positive Social Psychology is to help these people rebel against the confines of their past experiences and pivot in a more worthwhile direction, obtaining a belief in their own strength, adaptability, and power to change in productive ways. Instead of seeing group life as enemy territory, they can envision an opportunity to contribute and build new social skills. With this adjustment in approach, they can make useful contributions, earn others' respect, and strengthen their self-esteem, which can be an antidote to a disabling past.

Of course, there are others who are on a more solid footing with their development. They are buoyant and hopeful, more open and flexible in dealing with others. Still, small-group life can be confusing and difficult to manage at times. And how does one fully nurture one's leadership and social potential? The model puts them on a rewarding track, emphasizing the strategies that allow them to mature into enlightened, agile players, who are ready to guide diverse groups in constructive directions.

Central to this approach is the development of deep listening skills, listening with the ability to truly empathize with others in order to understand their motivations, values, and fears. With such perspective taking, one is able to hear with another's ears, see with another's eyes, and gain the ability to propose solutions that will have real validity for other group members. The use of psychological typology aids this process, enabling individuals to grasp how others take in information and make decisions in ways that are similar or different from their own. By grasping the system of type preferences, people can make adjustments that enhance their perspective taking and interpersonal communication, promoting a more fluid, meaningful dialogue in groups, which is at the heart of spirited collaboration.

With the information gained from deep listening, people can also learn to construct win-win solutions that provide benefit for every member of a team. Through this process, everyone gains something, which motivates people to be accountable and contribute their fair share to a project. Importantly, it tells members that everyone is valued and respected; everyone is a worthwhile partner in the enterprise. As this message is conveyed, it boosts morale, enlivens team spirit, and positions the group for high performance. It can also help to identify the lines of strength among members, so that responsibilities are delegated effectively, putting people in position to do their best work. With the win-win approach, people can build bonds that help them to strive together in the pursuit of excellence.

Another aspect of this philosophy is the promotion of shared leadership, in which multiple people take leadership roles in projects according to their skill sets and developmental goals. Again, this recognizes the different talents around a table and puts them into practical use. When people share leadership, they tend to become more engaged with the work, employing a strategy that can also incite creativity. From a Positive Social Psychology perspective, it also encourages people to collaborate in building and refining their leadership skills as they work together, adding another powerful learning dynamic to their social development.

The intent is to harness the fertile power of individual and team development, moving people in the right directions for constructive growth and potent performance. When people become more comfortable in social environments, they are better equipped to make strong contributions. As they develop greater rapport, mutual respect, and camaraderie, the demands of group life become more personal. It then becomes a matter of not wanting to let down valued peers and friends, which sparks a desire to contribute more to the cause and fosters a greater willingness to sacrifice for the team. Positive motivations therefore significantly increase, prompting more consistent, energetic effort. This provides a perfect context for thoughtful skill development, where people support each other in the refinement of specific leadership and membership techniques to achieve outstanding outcomes.

Positive Social Psychology, grounded on the KGI model, seeks to nurture healthy, mutually supportive relationships. For all individuals, this starts by activating their innate potential to become more fully functioning social beings. The approach instills courage in people to cultivate their own social development in an intelligent and systematic way, promoting the values of interpersonal respect, social awareness, and inclusiveness.

It also inspires the courage to be an active problem solver in group settings, so that one assists a group in becoming a high performing unit. For those who master the approach, team leadership flows very naturally, not simply because of the new skills that have been obtained, but because of a new attitude that is visible to others, influencing them to follow in these productive directions.

These skills enable people to deal with a wide variety of social settings—families, neighborhoods, schools, sport teams, businesses, professions, and religious communities. They prepare people to make a constructive impact in every context, enhancing the social interactions and raising the levels of collaboration. For individuals, this approach can create a new solidity and power in the personality, giving people fresh confidence in their social abilities and a deeper conviction about their capacity to relate to others. This experience can have a transformative, lifelong benefit. By opening up the social dimension of people's lives, Positive Social Psychology can add deeper meaning to life itself. After all, when people enrich the various relationships in their lives, they enhance the quality of their very existence. ✕

The Basic Script for Introducing the Klein Group Instrument® Assessment

The following information presents the core ideas that explain the Klein Group Instrument model. For consultants, counselors, coaches, or teachers, working in one-on-one or in group training situations, this series of ideas will orient their clientele to the design and enable participation in the skill-building process. This script is meant to serve as a handy reference for professionals working in assorted coaching and training contexts.

The Klein Group Instrument for Effective Leadership and Participation in Teams (KGI) assessment is designed for small-group situations in which there is a specific task to perform, such as in sport, educational, business, professional, or religious community settings. It targets four functions that are evident in all small-group life: Leadership, Negotiation Orientation, Task Focus, and Interpersonal Focus. These are essential group operations and by attending to them and guiding them in the proper manner, a group can flourish and produce high-quality results.

The design of the measurement can be expressed visually using a diamond model:

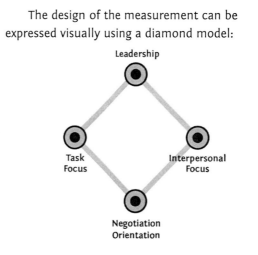

Leadership is essential for any task-oriented group venture. Whether there is a designated leader or not, someone must take the initiative to coordinate the efforts of the group—this is a primary dynamic. It may be one person, but it can also be more than one, who steps up to influence the direction of the activity and engage other members in the effort. Leadership guides the group in two main areas: Task Focus (working towards competent task completion) and Interpersonal Focus (promoting positive member relations). An underlying goal of Interpersonal Focus is to foster team cohesion that inspires the group to achieve its best results.

Negotiation Orientation enables the group to manage both task and interpersonal issues. With respect to the task, it seeks to resolve strategy differences so the team can arrive at a unified plan, with all members committed to the work. With regard to interpersonal relations, it strives to resolve personal conflicts that may emerge, as well as to connect members' interests to the enterprise to increase their motivation. Negotiation always plays a crucial role when discord occurs in the group, relating to either the task effort or interpersonal relations. It pursues agreements that encourage meaningful collaboration and favorable task outcomes.

Concise definitions for the four major scales are:

Leadership, as measured by the KGI tool, is the ability of members to guide the group towards effective collaboration and favorable task outcomes.

Negotiation Orientation measures the ability of members to listen closely to one another and to construct mutually acceptable agreements.

Task Focus measures the ability of members to devise a sound strategy for the task and to successfully carry out the plan.

Interpersonal Focus measures the ability of members to develop a team spirit and to address the feeling issues in the group.

Using the KGI diamond diagram, it is possible to detect some natural energy streams that are very significant in group life.

Effective leadership pays attention to both the task and interpersonal sides of the group enterprise. At the most basic level, the group must concentrate on the task because that's why it has assembled. But doing the job requires a collective effort, and how the members get along affects the levels of their participation and the quality of the final outcome. So, attention must be paid to individuals, because team harmony impacts productivity. As a result, leaders need to be flexible and stay alert to both of these domains.

One of the bedrock theories about small-group dynamics was articulated in the 1950s by Robert Bales (Bales 1950, 1955), a researcher who examined the relationship between task execution and the socioemotional aspect of group life. He found that when a group zeroed in on a task, trying to get it done directly, there were times when disagreements occurred among members due to competing strategies, values, and visions. Consequently, tensions could surface, and members could become angry, aggressive, or withdrawn. At those times, it was important for the group to switch its focus from the task to its social relations in order to reestablish harmony among the members. The goal was to resolve interpersonal problems, removing the emotional disturbances. Only then could the group go back to the task in a unified way, drawing on its full complement of human resources to achieve a quality outcome.

Bales saw that an elemental rhythm existed in groups, as the members' attention shifted back and forth between the poles of group task and group maintenance. Interestingly, the research on these twin aspects of group life indicated they were negatively correlated, so that focusing on one by necessity draws attention away from the other. Since a group can concentrate on only one at a time, there is a back-and-forth motion in group life, as the focus fluctuates between task and interpersonal concerns. This fundamental movement is the source of a core interactive dynamic, common to all small groups and teams. Being aware of this tension and managing it capably is an essential skill for leaders and team members. Attention to this dynamic is at the heart of the KGI diamond model.

Whether a group attends to the task, or examines interpersonal issues, negotiation plays an influential role. Members must strike agreements that provide the basis for their collective efforts. When a team constructs a task strategy, negotiation comes to bear as the group sorts out the options and decides on a joint plan. When the group implements the strategy, negotiation plays a role in the evaluation of appropriate adjustments to sharpen the plan's effectiveness. When conflicts emerge among members, negotiation helps to resolve the issues. When a team decides to take steps to build a more positive group spirit,

negotiation assists in the strategizing. So in a variety of ways, the negotiation process applies to the task and interpersonal functions of group life. Negotiation operates to ensure that voices are heard, that people remain involved, and that the team, to the best of its ability, stays unified. In the KGI model, energy from Negotiation Orientation rises up to address these different concerns.

In addition, an influential study on the factors that produce synergy in teams, i.e., the highest level of group performance, identified social awareness and inclusion as critical elements that ignite synergy (see Chapter 4). This maps out perfectly with the KGI diamond.

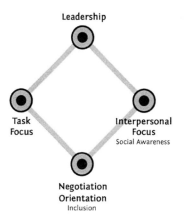

Interpersonal Focus strengthens social awareness by promoting positive member relations and by encouraging emotional sensitivity, which keeps members attuned to one another. Negotiation Orientation champions inclusion by deepening mutual understanding through perspective taking and by increasing member involvement through a win-win approach. Both of these KGI domains operate in support of Task Focus; they inject the extra social fuel that kindles potent job performance. With the KGI system, the efforts of both leaders and group members are directed towards the promotion of synergy in order to generate the strongest team outcomes.

The diamond model identifies central aspects of small-group life and shows how they are interrelated, orienting people to a series of pivotal group dynamics. This is the first step in the method. The next is to help group members become more proficient in operating in each of these domains, and more flexible in moving among them to nurture high-quality individual and team performance.

Toward these ends, the KGI tool defines a number of subscales for each major scale. The subscales designate *specific skill sets* for the four key sectors of group activity, identifying the practical skills people can employ to refine their behavior. As a result, the information that guides individual improvement and team improvement in the KGI system flows through the subscale sections of the KGI® Individual Profile and KGI® Group Profile, respectively.

Here are one-sentence definitions to explain the focus of each subscale.

Leadership Subscales

1. **Assertiveness:** the expression of ideas in the group.

2. **Group Facilitation:** the coordination of the group's efforts with regard to negotiation, task, and interpersonal relations.

3. **Initiative:** the willingness of members to assume primary leadership roles in different aspects of the group's work.

Negotiation Orientation Subscales

1. **Perspective Taking:** the skill of investigating and understanding other people's values, interests, and needs.

2. **Constructive Negotiation Approach:** the promotion of a win-win negotiation method so that all members benefit from an agreement.

Task Focus Subscales

1. **Task Analysis:** the examination of problems, opportunities, and task solutions.

2. **Task Implementation:** the competent execution of a plan with appropriate strategic adjustments along the way.

Interpersonal Focus Subscales

1. **Positive Group Affiliation:** the promotion of mutual respect, acceptance, and rapport among members, with the aim of forging a team spirit.

2. **Feeling Orientation:** attention to the emotional issues in the group.

When a client takes the KGI assessment online at the CAPT.org website, he or she receives a KGI® Individual Profile, along with the *KGI® Individual User's Guide* to orient the person to the material. The individual profile is designed in the following manner:

1. **An introduction that explains the profile's structure.** The first page outlines the document's design, which is divided into four sections according to the major scales of the instrument:

Leadership, Negotiation Orientation, Task Focus, and Interpersonal Focus.

For each segment, the most vital data are delivered in the subscale sections. They identify the following information: group behaviors that are personally enjoyable to perform; behaviors that are difficult or challenging; and new behaviors that will foster growth and social development. It is useful to note that for the second item—behaviors that are difficult or challenging—if an individual already functions in a very competent way in that skill area, there may be no data reported for the category.

An **important qualification** is emphasized in the introduction: the individual must evaluate for him-or-herself the profile feedback and select the most accurate, relevant ideas with which to work. While data are derived from extensive quantitative and qualitative research, each individual must personally validate the information and apply it in an appropriate manner. A counselor or coach, working with a client, will assist in this analysis.

2. **Results for the Leadership section.** The profile then moves along to the Leadership section, with information structured in this manner:

A. **A color graph.** The segment opens with a graph containing columns for the composite Leadership scale (the aggregate of all subscales), the Assertiveness subscale, the Group Facilitation subscale, and the Initiative subscale. The columns indicate high, medium, or low frequency of performance in each area.

The graph promotes a rapid appraisal of the individual's performance, with the opportunity to compare performance across the various subscales. A high score for the major scale or subscales indicates

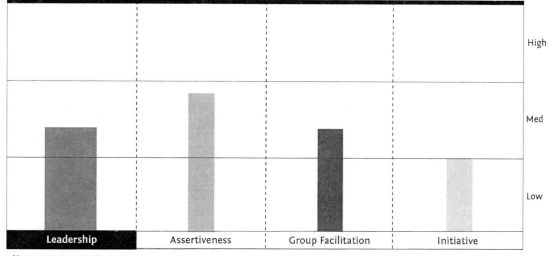

High

Med

Low

| Leadership | Assertiveness | Group Facilitation | Initiative |

*Represents a composite score
for all the subscales of the
Leadership scale

that a person performs the specific behaviors in the scale, or subscale, 75% to 100% of the time; a medium score signifies the person performs the behaviors 50% to 74% of the time; while a low score points to performance from 0% to 49% of the time.

B **Information about the Leadership scale and the respondent's personal results.** The section then introduces a brief explanation about the essentials of group leadership, followed by a statement describing the respondent's orientation in this area. This statement corresponds to the score in the first column in the graph, the composite Leadership score. The statement is calibrated to a low, medium, or high result.

C. **Information about the Assertiveness subscale and the respondent's personal results.** The report progresses to the first of the critical subscale areas, which supply the real meat of the profile. It starts with the KGI definition of Assertiveness, followed by a statement about the respondent's fundamental orientation in this area, which, again, is reflected in the column score for Assertiveness in the graph.

The report then provides detailed, personal information for the subscale, breaking out behavioral data in the following categories:

‣ What You Enjoy

‣ What You Find Difficult or Challenging

‣ Behaviors That May Help You Grow

For each of the categories, points are rendered in a *bulleted fashion*—clear, focused statements. This facilitates a *fast absorption* of the information, enabling the user to quickly transform ideas into action.

D. **Information about the Group Facilitation subscale and Initiative subscale results.** The report then introduces personal feedback for the other Leadership subscales, offering information in the same format as the Assertiveness section.

The report proceeds with information for the Negotiation Orientation, Task Focus, and Interpersonal Focus domains, introducing the information in the same manner as in the Leadership section.

4. **Composite Graphs.** On the final page of the profile are two composite graphs: the first displays the scores for the four major scales; the second depicts all of the subscale scores in a continuous sequence. These are the indispensable tools for evaluating personal performance and establishing a plan for skill development. As will be seen, based on the interpretation of these graphs, a consultant can organize a very powerful plan for a client's social development.

Your KGI® Major Scales

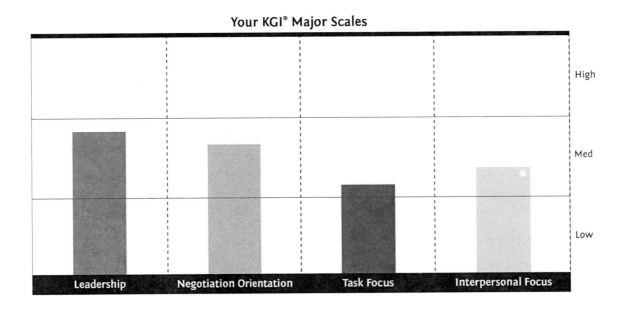

This graph brings together the scores for the major scales, allowing the recipient to evaluate frequency of performance in the large domains. What is useful to examine here are the *highest* score and the *lowest* score.

The highest score pinpoints the individual's primary focus in small-group events. This aspect of group life stimulates the greatest interest (even fascination), and it is the easiest area for the person to become involved in. The lowest score, on the other hand, holds the least interest and may be repressed and avoided, to a small or large degree. It takes greater exertion for the individual to participate in this activity. These two scores establish benchmarks for individual performance: what I tend to like most; what I tend to like least. They depict fundamental currents of energy in the person's social personality.

Your KGI® Subscales

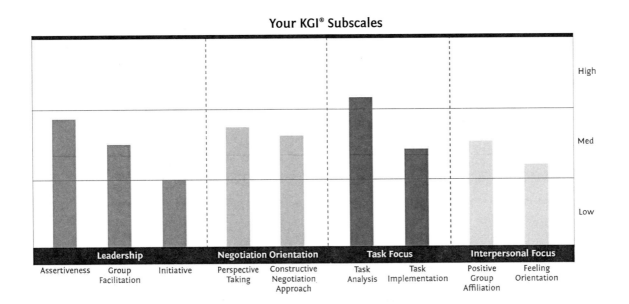

The subscale graph is the most crucial element in the profile. With it, a consultant and client evaluate performance across all skill domains, promoting a broad examination of group behavior. The graph displays areas of strength and areas of softer performance. It helps identify relationships among the skill areas, which will aid in balancing overall performance. In short, the graph serves as *the foundation for constructing a plan for personal development.*

After a close examination of this graph, a client and coach can designate certain subscales for improvement. It is possible, at that point, to identify two subscale priorities and initiate a process of new skill acquisition. For those subscales, one goes directly to the subsections in the KGI® Individual Profile and inspects the suggestions in Behaviors That May Help You Grow. These identify the behaviors to practice for skill development. Client and coach select certain options and the client can then begin to practice in an appropriate small group. This is the simplest, easiest way to use the KGI materials, and it will guide a client directly into skill acquisition.

However, research with the KGI model has shown that people who go on to acquire skills in **five KGI subscale areas** can really have a transformative social experience; they vault to a much higher level of social development, self-confidence, and leadership effectiveness. Therefore, the coach should encourage the client to think in terms of five subscales as providing the richest experience. It should be noted that some clients may be happy to simply work on a couple of subscale areas, ones they deem most important, and conclude the skill-building exercise right there. While it is fine to proceed in that way, development in five skill areas will provide significantly greater benefit. Working on five subscales will also extend the time for practicing new skills, usually for a number of months.

As part of the conversation, it is important to examine the client's **Initiative subscale score** and determine what skill development would enhance this area of performance. That is pivotal for the process of leadership development. (See the item about Initiative in the Inter-Subscale Combinations introduced below.)

The above information will orient people to the basics of the KGI model and the skill building venture. When working with individual clients, this information establishes the proper foundation and may suffice to advance a client into practice. Information in Chapter 11 will guide the personal coaching process.

It is possible, however, to take the graph and skill-building discussion to another level, by introducing the Inter-Subscale Combinations (ISC), which deepen the analysis and allow for the construction of a more comprehensive plan. Even if a client doesn't wish to advance to a five-subscale skill level, the ISC system will enhance this part of the consultation. In situations where a client has a composite graph with strong scores across all domains, the ISC system introduces a way to expand the analysis and identify suitable paths to refine such a solid performance.

According to the client's graph results, select the appropriate subscale pairings to target and discuss. The combinations include:

1. **Assertiveness** with **Perspective Taking**: creating an appropriate balance between speaking and listening skills.

2. **Group Facilitation** with **Task Focus** and **Interpersonal Focus Subscales**: refining facilitation skills across the two primary sectors of group life—task and interpersonal.

3. **Initiative** with **Negotiation Orientation**, **Task Focus**, and **Interpersonal Focus Subscales**: building a well-rounded leadership style by integrating skills across these vital areas.

4. **Constructive Negotiation Approach** with **Positive Group Affiliation**: perfecting skills that will promote synergy in a team, resulting in high-quality group outcomes.

5. **Task Analysis** with **Task Implementation**: achieving a better balance between these complementary skills in the task area.

6. **Positive Group Affiliation** with **Feeling Orientation**: nurturing team spirit through the effective management of emotional issues within the team.

Drawing on ideas from any of these combinations will initiate a more nuanced analysis of the graph data. At the minimum, it will elevate the previous phase of analysis and strengthen a person's understanding of group dynamics. It will add an important perspective to the skill-building enterprise. By integrating the ISC ideas, it will be easier to establish a skill-building plan with five subscales, or even six. In a step-by-step process, a person can practice a couple of skills at a time and steadily develop a variety of new skills. An individual can then climb to a higher level of leadership and membership performance.

KGI® Group Profile

If a professional is guiding a small group in a team-building enterprise, then the next phase of the consultation would be to introduce the KGI® Group Profile. This document is created by anonymously combining the individual results of all group members.

In a number of ways, the format of the KGI® Group Profile imitates that of the KGI® Individual Profile. The heart of the report flows in the same manner, moving systematically through the major scale domains, presenting graphs for each segment and offering suggestions for improvement in each subscale area. The graphs display the range of member scores for each subscale, promoting an informed analysis of group dynamics and group learning needs. The materials permit an examination of diverse issues related to leadership, communication, task execution, feedback processes, and team cohesion, presenting a series of options to address these concerns so the team can choose the most appropriate strategies for its particular needs. While an individual works on personal skills, the group seeks to improve its interactive processes.

The KGI® Group Profile contains the following elements:

1. **Introduction.** The report starts with the KGI diamond model, presenting the conceptual design of the instrument, and introduces the major scales and their subscales. It announces the goal of making the group a learning team, one in which members learn from and with each other to create a high-performing unit.

2. **Communication and Confidentiality.** This section explains that in analyzing group issues and developing team strategies, members will also refer to their individual results. This needs to be done with mutual consent, a respect for persons, and appropriate confidentiality. Through this endeavor, individuals gain personal skills and the team rises to a new level of performance.

3. **Team Results: Composite Group Graphs.** The report moves immediately into the team's collective results, which are displayed on two graphs, in a similar fashion to the KGI® Individual Profile.

A. **Group Composite Major Scale Graph**

The first graph reveals the results for the major scales: Leadership, Negotiation Orientation, Task Focus, and Interpersonal Focus. Like the KGI® Individual Profile, the graph has High, Medium, and Low sections, depicting the various levels of performance. Critically, each scale column contains a rectangular box indicating the range of members' scores in that domain.

The top line of the rectangle identifies the highest score, while the bottom identifies the lowest. Inside the rectangle is a line, with a diamond, indicating the average score for the group.

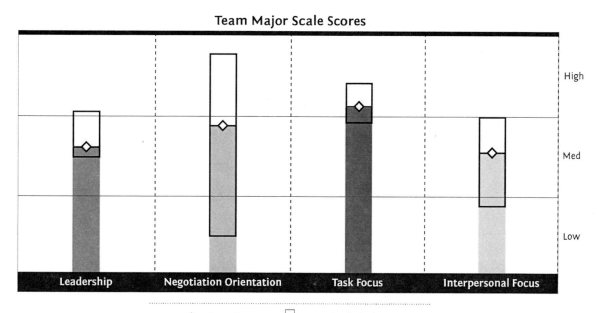

Team Major Scale Scores

High

Med

Low

| Leadership | Negotiation Orientation | Task Focus | Interpersonal Focus |

◇— Group Average ☐ Range of Individual scores

Important: When one analyzes this graph, it is necessary to be aware of a statistical fact that is counter-intuitive. In evaluating team performance on a specific column, pay attention to the diamond line marking the average score. **The greater cluster of member scores will be in the *smaller area* above or below this line in the rectangular box.** An initial assumption might be that there are more member scores in the larger area on either side of the line; in fact, the opposite is true: more members are clustered in the smaller area. **That's necessary to remember when interpreting the graph results.**

This section includes points for interpreting the Composite Major Subscale Graph, with an emphasis on the evaluation of the highest score and lowest score among the scales.

B. **Group Composite Subscale Graph.** The second graph displays all of the subscale scores in a continuous sequence. Each column contains a rectangular box with the range of member scores. This graph is an invaluable resource for team analysis, permitting a group to assess strengths, needs, and ways to balance group performance. *This graph is the centerpiece for determining team strategies.*

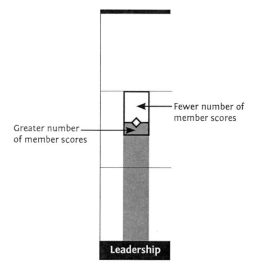

Greater number of member scores

Fewer number of member scores

Leadership

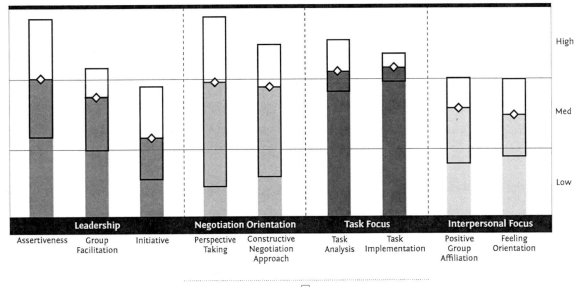

Leadership			**Negotiation Orientation**		**Task Focus**		**Interpersonal Focus**			
Assertiveness	Group Facilitation	Initiative	Perspective Taking	Constructive Negotiation Approach	Task Analysis	Task Implementation	Positive Group Affiliation	Feeling Orientation		

◇ Group Average   ▢ Range of Individual scores

This section includes points about interpreting the graph, including how to analyze it using the Inter-Subscale Combinations system. There is also information about the interpretation of the range of member scores contained in the rectangular boxes.

4. **Action Steps.** The next section outlines the steps for choosing which subscale domains to address, finding suggestions to improve the team's interactive processes in the appropriate subscale sections of the report, implementing those strategies, and pursuing an ongoing developmental process that will make the group a high-performing team.

5. **The Four Major Scale Sections.** The report now introduces specific information for each of the major scales and their subscales. Like the KGI® Individual Profile, the details in each section appear in the exact same format, so the first section to be described—Leadership—serves as a template for the later ones.

The information in the Leadership section proceeds as follows:

A. **A color graph.** The section begins with a graph displaying columns for the overall Leadership scale, the Assertiveness subscale, the Group Facilitation subscale, and the Initiative subscale. The graph displays lines that differentiate high, medium, and low frequency of performance.

As noted previously, each column contains a rectangular black box indicating the range of member scores. The diamond line marks the average team score, while the smaller section of the rectangle above or below this line signifies the larger cluster of member scores.

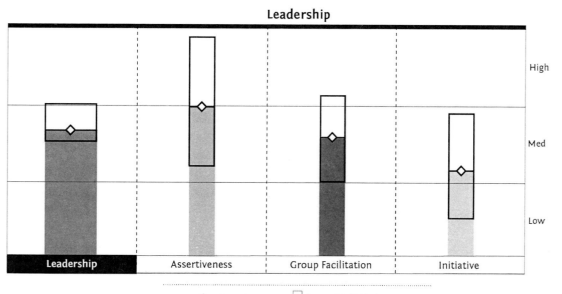

Leadership

Leadership	Assertiveness	Group Facilitation	Initiative	

—◇— Group Average   ☐ Range of Individual scores

B. Information on the Assertiveness subscale. The report then presents data about performance in the Assertiveness sector. It includes information in the following three subdivisions:

1. *In Brief:* Explains the significance of Assertiveness for effective team operations.

2. *Team Assessment:* Provides a short summary of the team's results in this domain.

3. *Suggestions to Improve Your Team's Performance:* Lists **5 to 8 recommendations** on how to upgrade performance in this area, according to the team's specific score. The number of options allows the team to choose the most appropriate strategies, which may be modified to create a more exact fit.

C. Information on the Group Facilitation Subscale and Initiative Subscale. Data for these subscales are presented in the same manner as the Assertiveness section, with the In Brief, Team Assessment, and Suggestions to Improve Your Team Performance categories.

The profile then introduces information for the Negotiation Orientation, Task Focus, and Interpersonal Focus segments, delivering data in the same format outlined in the Leadership subsection.

6. **One-Sentence Descriptions of the KGI Major Scales and Their Subscales.** On the last page of the profile are brief descriptors of the scales and subscales, providing an easy reference for the primary ideas in the KGI system.

Working with the KGI® Group Profile, a team can evaluate its performance in central aspects of group life, determine ways to balance that performance, and establish a learning team where members perfect group operations as they strengthen their personal leadership and membership skills. They possess the tools to take their team to a superior level of performance.

By introducing the above information, a professional will be able to orient people to the core ideas in the KGI system, and then move forward with the actual skill-development enterprise. ✕

REFERENCES

Adler, A. (1927/2010) *Understanding Human Nature*, Eastford, CT: Martino Fine Books.

Adler, A. (1964) *The Individual Psychology of Alfred Adler: A Systematic Presentation in Selections from His Writings* (Eds. Ansbacher, H. and Ansbacher, R.), New York: Harper and Row.

Adler, A. and Ansbacher, H. (1979) *Superiority and Social Interest: A Collection of Later Writings*, New York: W.W. Norton and Company.

Argyris, C. (2004) Teaching Smart People How to Learn. In *Harvard Business Review on Developing Leaders*, Boston: Harvard Business School Press.

Bales, R. (1950) *Interaction Process Analysis*, Cambridge, MA: Addison-Wesley Press.

Bales, R. (1955) The Equilibrium Problem in Small Groups. In Hare, A., Borgatta, E., and Bales, R. (Eds.), *Small Groups: Studies in Social Interaction*, New York: Alfred Knopf.

Branson, R. (2008) *Business Stripped Bare*, London: Virgin Books.

Brown, R. (2000) *Group Processes*, Malden, MA: Blackwell Publishing.

Caruso, D. and Salovey, P. (2004) *The Emotionally Intelligent Manager*, San Francisco: Jossey-Bass.

Conger, J. (2011) The Necessary Art of Persuasion. In *Harvard Business Review on Managing People*, Boston: Harvard Business School Press.

Coutu, D. (2009) Why Teams Don't Work (An Interview with J. Richard Hackman). In *Harvard Business Review*, Vol. 87, no. 5, p. 98–105.

Covey, S. (2004) *The Seven Habits of Highly Effective People*, New York: Simon Schuster.

Csikszentmihalyi, M. (2002) *Flow*, Rider: London.

Csikszentmihalyi, M., and Hooker, C. (2003) Flow, Creativity, and Shared Leadership: Rethinking the Motivation and Structuring of Knowledge Work. In Pearce, C. and Conger, J. (Eds.), *Shared Leadership*, Thousand Oaks, CA: Sage Publications.

Dweck, C. (2008) *Mindset*, New York: Ballantine Books.

Fisher, R., Ury, W., and Patton, B. (2011) *Getting to Yes*, New York: Penguin Books.

Goleman, D. (1995) *Emotional Intelligence*, New York: Bantam Books.

Goleman, D., Boyatzis, R. and McKee, A. (2009) *Primal Leadership*, Boston: Harvard Business School Press.

Gordon, M. (2004) Win-Win with Mark Gordon. In *Winning Negotiations that Preserve Relationships*, Boston: Harvard Business School Press.

Hackman, J.R. (2002) *Leading Teams*, Boston: Harvard Business School Press.

Hannah, B. (1997) *Jung His Life and Work*, Wilmette, IL: Chiron Publications.

Hicks, D. (2011) *Dignity*, New Haven: Yale University Press.

Jacobi, J. (1967) *The Way of Individuation*, New York: Meridian.

Jay, A. (1999) How to Run a Meeting. In *Harvard Business Review on Communication*, Boston: Harvard Business School Press.

Jung, C. (1921/1971) *Psychological Types*, Princeton, NJ: Princeton University Press.

Katzenbach, J., and Smith, D. (1993) *The Wisdom of Teams*, Boston: Harvard Business School Press.

Klein, R. (2007) *The Klein Group Instrument Manual*, Gainesville, FL: Center for Applications of Psychological Type.

Kouzes, J. and Posner, B. (2006) *A Leader's Legacy*, San Francisco: Jossey-Bass.

Maslow, A. (2014) *Toward a Psychology of Being*, Floyd, VA: Sublime Books.

Mithaug, D. (1993) *Self-Regulation Theory*, Westport, CT: Praeger.

Myers, I. with P. Myers (1995) *Gifts Differing*, Palo Alto, CA: Davies-Black.

Myers, I., McCaulley, M., Quenk, N. and Hammer, A. (1998) *MBTI Manual*, Palo Alto, CA: Consulting Psychologists Press.

Salovey, P. and Mayer, J. (1990) *Emotional Intelligence. In Imagination, Cognition, and Personality*, 9 (3), 185–211.

Schon, D. (1995) *The Reflective Practitioner: How Professionals Think in Action*, Suffolk, UK: Arena.

Stein, M. (2006) *The Principle of Individuation*, Wilmette, IL: Chiron Publications.

Wooley, A., Chabris, C., Pentland, A., Hashmi, N. and Malone, T. (2010) Evidence for a Collective Intelligence Factor in the Performance of Human Groups. In *Science*, Vol. 330, no. 6004, p. 686–688.

Robert R. Klein, Ed.D.

Robert completed his doctoral work at Harvard University, where he studied human development, psychology, and the teaching and learning process related to the instruction of group skills. His dissertation is entitled "A Study of Participation in Groups Using the Myers-Briggs Type Indicator." In collaboration with Center for Applications of Psychological Type (Gainesville, FL), he developed the Klein Group Instrument® (KGI®) for Effective Leadership and Participation in Teams, published in 2007. He is a certified MBTI® Master Practitioner. He has taught leadership and group skills at Harvard, Wheaton College (MA), Springfield College, and Western New England University. He is currently co-director of the Master's program Sport Leadership and Coaching in the College of Business at Western New England. He has been a faculty member at the C.G. Jung Institute in Zurich, Switzerland. ✕